Cosmopolitan Europe

Cosmopolitan Europe

ULRICH BECK AND EDGAR GRANDE

Translated by Ciaran Cronin

polity

The publication of this work was supported by a grant from the Goethe-Institut

Reprinted 2008

Polity Press
65 Bridge Street
Cambridge CB2 1UR, UK

Polity Press
350 Main Street
Malden, MA 02148, USA

ISBN-10: 0-7456-3562-8
ISBN-13: 978-07456-3562-0
ISBN-10: 0-7456-3563-6 (pb)
ISBN-13: 978-07456-3563-7 (pb)

1006568546

A catalogue record for this book is available from the British Library.

Typeset in 10 on 12 pt Stempel Garamond
by SNP Best-set Typesetter Ltd., Hong Kong
Printed and bound in Great Britain
by Biddles Ltd., King's Lynn, Norfolk

For further information on Polity, visit our website: www.polity.co.uk

The publication of this work was supported by a grant from the Goethe-Institut, Dachauer Str. 122, Goethe Institut e V, München, 80637, Germany, Tel: +49 89 1 59 21-0, Fax: +49 89 1 59 21-450, Email: zv@goethe.de, Web: www.goethe.de

Contents

Detailed Contents

Preface

Europe as a model must be rethought. It worked for fifty years but now it has outlived its usefulness. A new era of border-transcending and border-effacing cooperation began, if not at first, then emphatically with the eastern enlargement of the European Union. Yet what exactly has occurred? Where is Europeanization leading us and what has been its driving force to date? The euphoria (and the scepticism) over the new, enlarged Europe cannot disguise the fact that Europe still remains to be understood and conceptualized. This historically unique and distinctive form of intergovernmental and intersocietal community escapes all traditional categories and concepts. Europe exemplifies particularly clearly how historically unreal and blunt our political concepts and the theoretical concepts of the social sciences have become – for both remain trapped in the conceptual straightjacket of methodological nationalism.

What holds the enlarged Europe together? A new perspective on Europe – the cosmopolitan outlook! This book is a response to the new founding moment of the European Union and it presents and develops a concept for it, namely, 'cosmopolitan Europe'. It is an attempt to understand and to provide a new theoretical and practical specification of Europeanization in light of the theory of reflexive modernization.

This reconfiguration of thought and research cannot succeed in a single step. This book is part of a larger project of Ulrich Beck, a trilogy on 'cosmopolitan realism', which it also brings to a close. In the first volume of this trilogy, *Power in the Global Age*, Ulrich Beck explores the legitimacy of political authority under conditions of global interdependence. The second book, *The Cosmopolitan Vision*, deals with foundational questions and develops the principles of a cosmopolitan enlightenment. This third and final volume, *Cosmopolitan Europe*, which is co-authored with Edgar Grande, throws light on the unknown Europe in which we are living.

That this trilogy could even be begun and be completed with the present volume is a piece of luck that is due to the extraordinary support of many people. In the first place, we must mention the Deutsche Forschungsgemeinschaft which provides financial support for a collaborative research centre in

Munich on the topic of 'reflexive modernization', whose director is Ulrich Beck and to which Edgar Grande has belonged from the beginning. This book demonstrates in an exemplary way how such a special research centre can stimulate scientific cooperation across disciplinary boundaries even when it is not formally organized as a research project. The Deutsche Forschungs-gemeinschaft has, in addition, funded two empirical research projects of Edgar Grande within the framework of its special concentration programme 'Governance in Europe', from which ideas and findings have flowed into this book. Ulrich Beck owes an additional debt of gratitude to the Volkswagen-Stiftung for a grant that enabled him to work on these book projects over a long period.

Finally, we would like to thank our students in Munich, London and Toronto with whom, in recent years in numerous seminars and lectures, we discussed our ideas on cosmopolitan Europe in a globalizing world, and who repeatedly forced us to sharpen our view of Europe. Almut Kleine has survived many new revisions of the complete text virtually without losing her patience, which goes far beyond what one can reasonably expect even from the most obliging person. Oliver Buntrock undertook the laborious task of assembling the bibliography. Our warmest thanks to them both.

Ulrich Beck
Edgar Grande

1

Introduction: The European Malaise and Why the Idea of Cosmopolitan Europe Could Overcome It

1 Rethinking Europe

The world is out of joint. No, this is not a reference to 'globalization' or to the 'terrorist threat', to the 'eastern enlargement of the European Union' or to Europe's 'shrinking population', but referred to an explosion in population, to the scandal that 'servants were becoming kings', that the Reformation was leading to the collapse of a global order and that the first signs indicated that the new form of state was indeed having disciplining effects. Even allowing for the fact that the symptoms of crisis of the current European transformation are different, it is striking how similar the forms of speech in use at the beginning of the twenty-first century are to those used by people responding to the loss of certainty in the early modern period, at the end of the sixteenth and the beginning of the seventeenth century (Schulze 2004). The more societies are confronted with transformations that threaten their very foundations, the more fearfully people cling to what is familiar and the more likely they are to misunderstand the new realities. Even changes for the better then provoke anxious resistance.

Even the most advanced sciences and scientists were not immune to this infatuation with error intended to protect the foundations of one's thought – far from it. For example, the invention of the printing press was dismissed as a passing fad. Those who viewed the sciences as the source of renewal stood corrected: the 'friend of truth' had to 'guard with all his strength against all innovation'. For 'omnis novitas periculosa' (Lentulus), all innovation is dangerous! Moreover, according to Bacon, 'whatever has not already been invented and understood, can never be so hereafter' (*Novum organum*). The phenomenon that dramatic changes inspire intellectual and normative stasis has already been remarked by Jacob Burckhardt: 'Major historical changes are always purchased at great cost, often after people imagined they had got them on the cheap' (Burckhardt 1957: 89).[1]

However, the differences in reactions and mentalities among countries were as pronounced then as they are today. In France and England, there were elements of a 'libertine climate of thought'. The changes were accepted but at the same time attempts were made to comprehend them and relate them to older realities. The German reaction was quite different: 'The German discussion was framed by a kind of fundamental moral critique of the existing, "bad", world.' People felt endangered, for example, by 'a Turkish threat of apocalyptic proportions' (Schulze 2004: 10).

Like the printing press at that time, today the European Union is similarly misunderstood, for the simple reason that it is still perceived within the outdated political and scientific framework of the nation, whereas the realities which are producing Europeanization represent *the* classic historical counter-example to the political and social ontology of the nation-state. Because the European Union seems to have been exhaustively researched, the principle that whatever has not yet been discovered and understood cannot be discovered and understood in the future either also seems to hold for research on Europe. This book demonstrates precisely the opposite. Europe stands for the most misunderstood thing in the world, for a powerful negation – neither state nor society, at least not in the sense in which the United States, for example, is both a state and a society.

In contrast to the great European minds who developed their philosophical and political vision of Europe long before they could have had an inkling of what Europeanization would actually entail, today we are confronting the experience of Europeanization without knowing how to conceptualize and understand it. Europe in movement – Europe *as* movement – escapes our understanding because this permanent process of transformation contradicts the conception within which Europe hitherto seemed to be self-evidently situated, namely, the conceptual horizon of national societies and states. To be sure, social and political history is not the same thing as the history of ideas. Europeanization is also shaped by interests and institutions, and whether this experiment will fail or not does not depend on its false understanding of itself alone. Nevertheless, interpreting a permanent, thoroughgoing transformation like Europeanization for which we lack interpretive categories that are able to represent it as meaningful, and even necessary, multiplies the burden of innovation without revealing its chances of success.

That Europe is trapped in a malaise is by now a truism. However, it is more difficult to explain how this malaise could be overcome. In our view, it would be premature to discard the very idea of Europe as outdated. On the contrary, today Europe is the last politically effective utopia. The maxim 'in dubio pro Europa' remains valid, although Europe for the most part tends to think and behave in national terms. How can the really existing utopia overcome this debilitating malaise?

That the prospects are bleak is taken as a given in public discourses. The assumption is now that the EU can't amount to much, even though not long ago it was the target of impassioned appeals to form a military and political counterweight to America. Internally, the EU has been confronted with intensifying criticism from its citizens, as documented impressively by the failed national referendums on the Constitutional Treaty in France and the Netherlands in 2005. Economically, Europe's performance is still much worse than that of the USA and there is no evidence that the ambitious political objects of the Lisbon Summit in 2000 will ever be met.

Eastern enlargement has added to the current malaise. In its largest extension to date, the European Union expanded eastwards in early 2004, thereby bridging the deep chasm opened up by hot and cold wars during the bloody history of the twentieth century. However, the new Eastern European member states harbour the same scepticism towards the distant bureaucracy in Brussels that nourished their mistrust of Moscow. In the East, Europe belongs to the past. It has been lost and lingers only in memory. It is like a faded family photograph from the interwar years, tinged with nostalgia and longing. In the West, by contrast, Europe signifies a different future, one yet to be discovered and constructed. Thus, the states which have recently been accepted into the European 'family' represent a *terra incognita* for their Western neighbours.

There is currently much talk of the provincialization of Europe. But isn't Europe mainly preoccupied with its favourite topic – namely, itself – while the world is falling to pieces? From the perspective of the postcolonial world, globalization is synonymous with the decline of Europe. For globalization is the materialization of the American world spirit. The erstwhile colonial masters have suddenly been demoted to second-class status and hence no longer set their own standards of greatness or incompetence. On this point, the postcolonial countries are in agreement with the American 'lords of the world'. Europe no longer even figures in their power calculations. Since Europe cannot assert itself militarily and speaks with many voices in foreign and security policy, it need not be taken seriously and merits only cosmetic regard.

Europe is also mired politically. The uninspired, petty way in which it tried to give itself a constitution is just one example of this. All sides exhaust themselves in complaints, demands and appeals: Something must happen! Something should have happened a long time ago! But nothing is happening – or so it seems. In fact, a lot is happening – for some, even far too much. Though it may sound paradoxical, over the past decade the European process has been driven forward by its 'failures'. 'I've been pronounced dead, so I must be!' is Europe's motto. Europe has grown up amid doom-laden prophecies. If the prophets of doom and their prophesies were correct, then Europe would never have experienced its current major crisis. If it is not to disintegrate, it must answer the question: Who is to set the political agenda for this gigantic entity encompassing twenty-seven states and over 494 million people, and how? However, the fact that the phoenix has hitherto always arisen invigorated from the ashes of the declarations of its demise does not mean that the present malaise can also be overcome merely by being loudly trumpeted.

Yet, could it be that the perpetual diagnosis of 'crisis' and 'decline' also reflects the fact that the nation-state narrative of society and politics which we impose on Europeanization misses reality and leads to systematic misunderstandings? Perhaps it is not a matter of regret that Europe is still at the planning stage in spite of two and a half millennia of history; maybe the point is that this contributes to the reality of Europeanization. Maybe the main problem is that the political script being played out in the minds of Europeans is at variance with the script which is actually determining European reality. Maybe what is lacking is not a *single* European identity that unites everybody but a narrative of Europeanization that makes sense of the interrelation between new departures and declines. Maybe the real European crisis is just this inability to see the contradictory events as part of a common European undertaking. And maybe this, and not geographical distance, is the reason why the EU institutions seem distant, unreal and irrelevant to the citizens they are supposed to serve.

In fact, our thesis is that the process of Europeanization – because of its successes! – has reached a critical threshold and that the political energy reserves of the semantics and vision of Europe associated with the nation-state are exhausted. The internal conditions of European politics have changed abruptly with the completion of the European internal market and the eastern enlargement; and, at the same time, the external coordinates of European integration have been fundamentally displaced by globalization and the new global political conflicts. Under these conditions, institutional reforms alone, such as the creation of a European constitution, do not go far enough. Much more is called for, namely, *to rethink Europe*.

If Europe is to live up to its reputation as the world's most successful failing political organization, then it must achieve a new self-understanding comprising three elements: first, a narrative that enables us to situate and understand the contradictory realities of Europeanization as moments of a common European undertaking, second, a new political vision and, third, a new concept of political integration, where both vision and concept should be based on the narrative of Europeanization.

With the idea of *cosmopolitan Europe* developed in this book, our goal is to place such an analytical and political vision for Europe on the agenda. In our view, Europe is not currently weighed down by an excessive burden of tasks nor are its institutions poorly structured. The underlying problem is completely different. Europe is still labouring under a national self-misunderstanding that misrepresents its historical awakening and task and generates political obstacles. This national self-misunderstanding makes Europe and its member countries, behind their cooperative façade, into arch-rivals who threaten each other's existence in the final analysis because of the success of the European project. In a sense, they are conducting a 'war' against each other with the peaceful means of integration: *either* Europe *or* the nation-states – a third possibility is excluded. In this book, we are affirming precisely this third option when we speak of 'cosmopolitan Europe'. However, if this third cosmopolitan option is excluded analytically, and hence does not even appear as a possibility on the horizon, then the progress of Europeanization represents a persistent mortal danger to national identity and national sovereignty. In this view, talk of 'Europe' arouses deep fears that bolt doors shut and erect barricades; for the existence of nation-states must be continually defended and secured against Europe. Thus understood, European integration turns into an infernal zero-sum game in which both Europe and its member states are the ultimate losers.

2   What is meant by cosmopolitan Europe?

The concept of 'cosmopolitan Europe' and the associated idea mark a break with this 'either/or' logic of Europeanization, with the national outlook and methodological nationalism (see Beck 2005: ch. 1; Beck 2006: ch. 1) which consistently duped thought and action with the irreducibility of this alternative, and hence form one of the main reasons why debates about Europe always end up in the same impasse. However, when we speak of *cosmopolitan Europe* we do not mean to imply the dissolution and replacement of the nation but its reinterpretation in light of the ideals and principles for which Europe in essence always stood and stands, that is, in light of a new conception of political cosmopolitanism. The key question (not exclusively, but especially also, for Europe!) is: How can a new kind of society and politics be discovered and justified that does not rely on the old stabilizing factors, building both internally and externally on the historically established forms of nationality, while opening them up and extending them? How can social and political *integration through cosmopolitanization* come about? And how can this horizon of possibility and reality be opened up by dissociating basic social and political structures and concepts – society, state, politics, social inequality, mobility, ethnicity, justice, solidarity, etc. – from the national orthodoxy and redefining them from the cosmopolitan perspective?

The emerging cosmopolitan Europe opens up new possibilities of social organization and political participation, though *not* based on the model of a European demos or of a conventional European political monopoly based on homogeneity and uniformity. As this book demonstrates, de facto Europeanization has already developed in accordance with a different *empirical* logic over the past fifty years. For it was marked from the outset by the fact that the fundamental principle of cosmopolitanism was politically *institutionalized*, though at the same time *deformed* in the most diverse ways. The success story of Europeanization followed the route of limited, even contradictory, deformed cosmopolitanism, though one which is responsive to conflicts and generates conflicts of its own. This deformed institutionalized cosmopolitanism comprises multiple spheres and subjects; it is the point of intersection of the activities and strategies of a growing number of players involved in the discourse over the definition and shape of 'Europe', whether or not they are formally integrated into the European Union.

In the following chapters, we will offer a series of detailed answers to the question of what is meant by a 'cosmopolitan Europe', or a 'cosmopolitan integration' of Europe. Before we begin, however, we must clarify three prior questions: What is Europe? What is cosmopolitanism? And finally: How does the idea of the cosmopolitan Europe differ from other political visions and analytical concepts of Europe?

2.1   What is Europe?

Taking a closer look at Europe, whether in politics or in the social sciences, is like entering a hall of mirrors. Depending on one's standpoint, it is magnified or shrinks, and the slightest movement of the observer leads to a distortion of its proportions. There are no clear and simple answers to where it begins and ends, to what it is and what it should become. Whether one equates Europe with the European Union and its member states or understands it as a larger geographical and political space, Europe as such does not exist, only *Europeanization* in the sense of an institutionalized process of permanent change. What 'Europe' includes and excludes, the location and direction of its territorial boundaries, its institutional form and what institutional architecture it should have in the future – none of this is clear. Europe is not a fixed condition. Europe is another word for variable geometry, variable national interests, variable involvement, variable internal–external relations, variable statehood and variable identity. This also holds for the institutional core of Europeanization, the EU. At a first approximation, the EU can only be understood as the counter-image of a static state order. The EU is *an institutionalized 'more and further'*, it is geared to movement, to a process that transcends and interconnects the internal and the external. As we will later show in detail, its development does not follow the logic of state consolidation but of *post-hegemonic expansion*. In short, Europe is not a predefined spatial shell in which 'Europeanization' can unfold, and the goal of this process as yet lacks a conceptual blueprint and is without historical precedent. This innovation 'Europe' is a social construct, one which has until now obeyed a peculiar logic, namely, the *logic of side effects*, the logic of the unintended consequences of political decisions.[2] Therein lies the peculiar modernity of Europe, and it is exactly for this reason that the project of European integration represents an exemplary field of study for the reflexive modernization of modern societies. In what follows, we will elucidate this in five steps.

In a *first* step, we define Europe as an *open* political project, not as a fixed quantity of whatever kind. More precisely, we hold that Europe can define itself only in the form of a political project. In this context, one can certainly draw on the insights of research on nationalism, for the difficulties of conceptualizing 'Europe' are not completely new, historically speaking.[3] They already became apparent in a similar form at the end of the nineteenth century when the problem – sufficiently discussed in the meantime – was one of defining what the 'nation' is. This is shown in an exemplary way by Ernest Renan in his famous lecture at the Sorbonne of March 1882. As is well known, in answering the question 'What is a nation?', Renan concluded that it could be equated neither with a particular race nor with a language, a religion, an interest group or a naturally defined territory. In other words, the nation cannot be defined in terms of substantive attributes of any kind. And the same holds for Europe! However, this does not mean that these two concepts cannot be defined at all. Ernest Renan, and following him the later research on nationalism (see Gellner 1983; Hobsbawm 1990; Anderson 1991), concluded that the nation must be defined in *political* terms. More precisely, it must define *itself* politically and bring itself forth as a real community. Generalizing the basic ideas of Benedict Anderson's analysis of nationalism, one could argue that all modern collective identities must be politically 'invented' or 'constructed' (see Anderson 1991), where a constructed identity should not be confused with a *fictitious* one. This holds even more so for transnational, hence nation-transcending, collective identities, such as the European. Europe cannot be discovered [*gefunden*], it must be invented [*erfunden*].

A prime example of this is the adjudication of the European Court of Justice (ECJ), which, in accordance with its self-definition, elevated the European founding treaties to the status of a 'Constitutional Charter' in two leading decisions, in 1963 and 1964 (see Weiler 1991, 1999; Joerges 2003). As is generally known, with this it erected one of the two main pillars of the principle of European supranationalism, namely, the immediate jurisdiction of EC law and its priority over national law. Consequently, a European law emerged that claims constitutional *priority* and that was duly acknowledged and accepted as such by the key players in European politics. In this way, a European legal framework and culture developed that is potentially in a position to criticize the national legal systems and to replace them by the European administration of justice. This cosmopolitan overthrow of legal relations was driven forward by the 'legal conversation' with the national supreme courts (see Alter 2001) and, what is more, was adopted by national governments and parliaments as the basis of their further operations. Two things are especially noteworthy about this. First, this cosmopolitan self-definition of the ECJ gave rise to an authoritative form of constitutionalism in Europe *without* a formal constitution, based on a *practice* of law-making that is not founded on *any* worked-out theory or on *any* knowledge of where this is all leading or of its ultimate goal.[4] We will return to this unintentional aspect of the history of European integration in greater detail in chapter 2. However, this example throws light on a further feature of the construction of Europe. It shows that the 'invention of Europe' was a product not of public deliberation and democratic procedures but, in this instance, of judicial prescription.

This immediately raises the question concerning the European 'We'. Who invents and constructs Europe? Who decides on the legitimacy of changes in the rules of the game? Are transformations in the rules of power founded on the old basis of legitimacy of the nation-state system? Alternatively, are the national sources of the legitimacy of power and authority themselves up for grabs in the European meta-power game? The example of the self-empowerment of the ECJ in interplay with the member governments and the European Commission demonstrates that these questions admit very different and highly controversial answers. It nevertheless remains true that the 'We' in Europe is not the same before and after a surge in Europeanization.

However one interprets this in detail, it entails a change of 'We', a change in identity, subject and legitimacy. The 'We' who legitimize the cosmopolitan legal regime are the *prospective* Europeans who in this way become the subject of their own history. Ultimately, the legitimacy of the self-fulfilling prophecy is supposed to become (or be made) effective here. Through its adjudication, the ECJ is becoming a *cosmopolitan entrepreneur* who imposes an element of cosmopolitan Europe through the power of law against the national Europe. Here, it not only draws on a circular form of legitimacy but also produces it. The law counts on acceptance by the European subject which it brings into being through its law. Europeanization, thus conceived, is another word for Europe's *self-creation*.

This leads, in a *second* step, to the question of the political principles that are guiding, or should guide, Europe's 'self-creation'. There is no clear and straightforward answer to this question either. In recent years, the discussion concerning Europe has moved between two extremes. The minimal position, as contained in the Copenhagen principles governing the eastern enlargement, for example, demands only commitment to democracy and a market-based economic system from accession countries, plus the ability to put into effect the '*acquis communautaire*', the stock of existing European regulations. The maximal position found expression in the consultations of the European Constitutional Convention. The latter undertook the ambitious task of laying down a comprehensive, and in part highly controversial, catalogue of 'European basic values' in the Constitution, based on the 'Charter of Fundamental Rights of the European Union' of December 2000 (see European Council 2000). The Charter itself comprises a total of seven chapters and fifty-four articles in which the 'common values' of the European Union are contained. Its preamble not only refers to the 'spiritual and moral heritage' of the Union but at the same time lists a whole series of individual and collective rights, values and principles. The subsequent controversies in the Constitutional Convention showed that people have very different conceptions of what constitutes the 'spiritual and moral heritage' of Europe. Is it restricted to Western Christian culture, or does it go beyond this? And, if so, does it include the 'Orthodox cultural sphere', as defined by Samuel Huntington (Huntington 1996), or not? The answers to these questions have profound implications, for on them ultimately depends what is included in 'Europe' and which countries can be considered as possible future members of the EU (on this, see chapter 4).

In this book, we will adopt neither of these two positions. We will instead defend a historical argument that makes it possible to see the values and norms of the new Europe as an answer to the history of the regimes of terror of the twentieth century on both the left and the right. We will develop this argument in detail later (see chapter 4). Briefly, we maintain that these terror regimes and their consequences mark a break in the formation of a European collective identity. It is no accident that the institutionalized European cosmopolitanism which fosters respect for difference can be traced back to the Nuremberg Trials in 1945–6. The latter went beyond national sovereignty for the first time and established new ways of comprehending the historical monstrosity of the murder of the Jews in legal categories, namely, in terms of 'crimes against humanity'. This, in turn, gave rise to an original internal European contradiction. The traditions of colonialism, nationalism, expulsion and genocide originated in Europe; but so too did the values and legal categories against which they are measured and condemned as crimes against humanity. Commemoration of the Holocaust, in particular, becomes a beacon warning against the omnipresent modernization of barbarity (Levy and Sznaider 2001). Cosmopolitan Europe in this sense must be understood as a self-critical Europe. It represents its own institutionalized self-criticism. Could this radical self-critical confrontation with its own history be what distinguishes Europe from the United States and from Islamic societies, for example? Can we derive from this the shared norms which the cosmopolitan project needs to combine recognition of difference with the idea of European integration?

Third, it should be emphasized that the political construction of Europe has an internal and an external side. Large areas of research on Europe mistakenly conceive of European integration exclusively as an *internally* oriented process steered by national interests and supranational institutions. The various theoretical approaches differ primarily over which of these factors they accord the greatest weight. In this way, however, they overlook an essential aspect of Europeanization. An examination of the history of the process of European integration shows that the external side is particularly important in the European case. Europe was and is continually forced *from the outside* to define itself politically and to take stances on global political issues. The crucial point is that this is not left up to Europeans themselves, so that they cannot simply refuse to confront this question. Two examples of this are the Iraq War in early 2003 and Turkey's desire to become a member of the EU. It is no accident that both of these problems have provoked discussions of matters of principle and fundamental distinctions – between 'old' and 'new' Europe and between 'Christian-Western' and 'Islamic-Eastern' culture. This also revealed the kind of dead ends into which attempts to define Europe through pre-political, 'cultural' commonalities can lead. The discussion of where Europe stands on matters of foreign policy has ended up in a paradoxical situation as a result. On the one hand, the demarcation of Europe from Turkey is justified by appealing to the cultural, social, legal and political commonalities of its present member states; on the other hand, certain European heads of government presented precisely the same commonalities as an argument for standing alongside the United States during the Iraq crisis, and hence for the division of Europe.

Fourth, it should be noted that the political construction of Europe exhibits a peculiarity that distinguishes it from all projects of nation-state building. European integration was a *dynamic, open process* from the outset. To repeat, Europe does not exist, only Europeanization. Moreover, this process of Europeanization proceeds in two directions: *inwards*, through constant extensions of the powers of the EU and the resulting structural adaptations in the member states; and *outwards*, through the constant enlargements of the community and the export of its norms and rules.[5] The 'Europe' of the 1950s was very different from that of the 1970s, 1980s and 1990s; and, with the eastern enlargement in 2004, Europe again fundamentally altered its territorial shape. In recent years, both the territorial frontiers of the Community towards the outside and the internal 'political frontiers' between the Community and its member states have been shifting significantly. The Europe of the 1980s and 1990s was also different from the Europe of the 1950s with regard to the scope of its supranational tasks and competences. The decisive point here is that, whereas an end of this process has in the meantime become a topic of discussion, we are still far from clear concerning the 'finality' of Europe. Where does Europe end? What belongs to Europe? There is as yet no answer to these questions.

Fifth, and finally, Europe must not be equated with a specific institutional form, the EU (or, previously, the EC). From the outset, the European integration process exhibited a highly *variable architecture* of treaties and alliances. The European Communities (first the European Coal and Steel Community, later the European Economic Community and EURATOM) were not the first, or even the only, alliances and treaties formed in Europe following World War II. Alongside them were the Council of Europe, the Organization for European Economic Co-operation (OEEC), the European Free Trade Association (EFTA), NATO, the Western European Union (WEU), the European Space Agency (ESA), the Commission on Security and Cooperation in Europe (CSCE), EUREKA (the Europe-wide network for market-oriented industrial R&D) – the list could be extended a lot further. In this way, a highly complex architecture of forms of cooperation with extremely variable memberships and highly differentiated rights and duties for member states was created that extended far beyond the various

European Communities in the narrower sense, and some of them were even intended in part as direct competitors to them, as in the case of the EFTA. Hence, it would be fundamentally mistaken simply to equate Europe with the various European Communities or the European Union. If we transcribe this complex architecture onto a map, it becomes apparent that 'Europe' reaches as far west as Los Angeles and Vancouver and as far east as Vladivostok – and it included Turkey from the beginning, needless to say.

In sum, Europe is a highly complex and highly differentiated, politically animated and flexible political project. It cannot be defined clearly and precisely, and certainly not for all time, in a binding way. Consequently, from a nationally fixated perspective it inevitably appears that Europe does not exist, even that it cannot exist! Hence, Europe is an example of something known in fuzzy logic as the 'Law of Incompatibility': 'As complexity rises, precise statements lose meaning and meaningful statements lose precision' (McNeill and Freiberger 1993: 43). However, it by no means follows that meaningful statements are no longer possible. The concept of cosmopolitanism offers the key to this puzzle, as this book will show.

2.2   *What is cosmopolitanism?*

What does the concept of cosmopolitanism mean precisely? How does cosmopolitanism differ from other concepts situated beyond the particular, such as the concepts of universalism, multiculturalism and postnationalism? How is it related to modern society and its transformation? And what does the concept of cosmopolitanism contribute to our understanding of Europeanization? These questions are in urgent need of clarification because the concept of cosmopolitanism is currently in vogue and serves as a synonym for many things: globalization, globality, glocalism, globalism, universalism, multiculturalism, pluralism, imperialism. All of these, so it is claimed, contain a cosmopolitan element; nevertheless, their adherents also leave no doubt that there is a world of difference between these concepts. But which difference?

The concept 'cosmopolitanism' has both a very old meaning and one that points to the future. Indeed, what makes it so interesting for a theory of modern societies is that it is both *pre*-national and *post*-national. As is well known, it can be traced back to the Cynics and Stoics of antiquity who also invented the word. Subsequently, it played a role in European societies whenever they were faced with fundamental upheavals. It acquired central importance in the philosophy of the Enlightenment (in Germany, in Kant, Fichte, Schelling, Wieland, Forster, Herder, Goethe, Schiller, Heine and others) (see Schlereth 1977; Toulmin 1990; Kleingeld 1999; Thielking 2000); it was taken up again in the nationalistically oriented, culturally critical philosophy of the late nineteenth century (e.g., Meinecke 1907); and, finally, the current debates on globalization rediscovered it as a positive counterweight to the organizing power of the market and of the nation-state (see Pogge 1992; Held 1995; Archibugi and Held 1995; Archibugi, Held and Köhler 1998; Linklater 1998; Cheah and Robbins 1998; Kaldor 1999; Levy and Sznaider 2001; Beck 2005, 2006; Vertovec and Cohen 2002; Archibugi 2003b; Kaldor, Anheier and Glasius 2003).

In light of this long prehistory, it would be presumptuous to expect this concept to have a consistent meaning. Nevertheless, we can identify two premises that form the core of the cosmopolitan project. Cosmopolitanism combines appreciation of difference and alterity with attempts to conceive of new democratic forms of political rule beyond the nation-state (see Brennan 1997). Daniele Archibugi has summarized this normative core of cosmopolitanism in three principles: tolerance, democratic legitimacy and effectiveness (Archibugi 2003a: 11).

With our understanding of cosmopolitanism, we draw expressly on this strand of tradition. However, we want to use the concept in a very specific way – namely, as a *social scientific* concept – and for quite specific social facts and circumstances – namely, a specific way of *dealing socially with cultural difference*. In this way, the concept of cosmopolitanism can be distinguished in an ideal-typical manner from a number of other social ways of dealing with difference, in particular, hierarchical subordination, universalistic and nationalistic sameness and postmodern particularism (for a detailed account of the social scientific concept of cosmopolitanism and its counter-concepts, see Beck 2006, ch. 2). In the present context it is important that the concept of cosmopolitanism, whose specific point resides in overcoming the dualities of the global and the local, the national and the international, is not specified in *spatial* terms; in particular, it is not bound to the 'cosmos' or to the 'globe'. The *principle* of cosmopolitanism, as we define it, can be located and applied everywhere, and hence also to regional geographical units such as Europe. Indeed, understanding Europe in cosmopolitan terms means defining the European concept of society as a regionally and historically particular case of global interdependence, as we will later show (chapter 4).

In the first place, cosmopolitanism differs fundamentally from all forms of vertical differentiation that seek to bring social difference into a hierarchical relation of *superiority and subordination*. This principle can be applied, on the one hand, within societies insofar as they form highly differentiated caste and class systems. However, it was also used to define relations to other societies. Typical here is that one denies 'the others' the status of sameness and equality and perceives them in a relation of hierarchical subordination or inferiority. At the extreme, the others are regarded as 'barbarians' devoid of rights. Not only premodern societies tried to deal with difference in this way; the modern construction of colonial empires from the sixteenth century onwards also followed this principle. Moreover, as Huntington's (1996) concept of civilization and his thesis of a 'clash of civilizations' show, even the postmodern constellation itself is susceptible to a hierarchy of difference.

The *dissolution of differences* represents the countervailing principle to hierarchical subordination. It presupposes the development and recognition of *universal* norms that facilitate the justification and institutionalization of the equal treatment of others. The universalistic approach replaces the multitude of different norms, classes, ethnic identities and religions with one unified norm. In this context, we can distinguish between at least two variants of universalism: a *substantial universalism* that advocates the equality and equal value of externally different others on the basis of substantive norms; and a *procedural universalism* that is primarily geared to fair rules in dealing with otherness and to formal justice. Universalism in both of these forms is a typically modern way of dealing with difference, though not the only one. There are a number of other modes of dealing with difference, such as the principles of nationalism and of cosmopolitanism.

Nationalism standardizes differences while at the same time demarcating them in accordance with national oppositions. As a strategy for dealing with difference, it also follows an either/or logic, though instead of the hierarchical distinction between higher and lower it operates with the horizontal distinction between internal and external. Nationalism has two sides; one oriented inwards, the other outwards. Internally, nationalism aims to dissolve differences and promote uniform norms. It has this in common with universalism. However, because of its limited territorial scope, the dissolution of differences must always remain incomplete and difference is emphasized towards the outside. In this sense, nationalism dissolves differences internally while at the same time producing and stabilizing them towards the outside.

Here it is important that nationalism lacks an inherent regulator for dealing with difference in its external environment. It is as likely to tend towards enlightened tolerance as towards nationalistic excess (see Dann 1993). In its most extreme form, therefore, nationalism exhibits commonalities not only with universalism but also with premodern forms of hierarchical subordination. This is because it also has a tendency to reject the equality of other nations and to stigmatize them as 'barbarians' – and itself take on barbaric traits as a result. Thus, we can safely assume that nationalism is the typical mode of dealing with difference in the *first* modernity.

Cosmopolitanism differs from all of the previously mentioned forms in that here the *recognition of difference* becomes the maxim of thought, social life and practice, both internally and towards other societies. It neither orders differences hierarchically nor dissolves them, but accepts them as such, indeed invests them with a positive value. Cosmopolitanism affirms what is excluded both by hierarchical difference and by universal equality, namely, perceiving others as different *and* at the same time as equal. Whereas universalism and nationalism (and premodern, essentialistic particularism) are based on the principle of 'either/or', cosmopolitanism rests on the 'both/and' principle. The foreign is not experienced and assessed as dangerous, disintegrating and fragmenting but as enriching. My curiosity about myself and about difference makes others irreplaceable for me. Hence, there is an egoism of cosmopolitan interests. Those who integrate the perspective of others into their own lives learn more about themselves *as well as* about others.

The cosmopolitan principle of regarding others as both equal and different admits of two interpretations: the recognition of the distinctiveness of others may refer to *collectives* or to *individuals*. Both interpretations are constitutive for the principle of cosmopolitanism. On the former, collective reading, it becomes difficult to distinguish it from the principle of *multiculturalism*. However, the principle of multiculturalism refers exclusively to collective categories of difference; it is geared, first, to (more or less) homogeneous groups and, second, locates the latter within the nation-state framework. In this respect, multiculturalism is antagonistic both to transnationalization and to individualization. By contrast, this is *not* the case for cosmopolitanism but precisely the opposite: the cosmopolitan principle heightens awareness of the fact that the apparently sharp ethnic boundaries and territorial bonds are becoming blurred and intermingling at both the national and the transnational levels. As a result, under conditions of radical global insecurity, all are equal and everyone is different.[6]

Hence cosmopolitanism calls for new concepts of integration and identity that enable and affirm coexistence across borders, without requiring that distinctiveness and difference be sacrificed on the altar of supposed (national) equality. 'Identity' and 'integration' then are no longer different words for hegemony over the other or others, of the majority over minorities. Cosmopolitanism accepts difference but does not make it absolute; rather, it seeks out ways for rendering it universally agreeable. In this, it relies on a framework of uniting and universally binding norms that should prevent deviation into postmodern particularism.[7]

In the philosophy of the Enlightenment, this is particularly apparent in the cultural cosmopolitanism of Georg Forster. Forster's defence of cultural difference does not imply a pure form of pluralism but is based rather on the universal norm of human equality (see Kleingeld 1999: 516). Although cosmopolitanism is not an invention of the *second* modernity, we nevertheless assert that it is the typical mode of coping with difference within the second modernity. A cosmopolitan Europe would thus be, in the first instance, a *Europe of difference*, of accepted and recognized difference.

From this perspective, diversity, be it of language, of lifestyles, of economic systems, or of forms of statehood and democracy, would be primarily conceived as an inexhaustible source, perhaps *the* source, of Europe's cosmopolitan self-understanding, and not as a hindrance to integration (see Landfried 2002). However, European cosmopolitanism also signifies the need to restrict and regulate differences. Thus, a cosmopolitan Europe means simultaneously both difference *and* integration. It offers an alternative to the existing concepts of European integration, which either locate Europe above the nation-states and combat national particularities as obstacles to European unification, or want to subordinate Europe to the nation-states and national interests and regard every step towards further integration with scepticism.

Three of the approaches to dealing with difference sketched here – universalism, nationalism and cosmopolitanism – represent, heuristically speaking, *modern* variants. Universalism has one thing in common with each of the other two principles. With nationalism it shares the idea of equality and of the equal treatment of difference, and hence the goal of unity and uniformity. With cosmopolitanism, it shares the conception of the universal validity of norms and rights. For this reason, sometimes cosmopolitanism was (and still is) identified with universalism since both sought to overcome particularism, the local restriction of norms (see Kleingeld 1999: 516). Later, however, cosmopolitanism would also ally itself with nationalism and seek to realize notions of equality within a nationally circumscribed space or among several such spaces.[8]

There are two radical counter-proposals to these modern ways of dealing with difference. They are, on the one hand, the essentialistic hierarchy of difference, which is by no means restricted to the premodern period, and, on the other, the postmodern incommensurability of difference.[9] Cosmopolitanism should not be confused with postmodernism or interpreted as a variant of the latter (as in Smith 1995, for example). The postmodern strategy of tolerating difference consists in absolutizing otherness without a supportive framework of common substantive and procedural norms. This approach absolutizes relativism to such a point that shared ideals of order and criteria of selection are completely lacking. What cosmopolitanism values as a highly – namely, internalized and institutionalized – mutual perspective-taking with others is ultimately illusory in postmodern particularism, even culturally excluded, but always ideologically suspect. Although here equality among others no longer rests on essential differences, it does rest on the incommensurability of perspectives.[10]

In order to clarify a social scientific concept of cosmopolitanism, it is not only important to distinguish it analytically and heuristically from other premodern, modern and postmodern conceptions of how to deal with difference; it is equally important to recognize that the various modern strategies for dealing with difference not only differ from each other but, when conceived in terms of cosmopolitanism, also condition each other, indeed even complement each other. On the one hand, cosmopolitanism requires a certain fund of universal norms in order to regulate the treatment of difference and to direct the 'struggle for recognition' (Honneth 1995) into socially acceptable channels. Here, the question of how comprehensive this fund of shared norms must be, of whether it can be restricted to procedural norms, or whether it must in addition include substantial norms (however they are established), can remain open. However, one thing is certain: if these norms are missing, if there are no universally accepted criteria and there is no rule-governed procedure for dealing with difference, then there is a danger that cosmopolitanism will degenerate into postmodern particularism and/or into open violence.

However, this is not the end of the problem. If cosmopolitanism wants to guarantee collective, as well as individual, rights and identities, then it also needs a political mechanism for institutionally producing and stabilizing *collective* difference. This is precisely the strength of nationalism, which represents the historically most successful way of underpinning and stabilizing collective difference with universalistic norms. Where such *stabilizers of difference* are missing, cosmopolitanism is in danger of degenerating into substantial universalism.

This is of cardinal importance for the idea of a cosmopolitan Europe. Cosmopolitan Europe is not only the antithesis of, but also presupposes, a national Europe, i.e., a Europe of nations. It cannot simply abolish national Europe but must cosmopolitanize it from within. In this sense, we speak of a nationally rooted cosmopolitanism. Hence, it would be utterly false to think of the national and the cosmopolitan as two autonomous levels, or as two mutually exclusive political principles, and to play them off against one another. Rather, the cosmopolitan must be conceived as the *integral* of the national and must be developed and empirically investigated as such. In other words, the cosmopolitan changes and preserves, it *opens* the past, the present and the future of particular national societies and the relations among national societies (see chapter 4).

Viewed in this way, cosmopolitanism must not only integrate different national traditions and norms, it must at the same time balance various modern ways of dealing with difference. Its characteristic relation between the various modern forms of dealing with cultural difference is determined not by the either/or principle but by the both/and principle. We must discover cosmopolitanism as an at least partially effective real utopia and *bring it to awareness* in a twofold sense. In short, cosmopolitanism must become aware of its own conditions of possibility if it wants to be effective in the long run. If cosmopolitanism becomes aware of its ability to connect and balance the various modes of dealing with otherness and difference, then it can be understood, and theoretically and empirically developed, as *reflexive* cosmopolitanism. Reflexive cosmopolitanism, sociologically defined, would become the regulative principle through which the interaction between universalistic, national and cosmopolitan principles in the second modernity must be conceived and regulated. Under what conditions this can be successful is surely one of the key questions which will determine the progress or decline of the second modernity, and should therefore serve as a guide for its investigation in the social sciences.

2.3   *Sociological and political cosmopolitanism: from the national to the cosmopolitan outlook in research on Europe*

What does all this mean for Europe? How can the concept of cosmopolitanism be made fruitful for research on Europe and for European politics? What perspectives does this open up for the European political project? To these questions, which we will deal with in greater detail later, the present book provides a twofold answer.

A distinction that now plays a central role in the theory of reflexive modernization can serve as a point of departure, namely, that between *political* and *sociological* or *methodological* cosmopolitanism (for a detailed account, see Beck 2006: ch. 1). This is indispensable for understanding Europeanization and research on Europe – though not only for this. The former, political cosmopolitanism, is geared to the practical perspective of social actors and signifies the conscious renunciation of a nation-state-centred understanding of politics; the latter, sociological or methodological cosmopolitanism, by contrast, is geared to the analytical and methodological instruments of the social sciences and is opposed to the implicit nationalism of its system of categories. These two things do not necessarily coincide. The cosmopolitanization and Europeanization of nation-state institutions and national social conditions by no means necessarily leads social actors to adopt a cosmopolitan perspective – far from it; but the tensions and contradictions between transnationalization, renationalization and cosmopolitanism cannot be understood and analysed within the usual national conceptual horizon. What is required is that the social sciences should adopt a cosmopolitan perspective, specifically, a *methodological* cosmopolitanism.

This is especially true for research on Europe in the social sciences. Thus far, it has not succeeded in developing a perspective of its own that is appropriate to its object of study. Like European politics, it has been trapped in false alternatives and has viewed its object *either* from the national *or* from an inter-national perspective. If we want to understand the dynamics of Europeanization, therefore, we must make a methodological shift in perspective from the dominant national (or inter-national) to the cosmopolitan outlook.

Thus, methodological cosmopolitanism places the national catechism which informs social and political thinking and action systematically in question. This faith rests on the assumption that 'modern society' and 'modern politics' must be conceived as nationally organized societies and politics. The state features as creator, controller and guarantor of society. Societies (of which there are as many as nation-states) are thought of as containers that develop and exist within the state's sphere of authority. This conception, which identifies societies with national societies and conceives of them as territorially delimited units, is deeply ingrained in the understanding of the social sciences, their concepts, their way of viewing things, their way of conducting empirical investigations and accumulating and evaluating data – one might say, it is ingrained in the sociological imagination.

Here we must distinguish clearly between two aspects. When we encounter these articles of faith among social actors, we speak of the 'national outlook'; when they underlie the empirical terminology and observer perspective of the social sciences, by contrast, we speak of 'methodological nationalism'. This distinction between the perspective of social actors and the perspective of social scientists is important because, as we have seen, there is *no* logical connection between the two; they only exhibit a similar historical genesis. Moreover, the methodological nationalism of the social sciences is becoming historically false and, in addition, obscures the complex realities and spaces of interaction of Europe. In a word, it is and makes us *blind to Europe*.

In this way, methodological nationalism (mis)leads political theory into a *negative definition* of Europe, because the expansion of supranational institutions and freedom of action inevitably weakens intergovernmentalism – hence, the level of voluntary, limited forms of cooperation between states and their governments – and the sovereignty of the member states. This means that supranationality and international sovereignty are trapped in a zero-sum game; consequently, the issue is the extent to which the members of supranational institutions possess veto rights (as in the UN Security Council) or whether independent authorities can and should be established to implement autonomous decisions. The institutional reforms and logjams of the past thirty years turn on precisely this point: more majority decisions and institutional cosmopolitanism (which means extending the powers of the European Parliament and the European Commission), or more intergovernmentalism and more scope for exercising national influence.

In methodological cosmopolitanism, this negative conceptual approach is replaced by a *positive definition* of Europe. The negative-sum game is replaced by the *positive-sum game* based on the *both/and* principle: expansion of power at the supranational level is not equated with loss of power at the national level; rather, precisely the opposite holds, namely, power as a whole increases and, as a consequence, nationality, transnationality and supranationality reinforce and complement each other. Indeed, in this way, a *better* defence of the nation-state is even possible, via the detour of its cosmopolitan opening (see chapter 3).

When one speaks of Europe in this sense, it becomes clear that the formula 'cosmopolitan Europe' is at once a theoretical construct *and* a political vision. Hence, the aim of this book is also twofold: it seeks to open up a new theoretical and empirical perspective for research on Europe in the social sciences; and, at the same time, it wants to cure European politics of its dearth of imagination by, first, enabling it to understand the dynamics of its own activity and its own creation and, second, equipping it with a new political vision. The 'narrative' of cosmopolitan Europe can be summarized in *three theses* which this book will justify in detail: the thesis of institutionalized cosmopolitanism, the thesis of deformed cosmopolitanism and the thesis of cosmopolitan realism.

Institutionalized cosmopolitanism

The idea of a cosmopolitan Europe is at once radically new and yet forms part of the continuity of European thought and European politics. This can be shown in an exemplary manner by the (at the time revolutionary) reinvention of the word 'community' after World War II. Europe would not be Europe without the diversity already postulated at that time by the French foreign minister Robert Schuman. This identity-founding diversity represents a valuable source of possible ways of being European whose full utilization is central to the success of the eastern enlargement. Western Europe must also rediscover its cosmopolitan heart – that is, its curiosity concerning the 'internal other' of Eastern Europe – in dealing with the historical experiences of the post-communist countries. This also holds for the European integration process in the narrower sense. Thus, although the principle of cosmopolitanism offers a new perspective for understanding Europe and a new approach to its further integration, it does not mean that Europe has to be completely reinvented. On the contrary, our first thesis is that the European process of integration involved a *cosmopolitan momentum* from the beginning. It always differed from all other forms of regional integration – such as, for example, the North American Free Trade Area, NAFTA, the Asia-Pacific Economic Cooperation, APEC, or the Latin American alliance MERCOSUR – in that it transcended the idea of the nation and transformed national sovereignty. Europe was always supposed to be, and wanted to be, more than a form of intergovernmental cooperation in the traditional sense. The decisive point is that cosmopolitanism in Europe was from the beginning more than a mere 'idea'; it was already *institutionalized* with the creation of the European Coal and Steel Community. The core of this institutional cosmopolitanism was (and still is) constituted by the newly established supranational institutions out of which the European Commission, the Council of Ministers, the European Court of Justice and the European Parliament would later emerge. Through the agreement on common institutions that stand legally above the individual member states, all of the European Communities differed from other forms of regional integration, such as customs unions or a common internal market. Cosmopolitanism should not be simply identified with supranationalism, however. Supranationalism can also be grasped in the categories of the 'national', namely, as a 'European nation-state' or a 'European federal state'. Precisely for this reason, the European movement of the interwar years and the years immediately after World War II was committed to the dissolution of existing nations and nation-states, be it in a 'pan-European' nation or in new kinds of functionally defined spheres of action.[11] As we know, Europe did not follow this path. The European nation-states have successfully resisted their dissolution, in large part through the construction of strong intergovernmental counterweights in the system of European political institutions. Cosmopolitanism was institutionalized in Europe in precisely this way, namely, through the simultaneous institutionalization of two competing and conflicting principles: supranationalism *and* intergovernmentalism.

Deformed cosmopolitanism

If cosmopolitanism was institutionalized in the European Communities from the beginning, then what is novel about the idea of cosmopolitan Europe? Wasn't Europe cosmopolitan from the beginning? Aren't Europe and cosmopolitanism one and the same thing after all? How can cosmopolitanism rescue Europe from its malaise if it has always been a characteristic feature of the system of European institutions? Our answer to these questions is the concept of *deformed cosmopolitanism*. We argue that, although the process of European integration exhibited a cosmopolitan moment from the beginning, nevertheless thus far it has produced merely a *deformed* cosmopolitanism. These deformations have numerous causes: the egoism of the member states, economic self-interest and the asymmetries in influence on political decisions in the EU, the technocratic policy approach of the supranational institutions and the weakness of actors from civil society. Consequently, European cosmopolitanism has until now been shaped from above rather than from below, technocratically rather than democratically (on this, see chapter 5). Hence, the cosmopolitanization of Europe does not mean reinventing Europe or reconstructing Europe from the drawing board; rather, it means tracing the European malaise back to the cosmopolitan deformations and reforming Europe accordingly – in short, completing the incomplete European project.

Cosmopolitan realism

Isn't this a deeply idealistic project? Isn't this talk of European cosmopolitanism merely another variant of the 'idea of Europe' which has accompanied the history of European political unification since the fourteenth century (see Foerster 1963)? Why should the nation-states accept European cosmopolitanism or, what amounts to the same thing, renounce a substantial portion of their power and sovereignty? Our response to these questions is the theory of *cosmopolitan realism*. Its basic argument (summarizing for the sake of simplicity) is that, in the past, the member states of the EC/EU did not renounce power for idealistic reasons but for reasons of their own national interests. Thus, they acted on purely realistic motives (in the sense of realism in international relations theory), though in the knowledge that they can only (continue to) realize their interests in a particular way, namely, by recognizing the legitimate interests of others and integrating them into their own rational calculations. In this way, it was possible to achieve both national and European goals at the same time. The political premium generated by binding cooperative norms made winners of both the states and Europe. This does not mean that such a harmony of interests is always possible or that national goals coincide with European goals as a matter of course. It merely maintains that in the past European unification was less a product of idealistic enthusiasm than the result of rational calculations of interest. And the concept of cosmopolitan Europe assumes that this will remain the case in the future as well (cf. chapter 3, section 4).

3   European self-delusions

The criticism of Europe which underlies the idea of cosmopolitan Europe must be distinguished from four competing positions that have dominated public discussion in recent years. These four positions differ mainly over how much Europe they want to allow.

3.1   *The national self-delusion*

Much criticism of Europe, whether from the left or the right, rests on the assumption that there could be a return to the nation-state idyll in European society and politics. Everywhere we hear the lament that Europe is a 'faceless bureaucracy', that Europe is destroying democracy, that Europe is undermining national diversity. However undifferentiated, this criticism contains an element of truth; but it becomes problematic because it starts from false assumptions and becomes entangled in a false alternative. Of course, one can and must criticize the politics of the European Union and its democratic deficit. We will do so at length ourselves (see, in particular, chapters 5 and 8). However, this criticism becomes insidious if it accepts the premises of the national ontology, namely, that without the nation there can be no democracy. Here, the flaw is in the false nation-state logic of Europe and not in the European reality, for if we accept this logic, a postnational Europe *must* be a post-democratic Europe for purely conceptual reasons. The motto of this criticism is: 'the more EU we have, the less democracy'.

This line of argument is mistaken for a whole series of reasons and reveals the narrow-mindedness of the national outlook. First, its advocates fail to grasp that Europe's path to democracy should not be identical, and indeed cannot be identical, with the nation-state conception and mode of democracy that it employs as the standard against which to measure the European Union. Europeanization is, historically speaking, *categorically different*, something that is already evident from the fact that the EU is composed of democratic states, though it is not itself a state in the conventional sense but (as we will show in detail in chapter 3) an empire of consensus. Thus, it becomes questionable, second, whether the model of democracy developed for the modern state can be applied to the EU or whether different, postnational models of democracy have to be developed for the democratic legitimacy of European politics.[12]

Both the absolutization of the standard of democracy characteristic of the nation-state and the fact that the EU's specific historical path to democratization (utterly inadequate though it certainly remains) is misunderstood are rooted in the nostalgic self-delusion which absolutizes the national. This 'let's-return-to-the-good-old-nation-state' by no means dominates the thinking only of the duller reactionary minds. Even the most educated and cultivated thinkers and the most sophisticated political theories cling to this faith in the nation-state. While Europe and its ex-nation-states are interweaving, intermingling and interpenetrating, leaving not a single Europe-free corner in the European ex-national societies, the nostalgic imaginary of national sovereignty reigns more than ever in people's minds, becoming a sentimental ghost, a rhetorical habit, in which the anxious and disoriented seek refuge. However, there is no way back to the nation-state in Europe because all of the actors are caught up in a system of dependencies from which they could withdraw only at very high cost. After fifty years of Europeanization, the individual states and societies are capable of acting only *within* the European synthesis.

The national self-delusion comes in two variants, a hard and a soft one. The hard variant asserts that a complete retreat from Europe is both possible and necessary. On this variant, the EU would regress to the status of one of the numerous forms of intergovernmental cooperation and coordination – not less, but emphatically not more. Currently, this variant still has prominent supporters especially in Great Britain (Margaret Thatcher, Gordon Brown, among others) and in right-wing populist parties in Europe. The soft variant does not support a complete retreat from the EU but a precise, binding and permanent division of tasks between the EU and its member states, structured in such a way that the majority of the tasks should remain the preserve of the member states or would revert to them. This variant boils down to a European minimalism that continues to rely on the problem-solving capacities of the nation-states. Both variants rest on the assumption that a separation – a disintegration in accordance with the either/or principle – not only makes sense but also is practically possible. But *neither* is the case! There can be no return to the nation-state. And even if there were one, nobody could really want it since it would conflict with their rational self-interest. For such a regressive decomposition of the EU would be extremely dangerous; indeed, it would reopen the Pandora's box of Europe's war-torn history.

Thus, the national nostalgia is a schoolbook example of what we discussed at the beginning of this book, namely, how the utility of epochal transformations is misunderstood and is 'answered' by mental blockages, both in politics and in the social sciences.

3.2   *The neoliberal self-delusion*

Like the neonational self-delusion, the neoliberal self-delusion is based in essence on the assumption that it is possible and sufficient to integrate Europe economically. A farther-reaching social and political integration is not only superfluous, but even harmful. On this view, Europe should be nothing more than a large supermarket that exclusively obeys the logic of capital. However, such a conception ignores the tacit interdependence between the neoliberalization and the neonationalization of Europe. The creation of a European market, a European monetary union and, at least in its initial stages, a European legal system invalidates precisely the ideal of subsidiarity that legitimized this European project in the national outlook, thereby triggering a host of nationalistic defensive reflexes. For the modernization of Europe is pervaded by the rhetoric of global competitiveness. Under the banner of 'market integration', a process of modernization that undermines boundaries and foundations has been unleashed that annuls the national premises of parliamentary democracy, the welfare state and the class compromise. In this context, the talk of 'reforms' then atrophies into ever more deregulation of markets.

For many years, the neoliberal development of Europe was supported by a consensus among the European elites; for supranationally regulated economic cooperation was conceived and practised from the outset as the key to political reconciliation. Agreement on this lowest common economic denominator and overcoming national boundaries through the 'power of the economy', generalized into the neoliberal cure-all, led to the underdevelopment of the social and political basis of the European project. Granted, the European left has appealed to the social chapter of the Maastricht Treaty, which is supposed to defend social justice against the power of the economy. However, the principles of economic rationality produce just the opposite dynamic: possibilities for state control and public policy-making are minimized and the member states are bound to finance, economic and tax policies that tie their hands. Perhaps most glaring is the lack of effective means to combat unemployment, unless it be through the propagated magical power of neoliberal deregulation. In the neoliberal Europe, the overcoming of budgetary deficits and the principle of price stability have become the real criteria for the advance and decline of membership rights.

Such a neoliberal minimal Europe does not make economic sense nor is it politically realistic. The economic deficits of an exclusively 'negative integration' of Europe are sufficiently well known that they do not need to be elaborated upon here. Markets are not only politically constituted but also need continual political correction if they are to function effectively. If such market-correcting policies are not possible at the European level or if they lack support, then not only the European economy but also the European project as a whole will suffer in the long run. For the contradictions and inadequacies of the neoliberal minimal Europe cannot be politically neutralized; on the contrary, they are discovered and politically instrumentalized by growing right-wing populism. The power of the latter rests in large part on the neoliberal self-delusion that Europe can be realized as a non-political market Europe that leaves the old national social 'containers' unaffected. Even if this is surely unintentional, neoliberalism nevertheless sets in motion a dangerous anti-cosmopolitan dynamic in Europe, whose result could well be not only less Europe, but also less market.

3.3   *The technocratic self-delusion*

In contrast to the first two positions, which argue against Europe for different reasons, or at least against more Europe, the technocratic position is essentially pro-European. It accepts not only Europe but also the necessity of farther-reaching ('positive') integration. The backward-looking, national self-delusion is replaced by the future-oriented calculated optimism of (neo)functionalist 'spill-over integration'. Intended-unintended side effects give rise to permanent pressures to solve problems for which the enlightened European elites find 'objectively' required solutions, with the result that, lurching from one crisis to the next, the goal striven for, namely, 'integration', is reached over and over again.

What is problematic about this technocratic understanding of Europe is less the goal of integration itself, although its concrete form is naturally a matter of controversy; particularly problematic is the chosen path, hence the assumption that such a complex, contingent and colossal 'Europe of differences' can get by without democratic legitimacy of its own and that Europeanization is even possible in the long run without the democratic participation of those immediately affected by it. Since the conflicts and contradictions generated by Europeanization have until now not been resolved in a direct and open manner – along the lines of a European referendum, for example – the enlightened European elites had to resort to the *technocratic ruses of powerlessness*. In the case of the eastern enlargement, for example, this resulted in the EU attempting to graft a relatively rigid model of social order geared primarily to uniformity instead of diversity onto its new member states. The assumption was that those wishing to become members must submit to predefined, rigid, irreversible and conclusive criteria and take an oath of allegiance to the unspecific general project of 'European unification' as an end in itself without any precise goal.

Europe's questionable democratic credentials are not a new problem but belong to the construction flaws of European community-building, which, it would seem, were consciously accepted by its architects, such as Jean Monnet (Featherstone 1994). Meanwhile, however, this generates a danger for the European political project whose seriousness should not be underestimated. As the debate on Europe over the past decade has shown, the most convincing arguments against a further integration of Europe are provided by those who criticize the democratic deficits of the EU (see Grimm 1993; Offe 2000; Scharpf 1992, 1999). Like the neoliberal version, the technocratic vision of Europe is also in danger of ending up in the national blind alley.

3.4 The Eurocentric self-delusion

The fourth position which invites criticism is also in essence pro-European; indeed, it is the European position par excellence. Were we to associate it with specific persons, we would have to name such leading European political figures of the 1980s and 1990s as Jacques Delors and Etienne Count Davignon. Hence, the target of criticism in this case is no less than the guiding idea of European politics of the past twenty years. Its problem was that it was primarily inwardly oriented in a Eurocentric fashion. The external aspect of Europe, its role and responsibility in an unbounded world of dangers, was either effaced or, more problematically, interpreted negatively and instrumentalized in order to push through economic and political integration against the inertia of the nation-states. Along these lines, the 'American challenge' (Servan-Schreiber 1968) was invoked during the 1960s to kick-start the motor of European integration, and later, during the 1980s, the 'Japanese-American challenge' (Seitz 1990) was invoked as something against which Europe had to unite. In short, Europe was supposed to be welded together internally by dramatizing the danger from outside. All of this rests on the (mistaken) assumption that it is possible to create Europe as a culturally homogeneous and economically self-sufficient unit that is clearly demarcated from the rest of the world while (successfully) competing with it. Seen from the outside, the European internal market threatened to create a 'Fortress Europe'. It is somewhat ironic that this Eurocentric mentality contributed essentially to the acceleration of globalization because it led to a rapid increase in American and Japanese direct investment in Europe (see Rodriguez-Pose 2002: 23).

Aside from the fact that the Eurocentric position makes the mistake of ignoring the economic, cultural and political interdependencies of a globalized world (for a detailed discussion, see chapter 7), it rests on a twofold misunderstanding. To believe that one can separate Europe and America is to succumb, first, to a territorial misunderstanding of the European Union. On this conception, Europe constitutes a geographically limited community of states separated from the United States by the Atlantic Ocean. In addition, there is the *European* self-misunderstanding according to which the EU member states constitute the substance of the European Union and the glue that holds it together. Here Europe is mistakenly equated with the complex of treaties that constitute the EU, whereas what made the EU possible was precisely the overlapping, and in part the amalgamation, of America with Europe, hence the synthesis of America and Europe which stands for freedom, human rights and democracy. For the birth of the non-belligerent Europe after World War II and its 'integration' were and are made possible not least through the organizing power of the continental presence of America (see Katzenstein 2005). Consequently, to be European means to belong simultaneously to overlapping and competing spaces of power and spheres of identity. We are 'NATO citizens' (and hence also part-time US citizens), national citizens, communal citizens and, not least, European citizens.

This historical amalgamation of the Atlantic community, EU and NATO (thus of the 'old' West), becomes especially apparent at the historical moment in which it is threatening to fall apart. The extent to which a *merely* European Europe, one preoccupied with itself, is possible is highly questionable. Only a cosmopolitan Europe – and that means a transatlantic Europe that seeks and finds its global political role in the threatened world and does not confuse a cooperative balancing policy *towards* the United States with an antagonistic policy *against* the United States – can also stabilize itself internally (see Weidenfeld 1996).

With this specific background in mind, the title of this book, *Cosmopolitan Europe*, is intentionally ambiguous. If the emphasis is on 'Europe', then the title refers to *internally oriented* cosmopolitanism, to the Europe of difference. In this sense, the concept of cosmopolitan Europe represents a new regulative principle by means of which the national perspective in European politics and the blockages built into it can be loosened, and the project of European integration be injected with new life. If one emphasizes the adjective 'cosmopolitan', by contrast, then the concept points simultaneously *outwards*. It forces us to engage in self-reflection: What made Europe possible under the conditions of the Cold War? Was the United States not in a sense an informal founding member of the EU, so that the transatlantic conflict of loyalties over the Iraq War represents a threat to the EU? Was not overlapping membership in the NATO and the EU the tacit foundation of an EU without competence in security matters, so that the major predicament facing NATO in an era of terrorist threats is also a challenge to the EU to redefine itself? How is Europe possible? What role will Europe play in the world and in global politics in the future? What does cosmopolitan Europe mean at the level of foreign policy? Thus, the adjective 'cosmopolitan' compels us to think of Europe also from an external perspective in a globalizing world. It not only opens and sharpens our perception of the tensions, contradictions and limits to which cooperative regional institutions are subject in the global risk society; it enables us at the same time to grasp, or at least to inquire into, what global contribution the project of cosmopolitan Europe could make to the realization of a regime of multiple cosmopolitanisms.

Thus, this book represents in large part a *new critical theory of European integration*. Such a critical theory is urgently needed. For many years, the process of European integration was accepted uncritically by mainstream research on Europe; it was criticized, if at all, by the wrong people using (mostly) wrong arguments. This includes not only right-wing populists. The European left also viewed the project of European integration with suspicion from the outset because European transnationality seemed to represent a threat to the national welfare state. Both the Western European communist parties and European social democrats saw in Europe a danger for the nation-state with its extensive political steering capabilities, its democratic achievements and the social security it guarantees its citizens. We distance ourselves from this tradition in two ways; on the one hand, with the concept of deformed cosmopolitanism we open up a new approach to the critical theory of European politics and society; on the other hand, in contrast with the usual critics of Europe, we do not claim that the process of European integration has already gone too far, that we already have too much Europe. Our diagnosis, on the contrary, is that Europe is not European enough and that the appropriate therapy is, accordingly, *more* Europe – assuming that this is properly understood, that is, in a cosmopolitan sense! This new critical theory of Europe is also a *self-critical* theory. Cosmopolitan Europe is not a new mechanism for producing unlimited happiness but rather a set of instructions for dealing with ambivalences – ambivalences that are irreducible because they are characteristic of the second modernity.

2

The Reflexive Modernization of Europe

In the history of modernity (whose overconfident rationalism misleads it into thinking that it can understand and explain everything) the epitome of the unexpected has occurred, namely, Europe, the great misunderstood phenomenon – or, in plain terms, 'freak' – of world history. This institutionalized misunderstanding called 'Europe' emerged, from the outset, from the incongruity between concept and reality which presided over its birth following World War II. Here, behind the legitimizing shield of old categories (nation-state, national economy), a transformation of reality was institutionalized that annulled or recalibrated this conventional conceptual system of the national Europe from within, and the greater its success the more far-reaching its effects. It is high time to cast off the fetters of false concepts and to understand Europe for what it already is in part, a cosmopolitan Europe. For the political project of cosmopolitan Europe, the break with its belligerent history has already become a source of tradition. But what theory can provide sufficiently refined concepts to grasp Europe in all of its ambivalence – its past, present and future overshadowed by false notions of legitimacy – as a different reality, as a blurred modernity? Our answer is the theory of reflexive modernization.

1   From the first to the second modernity: Europeanization revisited – from the perspective of the theory of reflexive modernization

For pragmatic, methodological reasons, the theory of reflexive modernization operates with a distinction between first and second modernity that is free of any ontologizing intent. Here we cannot present the theoretical premises of this distinction in their full complexity and we certainly cannot exhibit its possible applications in all of their diversity. The latter extend from science and technology, through social inequalities, lifestyles and biographies, the organization of work, financial networks and forms of enterprises, to the state and politics in national and transnational contexts. In this context we can pick out only a couple of elements of the theory that offer useful analytical

and political instruments for clarifying the blurred picture of Europeanization, its dynamics and its impacts. We will proceed in such a way that these
theoretical components are not interpreted for their own sake but already in
their application to European society, politics and research.[1]

Generally speaking, one can divide the theory of reflexive modernization
into three complexes, namely, the theorem of risk society, the theorem of
forced individualization and the theorem of multidimensional globalization.
All three theorems extrapolate the same line of argumentation and thereby
mutually interpret and reinforce each other: 'risk society', 'individualization'
and 'globalization' are viewed as radicalized forms of a dynamic of modernization that, when applied to itself, annuls the formula of simple modernity.
This formula obeyed a logic of order and action that made sharp divisions
between categories of people, things and activities and drew clear distinctions
between spheres of action and forms of life that in turn allowed unambigu-
ous institutional ascriptions of jurisdictions, competences and responsibilities. This *logic of unequivocalness* – one could speak metaphorically of a
Newtonian theory of society and politics of the first modernity – is being
replaced by a *logic of ambiguity* – a *Heisenbergian* principle of indeterminacy
of the social and the political, so to speak. Of course, classical sociology is
also familiar with crises and functional disruptions; indeed, the analysis of
'systemic crises' in the political systems of 'late capitalism' enjoyed a vogue in
political science during the 1970s (see Jänicke 1973). However, these constitute an exception. The notion that the foundations of modern society become
porous or shaky, or must be recalibrated at the moment of their triumph, is
alien to the classics of social science.

However, this is precisely the law of Europeanization that must be conceptualized and investigated. The institutionalized dualities and coordinates
of the inner and the outer, the national and the international, society and
politics, 'we' and 'the others', are being broken down and recast in new
forms. The side-effects argument was also known to classical theory from
David Hume and Adam Smith onwards (see Beck, Holzer and Kieserling
2001). In the second modernity, however, the 'invisible hand' leads neither
to equilibrium nor to revolution. Rather, the boundaries, foundations and
basic distinctions of modern societies are dissolving and blending. The logic
of unequivocalness – the either/or model of society and politics – is being
replaced by the logic of equivocalness – the both/and model of society and
politics.

In other words, there are two kinds of dualistic concepts, exclusive dualities (the either/or logic) and inclusive dualities (the both/and logic), that is,
those which mutually exclude each other (such as national/international) and
those which mutually include each other (such as human being and citizen,
European and Frenchman, European and Christian, Muslim, etc.). The both/
and logic concerns concepts that complement and blend with each other,
though, contrary to what either/or thinking readily assumes, not everything

becomes blurred, but specific dualities can, and under certain circumstances must, be distinguished. However, precisely these specific, non-exclusive dualities are the defining characteristic of Europe (to speak in old-fashioned terms): Europeanness can only be conceived and lived as *civitas permista* in which the apparently necessary national either/or is presupposed, recognized, annulled and recast all at once. The European order is never seen as the polar opposite of the world of nations. The polyvalent European duality, the distinction between Europe and its national societies, between Northern and Eastern Europe, old and new Europe, serve to make the tension understandable and tolerable and hence to unmask the ontology of the national as ultimately unreal. When one analyses Europe in this way from the theoretical perspective of reflexive modernization, one is led to the following hypotheses which we will clarify in the remainder of this chapter.

(1)   Since the final quarter of the twentieth century the development of modern societies has been characterized by a fundamental discontinuity, a structural break, through which the basic institutions of politics, economics, science, etc., in the first modernity are being complemented and replaced by new kinds of institutional formations. Europeanization must be understood and analyzed as part of this comprehensive process of reflexive social modernization – the *structural break theorem*.

(2)   The relation between the first and the second modernity should be conceived in inclusive, rather than exclusive, terms, in accordance with the both/and principle. The second modernity is not situated within the duality of the non-modern and the modern (tradition and modernity), but within the duality of modernity and modernity (primary and reflexive modernity), in the sense that the second modernity presupposes the realization of the first modernity (i.e., a functioning state, the development of industry, democracy, science, etc.) – the *both/and Europe*.

(3)   How does the transition from first to second modernity come about? The unbounded, radicalized dynamic of modernization annuls the basic distinctions, the basic institutions of the first modernity; but this does not occur primarily through crises or revolutions, but as the unintended reverse side of the successes of primary modernization – the *side-effects theorem*.

(4)   The transition from the first to the second modernity does not follow from the collapse of the first, classical 'high modernity'; it occurs imperceptibly and must be attributed to a radicalized internal dynamic, thus to the growth of science, technology, mobility, basic rights, unrestricted capital flows, etc. – the *theorem of internal dynamics*.

(5)   Hence the transition from the first to the second modernity should not be understood as simple change but as 'meta-change', that is, as change in the parameters of change – the *self-transformation theorem*.

A conceptual shift and the associated change in outlook are certainly not a sufficient, though they are a necessary, condition for deciphering the still uncomprehended novelty of Europeanization and for disclosing a political perspective for Europe that makes different actors, different strategic fields, institutions – in short, a different political architecture – possible and real. The triumphal march of Europe presupposes a new theory of European society and politics and it can be understood only in this way. 'Can any cosmopolitan project ever be anything other than an inherently hegemonic and violent undertaking?' asks the neorealist Danilo Zolo (1997: 15). Yes, open your eyes! We are living in such a reality; Europe embodies it, albeit inadequately, and gives it voice (again, for the present, inadequately).

2   Europe and the reflexive modernization of state and society

What is actually new about Europe? Why is it worthwhile to approach Europe from the perspective of the theory of reflexive modernization? And what contribution can this perspective make to understanding Europeanization and to realizing a cosmopolitan Europe? At first sight, Europe seems to be a singularly unsuitable object of social science. The idea of Europe is ancient: it extends as far back as the fourteenth century; the process of integration which began after World War II was made possible by the highly specific experiences of two world wars and was marked by the constellation of threats of the Cold War; and the institution-building produced a unique new architecture of political power for which existing theories can provide neither suitable concepts nor useful standards of comparison. What more can one say about Europe than that it is unique, a '*sui generis*' construction that does not admit of generalizations for the simple reason that it is the only instance of its kind?

The theory of reflexive modernization asserts that Europe is not such an isolated case at all. On the contrary, the process of Europeanization can and must be understood as part of a comprehensive 'epochal break' in the development of modern societies. Only in this way can the potentials, dynamics, contradictions, crises and impacts of the European project be grasped completely and classified correctly. This project is about much more than the removal of toll barriers, the introduction of a common currency, the construction of new bureaucracies, etc. Europe's reflexive modernization gives rise to the structures of a new, transnationally interconnected society that breaks out of the container of the nation-state and simultaneously transforms its own basic institutions. Before clarifying this *structural break thesis* in greater detail, we would like to caution against a number of misunderstandings.

First, this break, the genesis of a second, modernized modernity, should not be misunderstood as a radically new beginning; rather it is shaped by the *dialectic of continuity and discontinuity*. The old is not simply replaced, but is complemented, extended and reformed. What sets apart the model of social change developed in the theory of reflexive modernization is precisely the resulting versatility and complexity (see Beck and Bonss 2001). The point here is not to advocate a new notion of arbitrariness. The thesis of discontinuity in the development of modern societies does not imply that everything changes or has to change or that all processes of transformation to which modern societies are subject are of equal relevance. Rather a very specific type of change features centrally in the theory of reflexive modernization: the transformation of the *basic institutions* of modern societies, by which are meant those norms, institutions and procedures which constitute the cognitive and institutional infrastructure of modern societies.

In the political sphere, the *nation-state* constitutes without doubt the basic institution of the first modernity. In the broadest sense, it is characterized by five features: first, by unrestricted sovereignty internally and externally, based on its monopoly on the legitimate use of physical force; second, by a specific form of bureaucratic rationality in its organization and operations; third, by a specific normative founding principle that presupposes and fosters a high degree of sociocultural homogeneity, namely, nationalism; fourth, by characteristic procedures of political participation and democratic political legitimation based on the principle of representation; and, fifth, by a constantly growing complex of tasks whose core is a comprehensive protection against individual and collective risks. These factors together constitute what one might call, paraphrasing Habermas (2001), the 'national constellation', that is, a historically evolved configuration of norms, institutions, techniques of power and procedures that made it possible to put the political integration of modern societies on a permanent footing and to make collectively binding decisions within them.

The theory of reflexive modernization assumes that the dynamic of reflexive modernization poses numerous challenges for the nation-state. Escalating civilizational risks increase the number of tasks assigned to the state while at the same time undermining the epistemological basis of their performance; the individualization of lifestyles entails intensifying claims to a say in political decisions, new forms of political participation and an upgrading of 'subpolitical' domains of action; finally, the globalization of markets, technologies, security risks, environmental problems and cultural memberships undermines the foundations of the modern nation-state, in particular the territorial restriction and restrictability of collective problems.

Our *central assumption* is that the nation-state, as one of the basic institutions of the first modernity, is being transformed from the ground up by the process of reflexive modernization. For present purposes, two aspects of this process of transformation are particularly noteworthy. The reflexive modernization of statehood leads, on the one hand, to the emergence of a plurality of diverse new forms of transnational 'governance beyond the nation-state' (Zürn 1998). The nation-state is not replaced or suppressed entirely but is integrated in a variety of ways into new international regimes and organizations, new supranational institutions, new forms of regionalism, and the like. The result of this development, insofar as it can already be ascertained, is new, complex systems of (global) governance (Zürn 1998; Held 2004; Slaughter 2004) with far-reaching implications for the possibilities and preconditions of conceiving and implementing national interests.

In addition, there is the increasing role of private actors in solving collective problems and producing public goods (see Cutler, Haufler and Porter 1999). This extends from autonomous self-regulation, through the creation of new, non-hierarchical connections and networks to trans-, inter- and supranational actors parallel or in opposition to state structures (O'Brien et al. 2000), up to and including transnational 'epistemic communities' (Haas 1992) with the ability to introduce and implement transnationally won scientific knowledge at the subnational, national or international levels in decision-making processes of the state. In sum, these developments indicate that the traditional structures and agents involved in the formation of the political will and in decision-making and policy implementation are entering into new groupings, are combining with new institutions and actors and are being amalgamated into a new architecture of political power (see Grande and Pauly 2005).

Our thesis asserts that the new basic institutions of the second modernity manifest themselves in these transnational political regimes. The new transnational systems of divided power differ from premodern models of political rule, as well as from postmodern concepts of politics, by the fact that they uphold the basic principles of the exercise of political power in the modern era, in particular the claim to provide collectively binding solutions to collective problems. In the 'era of globalization', however, this claim to provide collective solutions to problems can no longer be met through the old forms of the nation-state but only through new, transnationally oriented forms of governance.

The example of Europe makes it possible to examine the process of reflexive modernization of modern societies as though through a magnifying glass. Europe is at once the result and the driving force of this process. Europe exemplifies the forces of resistance of the nation-states as well as the new architectures of political rule; the tenaciousness of national bonds as well as the construction of new cosmopolitan identities; the defence of national interests as well as the constitution of new transnational solidarities. Hence, Europe is at once a model for processes of regional integration on other continents and a motor for establishing new global governance regimes.

3   The inclusive Europe

Europe is a 'society' of societies, an 'empire' composed of states. In the following chapters we will explain in greater detail what we mean by this. The important point for the present is that the process of Europeanization is marked by the both/and principle, which both presupposes and annuls the national either/or. For Europeanization is not a tabula rasa construction that emerges in a social and political no man's land and it cannot be conceived and fashioned in the image of nation-building. In general, the historical backdrops of the nineteenth century and the concepts and models derived from them are unsuitable for understanding Europeanization because the latter cannot be conceived as the modernization of the premodern, as the modernization of feudal structures and institutions, but only as the modernization of modern societies.

Thus, the formula 'both/and Europe' represents it as a product not of primary but of secondary modernization. Europe is not situated within the duality of tradition and modernity (of the premodern and the modern) but within the duality of first and second modernity. But this implies that Europeanization does not exclude, but rather presupposes, the triumphs and defeats of the national modernity. The European Union is also the *post-colonial* Europe, the Europe which confronts itself. Europe conquered, subjugated, colonized and exploited the rest of the world. It is the subject, not the object, of the colonial lust for power. Not least, the European community builds upon the devastation of World War II, the Holocaust and Stalinist totalitarianism; it is also the product of Europe's self-destruction, not of its destruction by others.

With the formula 'both/and Europe' is meant not least that the institutions of the first modernity remain an *integral component of the creation of Europe*. Europe is not a state, nor a national society, nor a sovereign; it is not autonomous, it does not have jurisdiction over taxation, it does not (as yet) have an independent foreign policy and it does not have a military policy or a police force. Yet, it presupposes all of these things. Without the nation-state of the first modernity, Europe is unreal, unthinkable.

The European Union has a strong legal system but lacks the machinery to translate it into practice. Legislation and the application of law are split between supranational and national institutions. Without the member states, the law cannot be applied and European legislation cannot be legitimized, and hence there can be no European politics, however this is understood. Europeanization can *only* be understood on the both/and principle and as the 'side effect' of first-level modernization, as something that can be traced back to deliberate actions of subjects, albeit as something unseen and unwanted. An essential distinction for Europe is that it is both seen and unseen, both wanted and unwanted – the master plan of not having a master plan. For only in this way (it was tacitly assumed by its founding fathers) can the 'idea of Europe', however vague its present concretization, be realized: a reconciled Europe that breaks with its belligerent past and even acquires and fosters a cosmopolitan identity and dynamic precisely from this deliberate historical break.

Can one understand the relation between first modernity and Europe on the model of the Hegelian dialectic, in the sense that the first modernity would be 'sublated' (i.e., both overcome and preserved) in Europe? Of course, 'sublation' [*Aufhebung*] in this context is a notoriously ambiguous figure of thought that can be understood in accordance with the either/or principle or with the both/and principle. On the former reading, the multinational Europe is replaced by the greater national Europe, France, Germany, Poland, Spain, etc., by a 'European people', a European demos, a greater European nation. On this reading, 'sublation' means something like 'replacing'; the former, the national constellation, has run its course, its ideas of civilization and key institutions are an extinct species to be stuffed and put on display for folkloristic edification. On this understanding, 'sublation' has the connotation of 'extinction': either a multinational non-Europe or a European nation.

On the both/and principle, by contrast, 'sublation' does not aim at a separate, completely independent European unit, but instead involves a doubling of the reference groups whose (mode of) existence is as a result transformed to its core. Every citizen of a EU member state should at the same time be a European and as such be 'sublated' in her national-exclusive existence. One can be a European without ceasing to be a German, or a Turk, or a Turkish-German, or a post-Marxist Pole, or an anti-continental and pro-Atlantic British Muslim. The old patterns of inner and outer are no longer valid. Consequently, cosmopolitan Europe (freed from inadequate descriptions) is the epitome of the interweaving, fusion and internal opening of the – still also, but no longer exclusively – national Europe.

In the logic of the either/or conception, the question 'How did or how does the EU become possible?' can ultimately be answered only by subjugation and hegemony, hence on the model of inner colonization. The Europeanization of the nation-states is the best historical reputation of this theory. Europe is the empire *without* an inner hegemon, the empire of *consensus* (more on this below). Without a doubt, there also exist enormous imbalances of power and hegemonic inclinations among the unequal equals within the EU. But membership in the latter does not rest on conquest, colonialism or imperialism, but is *voluntary*. This is impossible, says the national-realistic outlook of the either/or theorists. But it does exist and it is gaining ground all the time! When will the national-imperial hegemonic outlook recognize that it is outdated (if only in Europe) and blind to European realities?

4   Europeanization as regime of side effects

But how then is the transition from a Europe of nations to a cosmopolitan Europe possible? This question is difficult to answer, in particular against the background of the European wars (from the perspective of cosmopolitan Europe, one might say with hindsight, of the European civil wars, of world civil wars). Warring nations are not known as willing converts to peace.

By contrast, the model of the Europe of side effects proposed by the theory of reflexive modernization reckons with a kind of *cunning of reason* that makes possible the transition from the national to the cosmopolitan Europe in accordance with the both/and principle. European society does not emerge on the open stage in a heroic political act but evolves behind the backs of actors through the power of *side effects*. Expressed in terms of social theory, it is the reflexive modernization of European national societies that produces exactly that nameless and anonymous social reality, as well as the resistances to it, which will be discovered in this book as 'European society'. The trademark of this 'side-effects history' of Europe is a fundamental ambivalence. On the one hand, it reflects a cunning of reason that enables Europe to step out of the long shadow cast by its bloody history and to relativize its national egoism. On the other hand, a Europe of side effects is something that nobody really intended and authorized but nevertheless turns people's lives upside down, and thus provokes new national and ethnic resistance *against* Europe. The enigma 'Europe' stands for the unfamiliar transnational society in which we live, yet for which *as such* no, or only a rudimentary, political agenda exists which would make controversies over, and democratic legitimization of, its principles and futures possible.

A glance at the history of the European project shows that expectations concerning the ability of politics to shape reality purposefully should not be set too high. Until now, Europe has not been created by a single act of political will and strongmanship but in a completely different way. More than anything else, the progress of economic integration translated into law produced a social change in Europe through a kind of 'politics of side effects'. The notions of national autonomy, homogeneity and integration are being *annulled* through multinational diversity in the spaces of individualized European lifeworlds. Ever more individuals are producing internationally, working internationally, loving internationally, marrying internationally, living, travelling, consuming and cooking internationally; children are being educated internationally, that is, multilingually and in the nowhere-land of television and the internet; and even political identities and loyalties no longer obey the imperative of monogamous national loyalty. Thus, an *inner* globalization of European societies is gradually taking hold. This partial cosmopolitanization of societies that remain national in their understanding of themselves occurs in large part through side effects independently of the political agenda, in the form of a self-propelling 'meta-change'.

Who or what actually 'acts' when 'Europe' acts? Who or what constitutes the heart of European politics, a politics that promotes political integration as a side effect? What does 'Europeanization as side effect' mean? The side-effects argument does not deny, but rather stresses, that Europeanization was always the product of *political decisions* (which does not mean that these were always taken by democratically legitimate authorities). The side-effects argument is not a variant of the concept of technocracy. Our thesis of institutionalized cosmopolitanism asserts, *first*, that in Europe political opportunities were established whose constructive potential was seized by 'cosmopolitan entrepreneurs' and implemented, sometimes even against the individual member states, where the long-term *impacts* of these policies were largely unintended.

The regime of side effects means, *second*, that, although the *process* of Europeanization – the 'realization of an ever closer union of the peoples of Europe', as the EU Treaty puts it – was intended, its institutional and material consequences were unintended. Of primary importance is the fact that the individual stages of integration did *not* follow any master plan, that is, that the goal was deliberately left *open*. Europeanization 'takes place' and 'operates' in the specific mode of institutionalized improvization. It often remains systematically unclear who took the initiative and how the actual and staged roles and dependencies are interconnected, even in the historiography which hastens to document them. This hiddenness and anonymity of side-effect politics seems to have one major advantage: although the juggernaut of Europeanization presses ahead inexorably, it does not seem to require an independent political programme or a political legitimation. The development of Europe could occur through the transnational cooperation of functional elites with their own criteria of rationality, largely independent of national publics, interests and political convictions. But the technocratic façade stands in an inverse relation to the political content. The framework of European treaties exercises a 'meta-politics' that alters the rules of the game of national politics under the guise of technocratic utility maximization.

In (neo)functionalist theories, this side-effect politics plays a prominent role as optimistic speculation over the 'expansive logic' of 'spillover' effects (see Haas 1958, 1964; Lindberg 1963). In this context, it bears the main burden of explaining the 'political leaps' in the process of European integration. Neofunctionalism proceeds from the assumption that, once the integration of economies has begun, it will necessarily spread to the whole domain of the economy and politics due to the functional interdependencies between the various economic subdomains, on the one hand, and the increasing interrelations between politics and economics, on the other. In this way, the political pressure to act and make decisions is, so to speak, smuggled into the functionalist framework. Effects that overshoot their mark (but which can go in any direction!) create the preconditions for reflecting on 'new solutions' and for taking further 'revolutionary incremental steps'. Although our talk of a Europeanization by side effects links up with the idea of spillover effects, the cosmopolitan perspective of reflexive modernization goes much further. Thought through to its logical conclusion, it is even incompatible with neofunctionalism.

For the politics of side effects can, *third*, be seen as a prime example of what John Dewey in 1927 already prefigured as the inversion of the function of politics in founding publicity. Political controversy is not the result of collectively binding *decisions* but is ignited rather by the *consequences* of decisions that are perceived as problematic in various societal contexts (see Dewey 1991). This yields a specific figure of side-effect politics. If we succeed

(a) in organizing separate discussions concerning decisions, on the one hand, and their consequences, on the other, and thereby (b) invert the sequence of controversy and decision – i.e., *first* make the decision and only *then* engage in a controversy about it – the result is a double consensus effect that concretizes the regime of side effects: the decision itself remains uncontroversial and takes place – almost – without publicity. Accordingly, the transformative step can be taken in the form of an executive consensus among governments and European institutions, whereas the controversy and debates begin only *afterwards*, being sparked in effect by the 'side effects' for specific authorities and actors (for example, national courts and legislatures). In other words, the controversy is ignited *after* agreement has taken place, and *both* the uncontroversial decision and the cross-border dispute found and reinforce the power of Europe.

To the question of how political action is possible in multi-ethnic, transnational and cosmopolitan contexts, Dewey answers that the political – its binding power, its sensorium and nervous system, which generates and binds attention, morality and the willingness to act – emerges *only* in public controversies over consequences. Its scope does not correspond with national borders; rather, the public world includes everything that is registered as a disturbing effect of civilizational decisions. Consequently, it is always also the disruptive *resistance* to the national side effects of the decisions reached through a consensus among governments that promotes the European public sphere. Here 'side effect' becomes discernible as a specific *political construction*: the uncoupling of decisions from public controversies. This (temporal, spatial and social) uncoupling relegates, on the one hand, the actors of democratic collaboration and control to the role of *post hoc* prevention; on the other hand, the so-called internal dynamics of the process of Europeanization is politically produced and implemented in direct executive cooperation between governments and European authorities. Then the underdeveloped European public sphere and democracy can and must debate, reflect and contend over the negative effects of already executed decisions. The more far-reaching and revolutionary the side effects of the decisions reached and implemented through an executive consensus, and hence the greater and louder the controversies and resistances in the national spaces, the more effective will be a *negative*, fatalistic awareness of Europe across all borders in which the voices of the national losers find expression and gain a hearing.

Fourth, the 'Europe of side effects' must be outlined as a meta-power game that, in thoroughly selective and conflictual ways, changes *all* actors in their very substance and mutually extends the leeway for action of powerful actors. It is a major error of the national outlook (and of the related theoretical perspectives of neorealism, intergovernmentalism and federalism) to conceive of the interaction between the European centre and its member states or societies explicitly in terms of the dualism of the national and the international more or less as a zero-sum game: what European politics gains the member states must lose. European integration does not operate in accordance with this zero-sum logic, or, to be more precise, when it is conducted by the member states in accordance with this logic, then it does not function. Exaggerating somewhat, we can put the point as follows: Europeanization was successful when it was played as a positive-sum game in accordance with the principle of cosmopolitan realism. When this was not the case, it failed.

Until now the positive-sum game of Europeanization has functioned only *selectively*, however. Who are the winners of the creeping cosmopolitan over-throw of the nation-state? Both the apparently disempowered national governments and Europe's cosmopolitan entrepreneurs. The one power is inconceivable without the other. The European institutions, such as the Commission or the European Court of Justice, could not define their own role and maximize their influence independently, nor are the states as nation-states in a position to create a domain of power that affords them new European opportunities for power beyond their national boundaries. No member state, however powerful, can afford to disrespect or violate European norms openly, if only because the European Court of Justice, for example, claims and is acquiring European authority. All must listen to and consult with all others; they must learn to see things with the eyes of others and are drawn, indeed forced, into the collective decision-making process. In this way, barriers to unilateral decisions were erected especially in central areas of European policy. The fact that they possess a veto power allows the member states – all of them, even the smallest – to exercise their new status.

This presents an opportunity to study how the reciprocal extension of power functions: it is the right to erect barriers in particular that empowers both the European Court of Justice and the individual states. A European Court of Justice that was not recognized by the respective nation-states as a European-cosmopolitan authority that trumps national law would be an emperor without clothes or, even more, a suit without an emperor (see Weiler 1999). But the converse also holds: individual nation-states that fail to denationalize and empower themselves through the authority of a European Court of Justice remain what they are, namely, loners who must rely on themselves but certainly cannot solve global problems like lone wolves, and hence jeopardize their legitimacy even in the eyes of their own peoples.

At the same time, however, this also enables us to study the ambivalence of European institution-building. For the veto power of the individual states can not only be used to extend European authority; it is also the main instrument for limiting and blocking it. The example of the constitutional convention has demonstrated once again that when national power calculations dominate negotiations and initiatives at the European level, Europeanization grinds to a halt.

Analysis of the meta-power game of Europeanization (see in detail chapter 5) shows that, to date, this has been a highly *asymmetrical* process whose losers clearly are the European citizens (the *citoyens*) and the democratic institutions elected by them. This is what we mean by 'deformed cosmo-politanism': what empowers the governments and supranational actors dis-empowers the parliaments and democratic processes of citizen participation. The empowerment of the European-national intergovernmental cooperation is a major reason for the de-democratization of Europe (see Moravcsik 1994; Wolf 2000).

Finally, this already shows, *fifth*, that the side-effects regime runs up against its limits as the power of the Union increases. This can be seen from the fact that the internal distribution of side effects is becoming problematic. One can clarify this by reference to the neoliberalization of Europe. On the one hand, the governments and parliaments of the member states commit themselves to a budgetary policy that can be sanctioned at the *European* level; on the other hand, they have to compensate for the social and political side effects of this European policy at the *national* level. Although their freedom of action in combating mass unemployment, for example, is restricted, they nevertheless have to deal with its impact – exploding costs in the areas of employment, social and pension policy – at the national level. In other words, with the progressive expansion of the power of the Union, the EU's mode of decision-making becomes problematic because the consequences of these decisions have to be dealt with by the nation-states, which are increasingly restricted in their leeway for action. M. Rainer Lepsius presents a forceful account of the problem:

Decisions concerning distribution, and in particular redistribution, are among the most sensitive areas of policy, especially in times of economic stagnation, not to mention economic contraction. Complex systems for reaching decisions and compromises are then required. . . . Until now, these systems have functioned only at the level of the nation-state by drawing upon specific conceptions of solidarity, civic equality and national welfare guarantees. Both the prestige and the socio-political identity of the nation-state rest on the social and political process of mediation between different interests and interest groups and the consensual notions of legitimacy associated with the results of these negotiation processes. The more the European Union intervenes materially in these basic processes of social structuring and self-legitimation or formally restricts the scope for action of nation-states, the more the European Union will itself be drawn into distributional conflicts. As a result, it will not only be politicized but will also potentially expose itself to the threat of delegitimation. Hence it also needs to develop ordering ideas for the 'social space of Europe', normative conceptions of European social solidarity, hence of value-relations from which a common identity could emerge under conditions of serious internal inequality. (Lepsius 1997: 949)

5   Europeanization as transformative regime

When we also claim that until now Europeanization has not taken place according to a master plan but in accordance with the expansive logic of side effects, we do not mean that this process proceeds along the well-worn paths of business as usual. Europe was indeed produced in many small steps but it has already resulted in a fundamental transformation of European society (for a detailed account, see chapter 4). Europeanization is only properly understood when it is conceived as a politics of *structural transformation*. What is meant by 'politics of transformation'? A preliminary answer can be given through a retrospective examination of its results. During the 1950s, the European Coal and Steel Community developed into a structure whose member states have increased fourfold, whose population has grown to more than 450 million citizens and which constitutes the largest trading bloc in the world. However, 'transformation' as we understand it means more than what is expressed in these demographic and economic aspects. Transformation transcends the opposition between evolution and revolution; it means: evolution as revolution, revolution as evolution.

This hybrid concept of a 'revolutionary evolution' points, on the one hand, to permanently institutionalized change (evolution) and, on the other, to the fact that the nation-state paradigm has been overtaken, complemented or replaced by it. Under the title of 'political integration of the peoples of Europe', evolution has been institutionalized as a process of permanent change.

This revolutionary evolution is often driven forward by the 'motor' of crisis. Exemplary in this regard are the tensions which have recently broken out between the United States and Europe. The Iraq War not only revealed deep-seated fault lines and interest conflicts within Europe. It also awakened a new sense of European community that is necessary to strengthen Europe and to advance its transformation significantly. Europe could even emerge strengthened from this crisis if the European governments find the courage to promote the project of a cosmopolitan Europe. Especially at a time when the global order is dominated by a single major power, the United States, the European states have a future only within a European association of power. The British government learned this lesson the hard way recently when its policy of unconditional loyalty to the United States ended, as it were, in a shipwreck that has left it floating around in the middle of the Atlantic and having to reverse its course in order to reposition itself within Europe. Europe should draw the lesson from the Iraq War that it must counterpose its own cosmopolitan vision, in which the commitment to solve the problems of world risk society features centrally, to the policy of global hegemony of the United States. This would also entail new competences for the EU in security and foreign policy. For the economic strength of the EU must be complemented by the insight that the global political engagement of the Europeans cannot be founded on pacifism but is inconceivable without a military component. Europe can no longer afford the 'luxury' of predominantly national foreign and defence policies if its governments want to acquire worldwide validity, and hence also validity in the eyes of their own populations.

The essential point is to understand Europeanization as a political process based on an (at least partially) institutionalized cosmopolitanism. The role of the European Court of Justice again provides an excellent illustration of this transformative, non-intentional character of Europeanization. How could it happen, one might ask, that the revolutionary quantum leap from national to European legal sovereignty was made possible by a consensus among those involved, hence among the empowered and the disempowered? In answering this question, it is useful to distinguish between the *potential* of institutionalized cosmopolitanism, on the one hand, and its *activation* and implementation by particular 'cosmopolitan entrepreneurs', on the other. The administration of justice by the European Court of Justice is based (exclusively!) on the European treaties. Yet, at the same time, the treaties were first elevated to the status of constitutional law by the administration of justice of the European Court of Justice. More precisely, the European Court of Justice pressed forward with the application and expansive interpretation of the treaties wherever the member states (for whatever reasons) allowed them to do so. The European Court of Justice – as a 'cosmopolitan entrepreneur' – contributed decisively to the realization of the cosmopolitan *potential* of the founding treaties (as well as of the later treaties). Consequently, it would be mistaken to regard the later treaties (in particular, the Single European Act and the Maastricht Treaty) merely as the ratification of a new order introduced by the Commission and the European Court of Justice. The treaties always created something new, whether through institutional reforms (the extension of majority decisions, the expansion of the powers of the Parliament) or through the transfer of new powers (e.g., the economic and monetary union). But they established rather the preconditions on the basis of which the individual cosmopolitan entrepreneurs then advanced the process of Europeanization. A European law that trumps national law because it is perceived and *recognized* as having higher legal authority within the EU arose out of the interplay between the treaties, which made available the institutional potential, and the cosmopolitan entrepreneurs who exploited and shaped this potential.[2]

A prime example of this connection between European legal, constitutional and political developments is the (rightly) often-quoted 'Cassis de Dijon' judgement handed down by the ECJ in 1979 (see Joerges 2003: 195). The occasion for the judgement was a banal one. The case concerned a ban on the distribution of French blackcurrant liqueur in Germany due to the fact that German law prescribed a higher alcohol content for liqueurs than the French drink contained. The ECJ declared this norm to be an illegitimate restriction on trade and annulled it. The implications of this judgement went far beyond the concrete case, however. In its judgement the ECJ declared that the member states were obligated in principle to 'mutually recognize' each other's legal norms. In this way, it created not only the basis for a new concept of integration (the principle of 'mutual recognition') but also an important precondition for the subsequent establishment of a unified European market.

As a consequence of this 'integration through law', the European Union law *replaces* the conflicting national systems of legislation and adjudication by extending its competences and activities. Hence, this 'cosmopolitan over-throw' of the national legal conditions was impelled at least with the approval of the national governments and parliaments who, in accordance with the basic principle of the European treaties, in each case had to ratify the new order. Even the national courts, which, in a way, were disempowered by this Europeanization of legal sovereignty, agreed to this in principle.

What happened here? At first sight, nothing unusual. Without triggering major controversies in the governments and publics affected, another major step was taken in the process of permanent change called Europeanization. Once again, no public controversy broke out over basic principles, no more than there had been over the Schuman Plan or the Paris Treaties or the Rome Treaties. At the same time, this represented a historical step beyond national history without anyone knowing where it would lead and with the affected population remaining benignly indifferent.

In this regard, the intense public debates on the Constitutional Treaty in France, but also in the Netherlands, clearly marked a watershed in the process of European integration. This was the first time that the European project and its impact on national policies (in the French case the 'modèle républic-ain') were the object of a thorough and complete public inspection; and it also represented the first instances in which the European project has been rejected by the citizens of two of its founding members. Dissatisfaction with domestic politics certainly contributed to the negative referendums in both countries; but, on closer inspection, it becomes apparent that the controversy also concerned some of the basic principles of the European project.

In any case, viewed from the theoretical perspective of reflexive mod-ernization, this means that the nation-state (in the sense of the 'Westphalian state') can no longer be placed at the centre of the analysis of Europeaniza-tion. Rather, the principle of state sovereignty, which is equated with nation-state sovereignty in the context of the first modernity, must be freed from its national constraints both conceptually and in political consciousness and be opened up to the interdependencies and power relations of the global age. In reality, a twofold differentiation has long been apparent: on the one hand, a cooperative, transnational extension of sovereignty has been emerging via the renunciation of (national legal) sovereignty; on the other, this develop-ment is propelled within the various policy fields – for example, market regu-lation, social security, home affairs and justice policy, foreign and security policy – under different preconditions, at different rates, by different actors and with different follow-on problems and modes of resistance. European legal sovereignty may in this sense be incomplete, since from the national perspective it lacks the means of coercion to prevail in cases of conflict, for example. Yet from the cosmopolitan perspective the creation of a European rule of law must be understood and evaluated as an essential step towards a cosmopolitan legal system and mode of legitimacy, rather than as a mere departure from national legitimacy. From this point of view, it is then no longer so puzzling why governments and courts would disempower themselves by creating a higher-level European legal and court system in full awareness of what they were doing. For they are disempowering themselves only from the national perspective, not from the cosmopolitan one. In this way, a cosmopolitan vision is partially realized. For example, the European Court of Justice establishes itself as a cosmopolitan entrepreneur that upholds and implements European law – and hence, ultimately, the common European good – against the provinciality of the individual member states. As a European court, it is freed from the national legal systems and outlooks and has the authority to make autonomous decisions that direct the European regime of transformation into legal channels and keep it there.

However, this alone cannot justify the 'blind trust' with which the other actors accompany, indeed support, these revolutionary steps towards a cosmopolitan legal order in Europe. We have already discussed the positive-sum game of Europeanization. What is noteworthy here is that it is also primarily the governments of the member states themselves who benefit from the Europeanization of law. To the extent that a European legal space that is binding on all states emerges, the voices of the individual states gain power and influence. They essentially determine the results of European politics in cooperation with the European Commission and other European institutions. Here again we encounter a paradox that can be explained from a cosmopolitan perspective. The national outlook assumes that the law of the either/or governs the relation between the power of the European centre and the power of the individual states. What we lose, they gain (and the converse). This does not hold for the cosmopolitan outlook. Within this horizon, it becomes intelligible that Europeanization is *not* a matter of a change of subject. Rather the member states as political subjects can themselves propel the transformation of Europe *because* they are able to extend their political power and gain a hearing in a unified European legal domain.

This positive-sum game need not always function, but there can be no 'European integration' without strong transnational states. Only the latter, and not seemingly autarchic cosmopolitan EU actors, can initiate and continue Europeanization as a self-propelling dynamic. This statement *seems* to support the intergovernmentalists in research on Europe. However, that is only partly true. For the law of the *reciprocal enhancement of power*, from which both the states and the European actors at the centre benefit, holds sway in the European domain. The cosmopolitan perspective of reflexive modernization surmounts the controversy between federalists and intergovernmentalists by at once integrating and overcoming the main assumptions of both theories. For what is truly novel about the political integration of Europe is not that intergovernmental forms of cooperation between states were continually deepened and supplanted by supranational institutions. The crux of the European political construction is rather that these two principles were fused together. This is shown in multiple ways by the overall construction of the European Union: first, by the three-pillar structure of the EU which unites supranational and intergovernmental policy domains under a single roof; second, by the institutional architecture of the EU which is marked by the interplay of autonomous supranational institutions (primarily the Commission, the Parliament and the ECJ) and intergovernmental institutions (in particular, the Council and the ministerial councils); and, finally, by the internal make-up of the respective institutions in which the individual principles of integration are combined in the most diverse ways. For example, the European Commission is a supranational institution par excellence because of its formal independence from the member states; and yet it is pervaded by hundreds of committees, the so-called comitology committees, in which representatives of the member states exercise influence over the planning and implementation of community policies (see Töller 2002).

Assuming the concept of transformation as formulated here, the European integration process was always two things at once. In the first place, it was *revolutionary* because it was based on a few key decisions through which the legal, institutional and political bases – in other words, the potential – of Europeanization were generated.[3] However, it was also at the same time *evolutionary* because the supranational institutions (in particular, the Commission and the European Court of Justice) used these bases to exhaust gradually the potential thus created – and often in sharp conflict with the member states. Europeanization was always the product of the interplay between both developments; it is a 'permanent revolution' (but in a completely different sense from Trotsky's). This permanence explains why the process of Europeanization has until now never stopped or gone into reverse, even though it was repeatedly beset by crises. Nevertheless, this permanence is of course itself in need of explanation. A (realistic) explanation would be that until now the distribution of power between the member states of the EU has prevented any of them from gaining a hegemonic position or from exercising an exit option. Although one could in this way explain why there has never been a withdrawal from the EU, it would nevertheless remain open why the process of European integration has faltered but has never regressed behind a level of integration already reached. Even during the long period of stagnation from the middle of the 1960s to the 1980s, European integration progressed, slowly, unspectacularly and in small steps. The thesis of institutionalized cosmopolitanism suggests a different explanation for this phenomenon. According to this, the supranational institutions in their role as cosmopolitan entrepreneurs would be the main reason preventing European integration from regressing. These institutions function (assuming they function properly) as a ratchet mechanism that prevents the process of European integration from falling back behind a particular level of integration once reached.

However, Europeanization as a transformation regime must be understood in still another context, namely, as a 'meta-power game'. The new rules and basic institutions of cosmopolitan Europe are not fixed but are continually disrupted, rewritten and negotiated in the course of the meta-power game of Europeanization. The notion of 'transformation regime' here has a *twofold* meaning: on the one hand, the politics of permanent revolution, the intermeshing of revolution and evolution, through which Europe became, and is still becoming, the (at least partially) unintended product of an institutionalized cosmopolitanism; yet, on the other, also the product of a *meta-power game* in which supranational and national actors and institutions, such as the European Commission, the European Court of Justice, the European Parliament, national governments, national parliaments, courts, authorities, labour unions, enterprises, political parties and advocacy movements, among many others, contend over the future shape of the European project.

This poses the question of how the side-effects argument can be reconciled with the meta-power game argument: doesn't the meta-power game become pointless when its outcomes are not predictable and cannot be planned? Why should actors participate in such a game? In essence, this concerns a constellation in which it is assumed that, although the actors behave in a strategically rational way, the consequences of their actions are not intended. The concept of strategy is thereby refashioned into the concept of 'non-intentional strategies'. This concept of strategy can be distinguished from two others: first, the familiar rational choice models in which institutions are not only rationally designed but are also the intended consequences of strategic-rational action (see, among others, Shepsle 1979); second, models of organized anarchy ('garbage-can' models) in which not only are the consequences of action unintended but actors are also assumed not to act in a strategically rational manner, or to do so only to a very limited extent (see, among others, Cohen, March and Olsen 1972).

Our answer to this problem consists in making the meta-power game the engine of the mechanism which we take to propel the process of European integration, namely, the dialectical interplay between intergovernmentalism and supranationalism (on which see the following). For Europeanization is not a *perpetuum mobile* but is fuelled by the political energy which keeps the transformation process going, which in our view is the meta-power game of the political actors through which they seek to implement various power and integration strategies (for a detailed discussion, see chapter 5).

6   Europeanization as self-propelling regime

The transformation theorem can be summarized as follows: Europeanization is a political process based on an (at least partially) institutionalized cosmopolitanism (specifically, in the form of the European Court of Justice, the European Commission and the European Parliament). Correspondingly, talk of the 'self-propelling dynamic' as developed in the functionalist (or neofunctionalist) tradition in research on Europe must be reinterpreted. This theory is less attuned to the actor perspective; indeed, it misunderstands the analytical concept of the 'self-propelling dynamic' as a *strategy* of evolution-ary revolution. By contrast, it is a useful instrument in the doctrine which answers the question: How do we transform political strategies into law-like processes that unfold behind the backs of actors' motives and intentions with the force of inevitability? This accords central importance not to the contents of the theory but to its political effects in the meta-power game of Europeanization.

In this sense, the functionalism of the self-propelling dynamic fulfils the task of creating consensus. Europeanization, understood as a 'self-propel-ling' process, 'transcends' the ideological conflicts of national politics. In the national logic, functionalism becomes the counter-principle of nationalism (see Mitrany 1966). Here, a language and an associated practical perspective are created that, on the one hand, enable us to speak in analytically sensi-tive and morally uplifting ways about transnational economic and political interrelations, the spirit of cooperation, the overcoming of national egoisms and the European spirit of community. On the other hand, the political gun smoke is completely removed from the process of Europeanization – or so it seems, at any rate. What unfolds as a 'self-propelling dynamic' cannot become a focus of political conflicts; and it is at the same time possible to conduct very detailed negotiations about it in various policy fields. But in this way, a European *master plan* need not be worked out. Rather, the aim is to realize the revolutionary transformation through a kind of European 'millipede politics'. The idea is to concentrate on technically uncontroversial issues in order to implement 'major policies' one tiny step at a time, bypassing political institutions and the public sphere.

From the functionalist perspective, the highly political process of Europeanization mutates into an unideological, apolitical process of trans-formation – it is not a matter of a Europe *of* alternatives but of a Europe *lacking* an alternative. Conflicting ideologies and goals were reduced to the lowest common denominator of existing commonalities that scarcely allow room for a left–right polarization. It was simply assumed that the goal of European integration could be pursued and implemented in the member states and by the supranational institutions without being ground down in the mills of national political conflicts that dominate political debate in the member states. In this functionalist view, 'Europe' is regarded as a superior goal that 'transcends' everyday political conflicts. Functionalism preserves Europe as the ideologically neutral consensual goal of *all* states and popula-tions, parties and organizations. In this respect, the functionalist rhetoric of integration is the guardian of the 'European spirit of community'. The neo-functionalism of Ernst Haas (1958, 1964) and Leon Lindberg (1963), among others, already distanced itself at an early stage from the argumentative figure of the 'functional spillover' presupposed here and argued that political factors continue to play an important role in the European integration process. In this regard, neofunctionalism tried to supplement the 'functional' logic of Europeanization with a 'political' logic. The result was a broader concept of spillover in which functional spillover was supplemented by political and geographical spillover. Thus, neofunctionalists and intergovernmentalists do indeed share the premise that the European integration process is in essence a *political* process. They differ primarily over which political factors determine this process. Here, the neofunctionalists rely on two factors: the supranational institutions (Commission, European Court of Justice), on the one hand, and the national parties and interest groups, on the other. On this view, the 'self-propelling dynamic' of Europeanization is a consequence of the interplay of supranational institutions, parties and interest groups, who are expected to transfer their loyalties increasingly to the European level. By contrast, the (liberal) intergovernmentalists assert that the nation-states and their governments remain the masters of Europeanization (see, in particular, Moravcsik 1993, 1998).

Neither the (neo)functionalist nor the intergovernmentalist theory of integration goes far enough. Existing integration theory has convincingly analysed the deficits of both theories; but it made the mistake of playing the two theories off against each other in accordance with the logic of the either/or.[4] As a result it missed the opportunity opened up by the theory of reflexive modernization, namely, to comprehend the *political mechanism* responsible for the self-propelling dynamic of Europeanization. In this context, reflexive modernization of nation-states means that Europeanization is the unintended result of the conflict-laden *interplay* between the supranational and intergovernmental logics. It is (to repeat) the both/and character of these two logics that sets in train self-propelling Europeanization and keeps it on track.

Ingeborg Tömmel makes a similar argument when, in an analysis of the genesis of the EU, she concludes that

European integration as a whole must be viewed as a process whose progressive dynamic is the result of the tension between intergovernmentalism and supranationalism. When a supranational development results from a consensus among the member states in specific areas of policy, it induces in turn a reinforced intergovernmentalism that manifests itself, first, in the expansion of corresponding structures and decision procedures, then in the construction and extension of policies that take greater account of the divergences of interests among the member states and, finally, in a mode of integration that incorporates these divergences in the development and structure of systems in the form of flexible, variable or staged integration. However, each of these steps calls forth, in turn, a reinforcement of the supranational dynamic of the system or first makes it possible: the successive superimposition of policies, competences and authorizations at the European level; the extension of processes and procedures of decision-making that cannot be controlled exclusively by the member states but in which a multiplicity of non-governmental actors play a role; and, finally, an (apparently) self-propelling dynamic of system development. . . . The result of such a process is a system structure that neither replicates the familiar forms of the national states at the supranational level nor represents a specific variant of the established forms of international organizations; rather, it is a matter of *a system in which inter-governmental and supranational elements and modes of procedure are consolidated into a new structure.* (Tömmel 2003: 54f.; our emphasis)

This process is *always* highly political, but it *appears* unpolitical when it is implemented by independent supranational institutions or by national officials in the dense thickets of the Brussels 'comitology'. The functional-ist rhetoric of integration which is employed in this context must then be understood as part of a technocratic integration strategy (more on this later). Here it is important not to mistake this rhetoric for the thing itself; the fact that Europeanization is *presented* as an objective necessity should not be confused with the forms of policy which are responsible for the self-propel-ling dynamic of Europeanization.

This unpolitical-political character of the self-propelling transformation of Europe through side effects has undoubted advantages (as we have shown in this chapter). However, with increasing successes these advantages are mutating into disadvantages: the contradiction between reality and concept, proclaimed programme and emerging reality, can no longer be disguised, as we have witnessed just recently in France and the Netherlands. The reality of Europeanization outstrips the hollowed-out concepts of the national politi-cal ontology which continues to be articulated. The Union is in danger of becoming a victim of its successes, not of its crises! – this is what the theory of reflexive modernization teaches. More precisely, the self-propelling, non-intentional process of European integration has reached its limit and successes are threatening to mutate into self-generated threats – unless the Europe of side effects can find its way out of the sterile false alternative between federa-tion and confederation and become (or be made) in practice into what it has been from the very beginning: the project of cosmopolitan Europe.

3

Cosmopolitan Empire: Statehood and Political Authority in the Process of Europeanization

1 The national either/or Europe and its predicaments

Those who think of Europe in national terms fail to understand its reality and its future. The national outlook blocks not only Europe's self-description and research on Europe but also its ability to act politically. The European project, which has for a long time been institutionalized and promoted tacitly, urgently needs to be openly acknowledged and embraced as an explicitly political undertaking. Only in this way can Europe master the enormous challenges posed both by the internal, reflexive modernization of its societies and by the reordering of global politics and mobilize new energies. The necessary internal and external opportunities for action and organization can only be created through *negation*, through a radical critique of the customary concepts of politics and the state. The emerging order to be comprehended and developed is a *nova res publica*: the *cosmopolitan empire* of Europe.

The national outlook acknowledges two, and only two, versions of the European project of regional integration: either the confederation of states [*Staatenbund*] (intergovernmentalism) or the federal state [*Bundesstaat*] (supranational federalism). Both models are not only empirically mistaken; currently, Europe is neither one nor the other. We have already shown that Europeanization was marked from the outset by the fact that it integrated both organizational models. These models are also normatively and politically misleading, because they negate precisely the key issue for understanding both the reality and the future of Europe, namely, the Europe of *difference*.

The possibility of grasping the historical and theoretical novelty of the EU in a positive way is blocked by methodological nationalism with its fixation on the state, which continues to dominate the debate over Europe. This narrows the horizon of vision and diverts attention to false alternatives: either Europe is conceived as a 'superstate'[1] – more precisely, as a 'federal superstate' – thereby disempowering the European nations and relegating them to museum exhibits; or it is conceived as a 'confederation', an alliance of nation-states, in which the latter jealously guard their national sovereignty against the expansion of supranational power.

These false alternatives have also long dominated the discussion among social scientists. Thus it is hardly surprising that the process of European integration has generated considerable conceptual difficulties for theories of the state, primarily because European integration has entailed the transfer to external institutions of sovereign rights, which were previously regarded as the genuine property of states and as inalienable (see Grimm 1987: 81). The new political order that emerged from this process differed *from the beginning* – and not just with the steps towards deeper integration during the 1980s and 1990s – from all other international organizations by the fact that

- first, it has a legal system of its own independent of its member states, one which enjoys priority over the legal systems of the member states and exercises immediate jurisdiction over their citizens;
- second, it is equipped with its own institutions, the most important of which (Council, Commission, Court of Justice, Parliament) also have autonomous decision-making powers that they exercise in part independently of the agreement of the member states.

From the perspective of national sovereignty, this must appear as an *external dissolution of state power*, for 'the state no longer concentrates the entire legitimate coercive authority in itself but shares it with other, non-state, though also not private, institutions' (Grimm 1987: 81). In this way, two central features of modern statehood are jeopardized: the (internal and external) sovereignty of the state and its internal unity.

All attempts to comprehend the outcome of this development – originally, the European Community, later, the European Union – in terms of the standard categories of constitutional and international law and to classify it as either a 'federal state' or a 'confederation' have thus far failed to yield convincing results. The EU appears to elude straightforward and sharp categorizations; indeed, the 'neither/nor' seems to be its defining characteristic. Consequently, there is a consensus in the scholarly literature mainly over what the EU no longer is or has not yet become:

- the EU is not a 'state', neither a 'superstate' that has assimilated the sovereign rights of the member states nor a 'federal state' with a clear division of powers;
- but neither is the EU a 'confederation', an international organization or an 'international regime', hence none of the familiar forms of cooperation between states that leave the sovereignty of the nation-states fully intact.[2]

This both theoretically and conceptually unoccupied space of the neither/
nor has repeatedly inspired legal experts, in particular – not to mention
political scientists, historians and philosophers – to invent new concepts in
an attempt to do justice to the 'peculiarity and uniqueness of the Community by comparison with all forms of statehood' (Ipsen 1987: 202). In the
German legal literature, Hans Peter Ipsen's proposal to define the European
Community as an 'ad hoc association based on functional integration' (Ipsen
1972: 196–200) was for many years the most influential in the legal literature. Other authors described the EC (in critical opposition to Ipsen) as a
'parastate superstructure' (Opperman 1977) or as an 'integration association'
[*Integrationsverband*] (Zuleeg 1984).

With its Maastricht judgement of 12 October 1993, the German Federal
Constitutional Court also aligned itself with this tradition of juridical con-
cept-formation. It reached the following conclusion: 'the Union Treaty
[i.e., the Treaty on European Union] establishes a *compound of states*
[*Staatenverbund*] for the realization of an ever closer union of the peoples
of Europe – organized as states – not a state based on a European nation
[*Staatsvolk*]' (Bundesverfassungsgericht 1993: 155; our emphasis). However,
the court left open the question of the characteristic features which distinguish such a 'compound of states' from a confederation, on the one hand,
and from a federation, on the other.

Research on Europe in political science was for many years dominated by
the controversy between neofunctionalist and intergovernmentalist theories
of integration (see Caporaso and Keeler 1995). They were more interested in
classifying and evaluating the results of the integration process than in iden-
tifying its driving forces.[3] Later, attempts were made to apply some popular
'middle-range' theories to the EEC in an attempt to grasp the specificities of
political power and authority in Europe. In the context of these efforts, the
EC (or the EU) was defined, among other things, as:

- a *'network'*, a 'set of networks', a 'network form of organization', a
  'network form of governance' or a 'network state' (Keohane and Hoffmann 1990; Castells 1998; Kohler-Koch and Eising 1999; Ansell 2000),
  whose specific difference from the nation-state is that it does not have a
  clear decision-making centre;
- a distinctive form of vertical *'joint political decision-making'* [*Politikverflechtung*], typically displaying an interweaving and linking of decision-
  making structures and procedures (Scharpf 1988; Grande 1995). From this
  perspective, the EU is conceived primarily as a 'multi-level system', as a
  'multi-level system of governance' or as a 'multi-level state' (see Marks
  et al. 1996; Grande 2000a; Hooghe and Marks 2001, 2003; Benz 1998,
  2000, 2001);
- as a 'consociational system' (Puchala 1971) or a 'consociational state'
  (Schmidt 2000) whose characteristic features are cooperation and consensus among elites.

Each of these concepts exhibits characteristic weaknesses, either because they continue to adhere to an outdated either/or conception of the state, or because they lack a theoretical framework within which the various elements of the European both/and system of political authority can be integrated. However, they are certainly helpful in that they emphasize different, though in each case important, structural features of the EU. Taken together, they enable us to understand some important peculiarities of the institutional architecture and the political process of the EU. *The EU can currently be understood as a decentralized, territorially differentiated, transnational negotiation system dominated by elites.*[4] This transnational negotiation system into which both the nation-states and the supranational institutions are integrated forms the political-institutional core of cosmopolitan Europe.

However, the question naturally arises of how the individual elements of the European political order fit together conceptually. If the EU is not a state, but not an international organization either, then what is it? In our view, the primary challenge is to abandon the outdated, state-fixated concepts and develop an alternative understanding of state, society and social structure that overcomes the methodological nationalism of research on Europe. In an attempt to break the current epistemological deadlock, in this and the following chapter we will present a whole series of concepts in an experimental way, redefine and relate them and draw connections between them. Our goal is to create and test an appropriate conceptual framework to grasp what is novel about Europe. In this chapter, our aim is to update and test the concept of *empire* as a means of analysing the political and institutional dimension of European governance. Our argument is that the cosmopolitanization of the state in Europe has created a new political entity which we propose to analyse as a *post-imperial empire*. As post-imperial, this European Empire (unlike the empires of the nineteenth century) is not based on national demarcation and conquest, but on overcoming national borders, voluntarism, consensus, transnational interdependence and the political added value accruing from cooperation.

The point here is not to introduce the idea of empire as an isolated concept, whether in the sense of the new, global, postmodern political order, as Michael Hardt and Antonio Negri do in their book *Empire* (Hardt and Negri 2000), or as a *sui generis* European empire model, as often occurs in the case of the EU in research on Europe. In order to grasp the specificities of Europe as a (cosmopolitan) empire, what is required is rather to redefine the concept of empire as a new typological concept in the context of a broader historical and comparative sociology of political authority (Shaw 2002; Speck and Sznaider 2003; Münkler 2007). We will accomplish this in a number of steps. We will distinguish, as a first step, the concept of empire from that of the state and, in a second step, from other forms of international order; then in a third step we will contrast the European Empire model with other variants of empire; in the fourth step, we will analyse the internal structure of the European Empire more closely; in the fifth step, we will trace the transformation of sovereignty in the European Empire; and, in the final step, we will examine the various forms in which diversity is organized in the European Empire.

2   State and empire

In order to comprehend and rethink Europe, we must first keep our distance from the concept of the state. Our central thesis is that the concept of the state (and the concepts derived from it: federal state, confederation, condominium, etc.) cannot do justice to the distinctive features of the European project. This does not mean that the concept of the state has become entirely superfluous. As long as the European nation-state continues to exist, the idea of the nation-state remains important. But if it is true that Europe is not a state but rather a new kind of political order, then the concept of the state is inadequate for understanding the new form of political authority which is emerging before our very eyes in Europe. To continue to use it is like the futile attempt to open a door with the wrong key. But what are the alternatives? In the following, we propose to use the concept of *empire* to describe the novel forms of political authority which are acquiring exemplary shape in Europe.

2.1   What is meant by empire?

How could a revised concept of empire provide the key for developing a conceptual framework that would enable us to represent and investigate the macro-sociological political dynamics of Europeanization in an appropriate way? Wouldn't the concept of 'transnationalism' (see in particular Keohane and Nye 1972, 1977; Risse-Kappen 1995), which was already developed in the political science literature during the 1970s, also fulfil the same purpose? Without doubt, the concept of transnationalism has some advantages; but talk of 'transnational' Europe also remains tied to the principles of nationality and internationality, if only negatively. If one asks what really unites the transnational, not only in the microcosm of the lifeworld experiences and practices of individuals and groups, but also in the forms of institutionally legitimized power, then the concept of empire has undoubted advantages that parallel those of the concept of cosmopolitanism, as we will show in what follows. Hence, the discipline of 'international relations' must also awaken from its dream of the persistence of (inter)nationality and rethink the reflexive modernization of global politics in conceptual terms.

At first sight, however, the concept of empire seems to be extremely ill-suited to our purposes. In the legal theory of the state, 'imperium' functions as the counter-concept to 'dominium' and has the general meaning of the public property of a ruler as opposed to his private property (see Jellinek

1960; Krüger 1966). Analogously, Max Weber signifies by the concept of imperium all 'nondomestic powers' (Weber 1978: 651). Understood in this sense, *every form* of public political authority would fall under this concept, rendering it much too broad for our purposes. On the other hand, however, it can also be understood in a much narrower sense, namely, that of the 'imperial state' of the nineteenth and twentieth centuries. In this sense, imperium would signify a quite distinctive form of – territorially expansive and economically exploitative – statehood, and this variant of the concept would be too narrow for our purposes because it would remain linked to the concept of the state.

To avoid misunderstandings, therefore, we must first detach the concept from its existing contexts and define it anew. In order to make this difference terminologically clear as well, we will not employ the concept of imperium, or the even more vague (German) concepts of 'Reich' or 'Großreich', but instead make use of the concept of empire. In recent years, the concept of empire has undergone a renaissance, especially in the American discussion over the prospects of a new world order following the Cold War. It can be found in leftist critiques of globalization (Hardt and Negri 2000) as well as in neoconservative analyses of the role of the USA in world politics after 11 September 2001 (Bacevich 2002), and critiques thereof (see, among others, Todd 2003).[5]

How could the concept of empire function as a 'new paradigm' (Speck and Sznaider 2003: 14) in the discussion concerning new models of order and forms of political rule in the twenty-first century? To what extent does it offer a way out of the territorial misconception of political authority, in other words, the dead end of methodological nationalism? Can it replace the idea of a system of sovereign states which shaped the first modernity? In our opinion, the concept of empire has at least three significant advantages. First, it sensitizes us to new forms of political integration beyond the nation-state and liberates the analysis of political power from its fixation on the state. A second advantage is that talk of empire alerts us to the existing asymmetry of power among states, and hence breaks with the fiction of the equality of sovereign states. A third advantage of the empire concept is that it historicizes the division between the national and international and hence challenges the axioms on which politics and political science still act and think. We must ask how the pre-national and postnational constellations of empire-building, -reproduction and -dissolution can be compared. Or, more pointedly: does economic, cultural and political globalization necessitate a change in the basic unit of politics from the nation-state to empire? Hence, does the idea of the cosmopolitan state refer to the idea of empire? or, to rephrase the question, how can the one be specified more precisely through the other? In other words, talk of empire poses the question of the extent to which there exists an affinity between the premodern period and the second modernity, and hence the extent to which the brief eternity of the national era makes us blind to the long-range historical continuities and differences within and between the various global historical forms and epochs of empire, i.e., those of the ancient world, the Middle Ages and the second modernity.

2.2   *State and empire in comparison*

Our initial assumption is that state and empire represent two fundamentally different forms of the exercise of power. Following Max Weber, we define a state as a permanent political association based directly on the formal power of command over those subject to it. By empire, by contrast, we mean a mode of exercising power whose defining characteristic, bluntly put, is that it permanently strives for control over non-subjects. In contrast with a state, the subjects of a state retain a certain degree of formal independence. More precisely, empire combines direct and indirect, formal and informal modes of the exercise of political authority. An empire is not simply a territorially extensive state; it differs from the latter through a fundamentally different logic and fundamentally different techniques of political authority. But it is not a matter of purely informal relations of power either.[6] Although Max Weber acknowledged the imperial form of government, he could not understand it as 'a political association' because it does not rest solely on the power of command. It features only very briefly in his sociology of political authority, and then under the misleading heading of the 'empire state'. According to Weber, '[e]ven without any formal power of command an "empire state" . . . can exercise a far-reaching and occasionally even a despotic hegemony' (Weber 1978: 945). He cites as examples the role of Prussia in the German Customs Union and the status of New York 'as the seat of the great financial powers'. But since these are instances of 'forms of power . . . based upon constellations of interests', and not of those based upon 'authoritarian power of command' (ibid.: 946), consistent with this position Weber deliberately did not discuss them further in his sociology of political authority.

We intend to take up this loose thread in the sociological analysis of political authority. The key is provided by two differentiations in Weber's categories which we will explain in greater detail later: first, the distinction between (international) hegemony and empire; and second, the distinction between hierarchical power of command and consensus-based cooperation as modes of exercise of political authority. In this way, empire can be conceived as a non-hegemonic form of the exercise of political authority which does not rest, at least primarily, on a hierarchical 'power of command' but on the political premium which consensus-based cooperation produces for all participants.

In what follows, we mainly emphasize the differences between state and empire. Nevertheless, it must be borne in mind that, although they both fulfil the same *governmental functions*, they rest on different logics of political authority, and they employ different techniques to perform these functions.

They both have to guarantee the internal and external security of a political community and its material welfare.[7] Their success is ultimately measured by whether they manage to perform both of these functions in the long run. But they try to perform these functions in completely different ways. To put it baldly, the crucial difference between a modern state and an empire is that the state seeks to solve its security and welfare problems by establishing fixed borders, whereas an empire solves them through variable borders and external expansion. Neither strategy is unproblematic: the former runs the risk of *internal* overstretching (e.g., an immoderate expansion of the welfare state, or an excessive growth of the repressive security state), the latter that of *external* overstretching, with the attendant problems regarding resources, order, organization and identity.

In historical comparisons in political science, the modern state is treated as the superior form of political rule for good reasons. It clearly won out over its competitors, the late medieval city-states and alliances (e.g., the Hanseatic League) (Spruyt 1994), not least because (and only because!) it succeeded in establishing an optimal balance between the financial and military costs of exercising sovereignty over a territory, on the one side, and the promotion of public welfare, on the other. The precondition for this was both territorial and social demarcation. In this way, the costs of integrating a territorial jurisdiction were held within tolerable bounds. The modern state has also outlived all of the modern empires, whether post-feudal or colonial (e.g., Lieven 2002). Following the break-up of the imperial colonial regimes, the modern territorial state survived as the sole remaining form of the legitimate exercise of power in the second half of the twentieth century. However, it would be mistaken to conclude from this success story that it will also remain so in the future. On the contrary, in the age of globalization, the preconditions for the success of the modern territorial state have become precarious. Therefore, it is quite possible that it is no longer the state but a modernized type of empire which constitutes the most appropriate organizational model for political rule.[8] And Europe could be one of the paradigmatic cases to demonstrate this.

The *logic of political authority* of the state is based on drawing permanent, fixed boundaries; in particular, the modern state operates with a clear-cut scheme of inclusion and exclusion. Only its members, the citizens, are entitled to its benefits. The imperial logic of political authority, by contrast, is based on the logic of permanent expansion and transcendence of borders. Empires have a tendency towards comprehensiveness, even universality, not only in their practice but also in their self-understanding.[9] Their external borders are open and flexible.[10]

Perhaps the fundamental characteristic of imperial sovereignty is that *its space is always open*. . . . The modern sovereignty that developed in Europe from the sixteenth century onward conceived space as bounded, and its boundaries were always policed

	State	Empire
Function of political authority	Internal and external security; public welfare	Internal and external security; public welfare
Logic of political authority	Fixed, permanent and closed borders; logic of inclusion and exclusion	Flexible and open borders; logic of unlimited expansion
Techniques of political authority	Formal equality of members; uniformity of norms and public services; modern sovereignty	Asymmetry of forms and rights of membership; differentiated integration; imperial sovereignty

Figure 3.1: Constitutive features of states and empires in comparison

by the sovereign administration. Modern sovereignty resides precisely on the limit. In the imperial conception, by contrast, power finds the logics of its order always renewed and always re-created in expansion. (Hardt and Negri 2000: 167)

Consequently, empires also tend to overcome the distinction between 'inside' and 'outside' either by negating the outside (as in the case of the Roman Empire) or by integrating it through expansion (as with the Chinese Empire): 'the international order is merely the extension of the internal order, founded on the idea of a universal sovereignty' (Duverger 1980b: 17).

The *techniques of political authority* employed by state and empire in performing their tasks and ensuring their survival are also fundamentally different. This holds both for the organization of space and for the organization of relations with those subject to their rule. Modern states strive to create a uniformity of norms, entitlements and services within their territories, and they are based on the formal, legally guaranteed equality of their subjects. Empires, by contrast, tend to establish asymmetrical forms and rights of membership among their various territories and the associated groups of subjects so as to be able to control the space over which they exercise authority. At their simplest, they are organized internally through hierarchical centre–periphery relations;[11] at their most complex, they develop highly differentiated forms of integration and control.[12] These differences are rooted not only in the different spatial extension of states and empires but also in their different social structures. Whereas, ideally, modern states are organized in accordance with the principle of sociocultural homogeneity, all empires are marked by their sociocultural diversity. Indeed, this diversity is one of their central defining features.[13] As we shall see, however, empires can vary considerably in how they deal with sociocultural diversity internally.

2.3   *Empire and models of international order in comparison*

The concept of empire, however, must be distinguished not only from that of the state but also from the current models for the constitution of international order. If the new imperiums involve multinational, supra-state forms of political domination, how can they be distinguished from the familiar forms

Integration/symmetry	Symmetrical	Asymmetrical
Integrated	Field 1: World state; supranational integration	Field 2: Empire
Not integrated	Field 3: Westphalian system of international politics; intergovernmental cooperation	Field 4: Hegemonic order

Figure 3.2: Variations in the international organization of political order

of international and supranational order? For our purposes, it will suffice to explore the organization of political rule beyond the nation-states in two dimensions. First, these political associations must be distinguished according to the extent to which they aim at a formal, legal integration of their various territories; and then they must be subdivided into those which aim at this integration in symmetrical and in asymmetrical ways. The four possibilities resulting from these distinctions are summarized in figure 3.2. Based on these distinctions, *empires* should be conceived as a specific type of political rule which combines an integrated territory (where the mode and intensity of integration may take different forms) with asymmetrical relations among its constitutive elements, which are not only materially, but also formally, unequal. Important here is, on the one hand, the fact of integration. This integration may occur in a variety of ways: militarily, legally, administratively or economically. In each case, it is linked with explicit claims to authority. A whole range of differences may exist among the various elements of this political order, for example, with respect to their legal autonomy, their duties, their claims to public services and much else. And as we know, for example, from the British Empire, the modes of integration and their strength may vary considerably over time (see Ferguson 2003). According to Herfried Münkler, the exercise of imperial power is

ordered in accordance with a system of circles and ellipses that radiate outwards from the centre to the periphery. The manner and the degree of self-obligation of imperial power also vary with these circles and ellipses. It is strongest in the centre, in the heartland of the empire, where it approximates to what holds for the self-obligation of power in states. Towards the periphery, by contrast, it diminishes progressively, without thereby violating the functional principles of imperial order. (Münkler 2003: 112f.)

Empires must be distinguished primarily from two other forms of organization of international order – first, from *hegemonic orders* characterized by the dominance of one or a few 'great powers'. The territory over which their power extends is neither legally nor administratively integrated; power is exercised in the first instance indirectly, through military and economic superiority, and it extends primarily to the external affairs of states.[14] However, neither the zones of influence of such great powers nor these great powers themselves should be confused with empires. Great powers are not empires, but states. The model of international order they constitute is an asymmetrical system of international politics that leaves the foundations of the Westphalian model of formally equal and independent states intact, at least in principle. The other alternative to empire is supranational integration, by which is meant the formal integration of sovereign nation-states within a superordinate system of political authority. This finds its fullest expression in neo-Kantian models of the 'world state' or 'world republic' (for a recent example, see Höffe 1999).

How should Europe be classified in this context? At this point, the importance of distinguishing between the EU and Europe becomes apparent. As we have seen, the EU itself combines principles of intergovernmental cooperation and supranational integration. In essence, therefore, it combines the models in fields 1 and 3 of figure 3.2. At the same time, Europeanization is increasingly assuming asymmetrical forms. There are several reasons for this. On the one hand, integration in important areas within the EU is already proceeding in accordance with the principle of differentiated integration, i.e., it no longer embraces all member states in the same way. The best example of this is the economic and monetary union, which includes at present only twelve (of the initially fifteen and now twenty-seven) member states. At the same time, the EU is tied into a differentiated network of international organizations and treaties with other European (and non-European) states whereby the latter are formally integrated into the sovereign domain of the European Empire. Taken together, this implies – this is our *main argument* – that Europe has to be understood as an empire, indeed that the cosmopolitanization of Europe can only succeed if Europe abandons the state form and assumes the character of a *European Empire*. This is not to suggest that Europe is only conceivable as an empire. The four fields of figure 3.2 also represent the four most important paths for the future development of European integration. In principle, Europe could outgrow its intergovernmental limitations completely and acquire the form of a supranational state; it could also conceivably dismantle its supranational competences and regress to an intergovernmental arrangement, whether one with hegemonic power (which is becoming increasingly improbable considering the growing number of members) or one without a hegemon. However, as long as it does neither, as long as it combines and integrates both principles effectively, it can only be one thing: an empire!

2.4   Imperium and empire: historical variants of imperial constitution of order

Talk of the European Empire risks provoking not only opposition, but also misunderstanding. This is not only because in recent times the concept of empire has been reinvested with strong normative connotations, but also above all because it is used to describe very different phenomena that at first sight have little to do with one another (see Duverger 1980a; Doyle 1986; Koebner 1961; Eisenstadt 1963). The social, economic and cultural foundations of empires differ fundamentally; furthermore, empires do not appear as 'pure' forms of political rule, but are always bound to other forms.[15] Thus historical development throws up different types of empire that correspond in essence to the various forms of political rule or statehood (see the survey in Duverger 1980a).

Here we do not need to give a detailed description of these phenomena. For our purposes, it is sufficient to distinguish to begin with between the following basic forms of empires or, more precisely, of *imperial constellations*:

- *premodern empires*, characterized by the fact that their constitutive elements are *not states* in the modern sense. The power structure of these empires is shaped by premodern forms of political rule, namely, the ancient city-state in the case of the Macedonian Empire of Alexander the Great, clan structures in the case of the Mongolian Empire of Genghis Khan, feudal structures in the case of the Carolingian Empire and of the Holy Roman Empire;
- *modern empires*, whose constitutive elements are states and often nation-states in the narrow sense. In these cases, imperial rule assumes a state form – modern empires are not only militarily but also legally integrated. Their internal asymmetry is expressed in a tiered concept of sovereignty through which non-sovereign, semi-sovereign and sovereign states are integrated into a system of political authority. To this category belong not only the colonial empires of the nineteenth and twentieth centuries but also, for example, the Austrian Empire.

The question arises how the new forms of empire-building to be observed in the context of globalization fit into this classification. Hardt and Negri (2000: 187) interpret the new global order as a 'postmodern' one based on a new form of imperial sovereignty. Thus 'empire' in their sense would constitute, in systematic terms, a new, third type of imperium. Richard Cooper (2003) also distinguishes between premodern, modern and postmodern states, and within this framework he describes the EU as the most developed example of a postmodern system (see Cooper 2003: 36). However, we regard this dismissal of modernity as premature. Instead, we want to exploit the potential of the theory of reflexive modernization (see chapter 2; Beck, Giddens and Lash 1994; Beck and Bonss 2001; Beck and Lau 2004) to distinguish between empires of the first and the second modernity. The new forms of empire-building would accordingly represent a novel mode of political authority in the second era of modernity. They continue to be modern, since nation-states are their constitutive elements and the concept of state sovereignty functions as one of the central regulating features of authority. However, at the same time they mark a structural break in the development of modern societies, since political authority simultaneously transcends the nation-state and transforms its sovereignty. The theory also yields criteria of a postmodern conception of empire. We should speak of the latter only when basic principles of modern statehood have been completely annulled and the constitutive elements of empire-building are no longer states but other forms of organization of political authority.[16]

Both models contrast sharply with basic assumptions of first modernity, in which a quite specific combination of empire and nation-state evolved, i.e., the idea of the systematic rule of a nation-state over other territories. The result was 'a new type of empire' (Hobsbawm 1987: 57), namely, the colonial. Accordingly, the nineteenth and twentieth centuries produced the rivalry between imperial national and colonial powers in Europe, which were striving for world domination. Thus, the first age of modernity was characterized by a nation-state coding of global empire-building in which the principle of sovereignty was superseded by that of competitive subjugation: 'Between 1880 and 1914 . . . most of the world outside Europe and the Americas was formally partitioned into territories under the formal rule or informal political domination of one or other of a handful of states: mainly Great Britain, France, Germany, Italy, the Netherlands, Belgium, the USA and Japan' (ibid.). This nation-state empire system of the first modernity was, in Craig Murphy's terms, an 'inter-imperial system' (Murphy 1994).

After World War II, the nation-state system was transformed in accordance with the logic of the East–West conflict, though differently in the East and in the West. On one side, there was the subordination of the European and Japanese nation-states to the United States (see Katzenstein 2005); on the other, the Soviet Union established an imperial power in Eastern and Central Europe. Alongside and connected with it a new kind of empire initially emerged in 'Western Europe' that differed fundamentally from the national-colonial empires of first modernity.

2.5   Features of the European Empire

What are the constitutive features of the European Empire? If we apply the concept of empire to Europe and compare it with analyses of European politics, then at least ten features emerge, which we assume to be fundamental to the European Empire. Viewed as a whole, it becomes evident not only that the concept of empire is much more suited than the concept of the state (or other concepts of international politics derived from it) to understanding the peculiarities of the structure of authority in Europe, but also that a new form of empire is in fact emerging there. In analysing the European Empire, the findings of recent research on Europe in political science, in particular network and multi-level analyses of European politics, are definitely useful (see, among others, Hooghe and Marks 2001; Kohler-Koch and Eising 1999; Jachtenfuchs and Kohler-Koch 2003; Grande and Jachtenfuchs 2000; Ansell 2000). The change in perspective we are suggesting here does not invalidate these concepts. On the contrary, we argue that these concepts really make sense, and can realize their full potential, only in the context of the notion of empire.

Feature 1: Asymmetrical political order

The European Empire, like all empires before it, is an asymmetrical political order. Its members do not all have the same status, rights or duties. On the contrary, *formal* inequality (not inequality in effective power, whether military or economic) is constitutive – and indispensable. Only in this way can heterogeneity and integration be reconciled in the long run. Simplifying somewhat, the spatial structure of the European Empire can be subdivided into *four zones of power*. These zones may be distinguished, on the one hand, according to the *intensity of cooperation* and, on the other, according to the *number of countries involved*:

- first, a *zone of complete integration* that is made up of a small number of EU member states with a particularly strong willingness to cooperate. Representative here are the Eurozone, in which twelve of the then fifteen members adopted a common currency, and the Eurocorps, with which five EU member states created a common military force;
- second, a *zone of intensified cooperation* comprising the twenty-five member states of the EU (up to the end of 2006) in the policy areas of the first pillar. This includes those areas of policy (e.g., agricultural, competition, industry, research and technology, regional and environmental policy) in which the EU has powers of its own and which are handled by the supranational institutions;
- third, a *zone of limited cooperation* comprising the twenty-five member states and those policy areas of the second and third pillars which to date have not been integrated at all or only to a limited extent (home and justice policy, foreign and security policy). These are the policy areas in which the EU also operates in accordance with the principle of intergovernmentality;
- fourth, a *zone of extended power* comprising, on the one hand, those states which adopt European rules and participate in EU programmes without being formally members of the EU (accession candidates, associate states); however, this zone also includes regional organizations of intergovernmental cooperation located outside the treaties of the European Union

(such as WEU, ESA and EUREKA) and whose circle of participants as a rule is clearly distinct from that of EU members. Here cooperation also conforms largely to intergovernmental principles.

Note that this is not a utopian model for the future shape of Europe; what we describe here is the spatial structure of the European Empire in 2006, following the enlargement of the EU to twenty-five members. Neither Europe nor the EU is a homogeneous and symmetrical entity; a 'core Europe' of countries with a greater commitment to integration already exists; and with the eastern enlargement, the zone of extended authority of Europe was not dissolved and incorporated entirely into the EU, but simply (temporarily) reduced in size and displaced further east.

Feature 2: Open, variable spatial structure

The concept of European Empire is not one of fixed borders, but one that *annuls* fixed borders and makes them variable; not a static, but a dynamic concept. To put it paradoxically: its 'unity' is the process; 'integration' arises from the permanence of change and it does so in a number of respects:

- first, through *interweaving* – horizontally among the national societies, vertically among states, and diagonally among states, societies and international and transnational organizations;
- second, through *transformation*: the national units themselves change, the states and societies are becoming Europeanized and cosmopolitanized from within;
- third, through the *shifting of borders*: borders between states within the Union are being dismantled and a new kind of European border is being established, but one which is at the same time being moved ever further geographically, first southwards, then eastwards, so that transnational spaces of overlapping jurisdictions, identities and loyalties are being created;
- finally through *pluralization*: the more diffuse the 'European We' becomes, the more unclear becomes the 'cultural other' of Europe; the affirmation of difference itself is becoming the motor and the determining factor of the cosmopolitan both/and Europe (see Landfried 2002; also chapter 4).

The result is that the contours of the European Empire are becoming blurred. This should not be confused with principled openness or arbitrariness. The spatial organization of the European Empire follows the logic of contingency or, more precisely, *political contingency*. The borders of the European Empire are set, shifted and made more or less permeable for political reasons; membership is granted or refused for political reasons; opportunities for participation are exercised or rejected according to political criteria.

The result is a highly variable, multidimensional geometry of Europe with bizarre spatial structures.

Feature 3: Multinational societal structure

All empires are multinational, multi-ethnic, multi-religious power structures, and all empires face the problem of how to deal with (cultural, economic, social) diversity. The older imperiums generally tried to solve the associated problems of integration by making universalist claims, although, of course, they used completely different methods to realize these claims. Modern colonialism, as is well known, tried to enforce its universalist claims by brutal means.

The European Empire differs from earlier empires not in its greater homogeneity, but in a different, i.e., cosmopolitan, approach to dealing with difference. The European Empire cannot subordinate the multitude and variety of different national cultures and identities to a standardized 'European' culture. Where would it come from?[17] The integration of the European nation-states in a new supranational political order inevitably leads to a multinational form of political rule. Any attempt to impose uniformity, along the lines of the traditional model of the nation-state, is condemned to failure. Conversely, however, a historical model for a cosmopolitan Europe is not possible either, for a quite trivial reason, namely, because the European Empire presupposes the existence of nation-states, which were unknown to historically earlier empires. It is a well-known fact that the process of nation-state-building led to the break-up both of the major European territorial empires and of the colonial empires. The European Empire, therefore, is not the revival of an older political form, but the creation of a new one. This is what makes the EU a product of the second modernity. Just as the religious civil wars of the sixteenth and seventeenth centuries were brought to an end by the recognition of sovereignty and the separation of state and religion with the peace treaties of Westphalia, so a separation of nation and state – and this is the guiding hypothesis of the cosmopolitan empire – could be the response to the national world wars of the twentieth century. Just as the confessionally neutral state permitted various religions, so the cosmopolitan Europe would have to guarantee the cross-border coexistence of different ethnic, national, religious and political identities and cultures through the principle of constitutional tolerance. This cosmopolitanization occurs internally, within the member states (recognition of transnational lifestyles, civil rights and 'minority rights') as well as between them, but it also has an external dimension. In this context, the question of Turkey's EU membership is a key issue for cosmopolitan Europe. After 11 September 2001, the building of bridges to the Muslim world has become a necessity; and a European Turkey, which is at the same time Muslim and democratic, has a key role to play in this regard.

Feature 4: Integration through law, consensus and cooperation

In the past empires were established and maintained by force, above all military force: 'Major political formations are rarely the result of voluntary associations. In general, they are the product of fire and the sword. They arise from military superiority' (Duverger 1980b: 20). The European Empire is *the* great exception in this respect: it was constituted not through fire and the sword, but through pen and ink; and it is founded essentially on the consensus and cooperation of states, not on military subordination. The integration of the European Empire occurs primarily through *law*, through the voluntary agreement upon, and the acknowledgement and application of, European law (see Katzenstein 2005). The greatest threat to other European countries is not military conquest but the refusal of EU membership, i.e., accession into the inner circle of power of the empire. However, due to the specific mode of integration through law, the European Empire lacks an effective mechanism of exclusion from the outer zone of power. It cannot forbid other countries to adopt its legal norms or to open their markets voluntarily – that is, to Europeanize themselves (even against Europe's will) and to integrate themselves in the outer zone of the empire.

To outsiders, the European Empire appears curiously weak, 'a self-contained world of laws and rules and transnational negotiation and cooperation. It is entering a post-historical paradise of peace and relative prosperity, the realization of Immanuel Kant's "perpetual peace"' (Kagan 2003: 3). Such views fail to grasp the quintessence of the European Empire: it secures its internal domination not through force, but through a *taboo on force*. The monopoly of force as the most important attribute of modern statehood is not transferred to the empire but remains with the member states. The latter, however, handcuff themselves; they become executors of their own internal pacification. The key question 'Who enforces decisions and rules against resistance?' acquires a historically novel answer: not the state, not the imperial centre, not a UN or an EU armed force, not a hegemon, but those subject to authority, the member states of the empire themselves. The internal pacification of the empire is not based – as in the case of a sovereign association of states – on the disarmament of the members; on the contrary, these must continue to enjoy a monopoly on the legitimate use of physical force within their sphere, so that state force becomes controllable through the state's self-restraint. The internal pacification of Europe occurs through the establishment of a modern *taboo* – namely, the member states' self-restraint in the use of force to regulate their affairs – which seeks to annul, within the empire's domain of authority, the seemingly eternal laws of a history ultimately dictated by force.

The eastern enlargement of the EU in 2004 clearly demonstrates the constitutive importance of law and consensus for the European Empire. The eastern European countries have become members of the EU neither through conquest nor through submission, but through an altogether banal and yet highly rational act: they made an *application*, which was then scrutinized by the European Commission in a rational – at least in principle – *procedure*, in accordance with rational *criteria*, on which the heads of state and government of the EU member states agreed by *consensus*. The terms of accession were then *negotiated* by the Commission and the accession states; and, finally, the *subjects*, that is, the citizens of the accession states and of the EU member states, decided on admission, in part directly in referendums, in part indirectly in parliaments.

That does not mean, however, that force played no part in the genesis of the European Empire and in its development. On the contrary, the European Empire is also built on force, but indirectly, not directly. Europe is first and foremost the product of a conscious *negation of force*; after two world wars, the avoidance of war was the main imperative of European politics. It was then, in addition, the product of a quite specific organization and disciplining of global violence, the Cold War, which compelled the West European states to cooperate with each other.

Nevertheless, the European Empire remains a strangely flawed entity. Its military capacities are modest and they are not integrated under a centralized chain of command. It follows that the cardinal problem of the European Empire is fundamentally different from those of older imperiums. Their challenge consisted primarily in exercising military and administrative *control* over the territories over which they ruled; the problem faced by the European Empire is primarily to secure the *cooperation* of the subject states. In both cases, there is the threat of imperial overstretching, in one case because the costs of controlling a subject territory outstripped its utility, in the other because the costs incurred in ensuring the willingness to cooperate grow too large.

Feature 5: Welfare vs. security

Empires provide specific solutions for the security and welfare problems of societies. Security problems are supposed to be solved by extending borders outwards and bringing zones of insecurity under direct control; welfare problems are supposed to be solved by permanent control over scarce resources (raw materials, labour, capital) and unlimited access to consumer markets. These two functions of empires need not always have equal priority, nor need they be fully compatible, but they represent the most important driving forces of imperial expansion. All of this also holds for the European Empire. Initially, it was undoubtedly grounded in an immanent 'idea of peace' (Hardt and Negri 2000: 167) that marked the early phase of the European integration process after World War II, in particular. The aim was to eliminate the danger of further wars – above all that emanating from Germany – by sub-jecting the important war industries of the time (steel and coal) to common, supranational control.

Subsequently, however, the primary aim of its expansion was no longer to secure peace, but to increase affluence. Like the imperialism of the nineteenth century, the European Empire has to date followed a primarily *economic logic*. If 'the function of colonies and informal dependences was to comple-ment metropolitan economies and not to compete with them' (Hobsbawm 1987: 65), then the logic of expansion of a common market is also to open up an ever larger market for European industries and to impose uniform rules on economic competitors.

Pointedly put, thus far the European Empire has relied on the 'force of the economy', rather than on an ingenious 'economy of force' (Rosen 2003: 96). In the project of the eastern enlargement, both driving forces came together to create a political impetus that swept away all well-meaning incremental expansion plans. In a speech at Berlin's Humboldt University, the then German foreign minister, Joschka Fischer, got to the – national – heart of the interdependence between security and economic motives at work in the eastern enlargement of the EU:

Enlargement is a supreme national interest, especially for Germany. It will be possible lastingly to overcome the risks and temptations objectively inherent in Germany's dimensions and central situation through the enlargement and simultaneous deepen-ing of the EU. Moreover, enlargement – consider the EU's enlargement to the south – is a pan-European programme for growth. Enlargement will bring tremendous ben-efits for German companies and for employment. Germany must therefore continue its advocacy of rapid eastern enlargement. (Fischer 2000: 5)

Feature 6: Horizontal and vertical institutional integration

All empires differ from modern states in their more pronounced differentia-tion of spaces and functions of power. Aside from the asymmetric differentia-tion of political authority already discussed, the European Empire is marked by a high degree of vertical differentiation, which political science research on Europe has labelled a 'multi-level system of governance' (see Marks et al. 1996; Scharpf 1994, 1999; Benz 2000, 2003; Hooghe and Marks 2001, 2003; Grande 2000a). In other words, the European level is not simply superim-posed on the national and subnational levels of politics; the member states and their regions are not simply subordinated to the EU and its institutions.[18] Instead, there are highly diverse institutional and material interdependencies among the various levels of policy-making. These include the intensive par-ticipation of national and regional actors in supranational decision-making processes; they also encompass the major importance of national and regional actors and institutions in the implementation of European policies.

Crucial here is that, whereas the function of nation-states and their conditions of action change, they continue to play an important role. The member states of the EU are integrated in the European political process in the most diverse ways, whether formally or informally. At this point, however, the consequences of the asymmetry of the European Empire are especially evident. Whereas the members of the inner zone of authority are formally equal in drawing up the rules (although their voting power is weighted according to population), the members of the outer zone are mostly excluded. So even in an empire concept the question of EU membership makes a difference.

Feature 7: Network power

The exercise of political authority in the vertically differentiated, interlocking power structure of the European Empire is marked by two features:

- first, by the *non-hierarchical form* of decision-making and the inclusion of national political actors in the European decision-making process;
- second, by the participation of a large number of *societal actors* (interest groups, lobbyists, companies, actors from civil society) in political decision-making processes.

As a result, the European Empire has taken on a network-like structure. It is, in Chris Ansell's words, a 'networked polity':

The networked polity is a structure of governance in which both state and societal organization is vertically and horizontally disaggregated (as in pluralism) but linked together by cooperative exchange (as in corporatism). . . . The logic of governance emphasizes the bringing together of unique configurations of actors around specific projects oriented toward institutional solutions rather than dedicated programs. These project teams will crisscross organizational turf and the boundary between public and private. State actors with a high degree of centrality in the web of interorganizational linkages will be in a position to provide facilitative leadership in constructing or steering these project teams. (Ansell 2000: 311)

The key questions that arise here are: Where is power in such a network located? How is power organized in the European Empire? Is Brussels the new Rome? Our answer is that a double transformation of power occurs in the European Empire due to its multi-level structure. First, the power to command is transformed into negotiating power. In an interlocking multi-level system, political decisions can hardly be achieved by way of hierarchy and only to a limited degree by majority vote; instead they have to be reached through negotiations. Consequently, the European multi-level system is in essence an integrated negotiating system. Second, hierarchical power is turned into network power. This, too, can be substantiated in terms of organization theory (see Crozier and Friedberg 1979). In a multi-level system, power can no longer be entirely concentrated at the top; it becomes displaced to the interfaces and control centres between the individual institutions and system levels. In short, power emigrates from the centre and occupies the system's periphery and resource flows – power becomes network power.

The consequence of this double transformation of power is that the European Empire has a peculiar power structure compared to its historical predecessors. Although its power structure is asymmetrically graduated, it does not reproduce the straightforward centre–periphery relations of older territorial and colonial empires (see Eisenstadt 1963). This is because the European Empire does not have a power centre in the narrow sense, but also because its 'periphery' enjoys a greater degree of autonomy. This is precisely what typifies a cosmopolitan empire: it respects differences and is based on mutual respect among members – in spite of all legal and economic inequalities.

Feature 8: Cosmopolitan sovereignty

Unlike premodern and modern empires, the European Empire is based entirely on *sovereignty*. It does not mark a refeudalization of statehood or a 'new Middle Ages' (Minc 1994), even though it certainly does exhibit superficial similarities to the Carolingian Empire or the Holy Roman Empire (see Axtmann 2003). It also differs in a crucial way from modern colonial empires. The latter were based on a system of graduated sovereignty rights, which scholars of constitutional law tried to grasp within a differentiated conceptual framework: only the imperial centre possessed full sovereignty; the subject territories of the 'formal empire' were either non-state or non-sovereign (see Jellinek 1960: 489–96). In the European Empire made up of sovereign nation-states, this logic is reversed. The greatest losses of formal sovereignty are incurred by those states which constitute the innermost zone of power. The further we move outwards, the greater is the formal sovereignty of the subject states.

The point of the European Empire, however, does not reside solely in such shifts of formal sovereignty. In a globalizing world, such attributes are in any case becoming less significant (see Reinecke 1998; Grande and Risse 2000). Of greater importance is that in the European Empire the concept of sovereignty is itself being transformed, i.e., that sovereignty is developing into *complex, cosmopolitan sovereignty*. Two aspects characterize this transformation process. First, through the division of internal sovereignty and the consolidation of external sovereignty, the complexity of sovereignty is increasing; 'absolute' sovereignty as in Bodin and in Hobbes is becoming 'complex' sovereignty (see Grande and Pauly 2005). In this way, it also becomes possible to apply the concept of sovereignty beyond the modern nation-state. Moreover, the concept of European cosmopolitanism offers the possibility – only apparently paradoxical – of turning sovereignty losses into sovereignty gains (as we will show in greater detail below).

Feature 9: Ambivalence of delimitation and limitation

Empire, like the modern state, is not a clear-cut, consistent mode of organization of authority. It has its own ambivalences and contradictions. Characteristic of the European Empire is the ambivalence of delimitation and limitation. Every empire, including the European one, has an inherent tendency to expansion, to delimitation. As a *European* Empire, however, it cannot aim at universality; it must at the same time always limit itself. These limits or boundaries may vary over time and they may be politically contingent, but they must always exist.

From this follows a fundamental contradiction of the European project. It cannot, it *must* not offer an answer to the questions: Where does Europe end? What belongs to Europe? If Europe answers these questions conclusively, then it risks falling back into the *state* form – and becomes entangled in another contradiction, namely, that between national and supranational sovereignty. There is only one way out of this dilemma: the politics of reflexive self-limitation (for more detail, see chapter 7).

Feature 10: Emancipatory vs. repressive cosmopolitanism

In general terms, cosmopolitanism means the recognition of otherness. This recognition may be inspired by two completely different motives, namely, a repressive or an emancipatory one, leading to two fundamentally different variants of the cosmopolitan empire. In its repressive form, the aim of cosmopolitanism is to 'affirm' differences 'and arrange them in an effective apparatus of command' (Hardt and Negri 2000: 200). Cosmopolitanism in this sense represents an especially refined technique of power.[19] The aim of the emancipatory form of cosmopolitanism, on the other hand, is to create and expand free spaces. Here the acknowledgement and emphasis on difference serves to strengthen individual and collective *autonomy*.

However, it would be naïve to believe that this emancipatory quality is already imprinted in the structure of the European Empire: 'Empire does not create differences. It takes what it is given and works with it' (Hardt and Negri 2000: 199). *How* it works with it, is left completely open. At this point, we come to a final and decisive bifurcation. Just as we must distinguish in principle between two variants of reflexive modernization – reflexive pluralism and reflexive fundamentalism (see Beck, Bonss and Lau 2001) – so too we must distinguish between two variants of European Empire: a repressive one and an emancipatory one. It will be one of the most important tasks for the further elaboration of a theory of empire to work out in detail the conditions under which cosmopolitan Europe can realize its emancipatory potential.

For the purposes of the present analysis, it is neither possible nor necessary to examine every feature of the European Empire in detail. In the remaining sections of this chapter, we will explore in greater detail only the three aspects which are of central importance for the reflexive-modern character of the European Empire: (1) the role of the nation-states in a European empire; (2) the transformation of sovereignty and (3) the cosmopolitan organization of diversity.

3   European Empire and the transcendence of the nation-state

With the creeping constitution of a European Empire, the nation-states are not being dissolved but are instead being at once transcended and preserved (in the Hegelian sense of 'sublation'). They continue to exist but are being transformed into cosmopolitan states through their integration into a more inclusive system of political authority. Their function and the way in which they exercise it are changing, as is the nature and strength of their ties to their citizens.[20] We want to examine this *transformatory potential* of the European Empire in two steps. First, we will focus on the transformation undergone by the European nation-states. Then, in chapter 4, we will consider in detail the Europeanization of the national societies.

3.1   *The function of the nation-states in the European Empire*

The change in the function of the European nation-states has several dimensions. In the first place, it is clear that they are losing an ever larger part of their exclusive and autonomous legislative authority in the European Empire. In a cosmopolitan Europe, rule-making increasingly takes place at the European level and through supranational institutions; the remaining competences of the member states must frequently be exercised within a framework prestructured by European meta-rules. This also holds for those states which are not formal members of the EU but are integrated into the European Empire as part of its external zone of authority. These states, too, are compelled to adopt at least parts of the European system of rules, the *acquis communautaire*, and hence to relinquish their autonomous legislative authority. This affects not only countries that in this way hope to gain easier acceptance into the inner zone of authority of the empire as 'accession candidates'. Even countries such as Switzerland, whose citizens have hitherto stubbornly refused to join the EU, are no exceptions to this. Notwithstanding their rejection of accession, they could not prevent an increasing amount of Swiss legislation becoming merely an 'autonomous duplication' of EU rules.

From a national perspective, this development has provoked two misunderstandings. In the first place, it is generally interpreted simply as a loss: what the EU gains in term of powers, count as losses for the member states. On the other hand, it is often assumed that national and supranational competences can be clearly and permanently separated and allocated to the respective levels of decision-making. Both assumptions are false.

The notion that supranational and national competences can be cleanly and definitively separated is far removed from reality and reflects a misunderstanding of the peculiarities of the European Empire. Moreover, the idea of a precise division of tasks is part of the national self-delusion (see chapter 1, section 3). Numerous interdependencies and overlappings have transpired in practice between supranational, national and regional policies. This is not simply a consequence of the striving for power of the supranational institutions but has several reasons:

- the competing interpretations of the principle of subsidiarity in which the latter is read in very different ways;
- the cross-national divergences in the need for economic and social regulation resulting from different national models of capitalism and the welfare state;
- different national expectations concerning regulation, which reflect, for example, different state traditions;
- different national interests (poor vs. rich countries; large vs. small countries); and
- functional interdependences among the different policy areas.

None of these differences is easily removable. After all, heterogeneity and diversity are structural features of the EU, and the greater the differences, the more difficult it becomes to regulate the relations between the EU and its member states by means of the principle of subsidiarity. For this reason, we should expect that the distribution of powers and resources in the European Empire is subject to a *political dynamic* as we know it from federal systems (see, in particular, Friedrich 1964; Benz 1984, 1985; and more recently, with reference to the EU, Nicolaïdis and Howse 2001)

The constellation of problems and their expressions at the central and decentral levels, the definitions of problems and the specification of tasks, the internal distribution of resources and the forms of interaction are subject to constant change. For this reason, *federal systems cannot be stabilized through a specific division of powers and resources.* On the contrary, they prove to be reactive and changeable constructs. Thus centralization and decentralization, and the various forms of joint decision-making and cooperation within the federal state, represent different ways of coping with the main problems resulting from the interdependence among the tasks and developments in the problem constellations. (Benz 1984: 67; our emphasis)

What holds for federal systems also holds for the European Empire, even though it does not take the form of a federal state. Nevertheless, both conform to a similar logic of the distribution of powers and resources. This is due to a specific feature of the architecture of power, which distinguishes the European Empire sharply from other empires, modern ones included, namely, the reciprocity of resource relations and exchanges. Although the European Empire rests on asymmetrical relations of authority – i.e., a system of differentiated integration and tiered rights – it does not involve clear and straightforward relations of exploitation, such as were typical for premodern empires and the modern colonial systems.[21] A cursory examination of the 'net contributors' to the EU budget demonstrates this in an exemplary way. In the EU, the flows of resources do not proceed from the periphery to the centre, as is usually the case in empires, but in the opposite direction, from the centre to the periphery – and the eastern enlargement will reinforce this trend.[22] This is not to suggest that no relations of exploitation exist within the European Empire – of course they do; the point is rather that the structure of these exploitative relations is different and more complex than is typical for empires. This is due not least to the fact that the distribution of powers and resources within the European Empire is also more complex than in other empires.

The vertically oriented national perspective on Europe also overlooks something else: the member states not only transfer tasks to the EU, but they also acquire new tasks in the process. This exhibits a further characteristic of the European Empire, namely, the extensive delegation of the exercise of power to the subjects. The EU governs without being able to exercise control over those who control the means required to exercise power. This holds not only for those countries which are not members of the EU and belong only to the external zone of political authority of the European Empire; it also holds within the EU itself. The role of the nation-states within the power structure of the Union exhibits at least three defining features: first, that, in transferring their competences to the EU, they have not generally renounced their own competences entirely;[23] second, that they continue to enjoy exclusive fiscal sovereignty within the EU;[24] and, third and finally, by the fact that the financial, administrative and military capacities are for the most part established in the member states. In short, although the national administrations have been Europeanized through the process of European integration (see Knill 2001), there has not been any transfer of state capacities from the national to the European level.

As a result, the EU plays an ever greater role in *making* rules, but it does not possess the financial resources or the administrative capacities to *impose and implement* these rules. This remains primarily the task of the member states, and there is no sign of this changing much in the future. On the contrary, the European Commission is already quite often overstrained by the administrative implementation of its multifarious tasks. The obvious solution to this problem – namely, the establishment of additional administrative capacities in Brussels and an increase in the personnel at the disposal of the Commission – has hitherto been frustrated by the resistance of the member states. As a consequence, the chronically overburdened Commission had to develop a high degree of creativity in order to delegate its administrative tasks to commercial consultants, scientific experts, interest groups – and, above all, the member states.[25]

3.2   *The modus operandi of the European Empire*

The European Empire is an imperium without an emperor. Its governmental functions are concentrated neither in the hands of a personal ruler nor in a single institution. Europe has neither an emperor nor a president. In an era marked by the personalization of politics, the European Empire remains remarkably impersonal. The members of the European Court of Justice are probably unknown even to the majority of legal experts; the members of the European Parliament scarcely manage to step out of the shadow of anonymity even during election campaigns; the members of the European Commission (including its president) all too often present a picture of lamentable powerlessness; and the heads of state and government of the EU member states make only sporadic appearances on the European stage. This is not to say that the exercise of power in the European Empire is utterly diffuse or that Europe would need such a concentration of power in order to be recognized as an empire.

Europe has indeed an imperial centre of political authority, even though it is not to be sought in a single person or a single institution. It can be found in the institutional complex which constitutes the core of what we have called institutional cosmopolitanism. This institutional core of the European empire is constituted, in the first instance, by the supranational institutions such as the European Commission, the Council of Ministers, the European Court of Justice and the European Parliament. The architecture of this institutional core of the European Empire differs fundamentally from the political systems of all of its member states, as well as from earlier empires. This concerns, in particular, (a) the status and task profile of the relevant *institutions*; and (b) the *procedures* of decision-making and conflict resolution.

The institutional design of the EU's political system differs in numerous respects from the models of parliamentary or (semi-)presidential democracy on which the governments of the EU member states are based. This is, on the one hand, due to the different weighting of institutions, in particular of the Parliament and the Commission. It is striking that the parliamentary arena plays a much weaker role in the EU than in its member states. Although an extension of parliamentary rule is a running theme in debates on the reform of the EU, the reforms undertaken to date, notwithstanding all expansions of powers, have had only a minor impact on the fact that the parliamentary representation of European *citizens* still plays an ancillary role within the system of European institutions (see Maurer 2002).

However, at the European level the problem of the distribution and redistribution of powers among the institutions is complicated by the fact that the institutional architecture is characterized by a peculiar interlocking and fusion of power that is at least formally alien to the national systems of government. This atypical institutionalization of power is particularly apparent in the functions of the European Commission, which is in many respects a *hybrid institution* (Bach 2000; Nugent 2001). The Commission not only forms the executive of the EU (a function it shares with the Council and the member states, incidentally) but at the same time it also enjoys extensive legislative powers. It has the sole right to initiate legislation and has in addition some important decision-making powers of its own. The Commission is supposed to exercise all of these competences not only administratively, as the executive organ of the Council and the member states, but also in an expressly *political* sense – as the 'motor of integration', it is the main institutional agency of the cosmopolitan dynamic within the EU. In short, the Commission combines legislative and executive, political and administrative functions in an unprecedented way.

Consensus-oriented decision-making and conflict-resolution procedures play a much greater role within the EU than in the member states. Currently, approximately one-third of all EU decisions still require unanimity, and only two-thirds can be decided in accordance with the majority principle. As a general rule, majority decisions require a qualified majority (of almost 70 per cent of the votes); only procedural questions can be decided in accordance with the decision rule which represents the norm in the Westminster model of parliamentary democracy, namely, simple majority vote (see Scharpf 2000: ch. 7). Moreover, even these numbers overestimate the real significance of majority decisions in the EU. In fact, consensus among the member states is frequently sought even where an issue could be formally decided by a majority vote.

Consensus and cooperation not only shape the operation of the European institutions; they also characterize the functional logic of the European Empire as a whole. Its historical uniqueness ultimately resides in the fact that, at the most reckless moment in history of the world of states, a political invention succeeded that makes the impossible possible, namely, the erection and policing of the modern taboo on the use of force by the states themselves. Nowadays this state of affairs seems so obvious to us that it demands special emphasis. The threat of force as a political option – whether between the member states or towards the supranational institutions – has not only been banished absolutely, i.e., once and for all, from the horizon of the possible, but has disappeared from the horizon of the thinkable. Moreover, this is explicitly not felt as a castration but is valued and celebrated as a historical achievement, and hence presupposes the transnationalization of the politics of memory and commemoration (see chapter 4, section 3). How is this possible? First, the states must define their interests in cosmopolitan – hence simultaneously national and European – ways. Their national welfare can in this way be equated with the European, and this holds even in cases when the former seems to be at odds with the latter. This is a conflictual and contradictory process and it by no means always meets with immediate success. Our term for the outcome of this transformation of autonomous nation-states into self-disciplined members of the European Empire is '*cosmopolitan states*'. The logic of the self-constraint of state force in Europe presupposes the cosmopolitanization of the European nation-states.

Our second premise is that what is novel in this resides not in internal pacification but in the fact that the latter is accomplished not through disarmament and centralization – as in the state model – but through the controlled tabooing of national military force. Of course, the member states of the EU are not military eunuchs; the military was not disbanded at the national level and transferred to Brussels and concentrated there, but was instead subjected to a system of self-control within a European Empire.[26]

4 European sovereignty as a positive-sum game

The concept of sovereignty – more precisely, its redefinition – is the key to understanding the European Empire. On the common understanding of sovereignty, state sovereignty is absolute and indivisible (see Quaritsch 1970). This conception allows only an either/or: either sovereignty resides in the nation-states, or it resides in the EU. The idea that it might be possible to equip supranational institutions with sovereignty rights, without thereby restricting the sovereignty of the member states, is incompatible with this either/or logic. According to this logic, European integration would be a zero-sum game. For the European nation-states the only question would be whether and to what extent they play along with this game.

How can we overcome this either/or logic? Obviously, the only way is to abandon the prevailing understanding of sovereignty. For this purpose, it is useful first to recall the achievements of the classical conception of sovereignty. 'Absolute' sovereignty, as it was conceived by Bodin and Hobbes in the sixteenth and seventeenth centuries, achieved two things in particular: first, the claim to exclusive legislative authority contributed to reducing conflicts within societies, because it fostered clear definitions of decision-making powers and the elimination of the system of competing and overlapping authorities which had existed until then; this was, second, the necessary precondition for the state performing the most important function expected of it, namely, establishing and securing peace internally and externally. The former – i.e., 'legal' sovereignty – was the crucial presupposition for the 'material' functioning of the state.[27] In the terminology of organization theory, legal and material sovereignty were 'tightly coupled'. As conservative theories of the state correctly asserted, the emergence of modern welfare states during the twentieth century already loosened this close linkage between both dimensions of state sovereignty (see Forsthoff 1971); now, in the era of globalization, it has been completely dissolved. There is no important area of politics left in which legal sovereignty is anywhere near sufficient to allow the state to perform all of its important tasks effectively. The emperor is naked, not because he has no new clothes, but because he has lost his old ones – without noticing it.[28]

The distinction between legal and material sovereignty can serve as the starting point for transforming the zero-sum game of state sovereignty into a positive-sum game. For, under the conditions of globalization, the renunciation of legal sovereignty does not necessarily entail a loss of the state's ability to act and solve problems – on the contrary, under certain circumstances the latter can even be enhanced (see Grande and Risse 2000; Beck 2005). Briefly, the state renounces a portion of its legal sovereignty in order to recover its material sovereignty. Even more briefly, and with a paradoxical twist: the renunciation of sovereignty leads to an increase in sovereignty.

To cling to an outdated concept of absolute nation-state sovereignty under these conditions is either tragic or cynical. It is tragic if it represents an attempt – well meaning but necessarily futile – to achieve political goals in this outdated way and if 'national pacts for work' collapse and unemployment figures rise dramatically as a result. This is the tragic aspect of the national self-delusion. It is cynical if the shortcomings of nation-state policies are reinterpreted as a failure of the state as such, and the nation-state is reduced to a minimum state in order to safeguard its sovereignty. This brand of cynicism is typical of neoliberals.

The concept of European cosmopolitanism offers a way out of this dilemma. Cosmopolitan sovereignty presents the possibility of transforming the renunciation of sovereignty into an increase in sovereignty, thus finding new clothes for the emperor. In this conception, it is crucial that states should not be required to sacrifice their self-interest in favour of some altruistic ideals. In order to 'pool' national sovereignty (Keohane and Hofmann 1990), all that is required is that states should conceive of their self-interest in terms of the changed circumstances of 'world domestic politics' (Carl-Friedrich von Weizäcker) in a world endangered by civilization, and that they should redefine and pursue it in a specific – i.e., a reflexive – way. Thus what is expected of the nation-states is that they should acknowledge that their pursuit of their interests has been transnationalized and that they should realize that their interests are becoming reflexive. The concept of European cosmopolitanism, therefore, is not a plea for a return to the old idealism in the theory of international relations. It rests, first of all, on a globalized political realism that has become reflexive – on a cosmopolitan realism. At the centre of this 'enlightened cosmopolitan' realism is the concept of *reflexive interests* beyond the dualism of national and international.

The key question then is, of course: What are the conditions for such a transformation of interests to take place? In what follows, we will outline at least three sets of conditions that seem to be most relevant: (1) the politics of interdependence, which presupposes (2) the reflexive self-limitation of national interests and (3) some capital of trust.

4.1 The politics of interdependence

The result of the European integration process is not a new European 'super-state' but the economic socialization of states with the goal of reconciling them within a new form of empire. The success story of the EU – the taming of the bellicose rivalries among major national powers within the historically unique non-state 'Europe' without enemies – reflects an element of cosmopolitanism that is not at all banal, namely, the intermeshing of capitalism and a politics of reconciliation. Ironically, the construction plan of the EU has hitherto followed a Marxist realism with a political twist. Capitalism is given a 'pacifistic' turn because the dynamics of the economic substructure are intended to create the political superstructure, or to encourage, even compel, its creation. The European economic substructure has a specific political goal. In contrast to the imperialism of the nineteeth and early twentieth centuries, it excludes as its main ancillary aim war between the member states; in other words, it reorients Europe's bellicose history towards the goal of reconciliation and pacification. This policy of promoting peace in Europe through the economic back door was by no means illusory but, on the contrary, a highly successful endeavour. One could object that the declared goal of reconciliation was merely the ideological and rhetorical embellishment of a purely economic imperative. However, this criticism misunderstands the civilizing force of economic interdependencies and the new logic of Europe's economic pacification.

The secret at the very heart of this success story bears the name the *politics of interdependence*. The politics of interdependence has two aspects that mutually presuppose, complement and reinforce each other: the *perception* and the *creation* of interdependencies. First, without the perception of real, transnational interdependencies, be they military threats, mutual economic dependencies or civilizational dangers, there is no reason to redefine national interests. Perceived and publicly reflected interdependence is the necessary precondition for the transnationalization of politics. As long as states have, or assume that they have, the possibility of achieving their goals unilaterally, it suffices if they pursue their interests in an offensive manner. They neither have to take account of nor cooperate with others in pursuing their interests.[29]

However, the politics of interdependence also has a second meaning, namely, the conscious *forging of interdependencies*. In this case, mutual dependencies are consciously created in order to render national unilateralism more difficult or even impossible. The secret of the European politics of reconciliation was from the beginning a politics of interdependence in this sense. Subsequently, divergent perceptions of global problems were also exploited to forge interdependencies (more on this later; see chapter 7). Already at this point it becomes apparent that a *political* interdependence exists between the two aspects of the politics of interdependence. In Europe, an ever finer network of mutual dependencies arose, with the result that the costs of nations going it alone increased steadily. This can be made clear by means of a thought experiment. Imagine that the European Union were to be dissolved. What costs would be entailed by replacing the European currency again with twelve national currencies, by reintroducing all of the national borders to be policed and all the national customs, by replacing European regulations once again with twenty-seven national systems of regulation, by introducing national subvention programs for agriculture and underdeveloped regions, and so forth? We don't know whether such a calculation has ever been made,[30] but its result can be easily guessed at: the costs of dissolving the EU would be so high that the process of European integration has become de facto *irreversible*.[31]

Hence, the question of whether the member states of the EU have a *formal* right of secession, which plays a central role for political scientists and scholars of constitutional law and was hotly debated in the European Constitutional Convention, becomes de facto irrelevant. Even if they retain this right, and hence their formal sovereignty, they would do well to refrain from making any further unilateral use of it.

What happens, however, when individual states blockade the European decision-making and integration process *from inside* the European political system for strategic reasons through a systematic veto policy or a 'politics of the empty chair'? In fact, this is remarkably seldom the case. In effect, it has occurred only twice: in the mid-1960s when France blocked the Community with its 'politics of the empty chair'; and again in the mid-1990s when Great Britain for a brief period likewise withheld its cooperation in the decision-making process of the European institutions. This second case is especially instructive because it already shows that, at the current level of integration, the threat to refuse to cooperate does not harm the EU, though it may very well harm the refusing party. In addition, the fact that there has not been a *single* secession, or even a serious threat to secede, from the Community, tells the same story.[32]

Again, how should we understand this? In answering this question, it makes sense to differentiate the politics of interdependence not only in terms of the perception and the creation of interdependencies, but also in terms of the parties whose action is supposed to be bound, namely, whether it is a matter of *self-binding* or of the *binding of others*. In this context, the politics of interdependence means, first, *rational self-binding*. The classical example for this remains Odysseus, who had himself bound to the mast of his ship in order to avoid succumbing to the temptations of the Sirens. Jon Elster (1983) generalized this example and showed that under certain circumstances it can be rational to place restrictions on one's own freedom of action with the aim of preserving it. One can also call this the 'paradox of weakness' (Grande 1996); in what follows we will analyse it in terms of the 'politics of golden handcuffs'.

Second, however, the politics of interdependence can also be oriented to *strategically binding others*. Here we must ask *how* others can be obligated and, in addition, to what extent talk of 'interdependence' masks continuing or newly developing inequalities of power. This leads to the question of how (i.e., through what procedures) reciprocity between unequal member states can be assured.

As in the case of the perception and creation of interdependencies, here too rational self-binding and the strategic obligation of others presuppose and reinforce each other. Dependencies are created for rational reasons and in rational ways that compel the actors (in our case, states) to take account of the interests of others *if they want to avoid harming themselves* – and this solely to promote their own utility. This leads to a positive-sum game because the parties are at the same time compelled to promote the utility of *others*.

4.2   The politics of golden handcuffs: on the reflexive self-interest of cosmopolitan states

The apparent paradox to be understood and elucidated is the following: in the era of global crises and risks, only the self-conscious politics of 'golden handcuffs', in the sense of rational self-constraint, leads to the recovery of national independence – also and especially in view of the increased power of the highly mobile global economy. How, then, can the 'vicious circle' of the zero-sum game be replaced by the 'virtuous circle' of the positive-sum game of Europeanization?

In answering this key question, it makes sense to distinguish between *simple cooperation*, which leaves the cooperating actors largely unaffected, and *transformative cooperation*, which does not leave the cooperating entities unaffected but alters them. Drawing on the studies of Robert Axelrod (1984), we can safely assume that the probability of transformatory cooperation increases with the frequency of interaction. The longer the 'shadow of the future', the greater are the incentives for the actors involved to cooperate and the greater is the probability that the preferences of the actors, and ultimately the actors themselves, will undergo change as a result. This is precisely the case in Europe. Europeanization is not a single event and cannot be understood as a one-off cooperation or as a series of unique cooperations that ultimately leave the cooperating nation-states unaffected, as the intergovernmental perspective assumes. Europeanization must be conceived, rather, as transformative cooperation in which the actors undergo change. This can certainly occur in uncoordinated ways in the dimensions of institutionally enforced joint decision-making and public self-reflection. The political actors may delude themselves as to the degree of interdependency and self-transformation already achieved and they may formulate European policies as though they remained completely independent. The larger EU member states in particular tend to succumb to this self-delusion. However, the political actors can also foresee interconnections and dependencies and act in the expectation of possible interdependency. This is the anticipatory self-adaptation of the EU accession candidates.

Be that as it may, the gradual and abrupt transformation called 'Europeanization' has altered the forms of political authority concerned and the national sovereignty of the states involved *to their very core*. National states have become *trans*national states with advancing Europeanization,[33] and this in a twofold sense. On the one hand, an intermeshing and merging of national and European interests ensures that national interests can be pursued and maximized *as* European interests; on the other hand, the instrumentalization of the European public good, i.e., false cosmopolitanism, remains an option for *all* states. Every member state government must anticipate that the others may act likewise. It follows that the expectations of the expectation that the European interest will be instrumentalized, as a threatened reduction of one's own 'national-European' interests, are ever present. Accordingly, it makes sense to distinguish between a factual-institutional and a publicly reflected transnationalization of national interests. Only in the second constellation do *reflexive self-limiting* strategies of the member states *in their national self-interest* develop. The latter refrain from exercising their remaining sovereignty for good reasons and observe the European rules of the game, as interpreted by the European institutions, to ensure a permanent maximization of their national interests.

Once again, this demonstrates that cosmopolitanism does not mean altruism or idealism but realism, more precisely, the *reflected self-interest of transnational states*. This can be read, in turn, as an example of the *internal cosmopolitanization of the national* based on the interplay of three mechanisms.

1   The prospect of *increases in power:*   All member states – though not they alone! – gain access to new sources of power by internalizing the European rules of the game. They acquire a voice at the European level that matters. For the most part, they can directly influence the outcomes of European policy and hence also its (trans)national consequences. The solution to their 'internal' national problems – such as criminality, migration, the environment, agricultural development, technological and scientific cooperation, etc. – is achieved through the united power of the EU.

It is true that this logic of the increase in power is often ambivalent and that it can also be guided by the principle of the lesser evil. With increasing integration, however, its potential gains outweigh the threatened costs of exclusion and the establishment of a hegemonic power. If one asks, for example, how the implementation of a unified currency zone – i.e., the euro – succeeded, it becomes clear that countries such as France, Belgium, the Netherlands and Italy had their eye not only on the benefits of a common currency but also on the threat of a European Deutschmark system dominated by the Bundesbank. And the best way to avert this danger was to create a fully Europeanized currency system in which they enjoy equal representation and voting rights with the Germans. Here, too, the problem of asymmetries in power in the European Empire becomes apparent, for these imply exclusion from decision-making processes and the denial of the gains in power of Europeanization.[34]

2 *Interactive constraints and controls*: In the European power sphere, the interests of individual states are disciplined by the fact that their interests are bound into dense networks of interdependence and as such are objects of permanent interaction and revision. This is due primarily to a peculiarity of the EU negotiation system that clearly distinguishes it from other forms of international negotiation, namely, its permanence and transsectoral structure. Together they entail that the 'shadow of the future' (Axelrod 1984) cast over all negotiations is especially long and that, in cases of refusal of cooperation, undesirable displacements of conflicts from the political into other domains are a present danger. Hence, strictly egoistic conduct on the part of a single actor could have consequences such as were observed in the EC in particular during the 1960s and 1970s: 'The negative attitude adopted by one Member State led to a number of negative reactions in other areas on the part of its partners. The block on enlargement was answered by a corresponding block on the Mediterranean negotiations and on technology' (Sasse et al. 1977: 193).

3 Shifts in preferences through *policy learning*: Under these conditions, it would be fatal to assume (as does neorealism) that national preferences are unalterable givens. Politics would be in constant danger of being drawn into a vicious circle of refusal to cooperate; and, above all, once drawn in, it would have no chance of getting out again by its own efforts. Empirical research on Europe has shown that such a constellation is not unavoidable. The actors are quite capable of *learning* and changing their preferences, especially under conditions of strong interdependence and intensive communication (see Sandholz and Stone Sweet 1998; Eising 2001). This has far-reaching theoretical and practical implications, because then preferences are no longer independent but dependent variables, and the crucial problem is to identify the circumstances and factors that influence their variation.

In the 'politics of golden handcuffs', therefore, three components reinforce one another. Gains in power, interactive constraints and controls and reflexive transformations of preferences create the preconditions for breaking through the vicious circle of the national zero-sum game and replacing it by a transnational positive-sum game. The notion that power is like a predetermined 'cake' that the member states and the EU institutions compete to divide at one another's expense is simply false.

The transition from the autonomous nation-state to the reflexive transnational state, therefore, occurs insofar as national-transnational self-interest is made conscious and is institutionalized. In this regard, a programmatic shift from national to cosmopolitan common sense is indispensable. The fact that hitherto this has occurred in Europe only in secret and in confidence, while the national zero-sum game continues to hold sway in people's minds, indicates how much European consciousness remains split.

4.3   Capital of trust: obligating others

Talk of the 'politics of interdependence', especially if it is meant in a cosmopolitan sense, should not limit itself to its own perspective but must also include the perspective of others. Viewed from the perspective of others, interdependence can mean very different things, namely, either *hegemonic* or *reciprocal* dependence. In other words, in speaking of interdependence or in promoting it, one can easily downplay differences and inequalities and render them invisible. Talk of interdependence all too often merely feigns reciprocity. The politics of interdependence among unequals, however, may also be a euphemism for hegemonic dependence. It is no accident that 'interdependence' is not a neutral word or an intrinsic value for the Eastern European states which have recently cast off the yoke of their Older Brother, the Soviet Union. They aspire instead to independence while being confronted with eulogies from the West of the peace-promoting effects of voluntary interdependence.

Does a state have to be wealthy and powerful to advocate and pursue interdependence as a political goal, whereas other, weaker and poorer states must fear interdependence because it allows larger and more powerful states to lord it over them? This question is especially relevant in Europe because of the asymmetries of power within its new empire. Can all parties really play the game of interdependence politics under these conditions? And can all benefit equally from its positive effects? Or don't the mechanisms of interdependence politics sketched above necessarily lead to an unequal distribution of its gains? And what would that mean for the long-term integration of the European sphere of power?

Although these questions cannot be answered conclusively here, they should figure prominently on the agenda of future research on Europe in the social sciences. The advantage of the concept of empire in this context lies in the fact that it at least enables us to identify problems, instead of simplifying them as conflicts of interest within an integrated Europe, as does the national perspective. Here we should at least indicate the direction in which an answer to these questions could be sought.

Exaggerating somewhat, the answer is that the politics of interdependence as a positive-sum game – conceived as a social construction and the outcome of a historical learning process – presupposes the existence of a *capital of trust*. Two problems must be solved to get the process of accumulating trust capital going: first, reciprocity between participants must be guaranteed by designing appropriate procedures (participatory decision-making process, unanimity rule); and, second, the perspective of others must be brought to bear within the remaining domains of action. Thus, the positive-sum game of Europeanization must be related to the opportunities to act of different kinds of states, i.e., of larger and smaller, more powerful and poorer states, and the states' perception – including their perception of European power potentials – differentiated accordingly. In other words, interdependence only has a chance of becoming a positive-sum game if the following conditions of reciprocal interdependence are met:

- if, first, the preconditions of interdependence politics, its procedures and its results, are perceived and accepted by the states and societies concerned as *'equable' and 'just'*, by whatever criteria of fairness are deemed relevant;
- if, second, a credible barrier is raised to national-hegemonic forms of instrumentalization and infringements pursued under the guise of interdependence politics, hence if a *balance of dependence* arises (as held, for example, in the past for Franco-German relations and remains an enduring aspiration);
- if, third, in those cases in which it will not be realistically possible to remove *unequal* dependence completely, nevertheless its perception is counterbalanced by a corresponding *politics of reconciliation*;
- if, fourth, not only interdependence as such, but also a 'critical mass' of interdependencies, can be realized, so that the political behaviour of states can be transformed enduringly;
- and if, fifth, sufficiently strong *institutional guarantees* exist that prevent the exploitation of one-sided dependencies where they exist.

Only the link between interdependence and a capital of trust produces the commonalities across spatial and temporal boundaries which can finally trigger the 'political quantum leap' from the nation-state to the transnational state. Thus, the cosmopolitan statecraft which seeks to reconfigure the world in accordance with the law of irreversible interdependencies must integrate all of the components of the politics of interdependence outlined here. The perception and creation of interdependencies reinforce each other, just as do rational self-binding and the reciprocal obligation of others, though not necessarily in precisely this sequence. The perception of civilizational risks

– the ABC of world risk society: the threat of nuclear war, nuclear fallout, the terrorist threat, weapons of mass destruction, etc. – is ideally suited to forging global interdependencies. The perception of the dangers generated by civilization can serve very well to build and extend a common European 'house'. Here it is ultimately irrelevant whether these problems *really* exist or whether they merely shape the perception of key political actors. What is decisive is that they continually do the latter! Perhaps the neoconservative advisers of US President Bush do not really believe in the enormous threat posed by transnational terrorist networks. However, they know how to foment this danger and to exploit it to extend their power inside and outside the United States and make it permanent. Even though many people find ridiculous the way European politicians publicly express their deep concern for plant and animal life threatened by environmental catastrophes, it nevertheless shows that they have understood the interconnection between the global perception of danger and the forging of transnational and translocal interdependencies for extending the nation-state's scope for action. In fact, self-generated civilizational dangers represent a still largely unexplored resource for forging interdependencies beyond national borders and cultural clashes (see chapter 7). The answer to the question of when and how national states become transnational states is: when the *fear* of interdependence is superseded by the *desire* for interdependence.

policy 9

5   The cosmopolitan organization of diversity: the European Empire and its contradictions

The concept of the cosmopolitan European Empire involves a double, contradictory imperative (something which until now could be disguised only with difficulty). On the one hand, this empire is universally oriented and conforms *absolutely* and *unconditionally* to the principle of inclusive differentiation – without any spatial or temporal restriction. In the creed of universal human rights, one is neither German nor French, neither Christian, Muslim nor heathen, neither man nor woman, neither dark- nor light-skinned. All positions that negate individuals by emphasizing differences of caste, class, religion or gender are transcended in the cosmopolitan legal system, which includes all human beings. On the other hand, the concept of the *European* cosmopolitan empire only makes sense if the necessarily unqualified cosmopolitanism is *restricted* and tied to specific conditions. Both imperatives – both the unconditionality and the conditionality of cosmopolitanism – are necessary; precisely this constitutes its irreducible contradictoriness. On the one hand, therefore, the European Empire, according to its own cosmopolitan constitution, cannot deny any country potential membership. The official discussion concerning Turkey's desire for accession is focused on precisely this issue. Cosmopolitan Europe, therefore, is *potentially* universal and includes all countries in the world. *In reality*, however, this is ruled out and the politics of the EU ultimately contracts this non-excludability by constructing high border fences.

However, the decisive point is that this contradiction of the cosmopolitan European Empire does not block political action, but enables, indeed compels, it. Empirical examination and reconstruction of the political room for action must address the following complex of questions: How can diversity be organized in a cosmopolitan empire? What criteria, principles and procedures govern the treatment of otherness within this empire? How is it possible to draw boundaries and assign decision-making powers and authorities in a system that has made the cosmopolitan both/and into its foundation? Our answer to these questions is an empirical typology in which we distinguish six variants of the organization of diversity in the European cosmopolitan empire (for which we make no claim to completeness). Together these variants represent different interpretations, explications and practices of the 'both/and' principle.

Constitutional tolerance

Constitutional tolerance rests on two features: first, national peculiarities are recognized rather than annulled – more than that, they establish European identity; second, however, this principle of tolerating and reciprocally recognizing national peculiarities presupposes agreement on a basic stock of common procedural and substantive norms which ensure that national peculiarities are 'compatible with Europe'. In the case of democracy, this means that the member states of the EU must reach an agreement on the fact that both the political system of the EU and the national political systems satisfy certain minimum democratic standards; however, the member states are free to organize their national political systems as they see fit.

In this sense, the principle of constitutional tolerance was from the beginning fundamental for the development of the European Community. The European treaties always respected the distinctive characteristics of the national constitutions and have not generated any compulsion towards constitutional uniformity.[35] The new EU constitution, too, will not supersede the national constitutions but leave them unaffected. The problem from a cosmopolitan perspective is then the *problem of compatibility*. For the acceptance and stability of such 'composite' political systems, as Heidrun Abromeit has emphasized, 'is likely to depend essentially on whether the new, inverted structure is compatible with both the structures and the political cultures of the component parts' (Abromeit 2000: 63).

This problem of compatibility becomes apparent in the tensions between the European supranational institutions and the British democratic tradition. In Great Britain, the main controversy concerns the question of whether the principle of unrestricted parliamentary sovereignty is compatible with transferring decision-making powers to the EU. For the British model of parliamentary sovereignty, the problem of the twofold democratic deficit in Europe is particularly acute: Great Britain renounces parliamentary decision-making rights, thereby restricting its own democracy, in order to transfer them to an undemocratic EU. The same fears have been expressed in Switzerland concerning its model of 'referendum democracy'.

In both instances, the problem resides in the fact that national institutions claim an ultimate decision-making authority for themselves that is incompatible with the principle of the supranational Europe. Here the either/or logic seems clearly to have the upper hand: either Europe decides or the British Parliament or the Swiss electorate decides. A possible solution to this problem could reside in further differentiating the both/and principle, namely, in the fact that constitutional tolerance – in accordance with the principle of differentiated integration – can be given different procedural interpretations. More concretely, this could mean that national institutions (parliaments, constitutional courts, referendums) must preserve the de facto possibility of saying no, hence that 'the respective self-determining units must be granted the right to dissent from decisions made in the centre' (Abromeit 2000: 73). This should not prevent common solutions in principle, however, but only allow national institutions to refuse to participate in them. Thus, constitutional tolerance must be complemented and extended through a *practical tolerance* that accepts national unilateralism on specific policy issues, as in the case of the economic and monetary union.

Transnational diversity

In the national paradigm, diversity is regarded as hostile to integration, in the cosmopolitan paradigm, by contrast, as fostering integration. The question is no longer: How can diversity be restricted? but rather: How can diversity be enabled? Thus, the challenge of European cosmopolitanism consists in making deviations from the norm. The point of cosmopolitanism is that much of what appears as 'decline' to methodological nationalism can strengthen European identity and integration through diversity. The individualization process of the nation-states can be transformed into a process of Europeanization of identities. Something similar holds for the revival of the regions, i.e., regional pluralism. Of course, this should not be misunderstood as a plea for unlimited and unregulated diversity. Even cosmopolitan diversity requires universally accepted rules to ensure that diversity also remains compatible with community.

Hence, the key question is how European rules must be structured so that they regulate the behaviour of individuals, institutions and governments, whose 'differentia specifica' is that they are *not* determined by institutional rules. What kinds of rules enable individual and national actors to invent and follow their own rules? In answering this question, two distinctions are useful. First, we must distinguish between *constitutive* and *controlling* rules. Constitutive rule systems enable us to play a game; without them, there is no playing field. Controlling rules are prescriptive. They lay down *how* the game is played, what strategies and moves can be employed under what circumstances. For a more precise understanding of the regulation of transnational diversity, it is important, in addition, to distinguish between two kinds of controlling rules: *external controls* and *reflexive self-controls*. External controls are imposed on actors from outside and above; they are rigid and inflexible, like the rules of football games. Reflexive self-controls are invented by the actors themselves, designed according to their specific local and situational needs. Hence, they treat their 'autonomy' in a particularly gentle way (Scharpf 1994). Because the European Empire is based largely on the delegation of power, such reflexive self-controls are of major importance for regulating cosmopolitan diversity within it.

Applied to European cosmopolitanism, the question is: What kind of constitutive rules do we need to regulate the self-regulation of European actors? In what respects *must* European rules differ in character from national controlling norms that observe the principle of homogeneity? And how can we guarantee that self-controls are also compatible with the requirements of 'community', hence that they are reflexively oriented to the European public interest – however this is defined – and are not exploited by national egoisms? These are all open questions awaiting answers.

Transnational incrementalism

A further organizational principle for diversity in Europe can be derived from incrementalism. Here the parties concerned consciously renounce a formal order and hierarchy of common norms and rules and instead focus on *incrementalistic* practices that acknowledge the validity and authority of both national and European authorities and create a European de facto order through a pragmatic combination of coordination, harmonization and experimental development.

How this pragmatic incrementalism operates can be illustrated by the relation between European law and the constitutions and political systems of the nation-states. In this context, one of the most fascinating questions is: Why do the high courts of the member states acquiesce in the new European legal architecture? This question can be answered by drawing on the both/and principle of transnational incrementalism. For the latter implies procedures that lay down a specific sequence of recognition. Once some of the highest courts in some member states have accepted a new supranational norm, then the parallel courts in other member states have good reasons to reach similar conclusions. The point is that it becomes increasingly difficult for the remaining member states and their courts to resist this incrementalistic acceptance while at the same time preserving their credibility.

The decisive point is that this incrementalistic practice does not lay down *any* clear hierarchy of institutions, but instead leads to the mutual recognition and extension of the authority of both the European and the national jurisdictions. This is particularly true for the reciprocal enhancement of the status of European courts and of regional courts below the highest national level. Should national high courts in fact prove to be resistant to European decisions, then national legal authorities could seize the initiative on suitable occasions in resolving these dissonances. How should this be understood? 'Lower courts and their judges were given the facility to engage with the highest jurisdiction in the Community and thus to have *de facto* judicial review of legislation' (Weiler 1999: 33).

In other words, the incrementalistic order of a transnational both/and would afford the judges and courts opportunities for coordination above national borders and hierarchical systems. This means, in particular, that the European Court of Justice creates European law through mutual recognition and empowerment in interaction with subnational courts and legal authorities.

As this example also shows, using the logic of postmodernism to show that the line of demarcation between Europe and the member states breaks down in legal questions, and how it does so, does not go far enough. Instead, it must be shown how jurisdictions, responsibilities and decision-making powers are being demarcated and coordinated in new ways beyond national borders. Here the respective organizational principles of the both/and – in this case, of transnational incrementalism – explain why this transcending and drawing of borders need not entail a breakdown of order, but can instead provide the point of departure for a new order that makes possible an increase in influence and recognition for all parties concerned.

Ordered pluralism

Ordered pluralism means that European and national options are simultaneously held open. Nevertheless, the European option has priority; it lays down what counts as 'normal' and has priority over the others. Here the EU lays down standards of normality that not only do not exclude pluralization within individual national contexts, but actually facilitate it. This hierarchically ordered pluralism can be likened to the model of the 'normal family' which has in the meantime lost its monopoly position in European societies to plural forms of family life, though without being toppled from the pedestal of normality. Thus, the 'normal family' may continue to enjoy special constitutional protection, as in Germany, whereas 'deviant' forms of family life, including same-sex cohabitation arrangements, have in the meantime been recognized in the majority of European states as equally valid lifestyles for legal purposes. Thus, it is not necessary to abolish national peculiarities and rules in order to create Europe. On the contrary, the creation of a 'normal Europe' is very much compatible with recognition of the national deviations and variations which constitute Europe's diversity.

However, here the both/and principle may simply shift the problem it claims to solve. It remains open how much re-ethnicization can and must be accepted in Europe without lending the principle of ordered pluralism the appearance of shoddy indifference and abandoning Europe to the inner decay of its values.

Reflexive decisionism

A further possibility for dealing with ambivalences, ambiguities and eroding borders is to uphold the old boundaries in full awareness that they can no longer be justified either with the old or with new arguments. This amounts to building, as it were, a dam, a taboo, against the rising tide of uncertainties. 'Here I stand, I can do no other!' said Luther and appealed to his faith. 'Here I stand, I can do no other!' can also be declared by the nihilist, the aesthete, the postmodernist, the Machiavellian or a new Montaigne. They have all lost the foundation of faith, but they nevertheless do not want to drift into arbitrariness. The decisiveness with which boundaries are defended here is not based on the certainty of a binding conviction but, for example, by reference to the unforeseeable problems attending a displacement or dissolution of borders for which no one can accept prior responsibility.

However, one must distinguish clearly between decisionism and *reflexive* decisionism. The former involves the claim to a freedom of decision that rejects all norms of justification, whereas the latter implies a decision-making practice that generates its own justificatory norms. Reflexive decisionism in this sense is not a form of Europeanization, but its precondition. If it is correct that Europe is a 'political construct', then this urgently presupposes political decision-making. In short, Europe is produced by political decision-making; indeed, it must be so produced. And in this context we cannot fall back on existing criteria, such as natural borders, shared language, religion, etc. Rather, it can only be produced by political decisions. By this is not meant decisionistic arbitrariness (that would be the postmodern position), but rather that European politics must produce its own criteria (discursively!). Then reflexive decisionism would not involve decisions in a norm-free space, as Carl Schmitt would have it, but the binding of decision-making to self-generated norms.

The criteria for answering the question of whether the borders thus laid down can be stable would also have to be capable of being generated in this way. This, too, is an open question. Ultimately, the answer may depend on the consistency of its 'social construction', hence on whether these borders are also recognized by the citizenry and by other states.

Multiple memberships

The logic of inclusive differentiation, applied to European politics, means, finally, multiple memberships. This is the complementary principle to constitutional tolerance. Constitutional tolerance regulates relations between the member states within the Union; the principle of multiple memberships operates towards the outside. It does not conceive of membership in the EU as an either/or matter, but allows, as it were, 'polygamous loyalty' to different, overlapping international organizations and alliances. In this way, individual European states can differ in both the form and the intensity of their transnationalization.

This can be shown in an exemplary way by the regional security organizations in Europe and, in particular, by the relation between the EU, the WEU and NATO (see Buzan and Waever 2003). At no point in time did the regional security organizations and the supranational economic organizations which were founded in Europe after World War II have identical memberships. From the outset, the circle of NATO members extended far beyond the small circle of six countries that founded the European Coal and Steel Community (ECSC) and later the EEC. It not only included two non-European countries (i.e., the USA and Canada), it also included several countries (i.e., Great Britain, Iceland, Norway and Portugal) that were not simultaneously members of the ECSC or the EEC. In addition, already in 1952, thus three years before the accession of the German Federal Republic, Turkey and Greece joined the Western security alliance. Even after the eastern enlargement of the EU and NATO, this incongruence has not altered fundamentally. Although the memberships have since increased to twenty-seven and twenty-six, respectively, several European countries are still members of just one of the two organizations. The implications of this incongruence can be seen clearly in the case of the Western European Union, the European security alliance which arose as a parallel organization to NATO and has since functioned mainly as a link between the two communities. The WEU comprises ten full members who are all members of the EU; six 'associate members', of whom currently three (Iceland, Norway and Turkey) belong to NATO but not to the EU; seven Central and Eastern European countries, as 'associate partners', of which two (Bulgaria and Romania) were included in the last enlargement of the EU, on 1 January 2007; and five countries with observer status, of which four (Finland, Ireland, Austria and Sweden) are members of the EU but not of NATO. In 1993, the WEU was superseded by a joint military alliance, Eurocorps, to which at present five countries (France, Germany, Spain, Belgium and Luxembourg) belong who are all at the same time members of the EU and of NATO, and which is seen as the keystone of a future European defence structure.

This confusion is not only typical for the power structure of the European Empire, but there is a method in it – and it has its price. For in this way it is possible to respect the various security interests and basic political values (for example, the Austrian principle of 'permanent neutrality') of the states involved, while nevertheless integrating them into shared institutions and alliances. Hence, multiple (and selective) memberships need not necessarily be considered as expressing a lack of willingness for integration; they are also a necessary precondition for integrating diversity in a cosmopolitan Europe. How an effective foreign and security policy can come about under these conditions must remain an open question.

The interpretations of the both/and principle developed here differ in many respects, though not in their value. There is no hierarchy among them and they do not mutually exclude each other. Cosmopolitan diversity can be organized – and is organized – in Europe in very different ways. The diversity of forms, norms and principles is the construction principle of the European Empire. However, this should not mislead us into concluding that empire is a harmonious form of organization in which the principles of cosmopolitanism can be applied completely consistently. We will deal with the internal and external contradictions of Europe in greater detail later (chapters 6 and 7). Here we would only add by way of anticipation that cosmopolitanism means in essence the organization of contradictions and ambivalences, and that the latter must be endured and politically processed because they cannot be eliminated.

European Social Space: On the Social Dynamics of Variable Borders

In the previous chapter we examined the question of how *statehood* and *political authority* can be reconceptualized from a European perspective. The answer was through a new conception of empire freed from imperialistic and nationalistic connotations, one which must be opened up in a cosmopolitan fashion and reoriented towards consensus and law. In the present and the following chapters we want to redefine European *society*. That is, we want to ask: Which postnational concept of society, which alternative and supplementary concepts must we develop if we are to become receptive to the social reality of Europe? In this chapter we will proceed in three steps: first, we want to deconstruct a common misunderstanding of Europe through a *critique of the methodological nationalism of Europe research*; second, we will outline *the empirical parameters of horizontal Europeanization* and, on this basis, third, we will address the question of a *postnational social theory of Europeanization*.

1 On the Europe-blindness of sociology: critique of the fixation of Europe research on the state

The concept 'society' presupposes clear boundaries, at least to judge by the minimal consensus within sociology. Yet how should we understand a 'society' with variable boundaries and thus with variable internal–external relations? Is a society whose key feature is the political variability of its geographical 'boundaries' still even a 'society'? Is there even such a thing as a 'European society'? And on what alternative postnational concepts and theoretical traditions can we draw when we address these questions?

The irritating thing about these questions is at bottom that they are not even posed, let alone answered! There are many reasons for this but one in particular calls for criticism: the concept of society is the point around which methodological nationalism in sociology crystallizes. On the latter conception, Europe must be understood in terms of the plurality of *societies*, hence *additively*. In other words, European society is synonymous with Europe's national *societies*, namely, France, Germany, the Benelux and Scandinavian countries, Spain, Portugal, Poland, and so forth. These conceptual orientations pre-program sociology's incomprehension of Europe, indeed the sociological irrelevance of Europe, and set the seal on the blindness of sociology towards Europe. The additive, national view of society can grasp Europeanization sociologically at best

(a) *comparatively*, through methodical comparisons of national societies, or
(b) on the model of the *endogenous convergence* among national societies and national histories, or
(c) in terms of overlaps, that is, *intersections between social and historical commonalities*.

These ways of failing to thematize Europe are as fundamental as they are false because they prevent the key questions of a macro-sociological dynamics of and research on Europe from even entering the field of vision.

How should we understand the dynamics of a social space to which national societies belong, yet which does not conform to the national premises of social cohesion, cultural homogeneity, political participation and social welfare assistance? Isn't the distinguishing characteristic of Europeanization the very fact that the boundary and the division of labour between national and international politics are being undermined? Isn't it high time that comparativists developed appropriate research perspectives that enable them to uncover the European interdependencies of European integration?

Following the opening of Europe's internal borders and the liberation of the dynamics of the market in the common currency zone, how do the Europe-wide conflict dynamics and the nation-state conflict dynamics interpenetrate and influence each other? Can the emerging unequal Europe be understood and investigated on the national model of class society? Or will the increasingly radical inequalities in Europe be refracted and suppressed by the still dominant national gaze, hence be resolved into *national* inequalities and oppositions? Could it be that regional inequalities and conflicts are gaining the upper hand in Europe's social dynamics? And how do social classes, nations and regions in the evolving macro-dynamic of Europe as a whole relate to the religious conflicts which overlay this dynamic?

Is Deutschmark nationalism destined to be superseded by euro-nationalism? Is what politics is counting on – namely, the unifying power of the common currency – realistic or merely an illusion, because a currency without a state does not create a society but weakens social bonds? Are there distinctively European, and not merely a subnational multiplicity of, electoral constituencies, styles of consumption, worker and employee milieus, ethnic diasporas, advocacy movements, and so forth? Will the Europe-wide divisions and lines of conflict run along a centre–periphery axis or a North–South or West–East axis? Perhaps the main factors of a European unification are not to be found within Europe at all but outside it. Could the variable geometry of Europe be understood as a horizontal mode of integration in which graduated memberships acquire the binding force of differentiated, anticipated belonging? Will the question of what holds Europe together be answered by equating empire and civilization, with the European Empire rediscovering its 'civilizing mission', in Samuel Huntington's sense, to construct the non-European other, replacing the enemy image of the communist East with that of the Islamic East, so to speak? Or can we confidently and complacently dismiss all of these questions because the European project is in any case overcoming its self-produced obstacles under the dictate of consensus through a predetermined functionalistic mechanism and is completing its 'integration' – this unpolitical concept of the political?

The conceptual vacuity in which these questions are posed is a scandal – Europe, this social and social-theoretical vacuum which – to add insult to injustice – goes unnoticed, even by sociologists. (The rare exceptions confirm the rule.) In public and scientific debate, the European construct seems to be composed of politics and the market but, where other comparable constructs present a social face, it exhibits all of the features of a nameless void. It testifies to an astonishing naïvety to allow the internal European borders between nation-states to collapse, while continuing to assume blithely that the issue of the Europe-wide social dynamics can be ignored or taken for granted, that it collapses into national domestic inequalities and conflicts, as methodological nationalism assumes.

According to the asociological, state- and politics-fixated understanding of the European debate (and of research on Europe), Europe is an institutional framework for economic transactions and social interactions between national societies. Europeanization leaves the national societies in essence intact. Indeed, on this conception, institutional – and *not* social! – Europeanization is the very presupposition for the survival of the national societies under the changed conditions of globalization. According to this '27 + 1 logic'[1] the overcoming of all the barriers that represented a hindrance for (individual and corporative) transactions and interactions between the member states was the main focus of concern, hence especially the realization of the four fundamental freedoms and the further development of the institutional framework (under the heading 'institutional reforms').

On this conception, Europe is in the first instance a workplace for lawyers, economists and political scientists – sociologists are ignored; when they are involved, then it is as political sociologists, who are likewise interested mainly in institutional questions.[2] Two complementary questions – (1) To what extent is a Europe-wide social space emerging in which the variability of borders conditions new lines of conflict, modes of integration and a new process of institution-building? (2) How far has the Europeanization of national societies progressed over the past decades? – remain unanswered.

This is largely because research on Europe in sociology thinks in *one-dimensional* terms because it views Europeanization in national terms: it conceives of Europeanization as a *vertical* process between national societies and European institutions. Then Europeanization means, first, the emergence of supranational institutions (authorities, public sphere, citizenship, etc.) and, second, the repercussions of these supranational institutions for the national societies, for instance, the adjustment of national norms and institutions to European guidelines. Thus, vertical Europeanization means the opening of the national container *upwards*. This is just one side of Europeanization, however.

Europeanization can and must be conceived concurrently in a second, *horizontal* dimension. This horizontal dimension concerns, first, the emergence of a 'post-social' European social space with variable internal–external relations and, second, the relations between the European societies. Here Europeanization means the networking and mixing of national societies, national economies, national education systems, national families, etc., thus, horizontal Europeanization signifies the *lateral* opening of the national container.

If the vertical and horizontal dimensions are inwardly oriented, then turning outwards the question arises: How does the European Empire of variable borders and variable others delimit itself from non-European others, non-European civilizations? To what extent and in what forms does a European dialectic of cosmopolitanization and anti-cosmopolitanization develop? And how does the internal and external political management of borders respond to the explosive contradictions that accumulate here?

Until now, the discussion concerning Europe has proceeded as though Europeanization occurs only in the vertical dimension. Discussion turns constantly on the question of how much vertical Europeanization is reasonable and necessary. In particular, the neonational Eurosceptics assume that the containers remain closed to the side and that their opening upwards must be restricted to a minimum. The empirical proof that the European societies have also been Europeanized to a significant extent in the horizontal dimension allows us to introduce an additional argument of considerable weight into this discussion. For if this is the case then the return to the nation-state is already barred by the fact that its social foundation has begun to disintegrate.

Thus, the question concerning horizontal Europeanization resolves itself into two complementary complexes of problems which we will here address in turn.

The first concerns the question: What should we understand by 'horizontal Europeanization', what are its indicators and what empirical facts speak for or against it?

Second, there is the question of the postnational social theory of Europeanization: How can the social grammar of Europe be (experimentally) disclosed and studied?

2   Horizontal Europeanization: questions, indicators, empirical developments

What is meant by 'horizontal Europeanization'? It might be described as a regional concept of what is generally called 'transnationalization', one tailored to the peculiarities of the European Union. 'Vertical Europeanization', by contrast, corresponds roughly to the level of 'internationality' or 'supranationality'. 'International' and 'supranational' are *state-centred* concepts; the former has its intellectual roots and sensibilities in international relations, the latter more in public law and comparative constitutional theory. If the concept of internationality emphasizes the *separation* of national spaces, in the case of supranationality the *common* institutional framework of European law stands in the foreground and hence also the distinctiveness of European institutions. But whereas both perspectives thematize Europeanization *from above*, with transnational Europeanization the primary focus of research becomes Europeanization *from below*.

The point and at the same time the problem with these distinctions lies in the fact that, although transnational-horizontal Europeanization maintains a perspective opposed to the national and the international outlook, nevertheless it does not thereby annul the nation-state but presupposes and extends it.

(1)   The transnational-horizontal perspective throws into doubt the view that the national and international are two sides of the same coin and examines the third factor which is thereby excluded. It highlights forms of labour, production, life and action that escape, extend and redefine the national either/or through a co-national both/and. Transnational are co-national (hence anational) forms of life, production and interaction that in a sense permeate the walls of states. They involve forms and movements of *constant* boundary-crossing. Hence they can count as indicators of the fact that the power of national state borders to shape societies is diminishing. In the course of transnational Europeanization, new shadow realities are emerging that are lived and proliferate in the blind spot of the immigration authorities, as it were.

(2)   However, it would be a fatal misunderstanding to conclude that 'transnational' and 'national' designate mutually exclusive conditions or levels of analysis. Rather, the transnational dimension must be understood and deciphered as *integral* to the national dimension. Hence we must ask: How are the mutually demarcated spaces and histories of the national so interconnected, interwoven and fused with each other that we can meaningfully speak of a horizontal Europeanization?

Instead of the institutional architecture, horizontal Europeanization focuses attention on the everyday, familial-biographical, civic and economic integration of Europe. Characteristic here is that the national-international relations of exclusivity between membership and non-membership, internal and external, are in fact interwoven and merge with one another in a specific way. Consequently, we can distinguish different levels and indicators of horizontal Europeanization.

(3)   Transnational Europeanization is a relational concept whose meaning varies with certain relations (boundary-lines) and must accordingly be differentiated into a 'politics of scale' (Brenner 1999; Beck 2006, chs 3 and 4). One can (a) focus on the Europeanization of *one or more national societies* – for example, Germany and France – and study how many European languages are spoken there and how many European binational marriages (or divorces) occur there, or to what extent the German or French research communities can no longer be restricted by national borders but are networked at the European level. An indicator for the latter would be the level of foreign European research investment in Germany as a proportion of the total German investment in research. It is tempting to supplement this national standpoint on Europeanization (to the extent that current data permit it) with a comparative perspective whose goal is to produce *national comparisons of horizontal Europeanization*, e.g., to study the mode and extent of horizontal integration in Germany in comparison to France, Finland, Poland, etc., in different dimensions and areas.

However, here we must distinguish in turn (b) between Europeanization in the *broad sense* (including EU member states plus European countries that are not EU members) and 'EU-ization', Europeanization in the *narrower sense*, which includes only the EU member states. In addition, one can also (c) direct the spotlight on the Europe-wide perspective and study the *Europeanization of Europe*.

From the 'micro-cosmopolitan' perspective, the concept of horizontal Europeanization is (d) also applicable at the subnational level. Individual regions, federal states, municipalities or districts can be studied to determine to what extent marriages or areas of research, etc., are Europeanized, and hence decisively shaped by European actors and forms of cooperation. Finally, one can also (e) inquire to what extent *non*-European countries, groups of countries and continental regions are being Europeanized.

Here we must proceed in a highly selective manner by highlighting and explaining a couple of exemplary indicators and factors of national comparisons of horizontal Europeanization. To this end, we will concentrate on the following themes or dimensions: (1) language, (2) identity, (3) education and (4) the economy.

2.1   Language

For many people, the many languages and tongues that Europeans speak is an, or even *the*, obstacle to horizontal integration. Isn't Europe – it is often asked – an impossible undertaking if for no other reason than that each country not only speaks its own language but also insists on the *right* to its own language? Doesn't this of itself create a Babylonian linguistic confusion that negates everything that a functioning democracy needs to survive, namely, *one* language, *one* culture, *one* identity? Philosophers and linguists have argued that speaking one's own language is an indispensable source of identity. Here the specific form of identity founded by language must be defined more closely by comparison with identities shaped by religion, for example. Religion raises a claim to absoluteness, language does not. One can speak several languages, and thus continually traverse the boundaries between cultures and nations, but one cannot be simultaneously a Jew, a Muslim, a Catholic and a Lutheran. Whereas the either/or prevails among religions, native language is compatible with the both/and. Indeed, language is at once a source of identity and a medium of overcoming boundaries, of intercultural communication and of multiple belonging. The separation of language and identity is neither thinkable nor worth striving for; and language as a source of inner cosmopolitanization of separate worlds would have to be invented if it did not already exist.

Speaking different languages means having both roots *and* wings, being at home in several cultures at once, being able to see oneself from outside, living dialogically, but also having to tolerate contradictions – in a word, revelling in *linguistic polygamy*. A linguistically monogamous Europe would be a mononational Europe, an absurd 'community of autists'. Cosmopolitan Europeanization, by contrast, means not just speaking a common language (English) but loving many European national languages. If every European spoke, let us say, three European languages, had friends in all three countries, enjoyed *zuppa di pesce* in one and prime beef with chive sauce in another, and could even exercise her voting rights – in short, if each European needed the otherness of other Europeans like the air she breathes – that would be an internalized cosmopolitan Europe because it would be lived in a linguistically polygamous manner!

Monolingualism, by contrast, means blinkered vision. A Europe in which everyone spoke only English would not be a Europe, at least not a dialogical or a cosmopolitan Europe, but more an imperial Europe (as the monolingualism of US Americans demonstrates). The remaining borders of Europe are internal borders, linguistic borders; they could be made permeable with the strength, desire and ability to be at home in several languages. This is not at all an elitist idea because supposedly only the well-to-do can 'afford' and assimilate foreign languages and cultures. That multilingualism is not a luxury but necessary for survival is particularly true for migrants.

The myth of convergence – that all cultural differences are being levelled by the steamroller of globalization – is contradicted by the key area of language: 'In the single world there are more languages than ever before . . . and we are constantly witnessing the emergence of new languages before our eyes and among us' (Maier 1995: 657f.). Languages are becoming dissociated from territory; in other words, they are being spoken in many global locations. Cultural and religious differences are becoming ubiquitous. What divides and differentiates people is often present in a single place, increasingly often in a single family or a single biography. Linguists estimate that 75 per cent of people alive today speak two or more languages (ibid.: 81). Whether or not this is true, it seems certain that the number of people who possess a linguistic window on other cultures and are able to communicate with others in their own language is increasing; and this holds *independently* of the hierarchy of educational qualifications.

This has nothing to do with a nostalgic view of migration or exile. Hannah Arendt, the German Jew who emigrated to New York to escape the National Socialist lunacy, describes the strange emotion which overcame her when she once again heard the German language among the ruins of the German cities after the war. And she reports the experience of many emigrants who in the neither/nor of languages – really mastering neither their native language nor the language of their host country – were cut off from the authentic source of their thought.

Thus if every attempt to cut the umbilical cord that connects a human being to her native language is harmful, the following dilemma – applied to Europeanization – results: How can the right to one's native language hold in Europe without, on the other hand, Europe failing for this very reason? Is it really necessary to prescribe a *single* language for Europe as well as a single currency, a uniform legal system, and perhaps even an army and a police force, so that it can grow together? No, this very 'solution' succumbs to the error of methodological nationalism, namely, conceiving of Europe as a nation that speaks a single language. Against this, the cosmopolitan Europe must be constructed on a *weighted model of multilingualism*: 'nowadays everybody obviously needs three languages. The first is his language of identity; the third is English. Between the two we have to promote a third language, freely chosen, which will often but not always be another European language. This will be for everyone the main foreign language taught at school, but it will also be much more than that – the language of the heart, the adopted language, the language you have married, the language you love' (Maalouf 2000: 140). This polygamy of languages is the driving force of the internal cosmopolitanization of Europe, and it can be regarded at the same time as a quantifiable indicator of the extent to which the lifeworlds and biographies of people are being Europeanized, not only from below, but also *from the inside out*. For multilingualism is both the medium and the cradle of horizontal Europeanization. Multilingualism Europeanizes Europe. What appears to be a success from the cosmopolitan perspective appears often enough from the national perspective, by contrast, to be a problem. This also holds for multilingualism (Mokre 2003). The national educational systems, including the schoolbooks, the curriculums and the teachers, are poorly prepared for the multiple languages, passports and biographies of their pupils. This holds in different degrees for the contradictory language policies of European countries. Some of them conduct both a protectionistic and an imperialistic language policy designed to protect their national culture and the identity of their language and to extend their sphere of influence (a tendency particularly pronounced in France). Others, in turn, fight for the survival of their language. Still others can accept the global validity of their national language, as it were a global linguistic monogamy, 'as a given' (English).

The difficulties which the German school system, for example, has in dealing with the multilingualism of its clientele are one of the main reasons why the German education system fares so poorly in international comparisons. Yet here too the fatal reverse argument is confirmed: in public opinion and politics this is attributed largely to the fact that school classes are 'swamped by foreigners' [*Überfremdung*] but not to failure of an educational system that is still primarily oriented to reproducing the national rather than to active Europeanization.

Thus the proportion of schoolchildren in Germany who had a foreign passport in 2002 was surprisingly high: it comprised almost 1 million schoolchildren attending general schools and hence almost 10 per cent of all schoolchildren (Statistisches Bundesamt 2002). Four-fifths of them were citizens of another European country; a large proportion of this group, in turn – almost 44 per cent – had Turkish citizenship. Linguistic diversity becomes a 'language problem' in the context of national educational institutions. This is blamed, in turn, for the fact that foreigners comprise only 4 per cent of pupils attending the academically oriented high schools (i.e., the German *Gymnasium*), whereas they represent 18 per cent of those attending other types of high schools. The result is a dramatically lower level of high school graduation; 20 per cent of foreign students leave school without a qualification, whereas among their German fellow pupils the proportion is only 8 per cent. Compared to this, 26 per cent of German pupils, but only 11 per cent of foreign pupils, acquired an academic, or combined academic and vocational, qualification.

2.2   Identity

There can be no Europe without Europeans. But what is a 'European'? What characteristics distinguish trans- and multinational European identity (second modernity) from mononational identity (first modernity)? If one thinks of European identity on the model of national identity, one must conceive of it as a *shared* collective identity of the citizens of the European nation-states, and in such a way that the European 'subsumes' the national identity. Adopting this standard is a sure recipe for disappointment: a European identity as a greater national identity, and hence a demos, a European people, does not exist. If one nevertheless wished to create it, one would arouse fear concerning cultural assimilation and would end up turning Europeanization into a bogeyman.

With the archetype of national identity in mind, 'pathetic exercises in cultural engineering' (Delanty 1995: 128) have also been undertaken in the EU. Among these must be numbered the Eurovision Song Contest, Euro Disney and the annually awarded title 'European Cultural Capital'; but also the notion that a European passport, a European flag and a European anthem (the prelude to the 'Ode to Joy' from Beethoven's ninth symphony) confer the desired 'emotionality' on European national identity.

By contrast, empirical investigations have shown that when, for example, members of the European Parliament speak of and describe European – or, more precisely, *their* European – identity they fall back on the vocabulary of movement (Footitt 2002: 111–30). They do not experience and describe European identity as something fixed and predefined, territorially bound and restricted, but rather as identity *in* movement, identity *of* movement, as 'Europe under construction' (Günther Verheugen). The vocabulary and metaphors in which this *flowing* identity is expressed are derived from 'journeying', 'travelling' and the 'obstacles' to these: 'roads', 'ways', 'paths', etc., must first be opened up, 'maps' drawn up. In the spirit of Churchill's famous 1946 Zurich speech, one speaks, for example, of 'mapping out the way forward'; or one finds oneself 'on the road towards the European Union', on the 'road to Maastricht'; or one specifies 'that we must *pave* the way for a European foreign and security policy so as to *open up* a new dimension' – 'one step at a time', needless to say; and all the while one has to be on the lookout for 'potholes' along the way (Footitt 2002: 113).

Accordingly, the history of the European Union is also narrated in terms of metaphors of motion. Thus, an understanding of Europeanization is exhibited as movement in a space, but also as movement in time; and this movement has liberated European history from its belligerent past, and hence marks a decisive break with this past. It is oriented to the future. Neither the shared present nor the shared past[3] constitutes the European mobile identity. The guiding idea is rather the notion of a different time and a different future. Thus Europeanization means a future-oriented understanding of the present in which identity consists in being underway, creating, paving, founding, aligning, building, being lost and disoriented, seeking and searching, finding and discovering. Thus, European identity is not a matter of different contents of a different *understanding* of identity, a different *concept* of identity. In the self-understanding of those Europeans who have been studied, Europe – as Armin Nassehi formulates it – has already left behind the 'European metaphysics of identity, whose *basso continuo* . . . is the question concerning substance, constancy and essence' (Nassehi 2003: 1; Derrida 1992).

Getting under way in a European/un-European fashion, hence being at once identical and non-identical, can inspire the European founding spirit. Europe is not Europe in the sense that Germany is Germany or France

France. Europe means *doing Europe*. 'Doing Europe' here points to an unsentimental, effective Europe that is measured by the fact that its institutions consistently prove that Europeanization generates a better future for Europeans than the national governments can achieve on their own. In the global era, this is not unrealistic. In trade, in monetary, environmental, security and foreign policy, the EU would be better equipped than its member states to serve the interests of each individual independently of skin colour, place of residence and language.

In the idea of 'doing Europe', this unemotional image of history and self is simultaneously connected with a moral image of history and self. For the goal is to transform the bad past into a good future, a better life for all individuals beyond class, language and religion. As is well known, Max Weber identified the 'inner-worldly asceticism' of Calvinism as an essential moment of the 'spirit of capitalism' and also saw in it the power to intervene in the existing order of things and transform it (Weber 1992). The 'European spirit', by contrast, develops out of the inner-*historical* asceticism, from the recollected gaze into the abysses of European civilization. 'Doing Europe' is the 'never again' become act. Cosmopolitan Europe is permeated by the idea that the hatred and enmity among the peoples of Europe (and the world) is in the final analysis a delusion, an error – that the mutually feuding and slaughtering nations, ethnies and religions are indeed capable of working combatively towards the renewal of *their* world, of *the* world. The reconciled Europe which was still an unrealized dream for Churchill, de Gaulle, Adenauer, the leaders of the resistance against Nazi Germany – as it was also already for the Thomas Manns and Heinrich Heines – has so impressively become reality after half a century that one must almost be afraid again that it could be destroyed by bureaucratic routine. Yet, this inner reconciliation is the message that must prove itself, and can renew itself, historically with the eastern extension of the EU into the post-communist countries. Are the Eastern European countries awakening from the stupor of Soviet imperialism into the pre-1939 ethnonational self-understanding of Europe? Or are they discovering the blessing and utility that the creation of EU structures for peace, wealth and a supranational ethos can mean for each individual, not least because they put an end to nationalistic excesses for good? The 'cosmopolitan moment' – the heightened sensitivity to cultural others – arose out of the total exhaustion of acts and experiences of cruelty, from reflection on and commemoration of the unfathomable suffering and the unfathomable guilt inflicted on the world by the belligerent nationalistic Europe. This has made Europe, in conformity with the internalized standards of self-criticism, more sensitive, more open and at the same time more unrelenting in the struggle for a non-belligerent, post-religious humanity. This cosmopolitan Europe recalls only with shame and contempt the clashes of worldviews and the extermination camps produced by the entanglements of its national histories. This cosmopolitan Europe *could* be – or, more circumspectly, could become – undogmatic, unself-righteous, tolerant of conflict, free, cheerful and curious concerning the manifold contradictoriness of the world, full of liberal-minded provincialities, and shrug off ways of thinking in terms of exclusive absolutes – either us or them, either capitalism or communism, either the West or Islam.

This liberal-mindedness and openness concerning values should not be confused with postmodern arbitrariness. In addition to procedural norms, it calls for a minimal pride in values. For the new Europe should subscribe to *one* form of aristocracy, its own: the Europe of freedom, of freedom of the individual (see Heller 2004). The colourful, individualistic, secular culture in which religion does not determine politics is of greater value than a culture in which women are stoned. Everything that the fundamentalists hate is to be celebrated and cherished as what is authentically European: the much-lamented 'vacuum of meaning', the 'decadence', the 'loss of the middle', the rejection of the metaphysical image of 'the' human being and 'the' European West. Why? Because the cosmopolitan-European character of a society consists in the fact that nobody lays down what is right and good or how people should live their lives as long as they do not harm others.

What values remain when one casts one's gaze over Auschwitz, the gulag or the insanity of colonialism? The risky venture of Europeanization can be undertaken in the service neither of a universal God nor of a universal humanity nor of a universal truth and science. European values must be created; 'doing Europe' must be practised on a daily basis. Only this continual becoming can ultimately foster European cosmopolitanism and make it into a 'matter of act' [*Tat-Sache*]. And, here, neither divine nor human signposts can point the way.

2.3   Education

There is a clear answer to the question of where and how horizontal Europeanization can be 'performed'. 'Doing Europe' occurs (or fails to occur) in education and educational policy – specifically, first, with reference to the Europeanization of educational curriculums and, second, with reference to the Europeanization of educational flows, of educational *mobility*.

Educational curriculums

Educational policy was for many years a taboo subject in the corridors of the EU; in contrast to agricultural, trade and environmental issues, it remained largely within the sovereign discretionary power of the member states. Only in this way, it seemed, could one guarantee that cooperation in this area would respect the traditions of the countries and the diversity of their educational policies and systems. Even though responsibility for education policy has migrated to some extent to the Union since the Maastricht Treaty, and the Bologna Process, in particular, this has to date contributed little to the Europeanization of the educational curriculums; instead it has promoted the recognition of diplomas and professional qualifications or fostered connections and contracts between educational institutions, the establishment of training programmes for language instruction, etc. However, this is due to change by the year 2010 (Racké 2004).

Surprisingly, there are nevertheless – or perhaps for this very reason – thousands of activities that advance Europeanization from below, 'step-by-step', in the educational domain (as empirical investigations show, e.g., Soysal 2002; Popp 2004). One can subsume these activities under the general banner of NGOs: networks and advocacy groups, teachers' unions and associations, publishers of schoolbooks and instructional materials, minority organizations, all are actively involved in redefining Europe, specifically under the tutelage of UNESCO, the European Council and other supra- and transnational organizations. These discussion groups and workgroups are networked with advisory committees whose scientific experts have access to channels that enable them to influence the policies of the national governments and their decision-making procedures with a view to promoting the Europeanization of ideas of education and educational curriculums. Here it becomes clear that initiatives to promote transnationalization operate across borders, but for this very reason also *within* national spaces and at the same time beyond the scope of national or European authorities. This is how the horizontal networking of Europeanization operates.

This 'European subpolitics' has produced a remarkable result largely unnoticed by the wider public: as Suzanne Popp (2004) shows, current textbooks on European history employ a common canon of around fifteen historical images (photographs, paintings, lithographs) across countries that promote both the inculcation of a common European image of history and a common European historical outlook. This has the effect of systematically diffusing the struggle to define the past of Europe's belligerent history, yet precisely not insofar as European history is represented alongside or as supplementary to the respective national histories but rather as it is integrated into national and regional identities and histories. Thus, here, in the practice of historical dialectics, the either/or – either mutually opposed national histories or European history – is superseded by a cosmopolitan both/and that recognizes and preserves traditional national historical identities while at the same time integrating them into transnational European perspectives:

If this trend continues, soon all European history teachers, from Finland to Greece and from Ireland to Belarus, will be able to draw on a common fund of archival images of modern European history that are equally popular and historically informative and could form the iconographic core of a transnational historical 'image memory bank'. In contrast to a European historical textbook, for example, which stands alongside the national historical schoolbooks and aspires to a transnational-European perspective, the national textbooks themselves are generating the new inventory of images. Founded on a basis of national acceptance, it invites us to build pan-European bridges between the heterogeneous regional and national historical (instructional) cultures.

The starting points in one country – drawing parallels – could be the revolutionary uprisings for which the French Revolution may have played an important pioneering role (e.g., in Poland), whereas in another country – drawing contrasts, so to speak – a patriotic-national resistance against French foreign domination that became a national founding myth and a core element of patriotic self-understanding could come to the fore. Thus one becomes aware of both historical commonalities and differences when one highlights the historical images employed in national history instruction in the various countries throughout Europe not just with regard to their Europe-wide relevance but also when they are studied comparatively with a view to the diversity of historical experiences associated with them in one's own country and elsewhere. (Popp 2004: 23f.)

Since the 1990s, this way of 'doing Europe' has also spread to the history textbooks of Central, Eastern and Southern European countries as well as the Balkan countries. The corresponding committees have binational or multinational memberships and promote the aim of negotiating and inculcating a *European view of history* that makes it possible to transform the belligerent past into an amicable future. 'In one of their initiatives, Spanish, Dutch, Portuguese, Scottish and English history teachers gather together in Toledo to discuss the "controversial personality" of Philip II and his times – recasting his legacy as one of advancement in arts and literature, rather than entrenchment of Catholicism in Europe. These are efforts to rehabilitate the "unique national heroes and enemies" and the remaking of a European heritage, not of wars and conflicts, but of a positive collective past' (Soysal 2002: 271–2).

In this way, European history is being related less and less in ethnic and religious terms while increasingly highlighting the universalistic principles which it also contains. Thus, abstract, universalistic principles that are associated with Europe's past are accorded greater emphasis, although the fact that these same principles inspired most of the violent conflicts of Europe throughout its bloody history often recedes into the background. 'In recent schoolbooks, Europe appears as a much more peaceful land than what its history empirically dictates. Historically, Europe emerged and was sustained more by conflict and division than by consensus and peace, but now what holds Europe together, in textbooks, is a set of civic ideals and universalistic tenets' (Soysal 2002: 274).

However, this outlook permits the very cosmopolitan interweaving and amalgamation of European and national historiography in the textbooks alluded to above. For cosmopolitan identity incorporates national identity. In this sense, the European historical narratives coexist peacefully in the schoolbooks with the national and local narratives to which a significant amount of space continues to be devoted. In this way, European history becomes an integral component of national history, where the former is oriented to the future and the latter to the past. Thus, the Europeanization of schoolbooks also demonstrates that the European mobile identity does not require confrontation with and exclusion of cultural others, as many assume! This openness of European identity recently produced political effects when many millions of Europeans opposed in a cosmopolitan spirit the inversion of the 'war against terror' into a 'war against Islam' announced by US President Bush.

How typically these analyses of historical images and history textbooks reflect empirically the idea of cosmopolitan Europe is shown, moreover, by three structural characteristics.

- First, the educational canon of the historical images most often reproduced is confined to representations of *modern* European history, whereas the foundations of Europe in the ancient world, the Christian Middle Ages and the early modern period are virtually ignored (Popp 2004: 26f.).
- Second, the political history of revolutions and hence 'the genealogy of the system of values that, with the guiding concepts of civil and human rights, democracy, peace and tolerance, are supposed to constitute the basic normative components of the "European value-community", becomes the central focus of attention' (Popp 2004: 28). The historical legitimation of the '*minima moralia*' of cosmopolitan Europe is here cited with iconographic imagination.
- Third, the historical images relate how the hopes awakened by the political revolutions turned into disappointment, indeed, how nationalism and militarism lead to violence, terror and war (Popp 2004: 29). In other words, a dialectical relation of tension develops in the canon of images in which European values and European horror are not correlated with separate spheres but appear as inextricably intertwined. However, this occurs in a historically incomplete sense, for, in the images of the opening up of the Berlin Wall, the political revolutions of the eighteenth and nineteenth centuries are connected, as it were, in a circular fashion with the overcoming of Marxist and Stalinist totalitarianism.

Educational mobility

Over and above this historically induced Europeanization of image contents, we must pose the question concerning the Europeanization of educational *mobility*: To what extent has the European dream of studies without borders been realized? The first semester in Kassel or Munich, then an interlude in London or Barcelona, home again for the BA examinations and then on to Lyons for the masters – this is how the European education ministers imagine the academic training of the future. But what do things look like in reality?

Table 4.1: Germans studying abroad, 1991–2000

	1991	1992	1993	1994	1995	1996	1997	1998	1999	2000
Total	34,000	36,800	40,200	40,000	41,800	44,200	45,200	46,300	49,000	50,000
EU %	56.7	55.1	56.7	55.3	59.5	60.9	60.9	60.4	63.1	61.9
Europe %	72.1	70.3	71.7	71	74.5	74.7	73.9	73.3	75.4	75.1

Source: BMBF 2002: 14–15.

If one inquires into changes in the numbers of Germans studying abroad (table 4.1), one can observe a sharp increase in the overall number,[4] from 34,000 to 50,000 between 1991 and 2000. More than half of these students are enrolled in countries of the European Union;[5] this proportion also increased from 56.7 per cent in 1991 to 61.9 per cent in 2000. If one calculates the proportion of German students studying in European countries,[6] then the proportion is significantly higher, and it grew from 72.1 per cent to 75.1 per cent between 1991 and 2000. This last figure, which indicates that more than three-quarters of the Germans studying in a foreign country are enrolled in European countries, can be taken as clear evidence of a process of horizontal Europeanization.

If one asks how many Germans study abroad in tertiary level education, one finds here too clear evidence for horizontal Europeanization. In 1999, 250,000 students were studying abroad within Europe, but only 83,000 in countries outside of the EU, of whom 49,000 studied in the United States, 24,000 in other European countries and 10,000 in Asia and Oceania. The following facts speak for a progressive horizontal Europeanization.

- Two-thirds of the foreign students studying in Germany in 2000 came from Europe; however, students from the EU made up less than a quarter of all foreign students.
- Three-quarters of the German students studying abroad are enrolled in European countries.
- Of the half million European students studying abroad, less than a fifth study outside Europe.
- In Europe, there are more foreign students from other European countries than from countries outside of Europe.[7]

2.4   The economy

Labour market

After World War II, an intensive, though covert, horizontal transnationalization of the labour market began. A massive wave of migration washed over and transformed the societies of Europe. The migrants came not only from the European periphery but also from distant countries. Over the years the list of sender and host countries has increased remarkably, and new and previously unimaginable combinations of national-exclusive forms of life and works have arisen, for example, Vietnamese in Romania and East Germany, Chinese in Moscow, Nigerians in Turkey, Turks in Germany and Israel, and so forth. Corresponding waves of 'ethnic flows' (Appadurai 1991) were also triggered by decolonization. Former colonial subjects sought recognition of their universalistic rights in the countries of the colonizers.

Two things were connected with this. On the one hand, the 'postmodern' cultural mélange produced by colonial domination and slavery migrated into the metropoles of the centre and created a false impression of a historically *new*, postmodern form of diversity. On the other hand, a global discourse concerning human and civil rights was triggered. Transnational actors, such as the United Nations and UNESCO, and transnational social movements that inscribed human rights issues on their banners, codified the relation of equality and difference among cultures. In this way, the clear distinction between membership and non-membership, citizens and non-citizens, nationals and foreigners, became blurred (Soysal 1994; Beck-Gernsheim 1999, 2004). A large proportion of migrants in Europe find themselves in a status of neither/nor and both/and. They resist assimilation to the formal schemas of citizenship. At the same time, they have a whole range of rights and privileges connected with this very citizenship. One can even assert that European labour migrants form a diffuse, 'multi-ethnic class' of non-citizens.

Yet, the concept of 'European labour migrants' is thoroughly vague, for it can refer to internal mobility among EU member states or to the third-country mobility between the EU and non-EU countries, both within and outside Europe. Mobility or migrant flows that affect the EU labour market pose characteristic legal questions of horizontal Europeanization to the extent that here two legal spaces overlap in conflicting ways. On the one hand, in European law, the 'freedom to provide services' – that is, the right to 'post' employees abroad within the European internal market – is one of the European fundamental freedoms. On the other hand, key questions of labour and social law remain a matter for the sovereign discretion of the nation-states. Thus, we must ask which of the national legal systems involved in the numerous disputes – ranging from questions of legal certainty in welfare law and which court has jurisdiction, to the regulation of holidays and the minimum wage – is valid in cases of doubt and who should decide in cases of conflict, and on what basis: the European legal regulations governing freedom of movement and the equal treatment of employees (which prohibit discrimination against foreign citizens of EU countries in wages and working conditions) or the respective national laws, and if so, which (Eichhorst 1998: 93ff.)? The applicable 'conflict law' within the EU is a prime example of the legal transnationalization of Europe. In the overlapping and connection of the legal domains, the removal of boundaries between inside and outside, between citizens and non-citizens, and the resulting sources of conflict and need for regulation, are often treated in law with vague and unclear definitions.

At the end of the 1980s and the beginning of the 1990s, existing European and international law already explicitly regulated the posting of employees abroad as the legal situation had gradually assumed clear contours, though certain questions remained open. On the one hand, the posting of employees abroad was then at the latest clearly defined as a component of the freedom to provide services. On the other hand, already at this time the internationally binding interventionary norms of the temporary place of work held for workers posted abroad, even if, in the case of a temporary posting, the law of the customary workplace otherwise remained valid. However, there was no universally binding determination of the scope of the conditions of work in the respective host countries which had to be observed in the sense of protective rights of employees posted abroad. In particular, the ranking of negotiated and legal minimum wages remained vague. (Eichhorst 1998: 111)

In a certain sense, the estimated 15 million migrants from third countries in Western Europe remain 'foreigners' in their 'host countries'. As studies have consistently shown, this non-status has not triggered discontent. This is due to a circumstance that remains hidden from the national outlook: most of these migrants have acquired a permanent right of residence, a status that is not easily distinguishable from that of 'true' citizenship. In the European countries, the permanent right of residence includes the full range of civil rights, as well as the prospect of gaining access to economic rights, labour rights and social welfare entitlements quite comparable with those of normal citizens. Only the rights to participate actively or passively in national elections are excluded. By contrast, in certain countries, thanks to European law, participation in municipal elections is indeed envisaged. Moreover, those in Germany who measure levels of 'integration' and 'assimilation' in accordance with German norms overlook the fact that transnational forms of life have their own advantages, drawbacks and social logics.

Many people who live under these conditions have no desire to 'return' to the home country. They carry the 'myth of the return' around with them like a faded family photograph that refers to a time gone by. However, they do not suffer under the oft-invoked 'identity crises' of those living between cultures; this is a chimera produced by the national outlook with its false ontology of separate, mutually exclusive cultures. Yet, their rejection of integration does not imply a willing embrace of cosmopolitanism either. Rather, for them transnationalization is primarily a life and survival strategy: they have to defend themselves on a daily basis against the national institutions which erect barriers to their specific mode of life and somehow get by. Only in this way is it possible continually to re-create normal conditions of life across borders in precarious employment markets and under (il)legal working conditions in the face of tacit and open discrimination (Sassen 2003; Robbins and Aksoy 2001).

Table 4.2: Total number and percentage of national, European and international mergers and acquisitions

	1987	*1990*	*1993*	*1996*	*1998*
Total figure	2775	7003	5740	6327	7600
% national	71.6	60.7	63.4	55.7	50.1
% EU	9.6	21.5	15.9	17.4	16.5
% international	18.8	17.8	20.7	26.9	33.4

Source: AMDATA in *European Economy* (1999).

However, this partially coerced and partially chosen cosmopolitan way of life also exhibits reflexive moments. Multilingualism is as much a necessity of survival (and hence often more developed among migrants than among the successful native school leavers of the middle classes) as is living and thinking from an 'outsider perspective', both towards the dominant host country and towards the so-called home country, which one may know only as a tourist and from hearsay. In this way, the canon of established certainties in both countries loses its validity, and irony becomes a basic spiritual and intellectual necessity. An indicator of this daily transnationalization from below is the increase in binational marriages (and divorces) which by now constitute one in six of all marriages in Germany, for example; as a result, increasing numbers of children are growing up under conditions of multiple identities and multiple loyalties (Beck-Gernsheim 1999). Rudi Völler, the former trainer of the German national football team, put the point well: 'I'm a European and a German who is married to a Roman with two Italian sons' (*Frankfurter Allgemeine Zeitung*, 18 February 2004: 31).

Companies

The parallel question of how far research and development in business has been horizontally Europeanized also points to the peculiarity of the transnationalization perspective. For the point is to show that apparently domestic operations of German businesses are in fact to a considerable extent Europeanized activities that take place beyond national borders and at the same time within nation-states. When German companies conduct research, this is not German research but European research. This is what is meant by 'doing Europe'!

As regards the transnationalization of the economy, the facts are ambiguous. Let us take the fusions and acquisitions of firms as an indicator (table 4.2).

Here one can discern (Rodriguez-Pose 2002: 25), on the one hand, a clear trend towards transnationalization: the proportion of national mergers fell from 71.6 per cent in 1987 to 50.1 per cent in 1998, whereas transnational mergers (EU and international) shot up from 28.4 per cent to just under 50 per

cent over the same period. However, of these, 16.5 per cent were accounted
for by EU mergers in 1998, whereas extra-European international mergers
accounted for 33.4 per cent (by comparison, in 1987 the numbers for EU
and international mergers were 9.6 per cent and 18.8 per cent, respectively).
This points to a trend in which the general denationalization of the economy
is increasing enormously in the competitive struggle between Europeanization and globalization, yet in which globalization nevertheless is outpacing
Europeanization and is accelerating sharply. In the key area of the economy,
in particular, there is no easy answer to the question 'Why Europe and why
not the world?' (chapter 7).

3 Empirical cosmopolitan social theory of Europeanization

3.1 The problem

The first section of this chapter was devoted to the *de*-construction of social
science, namely, the critique of the methodological nationalism of research on
Europe. In the second section we posed the problem of *re*-constructing social
scientific knowledge initially with an empirical orientation and discussed
examples of questions, methods and phenomena of horizontal Europeanization. In this third section, we will now develop the theme of reconstruction
further from a *theoretical-conceptual* perspective. The guiding question will
be: What takes the place of the naturalistic understanding of society of the
first modernity, and in terms of which alternative concepts could Europeanization be conceived, described and investigated? One thing for sure is that
we do not need a new European grand social theory that repeats the errors
of methodological nationalism at the European level.

The analysis of horizontal Europeanization has shown that Europeanization must *not* be understood and analysed in an EU-centric manner; that
would be to repeat the error of assimilating the actor and observer perspectives. (It would be tantamount to 'methodological Europeanism'!) But how,
then, can or must Europeanization be understood from the perspective of
social theory? What does the cosmopolitan outlook mean in this context?
What are the historical premises of a cosmopolitan – hence *post*-social – social
theory of Europeanization? For this purpose, we must return once again to
the central claim of the theory of reflexive modernization: Europeanization
cannot be understood endogenously but only *exogenously*, i.e., as part of the
epochal perspectival shift of globalized modernity (see chapter 2, section 2).
What does this mean?

The first modernity was founded on the regulative idea of a global regulatory policy, the basic principle of Western-Occidental universalism and
rationalism. We do not need to recapitulate its basic commitments and
historical genesis here. What is important is rather the changed starting
point of the transition to the second modernity at the beginning of the

twenty-first century by comparison with the transition to the first modernity in the eighteenth and nineteenth centuries. In contrast to the major thinkers of the first modernity – Kant, Hegel, Husserl, Descartes, Adam Smith, David Hume – who developed and predicted the vision of a global unity *conceptually* long before it was possible to experience the world as a whole, today we are experiencing *the unity of the world in its fragmentation and vulnerability long before we know how we should think about it.* In other words, the cosmopolitan outlook on Europe has lost the very 'transcendental' certainties which oriented philosophical cosmopolitanism at the beginning of the first modernity. The cosmopolitan outlook is driven, rather, by the curiosity to trace, understand and explain empirically the boundary-transcending practices, side effects, compulsions, interdependencies and dangers which are spreading like wildfire outside the field of vision of the evolutionary theory of modernization (from Durkheim, Marx and Weber to Parsons and Luhmann)[8] (Beck and Lau 2004). Unity conceived in universalistic terms has been superseded by unity experienced *in* disintegration and *as* disintegration. The problem is to trace this simultaneity of unity and disintegration, at least in selective ways, empirically and analytically.

The cosmopolitan outlook forces us to view Europe with the eyes of others too and hence to confront and overcome the provincialization of Europe simultaneously. Which certainties of the global paradigm of modernization have evaporated (in the sense of the theory of reflexive modernization – see chapter 2) and how and why? Here, in rough outline, are *six theses* on this issue.[9]

1 In the paradigm of global modernization, power and knowledge were combined with a vision of the global order to be realized which spoke, as it were, *with a single voice*, that of Western modernity and rationality. Admittedly, the latter no longer dreamt the dream of the Enlightenment but instead that of the scientific-technical progress, of the increasing security and control, which goes hand in hand with the establishment of modern institutions. The vision and mission informing the evolutionary paradigm of modernization stated that, with progressive modernization, the world is taking on a 'Western' appearance and the division between 'the West' and 'the rest' is gradually being overcome.

In many respects just the opposite has occurred. The globalization of industry has annulled the division of labour and contrasts between the 'West' and the 'rest'. Thus islands of high industry have developed in South Korea, the Philippines and China, which conflict with the notion of separate worlds of centre and periphery. The progress of industrialization has everywhere led to a resegmentation of the world in which highly industrialized centres of rapid growth are emerging alongside unproductive wastelands, and not just 'out there' in Calcutta, Rio de Janeiro or Kinshasa, but also in New York, London and eastern Germany.

2 The *violence* which is becoming part of everyday life largely on account of these developments has also transcended the sharp boundaries between war and peace which were still characteristic even of the world wars of the twentieth century and has become strictly speaking uncontrollable. This was conceded by no less a person than the then American secretary of defence, Donald Rumsfeld, when he said that the transnational terrorist networks belong to the 'unknown unknowns', that is, to things of which we are unaware that we are ignorant. This amounts to a declaration of defeat by the greatest military power of all time. States, no matter how overwhelming their power, are no longer able to fulfil their original promise to guarantee the security of the citizens. At the same time, ubiquitous global problems are transforming the various global hemispheres into neighbouring parts of a single place. In short, the unity and disintegration of the world are becoming equally apparent and are undermining the familiar sense of geographical, ethnic, political and social distance and destroying the hope for global political order that informed the first modernity.

3 Although the globalization of the paradigm of modernization involved the claim to create ordering regimes in a unifying world, after almost one and a half centuries of expansive modernization the opposite result is becoming ever more apparent: legitimacy and political authority, which according to Max Weber comprise a unity in the forms of accountability, responsibility and democracy, are becoming uncoupled. In Europe, the container of the nation-state, which was supposed to unite *legitimacy and power*, has mutated into an empire of consensus in which zones of legitimacy without power (the European Parliament) coexist with zones of power without legitimacy (the comitology). Moreover, we are faced with the dissemination of largely anonymous, transnational exercises of authority residing in international organizations, networks and movements and in the system of banking and trade, which therefore elude the forms of legitimation and political authority of the nation-state. The social sciences have developed the metaphors of movement, flows, circuits, networks, hybridity and mélange for these forms of translegal power, which are neither legal nor illegal, neither legitimate nor illegitimate. Precisely *because* the phenomena escape the notions of global order, the concepts and theories which 'embody' this claim to order are blind to the processes and circuits of *real cosmopolitanization* (see Beck 2006: ch. 1, for a more detailed discussion).

4 *Global mobility* has experienced and triggered dramatic reversals. The beginning of the twentieth century was marked by a massive emigration of Europeans to North and South America and, to a lesser extent, also to Africa, Asia, etc. These flows ultimately served to uphold the existing order, in the sense both of an order-generating expansion and of the preservation of order *within* Europe. For the European order was jeopardized by the growth in

population. Not only has the direction of movement reversed, now that the poor of the world are streaming towards Europe, making it a meeting-place of global oppositions that used to be kept apart by geographical space. In addition Europe is marked by a general reduction of its population, and thus by an aging process that is not only undermining the foundations of its social security systems (pensions, health care) but is also making the 'old' continent look really 'old' in comparison to and in competition with the up-and-coming peoples and countries of the world with larger proportions of younger people.

5 During the twentieth century states were *the shock absorbers and mediators of globalization*. Their specific promise was to manage the global dependencies and involvements of an integrating world that 'national' politics had brought to fruition. Interestingly, today small states are in a better position to achieve this than large states, and large states are in turn better able to do so in certain policy fields (namely, environment and technology) than in others (taxation and social policy) (see Grande, Prange and Wolf 2004). In view of the pressing problems clearly no longer solvable within the national framework, or solvable only in bitter struggles with powerful interest groups, governments throughout the world face shrinking voter approval; meanwhile the various opposition parties enjoy temporary increases in voter approval, but only as long as they are not in government, for then the carousel of approval ratings turns once again. This raises the question: What use are nation-states as long as they fail to transnationalize themselves, and thus are incapable of controlling the real process of global change unfolding in flows, networks and movements beyond their sphere of control and of minimizing the risks generated by globalizing civilization?

6 Finally, the preconditions for *critique* and *protest* have also changed radically. All counter-movements opposing attempts to promote global integration have quietly transformed themselves into struggles in which the *conditions* of global integration are being negotiated. It is no longer a question of whether the world belongs together or not, but of who will lay down the norms which determine the autonomy, loyalty and identity of persons, countries and states, and how. Everywhere the question of how connection and cohesion in a world of multiple modernities is possible is tacitly or openly forcing itself onto the agenda. Thus what appears in Europe to be a 'European crisis' proves to be an *epochal change in perspective*. Nevertheless, it finds its specific expressions in the European experiment.

The methodological conclusion to be drawn from these theses is clear: there is no universalistic outlook or spirit, no old or new *world spirit*, which moves world history and is waiting to be 'elevated to the concept' [*auf den Begriff gebracht zu werden*]. The question of the new orienting concepts for understanding the new character of European 'society' must be given a methodological turn and transformed into the question of how alternative concepts of *sociality* can be discovered, invented and reconceptualized. It would be a grave error to understand this as a call for a new grand theory of Europeanization. Rather, what is involved is an experimental approach based on the following principles.

Globality: Neither Europe nor its member states can serve as the starting point for a European post-social theory. Rather globality must be chosen as the starting point. Then the task is to decipher Europeanization as specific internal–external variability, as contradictory politics of boundaries, as *regional* globality. This means that Europeanization must be conceived in terms of a pluralistic model of powers and counter-powers in which the European Empire seeks to mobilize its resources across all boundaries in cooperation and competition with other power centres, with a view to internal and external crises, variable borders and growing interdependencies. There is no royal road of modernization – especially no European one, but also no American one – only decentral sketches of multiple modernities that problematize each other.

Constructivism: Nothing that is thematized with Europeanization is predetermined; rather everything is constructed. Constructivism asserts that the realities confronting us in the global era are mediated through and through. They are both constructed and real (e.g., in the application of scientific and technical knowledge). Thus, constructivism is a matter of civilizational secondary realities that overlay, permeate and transform the existing institutions of the first modernity (Latour 2004).

In a constructivist spirit, in what follows we would like to explore in turn:

- European society as *interdependence*;
- *European society as mobility;*
- *European society as civil society;*
- *European society as civilization;*
- *European society as memory;*

and then in the following chapters:

- *European society as meta-power game (chapter 5);*
- *European society as dynamics of inequality (chapter 6);*[10]
- *European society as regional world risk society (chapter 7).*

3.2 *European society as interdependence*

Europeanization, we claimed, must be conceived in terms of the contradiction of unlimited limited globality. A key concept in this context is *global interdependence*.[11] What we mean by this can be best illustrated by an example.

In early 2004, a heated debate was being conducted in the United States and Europe over the 'off-shoring' of jobs, that is, the movement of jobs abroad or, more accurately, the creation of jobs without reference to borders. The information technology which enables Westerners to work in a café in New York or in a picturesque Bavarian village also exposes them to competition from well-trained, cheap 'non-Westerners' who are only too happy to perform a day's work for what Westerners earn in an hour. In the United States, in which (according to rough estimates) 70 per cent of this 'off-shoring' is taking place, this process is creeping up the corporate ladder and is now even affecting positions in software development, technical programming, and research and development. In the USA, as in Europe, the reaction is overwhelmingly nationalistic and protectionistic. Politicians accuse India of 'stealing American jobs'.

The categories in terms of which this process is framed and evaluated are rooted in methodological nationalism. Transnational corporations do not even have to *export* jobs; rather, because of the leeway to operate across borders afforded them by the global market and information technology, they can simply create new jobs in India or China; and they do this, not because they are 'unpatriotic' or because they want to do the Indians a favour and promote cosmopolitanism, but simply because the logic of the market forces them to do so. For the same reason, the term 'jobless growth' remains trapped in the national outlook because it absolutizes the national context and fails to realize that the creation of jobs is a transnational affair and must be analysed accordingly.

Ultimately, however, the key inference is that *the excluded, non-Western others are suddenly ubiquitous*, even at the core of the national interest of Western countries. The others against which the centre is erecting a fortress can no longer be kept out. And this holds even as the EU is simultaneously raising its ramparts and aiming the muzzles of its guns at foreigners.

This systematic confusion of inner and outer under the conditions of globality generates cross-border dependencies that any analysis of social structure must confront. The conclusion is that *national labour markets no longer exist*. More concretely, *there is no longer a German labour market* (or a French, British, etc., labour market, or a European or an American one). However, what do exist are the German, etc., employment *statistics* which preserve the counterfactual *illusion* that there is a German, etc., labour market that can be protected through national law and nationally organized force.

In thematic terms, global interdependence means, for example, that the history, the present and the future of the national labour markets *must* be rewritten from a cosmopolitan perspective if we are not to misunderstand their actual mechanisms, causality and dynamics. Only in this way will it become apparent that the Europe of shifting boundaries is undergoing an overlapping of 'on-shoring' and 'off-shoring' from which a new dynamics of inequality within and between countries is emerging:

- *On*-shoring: after World War II, millions of foreign workers were recruited and Germany and Europe were transnationalized, becoming global sites of divergent cultures.
- At the turn of the twenty-first century, these waves of on-shoring are being overlaid by waves of *off*-shoring, a process of transnationalization that initially affects low-skilled jobs, then jobs demanding higher qualifications (even in medicine, for example), with no end in sight.
- In the course of these movements and counter-movements, the hierarchy of centre and periphery and the associated global inequalities are being inverted: the centre no longer represents the future and the prototype for the periphery. Rather, the images which foreshadow the future of the former centre are being produced in the countries of the former periphery. 'Developing countries' are becoming suppliers of *cheaper, more highly skilled labour* that provides services in the national labour markets of the 'centre' across continents at the click of a mouse, thereby dismantling the national employment monopolies from 'within'. Former countries of recruitment (e.g., Italy and Spain) are becoming countries of immigration. Even the eastern countries of the enlarged EU (e.g., Poland) are acquiring the status of attractive countries of immigration.
- These border-transcending and border-effacing developments are blending with new waves of 'translegal' *on*-shoring: the labour migration of construction workers, cleaners, and workers in the hospitality and nursing professions, often (to use the official euphemism) *undocumented workers* without residence or work permits. However, this in no way alters the fact that they are *functionally indispensable* for these societies. The dominant reaction in the former centre is the call for ultimate security and an illusory policy of erecting barricades against the internal others (on issues of transnational inequality, see chapter 6).

Global interdependence means that reality is becoming cosmopolitan, though in a thoroughly uncosmopolitan way, one which no philosophical cosmopolitanism or cosmopolitan philosopher anticipated or even thought possible: without publicity, unintentionally, independently of political decisions and programmes, in other words, in a thoroughly deformed way. Real cosmopolitanization – unwanted, unseen, in varying degrees compulsory – is entering through the back door of side effects. This latent cosmopolitanization of the world is by no means an elite phenomenon. It is happening even *against* the express will of the wealthy Western countries; it is upsetting or destroying the monopoly on which the prosperity of their inhabitants is based. It is not taking place under the banner of a new global citizenry and it is not an expression of expensive tastes and business-lounge cosmopolitanism. A clear distinction between philosophical cosmopolitanism whose certainties belong to the past and the *terra incognita* of real cosmopolitanization is so essential for this very reason (Beck 2006: ch. 1).

The cosmopolitan outlook of the second modernity begins where notions of the 'one world', in which everything could have its proper place, at least in principle and in theory, have been forever shattered. Contradictory interpretations of global and local histories clash, as do multiple interpretations of modernity. The Western narratives of how Europe arose, and in terms of which concepts and theories Europeanization can be understood, collide, for example, with postcolonial counter-narratives from non-Western contexts. Our example shows that even what 'off-shore jobs' *really* are is controversial from a Western perspective. The dominant response of Western politics is: 'I am not a protectionist but . . .' Others argue that exporting American jobs to other continents reflects a cunning of reason, because the poor will become less poor and, consequently, the world will become safer for Americans. Occasionally one even hears the converse question, the outsider question: What does the 'export' of jobs mean for the receiving countries, for Indians, in the Indian context?

What appears here in an exemplary way holds more generally, namely, there is *no* privileged European standpoint or observer perspective, even for a social theory of Europeanization. What is becoming necessary is a *theoretical* cosmopolitanism, an experimental-dialogical theoretical perspective that accords central importance to global variability, interdependence and intercommunication: *Europeanization can be conceptualized as a special regional and historical case of the border management of global interdependence* (see chapter 3, section 4).

3.3   European society as mobility

More than anyone else, John Urry has proposed and developed a new paradigm of mobility for the social sciences (Sheller and Urry 2006; Bonss and Kesselring 2004; Kesselring and Vogl 2004). This criticizes the static, state conception of society, in particular, the fact that phenomena of movement – travel, migration, historical expeditions, slavery – were viewed in static terms as exceptions and hence have not been sufficiently studied by the social sciences (both theoretical and empirical). What sets and keeps people, goods and symbols in motion and how actual and potential movements structure social life – all this has remained a largely unsolved riddle for the static view of the state in the social sciences.

This way of viewing things has been disrupted by a whole series of new metaphors of streams, networks, landscapes, hybrids and mélange, concepts which, not unlike the transition from realistic to abstract painting, are intended to describe and facilitate the transition from a static structural sociology to the sociology of motion.

'Mobilities' in this paradigm is thus used in a broad-ranging generic sense, embracing physical movement such as walking and climbing to movement enhanced by technologies, bikes and buses, cars and trains, ships and planes. . . . Mobilities also includes movements of images and information on local, national, and global media. The concept embraces one-to-one communications such as the telegraph, fax, telephone, mobile phone, as well as many-to-many communications effected through networked and increasingly embedded computers. The study of mobility also involves those immobile infrastructures that organize the intermittent flow of people, information, and image, as well as the borders or 'gates' that limit, channel, and regulate movement or anticipated movement. And it involves examining how the transporting of people and the communicating of messages, information, and images increasingly converge and overlap through recent digitization and extension of wireless infrastructures. . . . Studies of human mobility at the global level must be brought together with more 'local' concerns about everyday transportation, material cultures, and spatial relations of mobility and immobility, as well as with more 'technological' concerns about mobile information and communication technologies and emerging infrastructures of security and surveillance, including a kind of self-surveillance. . . . Thus mobilities need to be examined in their fluid interdependence and not in their separate spheres (such as driving, travelling virtually, writing letters, flying, and walking). (Sheller and Urry 2006: 212; on this, see also Parker 2002; Wittel 2001; Gottdiener 2001)

Here too we encounter the question: What distinguishes mobility in general from *European* mobility? In what form must mobility be understood as a characteristic of Europeanization, that is, as integral to European identity and politics? In the last chapter, we discussed this question in connection with the concept of the European Empire whose peculiarity resides in the fact that *integration is equated with expansion*.[12] Here too the distinction between the EU and Europe is central, for the strategies, processes and political consequences of horizontal Europeanization can be analysed precisely with reference to the management of borders between the EU and the non-member, or not-yet-member, countries. The EU is an open project, which means a project of variable borders and variable geography. Thus the outside represents the future inside, and the anticipated membership of the not-yet-members represents a real political motivating force that simply does not feature in the script of national society.

Methodological nationalism recognizes only mobility of individuals or groups *within* societies; the idea of the mobility of *whole* societies, as exhibited for example by the eastern enlargement of the EU, is utterly foreign to the concept of society. The same holds for the notion that this 'country-mobility' (which is organized in a European manner as the 'elevation' of countries to membership of the EU) also throws relations *within* individual national societies into confusion. What is essential to Europeanization – the variability of borders and, consequently, the border-transcending internal–external axis, the macro-sociological dynamics both within European national societies and within the pan-European 'society' – remains undiscovered and is rejected as unreal by the stereotypical concept of society and the social theory and social research based upon it.

That this mobility and variability of whole societies, which is utterly unthinkable within the frame of reference of methodological nationalism, conceals the mobile identity of the EU, on the one hand, and the secret of its success, on the other, can be clearly seen in the case in which the opportunity presented by mobility was missed, namely, the wars of ethnic cleansing in the former Yugoslavia. Why did the Europeans offer the Balkan states the prospect of EU membership only after four wars, after the deaths of hundreds of thousands of people, after the horrific images of ethnic cleansings? Why didn't the Europeans offer the collapsing Yugoslavia a European perspective already in 1991, on the condition that it promoted democracy, the rule of law and a market economy? Could the Balkan wars have been prevented by the amalgamation of freedom and wealth which is the preventive promise of EU membership, because it would have obliged these countries to Europeanize themselves?

The remarkable thing here is this border-transcending *preventive* Europeanization. Horizontal Europeanization can be oriented outwards as well as inwards. What is peculiar in both cases is that, through the variability of borders and border policy, a specific internal and external nexus, respectively, is produced. Here we will sketch how this occurs in two problem areas, taking up and concretizing the empire theory (see Vobruba 2003):

- First: How does the integration of the EU through expansion occur?
- Second: How are external conflicts internalized through the variable geography of the EU?

European integration through European expansion

The methodological nationalism of classical sociology, most recently and explicitly in the work of Stein Rokkan (1999), assumes that social change and social structure-formation can be investigated on the premise that geographical spaces and spaces of membership are congruent. This perspective may be appropriate for the genesis of the first modernity, for questions of nation-state formation, of democratization and of the development of the welfare state. However, its intellectual orientation fails to do justice to the crucial point of Europeanization, which is that the variability of borders sets going an interaction between the internal and the external, between member states and non-member states, which presupposes a transnational, cosmopolitan observer perspective if it is even to feature in the methodological field of vision. Only in this way can the key question of the post-social, macro-sociological Europe research be conceptually posed and empirically investigated: What internally and externally overlapping dynamics of centre and periphery, and what forms of European 'movement-integration' built upon them, does the real or anticipated expansion of the European Union produce in the countries which already belong to the EU, on the one hand,

and in those which do not yet belong to the EU, on the other? Also: How are the variability of borders and the change and reform of the EU institutions related? Hence, how must we distinguish between 'nation-building' and 'EU-building' so that geographical space and the space of membership are precisely *not* congruent but are both in flux?

Security problems are key problems of empire-building. One can see this in the first instance in the case of the established and prosperous EU member states; however, one quickly encounters the complementary perspective of the non-EU European countries and hence must examine and explain the cross-border interaction between the internal and external perspectives. It is in the interest neither of the European Empire as a whole nor of the wealthy EU states to have unstable and potentially disintegrating countries plagued by civil wars and enmities on their borders. Correspondingly, the interests both of the nation-states and of the European Empire point equally to a successive outwards displacement of the distinction and the boundary between the EU and Europe, between member states and non-member states. Viewed from the other side, the variability of boundaries opens up the perspective of prosperity and freedom for the non-EU Europe.

To this extent, the internal and external perspectives can be connected and combined with one another through the politics of variable borders. On the one hand, the wealthy core EU can shift the burden of securing the borders to successively new countries; internally, at the centre of the EU, by contrast, 'borderless' countries and states emerge, the perfect example of this being Germany after the eastern enlargement. At the same time, the promise of EU membership is also a kind of insurance policy against the threats emanating from unstable neighbouring communities for the EU states. On the other hand, the promise of membership spurs the non-EU European countries to pacify themselves out of self-interest – to everyone's benefit. Border states form a security belt for central states. In this way, the key services of security and stability can be 'purchased' from states who wish to become members through a kind of 'division of labour' between countries, with negotiated compensations being provided by the member states. Thus, the horizontal integration between the EU and the not-(yet-)EU, between the EU and Europe, rests on a cross-border pact: *promotion into the EU in return for stability*.

In Europe in a state of flux, the promise of expansion (which was condemned as unbridled imperialism by the older theories of state and empire) opens up for the excluded Europeans and the non-EU member states the prospect of promotion from outside to inside, from the condition of a threatened and economically underdeveloped country to that of a protected country on the path to greater prosperity and democracy.

However, this does not yet exhaust the hope which a neighbouring country can derive from the 'Europe in flux'. Once membership has been achieved, there is the prospect of promotion from the periphery to the semi-periphery, and subsequently to the centre. Today the neighbouring countries of the EU are the peripheral countries of the EU of tomorrow, and maybe even the countries of the centre of the following day. The prospect of expansion leads to differentiated integration and to the switching of roles between the almost-member states and the would-be member states: the former can pass on the troublesome border-guard role to the new boundary and periphery states. Thus, given the prospect of membership, they come to enjoy the advantages which were conferred on the old member states and the wealthy central states when they acceded to the EU. They export stability by passing on the sensitive issue of defence policy to the next candidate.

Obviously, the social face of Europe changes with each new phase of enlargement. At the same time, new demands are made on the institutions of the EU. The interconnection between border policy and the reform of the EU is one of the many existential questions which occupies Europeans today and will continue to do so in the future.

The internalization of external conflicts

Shifting borders also mean that the boundary between us and the others in European space is becoming blurred. *Today's others are tomorrow's European 'We'*. Accordingly, the Western core-We of the old EU finds itself threatened in its identity by ever new waves of expansion. The 'East', the 'Balkans' and, in particular, the 'Islamic cultures', which constituted the classical others on the Western European understanding of the Union, are becoming the European 'We', really and potentially. This permanent 'changing of the guard', 'changing of fronts' and 'conversion' make the question of European identity as urgent as it is open – unless one accepts the cosmopolitan self-image of the horizontally open Europe which draws its self-understanding from diversity and difference.

But, in fact, this internal–external nexus does not only include the perspective of integration through expansion. Rather an *inclusion of global social conflicts* is also occurring on account of this variability of borders. Thus the anticipation of Turkey's membership of the EU has sparked a lively debate over the extent to which Europe and Islam, Islam and democracy, and Islam and human rights are even compatible with one another. It is not only the Western self-definition of the 'old' Europe anchored in Christianity that is being shaken to its core. More fundamentally, the almost exclusive monopoly of the Christian religion at all levels of the European social structure – from the municipalities, through the nations and states, to the transnational EU – is being placed permanently in question.

The conflicts with Europe's cultural others which were externalized during the nation-state era are being internalized under the conditions of variability of borders. Social inequalities which were disguised by national boundaries or were predefined as irrelevant are now coming loose from their national moorings as a result of the changing images of the mobile still-others and no-longer-others and can be politicized within the reconfigured national societies. Thus a major potential for conflict is brewing that has the potential to destabilize individual states and societies. The ghost of neonationalism is haunting Europe. And the power with which this phantom grips people's minds, and hence shapes reality, is likely to be enhanced by the eruptions triggered by successive boundary shifts in particular. The internal diversity of Europe, which renders the exclusion of cultural others illusory in practice, operates simultaneously as a sounding-board against which global conflicts can become internal European conflicts. Thus the anti-war policy adopted by the French government during the second Iraq War contributed inadvertently to a kind of 'French intifada'. France has both the largest Jewish and the largest Muslim communities in Europe, with 600,000 and almost 5 million members, respectively. President Chirac's opposition to the bombardment of Iraq spurred the anti-Semitism of French-Arab youths which discharged in acts of violence against French Jews. Thus, 'the outside is inside' also means that 'external' conflicts break out 'inside' the EU countries and jeopardize the national multicultural compromise.

3.4   European society as civil society

Controversy rages over the ultimate origin of the concept of 'civil society'. However, it is certain that it has European roots, and it was not least the revolt of Eastern European civic movements against the communist dictatorship which placed it on the global agenda. 'Civil society' is a complex phenomenon and it is not always clear what it means; but it always centrally involves human rights, democracy, progress, equality and dignity, though with the implication that these concepts and values have become a common possession, the property of all nations, cultures and religions, and seem to be resistant to a retrospective Europeanization. Precisely *because* the values of global civil society are negotiated globally, they prove to be an inexhaustible source of misunderstandings. When one person says 'justice', others hear the clash of cultures. Others, in turn, hear only colonialism whenever democracy is mentioned. How can European society be conceived as European civil society? What benefits, what added political value does it entail?

The uncoupling of nation and civil rights

The *Europeanization* of civil society can be seen first from how, with the internationalization of labour markets in Europe after World War II, what was originally regarded as an indissoluble unity became uncoupled, namely, national identity and civil rights (Soysal 2001). The large streams of migrants eroded the equation of territory, identity and citizenship through the power of facts (see above) and led to a Europeanization from below. De-territorial, trans-ethnic and transnational mobile identities were thus created, an experience that contravened the legal principles on which nation-states are based. Rights, which seemed to be indissolubly tied to the national community, became Europeanized, transnationalized, whereas national identities were simultaneously transformed from within under the influence of the mélange, both/and identities (e.g., *both* Turkish *and* German) of diaspora groups.

The German Basic Law states that 'Human dignity shall be inviolable', not that 'The dignity of *Germans* shall be inviolable'. Thus when the Basic Law protects the dignity of human beings, it must also protect the dignity of guest workers, their families and children, the dignity of German Turks, black Germans, Greek Germans and Spanish Germans. This means that human rights, whose implementation the EU has recently loudly proclaimed, yet which are equally protected by the Basic Law of the German Federal Republic and the constitutions of the other states, have led to an expansion of the rights of 'foreigners' within European national contexts. This means, in turn, that it is becoming increasingly difficult to distinguish any longer between nationals and foreigners. Thus, there are individuals who are nationals for educational purposes though they hold foreign passports, and nationals for residence purposes who also enjoy social welfare benefits, but who nevertheless remain aliens on the passport criterion. And this blurring of boundaries between national identity and civil rights, between human rights and citizenship, was also largely propelled in general by the new importance accorded human rights.

In light of the atrocities committed by the German state against its Jewish citizens – gazing into the abyss of European civilization – it is no longer possible to delegate the protection of human rights to nation-states. For the common thread of the horrors of the twentieth century is the realization that states themselves committed the most barbarous violations of the rights of their citizens whom they were obliged to protect. Thus the transnationalization of human rights *against* the national legal sovereignty of the nation-states represents one key to opening the door to the creation of a European civil society.

The boundaries of postnational citizenship are fluid; a Turkish guestworker need not have a primordial attachment to Berlin (or to Germany for that matter) to participate in Berlin's public institutions and make claims on its authority structures. By holding citizenship in one state (Turkey) while living and enjoying rights and privileges in a different state (Germany), Turkish guestworkers violate the presumed congruence between membership and territory. Another indicator of the fluidity of postnational membership is the increasing acquisitions of dual nationality across Europe. (Soysal 2001: 69)

Thus the basis of *European* civil society is the uncoupling of various moments that seem to be indissolubly bound together in the national model of civil rights: civil rights as a political principle of *democracy*, civil rights as a *juridical status of legal persons* and civil rights as membership in an *exclusive identity group* (Cohen 1999). Here, too, the dividing line that the nation-state established within the national community between members and non-members, i.e., between human beings and citizens, is crumbling. But these are precisely the opportunities presented by transnational Europeanization, the opportunities to create a European civil society. For example, the juridical dimension of civil rights – that citizens are legal persons but not necessarily political actors – can reach beyond borders precisely because these civil rights are not tied to particular collective identities and memberships in a demos. However, the reverse side of the coin is that these legal and social civil rights can also have genuinely depoliticizing and desolidarizing effects (at least within national contexts). The expansion of juridical human rights can lead to a weakening of the desire for political participation and to the willingness to submit voluntarily to 'integration' or even 'assimilation'. On the other hand, the Europeanization of civil society can create spaces for conducting the key experiment concerning how human rights and civil rights, legal status and identity, transnational forms of life and democratic political participation can be combined.

Civil society from above?

With the creation of European civil society as a juridical entity the various actors comprising the European executive have, on the one hand, opened up an autonomous field of action that has effects within the national social 'container'; on the other hand, civil society is viewed as an essential contribution to reducing the democratic deficit of the EU. European civil rights in this sense are supposed to create a space of European publicity and practice in which citizens and civic movements can practise and exercise their rights *beyond* the nation-state.

At the same time, there is an elective affinity between the European executive and European civil society: both have a transnational origin and see themselves as cosmopolitan entrepreneurs. The expansion of European civil society also makes possible both a critical and an inclusive access to globalization – critical, because civil society stands for human rights and political self-determination that can certainly come into conflict with neoliberal globalization; inclusive, because European civil society breaks open the container notion and container mentality of European national society and makes European societies receptive to global problems and the perspectives of others in a cosmopolitan fashion. In the final analysis, there can be no question of conceiving and practising European civil society in territorially limited ways. This European identity does *not* exist by closing itself off from others, because the recognition of others, both internally and externally, belongs to its very core.

It is the political constructivism inherent in the concept of civil society that makes it especially opportune and functional for the EU. Exaggerating somewhat, there is an inversion in the direction of causality (and legitimacy): neither society, the people nor the population fight for civil rights; in Europe, civil rights *create* a European civil society, that is, public spaces of citizen participation and identification. Thus the European domain presents the paradox of a civil society *from above* that is supposed to create and found civil society from below (see chapter 5, section 4).

A kind of European partnership in government is supposed to develop. With European civil society, the European executive acquires a 'co-ruler' that is supposed to quench the thirst of European politicians for legitimacy – beyond national parliaments.

The development of a European civil society had been identified by the EU as a solution to the problem of the democratic deficit and a means through which transnational governance can be secured. The role allotted to civil society is to mediate between the national and the supranational, thereby connecting national society to transnational governance. The integration of the EU opens up the possibility of transnational organizations participating in the development of transnational governance. In other words, European governance cannot be brought about simply by the establishment of a pan-European citizenship and rights regime, or through nationally sponsored moves towards greater integration, but requires the creation of new constituencies of European NGOs, citizens' groups, and other actors co-opted in the business of governing Europe, generating fresh momentum for European integration, and who can help advance genuinely European solutions to European problems. (Rumford 2003: 32)

Just as the nation-state in the nineteenth century created more than managed society, the concept of 'European civil society' offers the EU the opportunity to open up transnational space so that the latter organizes itself. This also involves a 'reorientation' from the past to the future: European civil society makes possible an orientation to the future that both remains tied to and breaks with the current concepts of the past of the national societies, insofar as European civil society opens the national containers and connects them horizontally. 'Civil society' is not the name for fixed structures, interactions and institutions administered by territorial states; it is instead a process concept, an experiment in inclusive differentiation, in which the predetermined European national societies are expanded, loosened and blended and made receptive for the global future. Thus European civil society can make a specific contribution to European integration. The question is not: What holds European society together?, but: What holds European *societies* together? The point is not to develop a new mode of integration of European society that *replaces* the national integration of the national member societies, but to Europeanize national societies, that is, to make them receptive, permeable and understandable to each other, *without* cancelling their specific diversity, including their narrow-mindedness and provinciality.

3.5   *European society as civilization*

The cosmopolitan outlook specializes in painful honesty, not false hope. Just as in the global domain all indicators point to the fact that cosmopolitanization lends impetus to anti-cosmopolitan movements, in the European domain anti-Europeanization movements are gaining force, both directly and indirectly. *Doing Europe* can mean becoming receptive to issues of reciprocal influence between East and West; but it can also mean employing the concept of civilization to construct a new outside against which Europe can delimit and define itself. This particular scenario was prefigured by Samuel Huntington as the 'clash of civilizations' (1996). A deeply unsettled Europe, which sees itself threatened from inside and outside by potential terrorist 'aliens' – this Europe can seek an ethnic refuge in the category of 'European civilization' which erects a fortress against other militant, terrorist and fundamentalist civilizations.

Understanding European society as civilization runs the risk of again essentializing cultural others. The temptation is to use the concept of civilization to establish a pan-continental European identity that incorporates and neutralizes the antagonistic nationalisms. The concept of civilizations is also a post-social concept that highlights the dynamic, conflictual character of global conditions, and hence affirms the transnationalization of Europe and seeks to overcome the fixation on the state – albeit by assuming the continuity of cultural boundaries and as a result tacitly essentializing them.

Here the key argument is that globality and interdependence are again carrying forward into the postnational era the clashes of civilizations which rest on a long, pre-national history of trade routes, cultural exchanges and bloody, religiously motivated campaigns of conquest. Sensitivity to collectively shared difference is being awakened, first, by the decreasing importance of nation-states, second, by the increasing importance of religion as a focus of identity. In contrast with national or ethnic identities which can be combined and merged, religious identities are mutually exclusive. But it is precisely this that is at the root of the new importance attached to the quasi-essentialistic civilizations conceived as ultimately resistant to any historical, political and social change and differentiated according to territorialized religious systems.

From Huntington's perspective, regional economic entities such as the EU can only exist if they position themselves in the global opposition between civilizations. 'On the one hand, successful economic regionalism will reinforce civilization-consciousness. On the other hand, economic regionalism may succeed only when it is rooted in a common civilization. The European Community rests on the shared foundation of European culture and Western Christianity' (Huntington 1993: 27). On this view, the membership of Greece as an Orthodox country already jeopardizes the integrity of the EU. But, at the latest, the EU must slam the door shut to Turkey if it is not to jeopardize its very existence.

The construction of a new essentialistic collective identity founded on 'the' European civilization in contradistinction to others is certainly connected with the dialectic between the dismantling of internal borders and the construction of a fortress against the outside which is a mark of EU policy. Thus understood, the civilization metaphor might even provide an antidote to the renationalization of European countries. For it could compensate for the loss of power of the European centre after the end of the Cold War. The pointers for this have been increasing since the terrorist attacks of 11 September 2001 in New York and 11 March 2004 in Madrid. The EU is also discovering the potential of the 'security issues' sparked primarily by migration as a source of self-authorization. The apocalyptic depression taking hold as a result of growing insecurities concerning employment, pensions, marriage, parenthood, etc., appears to be no less a threat that needs to be controlled. Here, it is difficult to underestimate the extent to which the fortress mentality permeates parties across the complete political spectrum.

The civilizing process is also undergoing a renaissance in the literature in social science (Delanty 2003). A range of authors – e.g., Benjamin Nelson, Norbert Elias, Shmuel Eisenstadt – attempt to merge the concept of civilization with that of modernization. Here critique of the concept of society and the associated methodological nationalism is used to justify the need for 'civilizational analyses'. The latter are supposed to rescue us from the impasse in which the concept of the nation and the state left us. In this way, the requirements of post-social discourse are being met by the modernization of the concept of civilization. The overcoming of borders and transnationalization are related to new boundary-constructions; de-deterritorialization, the rejection of homogeneity and the recognition of difference are combined with religious-ethnic essentialization. In view of the global pluralization of modernity, the analysis of modernization in terms of civilization promises to provide insight into the dynamics and fronts of the global social conflict constellations at the beginning of the twenty-first century. Europeanization is accordingly a process that unfolds *below* the global and *above* the national level. Precisely because globality is taken as the starting point, the figure of the clash of civilizations, which is no longer defined exclusively or primarily in religious terms but distinguishes between different historical routes to modernity – namely, revolution, war, colonization and communism – promises to be fruitful for the social analysis of a Europe of variable borders.

We need a broader historical notion of social change to conceptualize the four main transitions that will be involved in the event of major enlargement of the EU: the transition (1) from political authoritarianism to democracy, (2) from state socialism to market economies, (3) from industrial culture to postindustrial/postmodern culture, and (4) from a national to transnational order. (Delanty 2003: 7)

However, this good intention contradicts the essentialization and ontologization of difference that reannounces itself with the concept of civilization.

Encounters with cultural others are thought of in terms of large collective groups of civilizations that exclude the ubiquity of the mélange of cultures and 'entangled modernity' (Shalini Randeria). Thus, the concept of civilization is contaminated by the layers of meaning of cultural imperialism, Eurocentrism and even racism. It presupposes a cultural history of origins and cultural identity that reanimates the imperial and colonial Europe of the emerging first modernity but is alien to the cultural indeterminacy of the cosmopolitan Europe of the second modernity.

3.6   European society as memory

Does the era of globality and interdependence call for a world-historical perspective? Yes and no, according to Michael Geyer and Charles Bright (1995). No, because the classical analyses of world history presuppose a knowable or even known world unity, a conceptual Hegelianism, that outstripped reality but which has now been overtaken by it and has become false. This can also be shown by alternative projects that attempt to undercut Eurocentric universalism.

An alternative view, pioneered by critics of Western imperialism and theorists of dependency, would anchor twentieth-century world history in world-wide patterns of resistance against the imposition of Western rule. Nationalism and communism were the confluent currents of this program, and the (re)constitution of autonomy was its end. In linking the Soviet challenge (a 'Second World' break-out) with anti-colonial movements (a 'Third World' renewal), this approach sought to counter Eurocentric world history with the assertion of subordinated peoples engaged in coordinated struggle. Yet this proved no more secure as a framework of world history than did Western triumphalism, and not simply because communism has collapsed and the national project has fizzled. The century ends with the world being drawn together as never before but with peoples asserting difference and rejecting sameness on an unprecedented global scale. This is not a residuum of the past receding before a triumphant westernization . . . but it is not a renewal of autonomy either. . . . Rather, the recent waves of racism, nationalism, fundamentalism, and communism register, in the context of an accelerated global integration, the continuing irreducibility of the 'local'. Here lies the key to world history in the global age: for the progress of global integration and the attending struggles among would-be hegemons have persistently set loose contests over identity – or sovereignty . . . – and for autonomy that, time and again, have renewed difference in the face of integration and thus continued to fragment the world even as it became one. (Geyer and Bright 1995: 1043–4)

On this account, a world-historical perspective must seek out the global in the local, and it can do this by focusing conceptually and methodically on phenomena of boundary-transgression in a selective and topic-specific way. 'The next major stage of development will be constructed from building blocks such as these: a social history of Europe' (Osterhammel 2001: 470).

This talk of the 'next major development' refers to the unreflected national fixation of historiography, especially in Germany. Thus, Lutz Raphael (1999) summarizes the findings of a quantitative analysis of the first twenty-five years of the journal *Geschichte und Gesellschaft* [History and Society] in the judgement 'national-centric social history'. 'A scientific orientation that openly opposes all forms of German chauvinism, that embraces the universalist Max Weber and shows appreciation for more recent universalists such as Eric Hobsbawm, Barrington Moore, Charles Tilly and, more recently, Wolfgang Reinhart, exhibits an amazing degree of self-indulgence by any standards without even feeling the need to justify this' (Osterhammel 2001: 466). And Albert Wirz adds:

... especially against the background of the historiography hitherto cultivated in Germany, which was primarily preoccupied with the question of whether there was a special German way [*Sonderweg*]. Although it took the successful Western democracies as its point of reference, research was oriented largely to domestic social developments. And the representatives of the Bielefeld School in particular ... repeatedly invoked the primacy of domestic politics. A glance over the border to Central, Eastern and Southern Europe certainly can't do any harm! (Wirz 2001: 490)

Academic historiography can no longer adhere unquestioningly to the distinction between the national and international. This way of operating has become untenable in Europe with the end of the old polarity of the East–West conflict. With this, something qualitatively new entered European historical space. In the newly unfolding European space of memory, which breaks with the insularity of methodological nationalism, the national horror of the destruction of the Jews and the national wars and expulsions can no longer be studied in national terms but call for a systematic change in perspective, specifically, a Europeanization of perspectives (Diner 2003; Schlögel 2003).

As stated, the Europeanization of historical perspectives does not replace national history but enriches it with external perspectives and permanent boundary-crossings, and thereby makes it more receptive and inclusive. Europeanization does not have a fixed normative foundation. There is no greater European nation, no common European descent, no European community of fate, because the cosmopolitan Europe cannot supersede the national Europe, nor does it want to. Europe, understood as the horizontal Europeanization of the nation-states, *needs* a cosmopolitan humanism, but not a normative integration of the kind presupposed by the integration theory of national society from Durkheim to Parsons. Nevertheless, the experience of wars and dictatorships, of the concentration camps and gulags of the twentieth century, and their political processing in a still-to-be-created common horizon of memory, remains indispensable for this internal transformation of national societies.

It was Hannah Arendt who attached central importance to the relation between memory and political action (Arendt and Jaspers 1985). For her, too, no punishment is commensurable with this 'crime'. However, she gives the 'meaninglessness' of the Holocaust a political twist. All actions become ensnared in the irreversibility of their consequences. Not only God must grant forgiveness; human beings must forgive each other, and publicly, because only in this way can they recuperate the ability to act. Although this is true in general, it is particularly true in view of the monstrous crime of the destruction of the Jews. What is important for Hannah Arendt is that human beings can begin *anew* and not remain prisoners of the past. That is what forgiveness means. Only through the ability to forgive, which nobody can demand as a right, can action, which is more urgent than ever, regain its political efficacy.

Where can we analyse and document this interconnection? In the records and proceedings of the *Nuremberg Tribunals* against those responsible for the German Nazi terror. This was the first international court. It marked the creation of legal categories and a law court *beyond* national sovereignty, the invention of a legal-political practice to subsume the barbarity of the monstrous, state-organized destruction of the Jews under legal concepts and legal procedures.

In Article 6 of the *Charter of the International Military Tribunal*, we find three categories of crimes – crimes against peace, war crimes and crimes against humanity – on the basis of which the Nazi crimes and their perpetrators were tried and condemned. Interestingly, crimes against peace and war crimes presuppose national sovereignty and hence conform to the national outlook, whereas crimes against humanity, by contrast, annul national sovereignty and seek to comprehend the cosmopolitan outlook in legal categories. Thus, it is no accident that the lawyers and judges of the Nuremberg Tribunals ultimately had no idea what to make of the new category of 'crimes against humanity'. For with this, not just a new law or a new principle, but a new logic of law was introduced that breaks with the existing national logic of international law. Article 6c states: '*Crimes against humanity*: namely, murder, extermination, enslavement, deportation and other inhumane acts committed against any civilian population, before or during the war; or persecutions on political, racial or religious grounds in execution of or in connection with any crime within the jurisdiction of the Tribunal, whether or not in violation of domestic law of the country where perpetrated.'

In the formulation 'before or during the war', crimes against humanity are clearly distinguished from war crimes. In this way, the responsibility of individual offenders *beyond* national law before the community of nations, before humanity, is created. When the state becomes a criminal state, individuals who serve it must expect to be prosecuted and condemned for their actions before an international criminal court. The formula 'any civilian population' annuls the national principle on which responsibility within national borders is as absolute as is impunity beyond national borders, and replaces it with the legal principle of cosmopolitan responsibility. The cosmopolitan legal principle which breaks with national law does not protect the civilian population against violence from other, enemy states (this is already implied by the concept of 'war crimes') but, in a much more far-reaching and provocative way, against arbitrary acts of violence committed by sovereign states against their own citizens. Finally, this inverts the priority in accordance with a cosmopolitan legal morality: the principles of cosmopolitan law *trump* national law. Crimes against humanity cannot be legitimized by national law nor can they be tried and condemned by national courts. In this sense, the historical novum 'crimes against humanity' invalidates the principles of national legislation and national administration of justice.

Thus, morally, legally and politically speaking, a *genuinely European self-contradiction* finds expression in the Europeanization of memory. Although the traditions from which not only the horror of the Holocaust but also the colonial, nationalistic and genocidal madness spring are European, so too are the standards of evaluation and legal categories in terms of which these acts were tried *as* crimes against humanity before a global public. The victors could just as easily have summarily executed the elite responsible for the Nazi terror, as Stalin and Churchill originally demanded. Or they could have been brought before national judges and tried in accordance with national law (as in the Eichmann trial in Jerusalem or the Auschwitz trials in Germany). Instead, the European tradition of the recognition of others and the law founded upon it was mobilized against the perversion of law by the National Socialist state.

The cosmopolitan commemoration of the Holocaust becomes in this sense a cautionary memorial [*Mahnmal*] to the ever present modernization of barbarism, as Daniel Levy and Natan Sznaider (2001) have shown (see also Beck, Levy and Sznaider 2004). The negativity of modernity and its European consciousness does not merely reflect a pretentious ideology of the tragic. It expresses the history of the national and state deviations of the first modernity which fostered the merciless and self-destructively reckless potential for moral, political, economic and technological catastrophes.

Yet, there also exists an unrecognized but unbroken connection between European pessimism, the critique of modernity and *post*modernism which elevates despair to a permanent condition – Jürgen Habermas is right about this. In other words, there is a paradoxical coalition between the national and the postmodern Europe because postmodern theorists deny the possibility of answering the horror of European history with more Europe, with the radicalized cosmopolitan Europe.

Not only the national modernity but also postmodernity makes us blind to Europe. Europeanization means struggling for institutional answers to the barbarism of European modernity, and hence rejecting postmodernity which fails to understand just this. Cosmopolitan Europe, in this sense, is *the institutionalized self-critique of the European way.* This process poses many dilemmas, it is incomplete and incompletable. Indeed, it has only just begun with the series: Enlightenment, postmodernity, cosmopolitan modernity. Could this radical self-critique be what sets the EU apart from the USA and Muslim societies? Cosmopolitan Europe is the *self-critical* experimental Europe which is rooted in its history, breaks with its history and draws the strength to do so from its history.

5

Strategies of European Cosmopolitanization

The fact that Europe was created by the power of side effects, as the unintended product of the reflexive modernization of European national societies, does not mean that it was not, and cannot continue to be, the focus of strategic action. On the contrary, as in the case of globalization (cf. Beck 2005), Europeanization must also be conceived as a strategic power game, a *meta-power game*, in which the rules governing the state's exercise of power – their institutional architecture, their scope and the possibilities and conditions of their democratic legitimacy – are themselves newly determined. In this sense, 'Europe' – and that means not only the EU but the whole complex of national, international and supranational spheres of political power and authority – must be analysed as the (unintended) product of the competing strategies which have been employed over the past fifty years or more to shape the European experiment. We call the interim result of this meta-power game 'deformed cosmopolitanism'. This means, on the one hand, that until now none of the factors at work in this meta-power game has managed to reverse the cosmopolitanization of Europe, which was institutionally anchored from the outset; on the other hand, however, it also means that cosmopolitanism could only be realized in a damaged form. The principal aim of European cosmopolitanization, then, is to cure cosmopolitan Europe of its deformations and to redefine and reform it.

The meta-power game of Europeanization can be analysed from different perspectives (see chapter 4, section 2). When we speak in this chapter of the *European* meta-power game, then we mean neither the horizontal Europeanization of the national societies nor the Europeanization of non-European countries, but the Europeanization of Europe. In what follows, we will develop this understanding of Europeanization as a meta-power game in five steps. In the first step we will sketch the *logic* of the European meta-power game and its conflict dimensions; in the second, we will trace the most important *strategies* that have dominated this power game until now; in the third, we will identify the *deformations* which this meta-power game has thus far inflicted on the European project; in the fourth step, we will define the starting point for realizing Europe as a *cosmopolitan* project; and in a fifth step, finally, we will pose the question: What makes such strategies of cosmopolitanization realistic?

1   European cosmopolitanization as a meta-power game

What does 'meta-power game' mean? Isn't politics always a matter of power? Moreover, don't those involved in politics always act on the basis of rational strategies aimed at acquiring, preserving or expanding power? If we want to grasp what is distinctive about Europeanization as a meta-power game, it first makes sense to distinguish between two kinds of power game, namely, rule-setting and rule-transforming power games, on the one hand, and rule-applying power games, on the other. In the former case, the rules of the political game are themselves the focus of struggle; in the latter, the participants pursue their goals within a framework of predefined rules of the game. We use the term 'meta-power game' to refer to the first case, i.e., laying down and transforming the rules of the political game.

If we apply this distinction to national and European politics, a peculiar asymmetry becomes apparent. Whereas national politics is primarily rule-*applying* politics that accepts a pre-given constitutional framework and operates within it, in European politics, rule-positing, rule-applying and rule-*transforming* policies are constantly interwoven. The process of European integration initiated a new power game in which the old, national power games have lost their rules and basic concepts, and thus their substance, even though some political actors continue to play them. In short, the persistent conflicts which were fomented by Europeanization, and are supposed to be tamed by it, derive their particular political explosiveness from the fact that the political actors are forced to play a new game. Thus, Europeanization as meta-power game means four things:

First, it means that the old game, whatever one calls it – 'national realpolitik', 'national capitalism', 'national welfare state' – can no longer be successfully played in isolation. All of the positions in the power game of politics are being transformed by the Europeanization of the national societies – there is no way back. Even renationalization strategies must be conceived and implemented within the European context and as part of the European meta-power game; they are a reaction to Europeanization that has already occurred and been successful – in the sense of 'revolutionary transformation'.

Europeanization means, second, that neither the old rules and basic institutions of the national order nor the new rules and core institutions of cosmopolitan Europe are rigidly laid down, but are constantly reconfigured, redefined and renegotiated in the ongoing meta-power game of Europeanization. Hence, Europeanization must be conceived as an experiment, as the *heart of political constructivism*, as 'doing Europe', and this in the twofold sense of rhetorical and political conflicts over the transformation of reality (see chapter 4, section 3). Meta-power games are accordingly meta-*construction* games in which the rules of political constructivism are rewritten. This implies, on the one hand, that this meta-power game is in principle open and hence can at most be disciplined through European treaties and constitutions, but cannot be brought to a halt; on the other hand, it implies that the goals of this process and possible alternatives to it are as unclear as its results.

Third, the European meta-power game is characterized by the fact that *the military option is ruled out* (see chapter 3). The threat of military force, and especially its employment in internal relations between the member states and at the centre of the European Empire, has become unthinkable. As we have shown, this internal pacification of the European political domain is guaranteed by a taboo on violence. Although the member states preserve their monopoly on the means of coercion, they place handcuffs on each other – also because they are members of the joint military organization NATO.

Europeanization as meta-power game means, fourth, that the opportunities to act of the various political actors – the nation-states, the European cosmopolitan 'entrepreneurs' (European Commission and European Court of Justice), capital, labour unions and, not least, also civil society advocacy movements and external players such as the United States – depend essentially on how they *define and position* themselves within the European meta-power game. Note that Europeanization means that all actors must redefine their scope and radius of action, their goals and their strategies. Nothing is laid down in advance any longer by the nation-state or the bipolar Cold War order – even Europe does not (yet) provide a predefined framework as the nation-state did in the past. The actors certainly have a range of strategic possibilities for decision and action at their disposal when it comes to positioning themselves in the new meta-power game of European rule-setting. Neither their positions in this game nor their tactics are defined in advance. Rather, the meta-power theory rests on constructivist assumptions. *The players' room for manoeuvre depends essentially on their self-definitions* or, more precisely, changes in their self-definitions: only a change in outlook and orientation and the adoption of cosmopolitan categories provide the actors with a suitable understanding of their opportunities in the meta-power game of Europeanization (on this, see below, section 5).

This meta-power game is not merely a concomitant of the most recent treaty revisions and constitutional deliberations; the process of European integration and its preconditions were both a part and a result of this meta-power game from the beginning. The new delineation of the European power sphere began already in the early 1950s with the transfer of the first sovereign powers to supranational institutions. Indeed, even more, because the European integration process was conducted as an 'open project', it was simultaneously a permanent meta-power game in which the question of power was constantly posed and negotiated, whether openly or in secret.

This was apparent not only in treaty negotiations and at the summit meetings of European heads of state and government; this meta-power game has always also played, and continues to play, a role in detailed political decision-making. Consequently, European politics always exhibits a highly complex conflict structure (Grande 1995) in which three dimensions of conflict are inextricably interwoven: (1) institutional conflicts, (2) ideological-cultural conflicts and (3) material conflicts.

First, *institutional conflicts* over the division of powers between the Community and its member states, on the one hand, and among the supranational institutions (in particular, between Commission and Parliament), on the other hand, are at the centre of the European meta-power game. At what level can the respective powers be exercised most efficiently? What tasks follow for the Union? And, conversely, which tasks can best be left to the member states? This represents only a small portion of the comprehensive catalogue of questions which the European Council of Laeken in 2001 presented to the Constitutional Convention for consideration[1] – and these questions are far from new but are running themes of European politics. The same holds for the competences of the supranational institutions: How can the authority and efficiency of the European Commission be strengthened? How can the procedure governing joint decisions of the Council and the European Parliament be simplified? What role should the European Parliament play in the future?

The answers to these questions discussed for years appear at times highly technical. The consultations of the convention which drew up the Draft Constitution for the European Union were no different in this respect. However, the appearance is misleading, for behind apparently harmless proposals lurk the feints of the European meta-power game:

In reality, however, a huge tug-of-war is taking place. The one side wants to take a major leap forward in the direction of a European Union in which the Parliament and Commission, as the true Community institutions, play the leading role. The other side defends the position of the nation-states. Among the latter are some who really want to rein in the Commission, whereas others are primarily concerned to ensure that the governments work effectively to promote Europe. Almost more important than the composition of the committees in this respect are the working methods: will decisions be made by majority vote or can important decisions continue to be blocked by the veto of a single state? (*Süddeutsche Zeitung*, 17–18 May 2003: 4)

The second major source of conflicts over the construction of Europe which essentially shape the dynamics governing the European reality is represented by divergent *ideological-cultural* images of the future, and hence also of the past. In what kind of Europe do we want to live? Who determines the 'We' who speaks here and against whom does it demarcate itself? At no point in time was Europe a harmonious community of values; the process of European integration was riddled with value conflicts from the outset. We can distinguish at least three such normative conflicts. First, there were and continue to be often deeply rooted differences between the European countries over *the role of the state* in the economy and in society. In particular, the three largest member countries of the EU for many years stood for strikingly different models of capitalism – namely, French 'statism', British 'neoliberalism' and German 'corporatism' – corresponding to very different strategies of state intervention and different citizen expectations concerning public benefits and services (see Schmitt 2002).[2] This was reflected at the European level, in particular, by the persistent conflicts between neoliberal and interventionist policies.

The different national *philosophies of risk* constitute a further source of normative conflicts. On the one hand, the value of Europeanization is measured by the guarantee of security for citizens. However, the various national milieus often diverge widely over what counts as secure and what risks are acceptable (see chapter 7). The different national reactions to the Chernobyl reactor catastrophe in Germany and France and to the BSE crisis in Great Britain, France and Germany provided clear examples of this. The BSE crisis showed at the same time that national go-it-alone policies could be extremely risky for the other countries under the conditions of a European risk society.

Conflicts over the *construction of Europe's cultural identity* constitute the third variety of normative conflicts. Here the main question concerns the elements on which a European 'We-feeling' should be founded or created: common ancestry, common history, universal human rights, Christianity, the inclusion or exclusion of cultural and religious others (and which ones)? This problem became even more acute the more Europe developed from an economic community into a political union, and the wider the circle of (the actual and potential) members of this union became. In the most recent debate over Europe, these conflicts found expression in part in the controversy over the 'reference to God' in the preamble to the Draft Constitution for the European Union, on which confessionally oriented parties, such as the German Christian Social Union (CSU), were particularly insistent. However, this meta-power game of identity is also sparked by the question of the accession of Turkey to the EU. The critics of Turkey's desire for membership (in Germany, see Stoiber 2002, Winkler 2002, among others) attempted in the first instance to construct and use cultural differences between 'Europe' and Turkey as a reason for keeping the latter out of the EU. Some even went so far as to invoke again Europe's most authentic universalistic tradition, the Enlightenment, as a criterion of belonging, and hence of exclusion (Stoiber 2002).

Third, and finally, *material distributional conflicts* naturally play a key role in the European meta-power game. These conflicts not only dominate the day-to-day business of resource distribution in Brussels, in which the member states haggle over levels of agricultural subventions, payments from the regional and structural funds and the distribution of subsidies for research, transforming the European market into a bazaar. Behind these running clashes over appropriate shares of the European budget stand two much more fundamental conflicts that are part of the internal European, regional meta-power game over inequalities among different states: on the one hand, conflicts between 'rich' and 'poor' member countries and, on the other, conflicts between capital and labour. As we will show later (see chapter 6), these conflicts are the product of a twofold transformation of social inequality within Europe, i.e., the transformation of group and class conflicts into conflict between regions and states, and the Europeanization of the national welfare states with their frozen distributional conflicts between capital and labour. As a result, the old rules of the game for processing distributional conflicts are becoming obsolete and need to be renegotiated.

The fact that these conflicts are frequently interwoven is characteristic of the meta-power game of Europeanization. This can be shown in an exemplary way in the debate over the EU membership of Turkey, which would affect Europe in a number of respects. Accession to the EU would mean not only that global social conflicts would be internalized, but also that the relations of size, power and inequality within the EU would be mixed up. For example, given current demographic trends, Turkey with (at present) almost 70 million inhabitants would displace Germany in the not too distant future as the most populous EU member country. In this case, Turkey would naturally also challenge the German claim to the most seats in the European Parliament and the most votes in the EU Council of Ministers. And, not least, the preeminence of the two hitherto largest member states, Germany and France, who see themselves as the 'motor of the Community', would be jeopardized. Something similar holds for the question of whether the EU should remain a 'Christian club' or should alter its self-understanding to open itself up to other world religions. This would merely be to acknowledge reality – though the Christian churches would thereby lose their monopoly position.

This conflict, however, also has a material dimension: 'The economic power of Turkey, which currently amounts to just 22 percent of the EU average, would also pose a crucial test for the economic and social cohesion of the EU. By way of comparison: in the period between 2000 and 2006, Spain is due to receive around €56 billion in transfers from EU structural and cohesion funds. But Spain is only half the size of Turkey and has four times its economic power' (Stoiber 2002: 15). This example shows that the conflicts over the construction of Europe in the European meta-power game are *multiply coded* and lack the clarity and sharpness that characterized the conflicts during the formation of nation-states in Europe.[3]

2   Strategies of Europeanization

Who, then, are the *players* in this complex meta-power game? And what moves and strategies are open to them? In essence, we can identify three groups of actors who have dominated the game over the past fifty years: (a) the *states* (though it must be emphasized that not only the member states of the Community play a role in this game), (b) the *economy* and (c) the *supranational institutions* (in particular, the European Commission, the European Court of Justice and the European Parliament).[4] This constellation of players exhibits two striking peculiarities through which the meta-power game of Europeanization differs markedly from that of globalization (see Beck 2005). On the one hand, the supranational institutions play an important role in the European meta-power game. They are not merely passive recipients and executors of the decisions of the member states, as neorealism and liberal intergovernmentalism in international relations theory assume, but independent actors with their own interests, goals and resources.[5] On the other hand, actors from civil society and social movements for the most part played a minor role in the European meta-power game. Although the idea of European integration after World War II had the support of a broad and populous European civic movement that in many places drew on the 'spirit of the resistance' (Niess 2001), nevertheless this civic movement quickly lost its political relevance. Since then, Europe has failed to inspire the masses, either for or against.

2.1   State strategies

The states are the central players and objects in the European meta-power game. Their sovereignty and identity are the ultimate stakes in this game, for Europeanization means precisely wresting parts of their national sovereignty from them 'step by step' and transforming it into cosmopolitan sovereignty. It is true that numerous non-state actors are involved in this game. As we shall see later, this is precisely the secret of its success. But one fact is as trivial as it is consequential: the meta-power game of Europeanization could not and cannot function without the participation of the European nation-states.

The participating states generally pursued very different goals and strategies. In order to make this clear, we do not need here to analyse the full repertoire of strategies, ranging from renationalization to transnationalization, available to the states in the process of globalization (on this, see Beck 2005: ch. 5). For our purposes, it suffices to differentiate state strategies in two dimensions, i.e., in terms of the motives of action (realistic vs. idealistic), on the one hand, and the action orientations (egoistic vs. cooperative), on the other. By means of these differentiations, we can identify at least four different state strategies in the European integration process: (1) (neo)nationalistic egoism, (2) intergovernmental minimalism, (3) cosmopolitan realism and (4) cosmopolitan idealism (see figure 5.1).

Motive/practical orientation	Egoistic	Cooperative
Realistic	(Neo)nationalistic egoism/ intergovernmental minimalism	Cosmopolitan realism
Idealistic		Cosmopolitan idealism

Figure 5.1: Typology of state strategies in the process of Europeanization

Nationalistic egoism

The most problematic strategy in the European meta-power game is the refusal to cooperate that aims at one-sidedly maximizing one's utility, one's 'national interest'. This strategy can take different forms. A current example of the refusal to cooperate for reasons of national interests is the British government's decision not to join the economic and monetary union. The reverse side of this strategy is exercising one's veto to prevent the accession of a new member. France, as is well known, twice prevented the accession of Great Britain to the EEC in this way during the 1960s.[6] However, the strategy of refusing to cooperate can also be used by non-members, primarily by rejecting accession. Examples of this were Great Britain during the 1950s and later Norway and Switzerland.

The strategy of rejecting membership played a role mainly during the early years of European integration. The aim was to prevent the construction of supranational institutions and the transfer of sovereignty rights to the European Communities. Later, with the enlargement of the EU, a different strategy of national egoism became more important, namely, the exercise of the veto either to block decisions or to extort concessions from the other member states in one's national interest. A prime example of this was the policy of the British government during the 1980s, which involved threatening to veto EC agricultural policy to force a reduction in the British net contribution to the EC budget.

Intergovernmental minimalism

A minimalist strategy must be distinguished from this strategy of completely refusing to cooperate. In this case, the states are indeed willing to cooperate, but are unwilling to cede any sovereignty rights to European institutions. We find this strategy in different variants in the course of the integration process. Among them is, first, the attempt to establish alternative, intergovernmentally designed organizations alongside the supranationally organized EC/EU, as in the case of the European Free Trade Association, EFTA, at the end of the 1950s and the European research initiative, EUREKA, during the 1980s. Intergovernmental minimalism is responsible in part for the baroque profusion of forms of intergovernmental cooperation which has emerged in Europe outside the European Communities. The efforts to reinforce the intergovernmental elements in the internal organization of the EC/EU at the expense of the supranational institutions represent a further variant. The most well-known example was the granting of a right of veto to individual member states in 1966 as part of the so-called Luxembourg Compromise. The logic of intergovernmental minimalism was trenchantly formulated by Charles de Gaulle: 'He recognized only a Europe of states, but no Europe above the states. European unification could only mean cooperation between independent states, each of which retained its full sovereignty and its right of veto in all institutions' (Brunn 2002: 138 f.).[7] As the debates in the Constitutional Convention and the ensuing intergovernmental conference have shown, this either/or logic of national sovereignty remains present, indeed tacitly or explicitly ubiquitous, in European politics to the present day. The minimalist state strategy was particularly apparent in the refusal of the British government to renounce its right of veto in favour of majority decisions in European foreign policy.

Cosmopolitan realism

This strategy allows the member states to pursue their interests 'realistically', though in doing so they are expected to take account simultaneously of the interests of the other members and of those of the Community. The result is the maximization not only of their own interests but also of that of the Community, on the model of a positive-sum game. As we have seen, the success of the European integration process has hitherto been based primarily on this strategy (chapter 3, section 4). It was already exhibited by the foundation of the European Coal and Steel Community, which was largely free from idealism. The primary concern of the French side at the time was to counter the threatened dominance of the Germany economy. The German side – 'as far removed as possible from any enthusiasm for Europe', as Hans-Peter Schwarz (1994: 852) observed – was mainly concerned that 'there was no other way to get rid of the Ruhr Statute and its many inconveniences!' Schwarz accurately describes the logic of cosmopolitan realism that underlay the founding phase of the European Communities: 'Viewed in the clear light of day, the primary goal of the European constructions of those years was to solve genuinely German problems. Nevertheless, Adenauer, no less than Jean Monnet and the other "Europeans" of that decade, was convinced that European solutions, however structured in detail, *were as favourable to German interests as they were to the national interests of other Europeans*' (ibid.: 854; our emphasis). The same logic also informed the European constructions of the past twenty years. The main aim in establishing both the internal market and the economic and monetary union was to pursue national interests along European paths, and in this way to serve both one's own country and Europe.

Cosmopolitan idealism

Finally, we should not ignore a state strategy that is at once the most ambitious and the most improbable. In this case, states do not pursue their own, 'national' interests when they cooperate with other states but instead subordinate their interests to the goals of the Community. In short, they act 'idealistically' rather than 'realistically'; they are not guided by interests but by higher ideas. Thus Frank Schimmelfennig (2003) demonstrates that the eastern enlargement of the EU not only served national interests, but also obeyed a normative logic of democratic community-building – though this is certainly compatible with the cosmopolitan interest of the European Empire in expansion as a strategy for controlling new zones of insecurity.

The 'Schuman declaration' of 9 May 1950 shows how difficult it is to distinguish between cosmopolitan idealism and realism (especially when one accords central importance to rhetorical constructivism). It states:

[T]he French Government proposes to take immediate action on a limited but crucial issue . . . to place the entire Franco-German production of coal and steel under a single joint authority within the framework of an organization open to the participation of the other European countries. . . . *Solidarity at the level of production, once achieved, will make it clear to all that a war between France and Germany is not only unthinkable, but materially impossible.* (Cited from Fontaine 2000: 14; our emphasis)

In this case, the creation of economic interdependence is wedded historically to the promotion of peace. One could even say that national idealism is wedded to supranational idealism. The creation of economic interdependencies becomes a means of immunizing the values of the nation from being corrupted by nationalistic insanity and militaristic misappropriation. However, one should not overestimate the idealistic moment either: 'One certainly cannot deny that Robert Schumann and the architect of the plan, Jean Monnet, were motivated by European idealism. Nevertheless, in view of the decidedly national aims of the proposal, one can also rightly assert that the plan equally involved an instrumentalization of European policy for national purposes. In other words, it was a continuation of national politics by European means' (Brunn 2002: 77).

What status European idealism actually enjoyed in this case need not concern us here. Idealistic motives undoubtedly played an important role in the political construction of Europe and they remain important (see Weiler 1999: 250ff.; Brunn 2002: 104). Nevertheless, the crucial point is that in the past the European project was not founded exclusively on the idealism of states and their governments and that its further cosmopolitanization need not be made dependent on such idealism either.

Strategy/level of action	National	European	Global
Neoliberal	National neoliberalism	European neoliberalism	Global neoliberalism
Interventionist	National protectionism	European protectionism	Global interventionism

Figure 5.2: Typology of capital strategies in the process of Europeanization

2.2 Capital strategies

Europe is indeed a project of the states, but it was also shaped from the outset by economic interests and strategies.[8] This is grounded, of course, in the peculiar starting point of Europeanization, i.e., economic integration, which made Europe a primarily economic project. We should not forget, however, that it was at no time a purely neoliberal project. On the contrary, the original European Communities – the European Coal and Steel Community, the European Atomic Community and the Common Agricultural Policy in the EEC – all observed the logic of 'planned', 'organized' and 'regulated' capitalism in the service of promoting peace. All of these communities were based on interventionist policies and their architects came primarily from the French tradition of *'planification'*. The most important exception to this was the Customs Union, which came into being with the EEC and observed expressly and exclusively the neoliberal logic of 'negative integration' and provided the basis for the subsequent development of the Community, i.e., the completion of the internal market and the establishment of the economic and monetary union.

In order to clarify the aims and strategies of economic actors in European politics, it is useful to differentiate capital strategies in two dimensions, i.e., to distinguish between neoliberal and interventionist strategies in the horizontal dimension and between national, European and global strategies in the vertical dimension. There result six possible capital strategies, of which four are especially important for the European integration process (see figure 5.2).

National protectionism

National protectionism is the most pronounced anti-European strategy. Its aim is to preserve the competences of the nation-state in order to protect national markets, companies, industries and welfare systems. Striving for national protection in the form of government subventions, market monopolies, import quotas, supply guarantees, procurement contracts, etc., was for a long time the dominant strategy of capital during the decades following World War II in all industries that came under international competitive pressure, whether 'old industries', such as the coal and steel industry and shipbuilding, or the 'industries of the future', such as nuclear energy, electronics and aerospace.

European protectionism

Protectionist and interventionist capital strategies, however, do not depend exclusively on the nation-state but can also be realized at the European level. Moreover, with the establishment of the common internal market, protectionist capital strategies were increasingly geared towards Europe. The idea was that Europe would ensure uncompetitive capital the protection which the nation-states were no longer permitted to guarantee as a result of Europeanization. European protectionism is accordingly the strategy of capital that links the creation of a single internal market to protecting European industry against external competitors. This strategy advocates market-correcting interventions, but in extremely one-sided and selective ways that exclusively favour the European economy. The most striking and well-known example of European protectionism is to be found in agricultural policy, which is dominated by internal subventions, export compensation payments and restrictions on imports. However, numerous instances of interventionist strategies can be found in European industrial policy as well, for example the research and development subsidies for the large companies in the information technology and biotechnology industries.

European neoliberalism

This is also a pro-European strategy, a capital strategy that seeks to reduce the European project to the creation of a large, unified and weakly regulated internal market. In this context, the European internal market project was interpreted as 'a political offensive for economic deregulation and technological-industrial revitalization. It loosened encrusted structures and introduced greater competition into the national markets in Europe' (Grewlich 1992: 33). The primary concern of the European Commission during the 1980s and 1990s was to establish a link between the Europeanization of markets and the international competitiveness of European industry. The rhetorical constructivism of the Commission found exemplary expression in the so-called Davignon Report of 1979, which concluded that

purely national strategies are not sufficient to bring our companies up to the level of the global market. The resources and markets of the European states no longer correspond to the dimensions of this technological revolution . . . The limited scope of national markets meant that too small firms survived which were not competitive with American and Japanese firms, and that in the key technological developments for the future they fell behind and American and Japanese firms conquered the market. (EG-Kommission 1979: 9)

Within Europe, the neoliberal strategy has two main goals. First, it aims to remove restrictions on the economy completely, physical (abolition of border controls for people and goods) as well as technical (elimination of barriers to cross-border services and capital mobility) and fiscal (harmonization of taxes, among other things); second, it seeks to remove all national market distortions (subventions, etc.). However, the neoliberal strategy aims solely at a 'negative integration'; it rejects more far-reaching, market-correcting activities at the European level.

Global neoliberalism

Although neoliberalism contributed essentially to the promotion of the European project during the 1980s and 1990s, its attitude towards Europe is ambiguous. It can serve not only pro-European but also anti-European capital strategies. For, in essence, neoliberalism cannot form or accept any exclusive preference for a particular territorial level, whether global or European. The ideology of neoliberalism may promote 'denationalization' and removal of borders within Europe, but it does not have an answer to the key question: Why Europe and why not rather the world? Accordingly, the goal of global neoliberalism is not only to create a single market in Europe but also to liberalize the global economy. And where these two goals conflict with each other – where attempts are made to build Europe into a 'fortress' and to restrict the free movement of capital – neoliberalism becomes anti-European. This global neoliberalism is not a concomitant of the most recent wave of globalization. As early as the 1950s, the German export economy viewed the project of European integration as 'economic nonsense' (Ludwig Erhard). Its slogan at the time was: 'Our field is the world' (quoted from Brunn 2002: 103). Consequently, for global neoliberalism, Europe can be at best a means to an end, an instrument for disempowering (national) politics, but one which has no deeper intrinsic value for this capital strategy.

2.3   Technocratic strategies

Technocratic strategies are distinguished by the fact that they are guided neither by the political logics of states nor by the economic interests of industry, but by functional rationalities. Technocratic strategies can also be pursued in various forms by very different actors. Among them are the efforts of national administrations to preserve their domains and resources as well as the activities of supranational institutions. The latter are especially important in the present context. For the technocratic strategies of the supranational institutions are in essence pro-European and are aimed at the expansion and strengthening of the supranational elements in the Community. These ambitions are justified essentially in functional terms. This holds both for the European Commission and for the European Court of Justice, the two most important supranational motors of integration.

From the beginning, the European Commission exhibited the technocratic strategy in a particularly clear form. Its technocratic approach has two characteristic features: first, the idea of beginning European integration in a small number of clearly defined, technically limited and politically uncontroversial areas and then extending it to other areas; and, second, its emphasis on functional, technical requirements in justifying new activities. Correspondingly, the European Commission always regarded its role as that of the advocate of the 'Community interest' who had to impose functional requirements and technical best practice in the face of political idiosyncrasies and national particularism. A prime example of this was the justification of a common technology policy in 1970. 'In Western Europe', wrote the Commission, 'cooperation in the field of technology in recent years was marked by the fact that not even a minimum of homogeneity existed . . . Cooperative initiatives at the financial and industrial levels could not be shaped in accordance with the most rational considerations. They are mostly short term, subordinated to political and economic considerations determined by national interest and lead to compromises which cannot be reconciled with the principle of economic efficiency' (EG-Kommission 1970: 347f.). What was needed was rather a 'pooling of forces', a 'joint course of action' (ibid.: 356f.) – by which were meant, of course, activities of the European Commission.

A further variant of the functional logic is to be found in the adjudication of the European Court of Justice. The ECJ is seen as primarily responsible for the form of Europeanization termed in the jurisprudential literature 'integration through law' (Cappelletti, Seccombe and Weiler 1986). By this is meant in essence that the ECJ made an essential contribution to the dynamics and scope of the European integration process through its administration of justice over the past forty years (Burley and Mattli 1993; Alter 2001). The ECJ also took its principal orientation from 'functional' considerations, from the 'letter and spirit' of the European treaty complex (Joerges 2003).[9]

None of these three strategies – state strategies, capital strategies or technocratic strategies – has consistently dominated the project of European integration. They were particularly effective whenever they succeeded in forming coalitions. European policy was always the product of competition among the most various cooperation strategies. During the 1960s and 1970s, a coalition of nationalistic state strategies, national-protectionist capital strategies and national technocracy dominated; in the 1980s, a coalition of cosmopolitan realism, European neoliberalism and supranational technocracy developed in opposition to this. This strategic constellation brought the European project forward a couple of important steps, but it is also responsible for the current parlous state of Europe. For the European project was only partially realized by this strategic constellation, and in addition it was *politically deformed*. Europe, on our argument, is suffering from a politically divided and half-hearted cosmopolitanism, that is, from a *deformed cosmopolitanism*.

3   Deformations of cosmopolitan Europe

In chapter 2, we showed that the European integration process was a cosmopolitan project from the start. This is precisely what distinguished it from all previous forms of state-building, regional integration and construction of international organizations, which were shaped by either a national or a universalistic perspective. However, this cosmopolitan project has been realized to date only in a deformed manner due to the weakness of European civil society and the dominance of state, capital and technocratic strategies. On closer inspection, each of the three strategies we have presented proves to have led to characteristic deformations of the European project.

3.1   The economic deformation

The first and most important deformation of cosmopolitan Europe is its economic deformity. By this we do not mean the deleterious effects of European protectionism and the Brussels subvention economy, which are the bane of neoliberal economists, but the consequences of neoliberalism itself. Where neoliberal capital strategies are successfully implemented, 'negative integration' dominates the European project. Market restrictions are being torn down without politics acquiring the possibility of counteracting the negative effects of unrestrained economic competition (see Scharpf 1999, 2003).

Hence, neoliberalism is not just an economic but also a political ideology of the self-transformation of the world of states or, more precisely, an ideology of the self-liquidation of states. As such, it is the precise opposite of a status quo politics, for it advocates and promotes the systematic transformation of the political under the banner of 'economic necessity'. The neoliberal reformers in Europe are consequently (to adopt a term used by Enzensberger about Gorbachev) 'artisans of liquidation'. Like managers who use their power to rationalize away management positions, the acme of their success is to put themselves out of a job. For the neoliberal mission of minimizing the state, the construction of a European institutional architecture is merely a means to the end of creating an agency for dismantling the state. The intentional strategy of unintended side effects plays an important role in this process. Its goal is to start an economic dynamic whose follow-on problems generate pressure on the member states either to fail or gradually to strengthen, indeed to create, the postnational Europe by political means.

Accordingly, the dynamics of neoliberal Europeanization congeal into an institutional paradox. Under the banner of 'integration', a process of undermining borders and basic foundations of modernization was triggered that explodes the frame of reference of the Europe of nation-states, in particular, the projects of the welfare state, of class compromise and of subsidiarity among states. In this way, the neoliberalization of Europe annuls the very historical social and political foundations on which the European project was based. Whereas politicians of the 'new left' in particular appeal to the social chapters of the Maastricht Treaty which are supposed to guarantee social justice against the threat of economic anarchy, the implementation of the principles of unconstrained economic rationality creates a countervailing dynamic. State controls are minimized and the member states are committed to principles of financial, economic and tax policy that bind their hands. 'Reform' then degenerates into an ever further deregulation of markets. As we have noted, this kind of 'reflexive modernization' destroys the complex lifeworld architecture of solidarity that lent the European nation-states their social-moral frame and shaped the bonds and conflicts which have generated social meaning. In the interplay between the individualization and postnationalization of societies, Europe is becoming at once depoliticized and privatized and as a result is succumbing to capital accumulation and, importantly, to right-wing populism. In short, a neoliberal Europe is a Europe shaped by the primacy of the economy, and thus is an economically deformed Europe.

3.2 The nationalist deformation

Europe suffers from a second, nationalist deformity when national egoisms on the part of states or national-protectionistic capital strategies gain the upper hand, and this becomes especially pronounced when the two operate together, for example, to protect national subventions for threatened companies and industries. In this case, both the logic of economic competition and the logic of European cooperation are undermined. Europe degenerates into a bazaar especially when money is at stake.

National egoisms manifest themselves in Brussels in many places. Be it the size of the agriculture budget, the volume of cohesion and structural funds, quotas in fisheries policy, the establishment of new funding programmes, decisions over the location of European institutions or the granting of national subventions – there is hardly a decision in which the representatives of member states do not attempt to squeeze out material advantages for their own country. In these bargains, politicians of all member states and of every political affiliation are involved. National egoisms play an especially prominent role in European politics whenever decisions have to be made in accordance with the principle of unanimity, thus enabling individual countries to blackmail the others. The successful threat of the Greek prime minister Papandreou to use his veto to block the admission of Portugal and Spain into the EC unless Greece received guarantees of compensation payments is legendary (see Thatcher 1993: 545–6). The Spanish government played the same game in the negotiations over the eastern enlargement. It linked Spain's agreement to the condition that the structural funds, which until then benefited primarily the Southern European countries, would continue even after the eastern enlargement. Finally, in the interests of its agro-industrial complex, France has stubbornly opposed reforms of the EU agricultural policy intended to eliminate the existing system of overproduction.

The structural funds, in addition to agricultural policy, are a particularly egregious example of the impact of the political illogics which drive national egoisms on European policy (see Peterson and Bomberg 1999: 157f.). The funds were originally supposed to be reserved for the regions in the Community whose gross national product amounted to less than 75 per cent of the EU average. At the end of the 1980s, regions in four member states (Spain, Portugal, Greece and Ireland) satisfied this criterion. Northern Ireland had already been admitted into the group of Target 1 regions in 1988, despite the fact that its gross domestic product was almost 79 per cent of the average, primarily to facilitate the agreement of the British government to the establishment of the structural funds. In 1993, the criteria were watered down even further. Great Britain insisted on the inclusion of the regions of Merseyside and of the Scottish Highlands and Islands among the recipients; Belgium pushed through the inclusion of the Wallonian region of Hainaut, whereupon France insisted on including the bordering French region of Nord-Pas-de-Calais; the Netherlands promoted the inclusion of the region of Flevoland; and, finally, Italy insisted on the inclusion of the Abruzzi region, although its gross national product was almost 90 per cent of the average. It is hardly surprising that they all got what they wanted in the end; nor is it any more surprising that analysts of EU cohesion policy have concluded that its goals – solidarity among states and the reduction of territorial inequalities within the Community – have to date been realized for the most part only symbolically and that their effective contribution to economic convergence is minimal (see Peterson and Bomberg 1999: 170f.). Fritz Scharpf concluded already in the mid-1980s that the institutional structures of the European Community systematically promote suboptimal policies because they concede too much scope to national egoisms (Scharpf 1988).

Europe's nationalist deformation is exhibited not only in its policies but also in its institutions. Whether it is a matter of the 'major' institutional questions, such as the division of powers between the EU and the member states, changes in the decision-making rules or the establishment of new institutions and functions, or of the fine detail of the design of the supranational institutions and their modus operandi – everywhere national egoisms predominate. This is particularly clear in the case of the European Commission, which is frequently made the scapegoat for the deficiencies of European politics, but whose inefficiency is often due to the self-interest of the member states. This starts already with the size of the Commission, which is determined not by its functions but by the interests of the member states. In spite of several enlargements of the EU, each member state continues to insist on the right to nominate a commissioner, though this is strictly speaking irrelevant because the EU Treaty obligates the commissioners to exercise their office in a cosmopolitan manner in the European sense, thus in complete independence from the member states. It continues with the distribution of responsibilities within the Commission, where the member states jealously take care to ensure the area of responsibility of 'their' commissioner appropriately reflects the weight of the country. In the past, this meant that the tasks assigned to the commissioners were determined not by professional considerations alone but also by criteria of national proportionality: 'Since there are not enough "important" tasks, or since certain areas of responsibility are too important to be assigned to a single commissioner, completely independent tasks are often bound together into bundles at the political level . . . ; portions of complex areas are frequently split off or policy fields that belong together are separated' (Starbatty and Vetterlein 1990: 43).

Finally, the self-interest of the member states has also contributed to hundreds of committees – the so-called comitology – emerging under the umbrella of the Commission in which representatives of the member states collaborate in European policy-making (see Töller 2002). Although the Commission itself promoted such committees in order to enhance acceptance of its activities among the member states, and although the regulatory accomplishments of these administrative committees sometimes receive quite positive ratings, nevertheless their primary task from the perspective of the member states is to control the Commission in the implementation of European programmes and to ensure that national concerns are taken into account in this process. In short, the European Commission is a bureaucratic giant that has been deformed and chained by the member states – only to be criticized by these very states for its ineffectiveness.

3.3 The bureaucratic deformation

The third deformation of cosmopolitan Europe, the bureaucratic deformation, is a negative concomitant of technocratic strategies (on this, see also Bach 2000; on bureaucratic rationality in the EU, see Peters 1992). Notwithstanding the frequently heard laments, this is not a matter of the absurd influence of power-hungry 'Brussels bureaucracies'; the bureaucratic deformation of Europe is manifested in completely different ways. Its primary reason is that European integration has until now clearly strengthened the executives, both national and supranational; the losers at both levels were the parliaments and the citizens (Moravcsik 1994). In other words, Europeanization means bureaucratization.

In this context, a new type of bureaucracy has emerged that differs in important respects from the Weberian one, among other things through the pronounced networking of national and supranational bureaucracy. Maurizio Bach (1992, 2000) has called this new type of bureaucracy 'transnational fusion-bureaucracy'; but a more accurate description would be 'transnational cooperation-bureaucracy'. The crucial point is that the bureaucratization of Europe does not take place in Brussels but all over Europe, right down to the level of municipalities. According to estimates of Wolfgang Wessels (1996: 178f.), already by 1990 approximately 25 per cent of the higher-level civil servants in the German Federal Government had collaborated directly with committees of the EC; and there are estimates that at the same time around 40 per cent of all higher-level civil servants in the German ministerial administration were working on EC issues as part of their respective areas of responsibility.

Deformed cosmopolitanism, as it has evolved in Europe over the past fifty years, has up to now been amazingly successful. Although its various rationales – the economic, the nationalistic and the bureaucratic – often conflicted with each other, they have not (yet) blocked or annulled each other. This is not to imply, however, that this development will simply continue. Deformed cosmopolitanism has a highly sensitive weak point: its *legitimation problems* are its Achilles heel. Neither the neoliberal rationality of the market nor the bureaucratic rationality of supranational technocracies, not to mention the political rationality of national interests of states, is capable of providing the necessary legitimacy for the European project. And this ultimately means that they are incapable of making Europe indispensable. For Europe can only make itself indispensable through the legitimating power of politics, not through objective necessities or economic achievements or Western reason.

Our analysis has shown that Europe is suffering from a double legitimacy deficit: a participation deficit and a performance deficit. Europe neither possesses the input legitimacy, i.e., the permanent support of its citizens, generated by formalized rights of participation in political decision-making processes; nor has it succeeded in compensating for this deficit through output legitimacy, i.e., through the achievements and problem-solving capacity of its policies.[10] Citizens' opportunities for participation currently boil down to the five-yearly elections to a European Parliament that is weak in comparison with most national parliaments; and although the capacity of European politics to solve problems may be considerable in some areas (cf. Scharpf 1999; Grande and Jachtenfuchs 2000), it nevertheless exhibits such serious deficiencies in key areas such as agricultural policy, industrial policy and foreign and security policy on account of the dominance of national interests that it seems improbable that Europe can reliably legitimize itself in the eyes of its citizens in the long term through its political effectiveness. In short, Europe needs more, not less, cosmopolitan Europe if it is to overcome its deformity.

4   Strategies of European cosmopolitanization

How can the deformations of cosmopolitan Europe be overcome? How can a deformed cosmopolitanism be transformed into a genuine cosmopolitanism that also finds expression in the self-understanding of the political actors? On which actors can we count in this regard? And what strategies are open to them? In principle, these questions admit two kinds of positive answers that must be examined. The first possibility would be that one of the dominant actors to date – i.e., states, capital and supranational institutions – would successfully impose itself and advance the project of a cosmopolitan Europe; the other possibility would be that new actors – for example, civic movements – would emerge and drive the process of cosmopolitanization forward.

4.1   Cunning of reason? The side-effects power of the global economy and its limits

When it comes to breaking down national egoisms and encrusted bureaucracies, neoliberal capital strategies have until now proved to be a truly revolutionary force. Is it not conceivable that the bourgeoisie could also sweep away the outdated institutions of the nation-state, just as it brushed aside the political institutions of feudalism in Europe? Moreover, what is to prevent a cosmopolitan democracy in Europe becoming the heir to the democratic welfare state, just as the latter superseded the feudal monarchies? In other words, couldn't the neoliberal assault of the global economy on the world of states signal the birth of a cosmopolitan Europe on the model of a politics of unintended side effects?

As early as the end of the eighteenth century, Adam Smith argued that whoever possesses land is necessarily a citizen of a particular country, whereas shareholders could become world citizens because they are no longer bound to a particular country. Thus, it does not appear so far-fetched to rely on the 'cunning of (economic) reason' and the side-effects power of the global economy. For an 'enlightened' global capitalism would at least force national societies, states and political parties gradually to overcome the narrow-mindedness of the national outlook through the negative global power of non-investment. At any rate, capital strategies are intrinsically coercible through non-intervention. This could awaken the self-interestedness of the pro-European nations and tempt them onto the thorny path of political self-transformation into transnational cooperative states. The neoliberalization of Europe *could* thereby become a preliminary stage that prepares the way for the cosmopolitanization of Europe. This possibility is reflected in Samuel Huntington's (2004, 2005) anxious vision that 'economic transnationals are the nucleus of an emerging global superclass'. He estimates that this transnational elite already comprised around 20 million in 2000 and will double by the year 2010 (Huntington 2004: 8).

This idea is open to two objections. The first was formulated many years ago by Fritz W. Scharpf (1994, 1999, 2003) and Wolfgang Streeck (1995) with their thesis of the 'negative integration' of Europe. They argue that the European integration process is necessarily characterized by an asymmetry. The institutional rules governing decision-making, on the one hand, and the constellations of interests among the member states, on the other, make it possible to abolish national regulations and create a single European market ('negative integration'); yet agreements on common rules for regulating and correcting the European market in analogous ways to the national markets ('positive integration') can be reached only with great difficulty. This con-stellation involves the danger 'that the European democracies would ruin themselves if, in an ever increasing number of urgent problems, national poli-tics could no longer act but could only call for "European solutions", while in Brussels long-drawn-out negotiations at best produce compromises that satisfy nobody and for which nobody wants to accept political responsibility' (Scharpf 1993: 6). For Scharpf, there is only one realistic option: 'to curtail as little as possible the room for manoeuvre of politics *in the member states*' (Scharpf 2003: 240; our emphasis). On this conception, in other words, the neoliberalization of Europe would be not the *first*, but the *last*, step towards a cosmopolitan Europe – only a neonational state strategy can successfully counteract a neoliberal capital strategy. Exaggerating somewhat, neoliberali-zation would not prepare the way for a cosmopolitan Europe but would be a dead end on the road to further Europeanization.

The notion that neoliberalism could be the midwife of a cosmopolitan Europe is open to a second objection. For it is also doubtful whether the neo-liberalization of Europe prepares the ground for a *cosmopolitan* project. This is due, on the one hand, to the fact that neoliberal Europeanization aims at the *complete* abolition of national rules. According to this capital logic, public services must be minimized while at the same time becoming exchangeable. National peculiarities are not acknowledged and used productively, but are levelled out.[11] This destroys the basis of any cosmopolitanization, namely, the existence of substantive difference. The neoliberal ideal, applied to Europe, amounts to the destruction of Europe. Ultimately, neoliberalism is not cos-mopolitan, but postmodern.

Moreover, neoliberalism is not suitable for establishing a *European* project. In the final analysis, it aims to dismantle borders completely (Ohmae 1990) – for neoliberalism, European borders are as superfluous as national borders. Why does it have to be Europe? Why not rather smaller political units (as pro-posed, for example, by Ohmae 1995)? And if collective rule-making beyond the nation-state is already necessary, why not simply reinforce the WTO directly? The logic of global neoliberalism does not provide any answers to these questions.

4.2 Cosmopolitanization from below: the role of civil society movements

Notwithstanding its system-transforming potential, neoliberalism is a thoroughly unreliable and inadequate midwife of a cosmopolitan Europe. Although it has made an essential contribution to undermining the bastions of the Europe of nation-states, it can contribute only minimally to constructing a new cosmopolitan Europe. On whom, then, can this project rely? Our answer to this question is: on European civil society! – more precisely, on a new coalition between the state, supranational actors and civil society.

This answer appears at first sight utopian, for civil society is by far the weakest actor in European politics. To date, a European public sphere has developed in at best a rudimentary form; European parties currently exist only as loose federations of national parties, and even the interest groups which have developed in great numbers in Europe count as mainly weak and ineffective. Those interests which exercise the greatest weight in European politics – namely, economic interests – have had the best chances of developing and articulating themselves in European civil society (see Greenwood 1997, 2002, 2003; Grande 2003). European civil society seems to be a mere reflection of the general parlous state of European politics and unable to contribute much to overcoming it. Numerous reasons can be cited for the miserable state of European civil society: citizens' lack of interest in Europe, the tenacity of national organizations and their interconnections with national politics, the heterogeneity of social interests and political values in Europe and, not least, the institutional peculiarities of the European Empire.

However, an examination of the early phase of the European integration process shows that not all of these reasons are compelling:

The years 1947 and 1948 marked the flowering of the movement for Europe. In all of the democratically governed countries of Western Europe, clubs, associations and movements, as well as sectarian groups, devoted to the European idea arose and called for the political and economic unification of the nation-states, although they had very different conceptions of what this involved. The resonance of the idea of unifying Europe was so broad and won so many influential sympathizers that the activists occasionally got the impression that the movement would grow into a European popular movement, and there was much optimism that a unified Europe would soon be achieved. (Brunn 2002: 52)

At the time, there were more than half a dozen major pan-European associations for Europe, with numerous affiliated associations at the local, national and international levels (Niess 2001: 158). 'Federalists', such as Denis de Rougemont, propagated the idea of 'grassroots federalism', 'which sees the acts of federating as coming from below, from the individual or the community of individuals, etc., rather than from state actors' (ibid.: 109). In short,

Europe was supposed to be founded *from below* by actors from civil society, not *from above* by the states!

A backward glance at the strength of the European civic movement following World War II proves that Europe is indeed capable of exerting a fascination over its citizens and mobilizing them. If European civil society is in the meantime underdeveloped, then this has less to do with the indifference of the citizens than with the fact that European politics was taken over by the states with the foundation of the European Communities and the European citizens were accordingly incapacitated. This process must be reversed. European civil society must be brought back into European politics and the European citizens must once again become the subjects rather than the objects of cosmopolitan Europeanization.

How could the European civil society movement be strengthened, and by whom? How could it regain its lost vitality? We propose three answers to these questions.

- The first is that actors from civil society can and must exploit the contradictions and legitimacy deficits of the neoliberal-technocratic project to strengthen Europe from below.
- The second is that Europe's civil society actors must seek external support. Here the global contradictions of neoliberalism and the new threats generated by global risk society can serve as points of reference.
- And the third answer is that European civil society must be reinforced from above through the supranational institutions. Here the legitimacy deficits of state and technocratic strategies can serve as a starting point.

Thus, actors from civil society can indeed benefit from the deformations of the European project. They can exploit the neoliberal barriers to political interventions in markets and the poverty of vision of technocracy to transform themselves into advocates of a redefined 'European public interest' that is systematically violated both by short-term capital interests and by the egoisms of the nation-states. The strengthening of European civil society then means, above all, the rediscovery of the ambitious goals of Grand Politics.

In view of the current subversion of European policy by power and its domination by states, however, it would be illusory to believe that European civil society and its actors could regain their former strength on their own and construct a cosmopolitan Europe. Because of their political and organizational weakness, European civil society movements need support from two directions, *from above* and *from below*.

4.3 Cosmopolitanization from outside: Europeanization and global political cosmopolitanism

The political integration of Europe was always contingent on external conditions, whether favourable or unfavourable. At the end of the 1940s and the beginning of the 1950s, as the Cold War was beginning, the United States served as the 'midwife' of Europe (Neuss 2000); later, during the 1980s, the 'Japanese-American challenge' (Seitz 1990) brought the European states closer together; and, in the 1990s, the collapse of the Eastern European communist regimes had a major impact on the conditions of political integration, its scope, its dynamics and its goals. At the beginning of the twenty-first century, a close relation continues to exist between external conflicts and tensions and internal integration. We can think of at least two scenarios in which external circumstances could promote the project of a cosmopolitan Europe.

First, through a redefinition of Europe in relation to the United States. US hegemonic power not only has the capacity to split Europe but it could also force Europeans into jointly redefining their role in global politics, and in this way bring them closer together. The Iraq War accomplished both at once: it split the governments and simultaneously brought hundreds of thousands of citizens onto the streets of the European capitals. It provided a further example of the impotence of a politics of states dominated by special interests and veto rights – and it mobilized the citizens of Europe to the largest mass demonstrations since the end of World War II. Now the question is how this political potential for reinforcing European civil society and constructing a cosmopolitan Europe can be utilized (for a detailed discussion, see chapter 7).

Second, the weak civil society movements inside Europe could conceivably be strengthened from outside by the so-called anti-globalization movement. The global lip service paid to the challenges of climate change and other forms of environmental destruction and questions of global justice spring to mind here, as well as questions concerning the implementation of human rights against states and other global questions to do with the realization of political freedom and democracy and, not least, securing peace in a world without borders. Such goals of cosmopolitan politics threaten to become empty rhetorical formulas that heads of government, company directors and leader writers readily employ at the regularly recurring international conferences. Thus, the heads of state of the G8 countries have repeatedly called in solemn declarations for political restrictions to be placed on current 'turbocapitalism' and for it to be reconciled with principles of social justice – though, needless to say, solutions should no longer be sought at the national level but in new transnational structures. To date, however, concrete proposals for translating this rhetoric of a politics of 'global justice' into legislative initiatives and suitable institutional architectures have been almost completely lacking.

Europe could make a twofold contribution at precisely this point. The meaning of 'global justice', 'cosmopolitan sovereignty', 'sustainable development' or the 'recognition of cultural difference' not only needs to be spelled out theoretically and programmatically but above all must be tested and politically implemented. Europe could function in this context, first, as a large-scale experiment in exemplary ways of dealing with self-produced civilizational dangers, thus restoring Europe's charisma both internally and externally for the global era. At the same time, a cosmopolitan Europe could become an important ally of the anti-globalization movement in its struggle to tame global capitalism. Briefly, the transnational anti-globalization movement would have good reasons to support the cosmopolitanization of Europe. Moreover, a number of important preconditions for this are indeed satisfied by the anti-globalization movement. The empirical study of Andretta, DellaPorta, Mosca and Reiter (2003: 201) has shown that the European Union enjoys a markedly higher level of trust among anti-globalization activists than the national governments.

4.4   Cosmopolitanization from above: supranational institutions and civil society movements

Finally, it is even conceivable that the cosmopolitanization of Europe would be supported 'from above', by the political elites themselves. The idea that the European elites are ready to form coalitions with actors from civil society in their enlightened self-interest is by no means unrealistic. The European Commission has always been open to cooperation with interest groups, especially when it could thereby enhance its power vis-à-vis the member states. For example, such coalitions underlay the European internal market programme and the strengthening of the competences of the EU in technology and industrial policy.

The new governance approach propagated, and in part already implemented, in recent years by the European Commission (see, in particular, European Commission 2001) offers a number of points of orientation for new coalitions between supranational actors and civil society. It is no accident that it was precisely the European Commission which took up the idea of strengthening the role of social actors and civil society movements within European politics. For the Commission would be the institution most deeply affected by the loss of legitimacy of European policy and its subsequent renationalization. As Jacques Derrida and Jürgen Habermas correctly stated,

at present the policy of further expanding the EU is running up against the limits of the existing administrative steering mechanisms. Until now, the functional imperatives of creating a common economic and currency zone have propelled reforms. However, these driving forces are now exhausted. An *active* policy that calls not just for the removal of obstacles to competition but also for a common will on the part of the member states is dependent on the motives and convictions of the *citizens themselves*. (Derrida and Habermas [2003] 2006: 42)

Cosmopolitan realism, therefore, might be found not only among the nation-states but also among the supranational institutions; the latter could also propel cosmopolitanization in coalition with civil society movements out of a 'realistic' sense of self-interest. The European executive, in particular, within whose power sphere the original cosmopolitan project has run aground for technocratic reasons, needs a coalition with civil society in order to refloat the European project.

The idea that civil society is seizing power in Europe is untested, but for that very reason seductive. We call such a symbiosis between civil society and Europe 'cosmopolitan empire' or 'cosmopolitan Europe'. A new coalition between the state, supranational actors and civil society movements must supersede the coalition of economy, state and supranational technocracy which has been dominant until now. It is precisely this internalization of the civil society criticism that could become the source of the revival of European identity and power.

5   What makes cosmopolitanization strategies realistic?

Many people will now object: 'I hear the message, but I don't believe'. Hence, the *question of strategy* is crucial for the further development of the cosmopolitan project in Europe. Or, to put the question differently: If it is correct that the political premium for the member states results from their active self-Europeanization, why then is Europeanization proceeding so painfully slowly, meeting with so much resistance, plagued by contradictions and crises and threatened with collapse? 'Neorealist' or 'rational' kinds of explanation offer a seemingly trivial answer to this question: because national interests remain dominant and are essentially invariant. Even if the earthly paradise of cooperation is tempting in principle, no state can overcome the gravitational pull of its national interests. If this argument were sound, however, the EU would not exist at all. Moreover, this point of view is continually refuted by two central problems of the EU: the desire of countries for accession and flows of migration. In view of the fact that the EU is both a political and a theoretical impossibility, it remains amazingly and stubbornly attractive to both countries and individuals!

The theory of cosmopolitan realism developed in this book turns the tables on this argument. The problem is not the goal, namely, the cooperative, cosmopolitan premium afforded by Europeanization; the problem is the path thereto, that is, overcoming the national ontology and the bracketing effects clearly triggered by the dominant rhetoric of Europeanization and globalization. How can national realism be *transformed* into cosmopolitan realism? The question: 'What makes cosmopolitanization strategies realistic?' is translated into the question: 'How does cosmopolitan realism gain *credibility*?' How does the *change in perception* become possible as a *process of social and political construction* and how can it be reconstructed by social science? This inversion of the problematic rests on three premises, as follows.

Europeanization as positive-sum game

First, the state's capacity to act in cosmopolitan ways must be conceptualized and developed politically independently of existing notions of sovereignty and autonomy. The focus then becomes the effective capacity of the state, its ability to contribute to solving global problems, and no longer its faith in national sovereignty. The adjective 'cosmopolitan' designates the *extension* of the state's capacities for action both internally and externally which are opened up by international as well as various other more advanced forms of cooperation. Thus, the cosmopolitan state – no longer tormented by scruples concerning sovereignty – exploits the political premium generated by the gratuitous contributions of other governments, non-governmental organizations and international organizations. The 'cosmopolitan' capacity and power of a particular state, reduced to a formula, would accordingly be the *sum* of the national options *plus* the cooperative capacities of transnational political networks (European Union, NGOs, supranational organizations, transnational corporations, etc.).

Problems of perception or conversion

Second, however, this cosmopolitan realism of cooperation is unreal, i.e., unattainable and unrealizable, because or as long as the national ontology dominates people's minds and institutional norms and rules – as long as the national bird in the hand is, so to speak, more real than the two European birds in the bush. To put it less metaphorically, the resistances to cosmopolitan realism are real but they are based on a collective self-misunderstanding according to which (a) definitions of national and cosmopolitan interests are mutually exclusive and (b) national problems can and must be solved nationally. Both of these assumptions are false. Cosmopolitan self-definitions extend state sovereignty without superseding it; and almost all of the key everyday problems that plague populations and are dramatized by the mass media present an open flank to the global – they can be adequately handled for the most part only in transnational, hence at least European, agreements and institutions. The decisive problem, therefore, is that of perception or conversion: those who seek salvation in national sovereignty must learn to see the renunciation of sovereignty as a gain in sovereignty.

The problematic of interest-transformation

Third, in other words, we must ask: What conditions and what dynamics render this *shift in perception* possible? How can the transition from the national 'bird-in-the-hand strategy' to the cosmopolitan 'two-birds-in-the-bush strategy' be accomplished in reality? The epistemological aspect of this question is important. For, in this perspective, it is no longer a problem of interests, but of the *perception, construction* and *transformation* of interests. In terms of political theory, social-constructivist theoretical perspectives and research programmes acquire key importance in conjunction with neo-institutional theoretical perspectives and research programmes. The question of how the 'politics of golden handcuffs' (see chapter 3) is transformed into a realistic option becomes the question: Through what strategies can the shift in perception from national realism to cosmopolitan realism be achieved, or how can such strategies be observed and reconstructed in the social sciences? Here we would like to explicate, rather than answer, this question by taking three strategies by way of example, namely, (1) risk shock and its strategic utilization, (2) the pioneering strategy and (3) the value strategy.

5.1 Risk shock and its strategic utilization

Neither methodological nationalism's unreflective assumption that political problems are essentially national and must be solved at the national level nor the resulting obstructions to action can be overcome voluntarily and through unilateral national initiatives, but only through the shock exerted by social and political explosions, such as those triggered by civilizational catastrophes. The Chernobyl reactor catastrophe, the BSE crisis and the terrorist attacks of 11 September 2001 in New York and Washington, and subsequently in Madrid and London, provide exemplary objects of study in this regard. Here we must distinguish clearly between the catastrophic event itself, which – as in the case of the terrorist attacks in New York, Madrid and London – can remain spatially, temporally and socially restricted (in contrast to the Chernobyl reactor catastrophe, for example), and the strategic utilization of the risk shock which creates a spatially, temporally and socially *unrestricted* perception of danger. The latter is conveyed by the mass media and, under certain conditions (e.g., corresponding cultural sensibilities and existing political reform strategies), alters the premises of people's everyday lives and those of the institutions of the nation-state (see chapter 7). This is demonstrated most clearly by the risk conversion undergone by the United States under the impact of the terrorist attacks. Assuming that Americans were still risk *atheists* on 10 September 2001, since 12 September 2001 they have been risk *converts*, risk *believers* – though only in a very limited sense, namely, *not* in questions of impending climate change, global environmental dangers, the risks of human genetics and genetically modified food, which are all dismissed as 'irrational', but all the more so with respect to the global terrorist danger and its strategic utilization. Plans for foreign and defence policies that were lying around in the bottom drawer for years – the post-Cold War strategy of US foreign policy – were suddenly put into practice. The 'War against Terror' has made it possible to upgrade military options and interventions and to downgrade international organizations and alliances (UN, NATO) and international law. Note that it was neither the terrorist attacks nor the terrorist networks as such that led to this change in strategy. It is rather the national and international construction of the problem of terrorism, the political debates in parliaments, by governments, in the mass media and at the dinner table or in the pub, which transform the shock experience into a perception of dangers that demands and legitimizes global, preventive intervention. Three moments undoubtedly came together to produce this shift in perception: first, the delayed adjustment of US foreign policy to the changed global situation after the end of the bipolar East–West system; but also, second, the global experience of interdependence implicit in the experience of risk shock; and, third, the experience of collective self-endangerment.

The interplay between these moments can also be demonstrated by another form of risk, namely, global financial risks. In a study on the banking crisis of the 1980s, Philipp Genschel and Thomas Plümper (1997) show how the experience of global interdependence and collective self-endangerment intermesh, thereby converting powerful players in the global financial system from deregulation to re-regulation and – successfully! – forging a coalition to push through regulatory norms. Here, too, the side-effects argument plays a key role. Following World War II, the integration of the global financial markets was at a very low level. The national markets were sealed off from one another. The national outlook was oriented inwards. This began to change during the 1960s as controls on capital were dismantled and the European market was opened up, with the result that the volume and speed of the financial flows increased. As a consequence, however, the vulnerability of the whole system also grew – as a side effect of its efficacy. This explosive susceptibility to risk discharged in a series of spectacular banking collapses, which in turn clearly demonstrated that the insolvency of a single bank could trigger chain reactions that endanger banks and the banking system throughout the world. Thus the experience of interdependence and the realization of self-endangerment combine to generate the perception that no country can evade and immunize itself from these civilizationally generated dangers. All borders and internal–external constructions are broken open by the globally reflected danger of infection. The feeling of security, based on the national outlook, is giving way to the fear of the global uncontrollability of terrorist, financial and environmental dangers.

The former German Chancellor, Gerhard Schröder, formulated this 'new quality' as follows, shortly after assuming office in 1998:

The political challenge posed by the financial markets is greater than that in the area of trade. It is no accident that the risks of globalization have become particularly apparent especially on the international financial markets, that is, where globalization and deregulation are most advanced. When Alan Greenspan himself admitted recently that he did not fully understand how the international financial system operates, it reminded me of Goethe's sorcerer's apprentice: could it be that politics has reached a point where it can no longer restrain the speculative spirits which it has helped to conjure up through deregulation? (Quoted from Bittner 2002: 209)

5.2 Pioneering strategy

However, neither the shock experience as such nor the perceived danger of infection owing to the experience of interdependence can overcome the resistances of national realism. This calls for *pioneering coalitions*. Forging such coalitions is an extraordinarily difficult undertaking, however, because the aggregated national conflicts of interest have to be overcome and norms must be laid down and implemented in transnationally binding ways. Since the conversion effect produced by the experience of risk shock alone is scarcely able to extinguish all national differences, conflicts, rivalries and enmities at a single stroke, the need to achieve and generalize capacities for action through pioneering coalitions remains. The latter, however, generate contradictions of inclusion and exclusion that are difficult to reconcile. On the one hand, one must forge small coalitions to minimize dissent and maximize consensus; on the other hand, however, the need to implement the corresponding norms broadly, transnationally and, at the extreme, globally demands the inclusion of as many parties as possible. But this, again, increases the risk of failure. The former strategy – i.e., forming small, effective pioneering coalitions – externalizes the problem of failure, whereas the latter strategy of including opposed positions displaces the risk of failure inwards. From this perspective, the only remaining choice seems to be when and where one fails.

Yet, as the studies of Genschel and Plümper (1997) and Bittner (2002) demonstrate, it is possible to solve this dilemma. In the case of the banking crisis, the key to success lay in the power of the pioneering coalition and the strategic skill with which it succeeded in outsmarting the national resistances. The American and British central banks formed an alliance, brought their global market dominance to bear, took Japan on board following tough negotiations and presented all of the other sides which hesitated and offered resistance with a fait accompli. The result was that these actors had no other choice but to accept the Anglo-American norms and regulations and to redefine their own interests and options to act accordingly (Genschel and Plümper 1997: 628ff.).

The risk policy of the G8 countries played a similar pioneering role in the re-regulation of the financial markets:

If one examines the risk policy strategies of the G8, one can discern a shift at the end of the 1990s. Its clearest expression is the foundation of the *Financial Stability Forum* in early 1999. Until that time, the risk policy of the G8 countries was restricted primarily to crisis management. Preventive measures to stabilize the international financial system, such as laying down internationally binding norms, were the responsibility of international regulatory authorities. Their operations are restricted to specific sectors without any overarching coordinating authority and they pursue purely technical goals. Consequently, their effects are often quite limited. By contrast, the Financial Stability Forum is an institution in which all of the key players in the international financial system are represented. The clear dominance of national political actors shows that the buttressing of the international financial architecture is part of a new political programme of the G8. Thus, the approach of the forum is no longer limited technically and sectorally; rather it is politically and globally oriented. It becomes clear that the strategy is no longer restricted exclusively to crisis management, but that the primary emphasis is increasingly on a precautionary policy of prevention. (Bittner 2002: 192)

The power on which the effectiveness of pioneering coalitions is based, however, need not be given in advance; it can also result from the dynamics of the pioneering role itself, specifically, from the fact that the latter creates possibilities of cooperation and power across boundaries, between the internal and the external, the national and the international, through which domestic vetoes can be successfully overcome.

There is a close and positive correlation between states' national capacity for reform and their capacity for international cooperation. The necessity of engaging in international cooperation not only limits the autonomous room for manoeuvre of states but can under certain condition enhance it as well . . . Dutch environmental policy is instructive in this regard. Since the 1980s, the Netherlands has linked its pioneering role in environmental policy consciously and strategically to a cooperative approach in the EU and in international organizations. In this way, the Netherlands succeeded in exporting in considerable part its concepts and instruments of environmental policy, thereby reducing national pressures to conform to international norms. At the same time, the international norms thus agreed upon made the acceptance of national norms and their refinement easier. This policy approach is based not least on a close coordination between national environmental policy and foreign policy in this field. (Grande, Prange and Wolf 2004: 37f.)

All attempts to harmonize European tax policy, by contrast, have hitherto failed, though the initial conditions were by no means unfavourable. Many governments feared that the liberalization of the European capital markets would lead to an increase in tax competition and thereby cause tax revenues to fall. France and Italy, in particular, voiced the concern that the European Union could as a result become a tax haven and hence undermine the position of the member states. The British government, by contrast, took an emphatic stance against any European tax coordination. Such a tax on capital, it claimed, would be 'anti-European' since it would divert flows of money out of Europe and into other global financial centres. Other governments made forceful pleas in favour of a harmonization of tax laws with the argument that a unified capital market demanded common regulations against tax competition. There were also proposals, in particular from the Dutch side, supporting the creation, if not of a unified European tax system, then at least of a unified information system that would oblige banks to track financial flows and publish the relevant data. The German government tried to initiate a European regulation in a pioneering coalition with the European Commission, but then withdrew its proposal with the argument that it would damage the national capital markets. Thus, the dice were cast in favour of the blocking coalition with Great Britain and Luxembourg in the pioneering role, because the remaining parties could not overcome their national fragmentation in spite of their interest in doing so (Genschel and Plümper 1997: 632ff.).

The blocking countries repeatedly emphasized that the European Union was not the appropriate place to implement such a regulation, which should instead be pursued within the framework of the OECD. However, this argument fails to appreciate the political construction process and the power dynamic which pioneering initiatives can generate, as the example of the banking crisis and the Anglo-American regulatory avant-garde demonstrates. But perhaps this also makes clear that a Europe of many voices that is preoccupied with itself does not (yet) have the stomach for a truly global-*cosmopolitan* regulatory initiative in this field.

5.3   Value strategy

The resistances to decisions promoting Europeanization can be overcome not only through the pioneering role assumed by alliances of states, by the resources at their disposal and by the political dynamic they unleash. These resistances can also be broken down – as Frank Schimmelfennig (2003: 565) argues – through the power of collective ideas (identities, values and norms). Schimmelfennig adduces the example of the eastern enlargement to support his argument. Here, too, a pioneering coalition and a blocking coalition stood opposed to each other. The author explains their options to act and their modes of action, on the one hand, in terms of the rule system of the EU which prescribes unanimity and hence grants veto positions completely independently of the location and size of a member state. On the other hand, the preferences of the member states concerning the eastern enlargement largely reflected their geographical location. With the exception of Greece and Italy, the neighbouring member states of the Eastern European countries formed the vanguard of the eastern enlargement, whereas, Great Britain aside, the distant member states belonged to the blockers.

In general, international interdependence increases with geographical proximity. Hence, member states on the eastern border of the Community are, on the one hand, more seriously affected than others by negative developments in the Eastern European countries, such as economic crises, wars, migration and environmental pollution (negative interdependence). The enlargement is from their point of view

an instrument for stabilizing the Eastern European countries and controlling negative externalities. On the other hand, however, geographical proximity enhances the
preconditions for trade and investment by lowering the costs of transportation and
communication, among other things. The member states neighbouring the Eastern
European countries derive special benefits from the opening up of the Eastern and
Central European markets (positive interdependence). (Schimmelfennig 2003: 546)

But how could the accession aspirants break the resistance of the
blockers?

In view of the weakness of their negotiation power – that is, the implausibility of
threats against the blocking coalition – they relied on the strength of arguments based
on the fundamental and universally recognized values and norms of the Community.
By strategically employing concepts and arguments, they linked the distributional
conflict over the costs and benefits of the eastern enlargement with the question of the
identity, legitimacy and credibility of the Community ('framing'), and, through the
moral pressure created as a result ('shaming'), they succeeded in inverting the asymmetry in power between the blockers and the pioneers. (Schimmelfennig 2003: 554)

By referring to the institutionalized norms of European cosmopolitanism,
therefore, they succeeded in framing the eastern enlargement as a question
of principles and values and in discrediting its rejection as betrayal of these
same principles and values. This line of argumentation could be effective,
however, only insofar as the countries which were seeking EU membership
for their part voluntarily Europeanized and cosmopolitanized themselves,
and hence integrated themselves into the European Empire. They had to
become European converts themselves, that is, to frame their national history
and their national interests in one way or another as immanently European.
Here symbolic (or rhetorical) Europeanization is hard to distinguish from
the real thing. However, even with this qualification, the fact remains that at
least the semantics of cosmopolitan realism are becoming universally binding
– with all of the associated contradictions, ambivalences and opportunities.

5.4   The prospects of strategies of Europeanization: the examples of
migration and provision for the elderly

In conclusion, we want to show how the room for manoeuvre of politics could
be extended through Europeanization with reference to a central problem
area, namely, the connection between migration and demographics.

The facts tell a clear story: it is not only individual countries but Europe
as a whole that is experiencing a dramatic decline in birth rate. If the current
trend continues, the population of Europe will have shrunk by more than
15 per cent by the year 2050 and by a half within a hundred years. Among
all European countries, only Albania has a birth rate sufficient to reproduce

its population at a constant level. Europe is greying, and is doing so at a dramatic rate. This creates, in turn, grave knock-on problems in the social security systems (pensions, health care), in politics and in culture and, not least, it also generates an enormous need for migrant labour.

Here, of course, two opposing imperatives clash. On the one hand, the European Union must keep its borders open and implement a corresponding migration policy in the new accession countries as well. On the other hand, such a policy foments neonationalism and xenophobia; even centre-left and centre-right governments already find themselves compelled to absorb right-wing populist themes in order to win elections. Hence, the question which confronts European politics is: How should this contradiction between the imperative of inclusion and the rhetoric of exclusion be resolved, or at least channelled? Here Europe is paralysed by two factors. Following the terrorist attacks of 11 September 2001 in the United States, the security questions affect in particular those Muslim cultures from which legal and illegal migrant labour is recruited; but this in turn foments anxieties concerning foreigners that influence voting behaviour. From Austria to Australia, elections are increasingly being won with protectionist, neonationalist slogans.

The key insight here is that the decline in population is neither the national problem of individual societies (although until now it has been discussed in such terms by demographers in public political debates under the spell of methodological nationalism), nor can it be adequately solved through unilateral national policies. Wherever one looks in Europe, one encounters the same situation: the percentage of elderly people is increasing inexorably and the pension systems are coming under increasing pressure, but the necessary reforms are being blocked by the organized resistance of the affected groups. This holds for France as much as for Austria, Great Britain and Germany, but also for Italy and Spain. Once a government has finally succeeded in reforming the pension system, it encounters a storm of angry protest. And since governments want to be re-elected, to be on the safe side they avoid the controversial issue altogether or limit themselves to symbolic corrections. For example, in 2003, the red–green coalition in Germany watered down its reforms of the old-age pension system once the labour unions intervened.

An important step out of this trap could be to define the relation between the decline in population, the greying of society, needed reforms of the social security systems and a targeted migration policy as a *European* problem and to address it in a cooperative way. Here the idea of cosmopolitan realism shows its strength. All governments, which have to limit themselves to phoney measures because they are trapped in the national dead end, can benefit from it. Assuming that the EU were to develop and enact a plan of action to address the problems of old-age pensions and migration in view of declining populations, these guidelines would reduce the pressure on the national governments. On the one hand, appreciation would grow for the fact that this is not a national failure, but a question that all European societies and governments are forced to answer in one way or another. On the other hand, such a plan would enable national governments to arm themselves with European arguments. Some national governments are already well versed in this game: appealing to European obligations can make it easier to push through difficult measures in one's own country.

However, a cosmopolitan Europe could also serve as a laboratory in which the various national approaches to the problem – such as the Danish model of financing pensions solely through taxes to reduce labour costs, or the clarity of the Swedish formula for converting aging directly into pension cuts – could be connected and harmonized with each other, and thereby ameliorated. In this process, certain indispensable minimal principles could also crystallize out at the European level, such as the insight that people who live longer must also work longer. A European problem definition and strategy becomes absolutely indispensable when the connection between aging and migration comes to the fore. The question: 'Where will we find the young Europeans to lend vitality to the aging Europe?' can no longer be answered at the national level. The insights provided by this example can be generalized: the Europeanization of the challenges facing the EU member states and their governments does not constrain the room for manoeuvre of the latter, but extends it.

This is not to imply, however, that a cosmopolitan Europe is completely free of contradictions. The cosmopolitan completion of the European project does not mean the realization of the promises of harmony and prosperity of the first modernity; on the contrary, European cosmopolitanism does not promise to resolve European contradictions, but rather to acknowledge them. We will elaborate on this contradictoriness of the European project both internally and towards the outside in the next two chapters.

6

Inequality and Recognition: Europe-Wide Social Conflicts and their Political Dynamics

Europeanization is not merely a 'side effect' (chapter 2), a horizontal process that permeates and transforms the national member states (chapter 4). Europeanization also creates a Europe-wide space of conflict (chapter 5). However, this poses the question which will be addressed in this chapter: Which *Europe-wide dynamics of inequality* are produced by European political integration? And does a Europe of conflict signal the decline or the birth of Europe?

First, a correct assessment of the epistemological character of this problem is important. The question of the pan-European dynamics of inequality concerns not just which conflicts are already emerging in the process of Europeanization, but the prior issue of which *concepts and coordinates of inequality* are characteristic of the Europe-wide conflict dynamics. Can we simply assume that the same patterns of inequality – e.g., class or regional differences – which apply in the nation-states and national societies also prevail at European level? Taylor's 'politics of recognition' points to the paradigmatic line of conflict at the beginning of the twenty-first century (Taylor 1992). Will the demand for 'recognition of difference' raised under the banner of nationality, ethnicity and religion also determine the conflict dynamics of the cosmopolitan Europe and, if so, in what form? The question of cultural dominance conceals and downplays the issue of socio-economic redistribution; 'injustice' is no longer understood in material terms alone but also in cultural terms. How, then, are questions of material and cultural (in)justice related in a Europe-wide conflict dynamic?

The eastern enlargement of the European Union did not involve the colonization of countries, nor are unforeseeable migratory flows likely. But, something much more serious happened: whole countries immigrated into the EU; European 'foreigners' became European 'nationals'. Voluntary collective immigration by states is a historical novelty. What does this mean for the EU's 'ethnic' self-definition, which has hitherto been marked by a kind of 'Western European racism', albeit one which scarcely needed or was able to recognize itself as such? Moreover, what does it mean for the web of inequality and conflict within the nation-state and in Europe as a whole?

The European Union is a club of greying societies confronting extremely young societies in many developing countries. The antagonism associated with the age pyramid can be either the making or the undoing of Europe. One way or another the balance between the pressures of migration from abroad and the domestic need for immigrants will become the central topic of political debate. Only if Europeans succeed in overcoming their rigid, quasi-ontological differentiation between 'Us' and the 'Others', between Europeans and non-Europeans, can the aging continent withstand competition with the world's youthful powers and regions in the long run. Europe's cosmopolitan opening is becoming both a necessity of survival and an opportunity. Only in this way can the aging Europe simultaneously rejuvenate itself and recover its economic prosperity. What, therefore, are the effects of the superimposed conflicts over cultural recognition and material redistribution in an open and cosmopolitan Europe? Will Europe become more European or more national, more neonational – or both at once?

The national perspective has marked the answers offered to these questions in three respects: by the methodological nationalism of both the sociological treatment of inequality and the sociological study of migration and minorities, and by the national outlook of politics at the state level. All three forms of myopia have hitherto complemented each other perfectly. Cultural differences and social inequalities were perceived (almost) exclusively within national boundaries, and were only really taken seriously and dealt with politically within this framework. This is at least the case for the material core of the welfare state (in whatever form) and its comprehensive social security systems, which remains almost exclusively a *national* welfare state. Over the past fifteen years, the European institutions have acquired new competences in the area of social policy (Falkner 1998; Hartenberger 2001), but these powers are purely regulatory. The European welfare state is a 'regulatory state' (Majone 1996), not an institution for redistribution. The key function of European institutions consists precisely in *not* redistributing money.

In the case of intergovernmental institutions and agreements, the rejection of redistribution among the states concerned is one of the most important organizational principles. They either function in accordance with the principle of '*juste retour*', as in the case of the European Space Agency (ESA): each country gets back (e.g., in the form of orders for industry) what it paid in contributions to the programme – with the well-known costly and complicated allocation of production to various European industrial locations in the case of the Airbus consortium; or these institutions completely lack a budget of their own, as in the case of the European research initiative EUREKA. In the latter case, national research activities, assuming they receive any public funding at all, are financed from the respective national research budgets. In both cases, redistribution of money between the states concerned is avoided.

The exceptional status of the European Economic Community (EEC) – and, subsequently, of the EU – was also evident from the outset from the fact that it was not organized according to the *'juste retour'* principle. Redistribution of funds was expressly provided for, albeit within a strictly limited scope.[1] This has meant that in the EU there have always been two groups of countries, so-called net contributors and net recipients. It is a well-known fact that the Federal Republic of Germany was the largest 'net contributor' to the European Community from the beginning. The focus of this transfer was for many years agricultural policy, which continues to account for the largest share of the EU budget. The redistributive logic of the 'Common Agricultural Policy' was straightforward: the Community's more industrialized countries, in particular, Germany, subsidized the agriculture of the less industrialized countries and obtained in return a larger market for their industry. Since the 1980s, Regional and Structural Policy, which allocates funds for development programmes in economically less developed regions, represents a second major area of redistribution. The regional and structural policy was also based on a simple redistributive logic: the economically weaker member states (primarily in Southern Europe) gave their assent to the completion of the European internal market on the condition that they received development funds from the economically stronger member states to help them improve their economic infrastructure.

In sum, with this and countless other programmes (in the field of research and technology policy, among others), undoubtedly a substantial level of redistribution has been established between the states at European level, albeit one markedly different from national transfer systems. The area of welfare-state redistribution is entirely excluded and remains under the exclusive control of the member states.[2]

From the national perspective, this constellation generates two main problems. First, governments face the challenge of protecting the national welfare states from the dynamic of expansion of the neoliberal market logic which is set going at the European level. Here a European–national contradiction is looming with potentially grave consequences for the policy competence of the European nation-states. How can we preserve national social security systems from suffering the same fate as the former state-owned enterprises in the infrastructure sector (telecommunications, electricity, etc.), that is, from being disqualified as competitive distortions and market hindrances, and being liberalized and privatized?

Second, assuming that this is a success, a complementary problem arises: What form could a *European* welfare state take that would not bring about the ultimate collapse of the already fragile national welfare states of the 'rich member countries' under the burden of large-scale European transfers? How should we envisage, or is it even realistic to believe, that the Europeanization of both markets *and* welfare states, which is a contradiction in terms, can be coordinated?

The discussion to date gave the impression that these problems allow only perverse – and hence equally undesirable – alternatives. One option – the neonational option – would be to restrict the scope of Europeanization drastically to preserve the supposed room for manoeuvre of national economic and social policy. A second option – the neoliberal option – would be to dismantle the national welfare states in order to improve the efficacy of the European market. Is there also a third, *cosmopolitan* option? And, if so, what would it look like?

What social conflicts, therefore, are characteristic of cosmopolitan Europe? And how can these conflicts be dealt with? However these questions are answered – or, more modestly, made answerable – one thing is certain: the sociology of social inequalities and research on the welfare state in political science are poorly equipped to address them, let alone resolve them, and hence to contribute to clarifying the problem of inequality in Europe.

1   Critique of methodological nationalism in the sociology of inequality and research on the welfare state

The methodological nationalism of the sociology of inequality and research on the welfare state is as obvious as the self-confirming relation between these two sociological disciplines. The basic assumption is the nation-state as the basic unit of social conflicts and their regulation by the state, generally without giving a single thought to the presuppositions which guide research. The problem with this congruence between the perspectives of actors and social scientific observers is that it transforms practical categories uncritically into analytical ones. The concepts informing the actions of social agents and state actors are tacitly transposed into the conceptualization and empirical investigation of social inequalities and the welfare state. Thanks to this analytical mindset, this kind of theory and research is blind to Europe. The result is the failure to appreciate that the mixing, blurring and redrawing of boundaries between member states, and also between Europeans and their others, has far-reaching implications for the pan-European conflict dynamic – for questions of social recognition, social inequality and social redistribution. Likewise, the problems and dilemmas resulting from the intersection of these issues are not appreciated.

To gauge the scope of our critique of the methodological nationalism of the sociology of inequality and welfare-state research, we must question a distinction that deeply marks the sociological and political debate about the stability of societies, namely, that between the *reproduction* and *fragmentation* of societies. Within the horizon of methodological nationalism, social reproduction – i.e., processes by which societies maintain themselves over time – and social fragmentation – i.e., processes that endanger the social reproduction of societies – are quite naturally related solely to *national* societies and *national* states. Europeanization, however, involves a *revaluation* [*Umwertung*] of the positive connotation of reproduction and of the negative connotation of fragmentation. Europeanization *demands* 'fragmentation' of Europe's system of nation-states and also new social differentiations and conflict dynamics. It is not social reproduction but the *non*-reproduction of national societies and nation-states that opens the latter up for Europeanization. To put it succinctly: it is not the conflict over Europe but the self-reproducing integration of national societies that is Europe's downfall.

Two problems follow from this dilemma. First, which of the Europe-wide conflict dynamics that grip and 'fragment' the national societies concerned *promote*, and which *impede*, the progress of European integration? Political Europe could be brought about or promoted by the side effects of conflicts to which a blind eye is tacitly turned or which are utterly unexpected. The architects of the euro, i.e., the single currency zone, must surely have had the consequences of this process in mind, namely, the deeper political integration it requires.

Second, how can *Europe's reproduction* as an integrated society be understood and what does it mean for the 'integration' or 'fragmentation' of Europe's national societies? What new forms of differentiation arise in the Europe-wide domain of social inequalities that contribute to buffering or counterbalancing Europe's national divisions? What kinds of European conflicts and conflict dynamics can stimulate European alliances across national frontiers, with the result that both the pros and the cons propel Europeanization (in the sense of denationalization and transnationalization) further? To rephrase the question: Must Europe-wide conflicts always endanger Europe, or can they also, on the contrary, contribute to its construction? Can the neonational, isolationist tendencies within Britain, France, Spain, Italy, Germany, and Poland, etc., for example, be tempered by a Europe-wide pro and contra?

We want to analyse these problems in terms of four questions: (1) How does the mobility of European borders affect the European dynamic of inequality (assuming provisionally the conventional concepts of inequality)? (2) What new patterns and coordinates of social inequality arise? (3) Given Europe's variable geography, how are inequality and recognition conflicts related? (4) To what extent do these conflicts lead to a recognition–inequality dilemma?

2 Mobile borders, mobile patterns of inequality?

How does the national perspective affect perceptions of social inequality? What do national borders contribute to the perception and legitimation of social inequality (see Beck 2005, ch. 1.11)? The key issue is that it leads to curious distortions in how social inequality appears. Inequalities within national societies are grossly *magnified*, whereas inequalities among national societies are *diminished* beyond recognition. This is the prerequisite for the political legitimacy of social and political activities at home and passivity towards others abroad. For if the political criterion were 'need', then it could hardly be justified that affluent European societies organize financial transfer systems at home at enormous costs based on national criteria of poverty and need, while a large proportion of the world's population faces the threat of starvation on a daily basis.

What consequences does the 'European border' and border policy have for patterns of social inequality in Europe? Two answers, starting from different ways of pluralizing and relativizing frontiers, are normally offered to this question:

- *First*, Europeanization changes the nature of European borders. Inside they become lower and more permeable, whereas towards the outside they become mobile, flexible and imprecise – but also higher and less porous.
- *Second*, borders between (national) societies lose their significance; the barriers between societies (especially their economies, education systems, etc.) are removed.

In what follows, we will develop the associated argument that distortions in the perception of social inequalities – i.e., the production and maintenance of the incomparability of the same inequalities between and across national borders – are *dissolved* in the course of the border-transforming process of Europeanization. In this way, Europe becomes enmeshed in internal contradictions that hold an enormous potential for political conflict.

The problems can be illustrated by a simple example. The demand for 'equal pay for equal work' was and continues to be one of the central demands of the labour movement. In the highly industrialized countries with strong trade unions, this principle has been realized to a very large extent – not just within companies, but also far beyond them. However, the trade unions' campaign for equality came to a halt at a 'natural' border, that of the nation-state. Just as it has been natural since unification to campaign within Germany to maintain nationwide collective bargaining agreements and to equalize wages in the eastern and western parts of the country, it also for a long time seemed natural to ignore differences in pay relative to other European countries. Viewed through this national lens, differences in pay between Bavaria and Saxony are illegitimate, whereas the same differences between Bavaria and Belgium are legitimate. What happens then if the same differences are viewed and judged through a European lens? Don't differences in pay between the European countries then become illegitimate? Shouldn't the European trade unions then demand 'equal pay for equal work' for *all* European workers? Or must this principle be abandoned? And if it is abandoned, how can the differences be legitimized?

These questions are far from academic, as became clear in January 2004 when there was a heated debate among the publics of the various member countries over the initiative of a number of MEPs to strengthen the European Parliament's identity by standardizing parliamentary attendance fees. In immediate proximity, there are huge inequalities in payment for the same work: an Italian MEP receives €11,000 gross per month, his German party colleague, by contrast, around €7,000, the Spanish colleague alongside him has to make do with €3,000, whereas the new colleagues from the recent Central and Eastern European accession countries receive no more than €1,000. For the present, there will be no mitigation of this extreme inequality in parliamentary allowances for the same MEP job, because the EU foreign ministers rejected this initiative under public pressure.

The explosiveness of these issues is also evident from the fact that they represent one of the main lines of conflict between neoliberals and neonationalists in Europe. In recent years, neoliberalism has tried systematically to delegitimize the differences between levels of pay. Its concern was not to raise the low wages in Portugal and Greece to the German level but, conversely, to criticize high wage levels in Germany (Malcolm 1995). Neoliberalism thinks in European, indeed global, terms, in the categories of a European or global *market*. Social differences are thus reduced to simple cost–benefit calculations and registered as differences in wage levels. Neoliberalism has appropriated the old workers' movement slogan 'equal pay for equal work' – but at the lowest level!

This means that the trade unions seem to face two equally unpalatable alternatives. One is to oppose this development and demand 'equal pay for equal work' – but at a high level! This was the option chosen following German unification (Sinn and Sinn 1991); no one disputes that it is economically disastrous and politically utopian. The second alternative is no less attractive; it puts the trade unions in the perverse position of adopting the old catchphrase of their opponents and demanding 'unequal pay for equal work'! – in effect, defending the existing differences in pay between the European countries. In this way, societies are forced into a neonationalist position, for the existing differences in pay can be maintained only if national frontiers are maintained and effectively controlled.[3]

This example shows that the dismantling of borders does not defuse the explosive potential of European inequalities. Rather, conflict threatens to flare up because the perceptual barriers to comparing different national situations are being removed so that equal levels of inequality can be assessed equally and corresponding adjustments can be demanded. In other words, current Europeanization policy has led to the paradoxical situation that the Europeanization of markets, but also of societies, actually appears to necessitate a neonationalist reaction because to date there has been no success in defusing the conflict potential of European inequalities by other means.

Moreover, this pattern of conflict holds an enormous political potential, which at present is not yet clearly politically defined (see Kriesi 2001; Kriesi and Grande 2004). It can be exploited by post-communist parties as well as by right-wing neonationalist movements. This enabled the right-wing populist parties to come into possession of a second 'winning formula'. Their 'winning formula' during the 1990s was a combination of neoliberal economic policy and authoritarian domestic policy (e.g., restrictive policy towards foreigners) (Kitschelt and McGann 1995). In a new 'winning formula', the authoritarian domestic policy would be combined with a neonationalist economic and social policy. Even social-democratic parties are not really immune to this neonationalist temptation. All these parties and movements can make themselves the advocates of those whose standard of living is endangered by neoliberal Europeanization.

3   European regions as conflict patterns of European inequalities

It was stressed early on that inequality can be judged according to different measures. From the Enlightenment onwards, discussion of inequality was marked by the juxtaposition of *individual* and *social* inequality. This applied not only to the causes of inequality, but also to its manifestations. The magnitudes in terms of which social inequality was measured were generally *social* units such as social classes, strata, milieus, situations, etc. The classification of equals and unequals was regulated via these aggregates. One was 'equal' within a stratum or class, and the relevant inequality existed between these. If one analyses European inequalities, it becomes immediately clear that we need a third category: *geographically/territorially* defined inequalities. This means, in the first instance, inequalities between states and regions. In this case, individual life chances are determined not by class or income group membership, but by membership of a nation or region.

Of course, geographically defined inequalities already existed even within the old nation-states, for example between Italy's 'rich north' and 'poor south'. Moreover, conflicts between centre and periphery were one of the key forces in the formation of nation-states (Lipset and Rokkan 1967). These regional disparities within the nation-states can nevertheless be compared only to a limited extent to the new forms of inequality in Europe. Within the nation-state, these disparities were *illegitimate*; the nation-state raised the claim to maintain 'uniformity of living conditions' at least in principle, as the old Article 72 of the German Constitution put it. Government policy was supposed to take its orientation from this principle of uniformity, which also means that it had to intervene and lend support where this uniformity did not exist.

With the intensification and multiplication of regional inequalities, the uniformity principle is no longer viable in this form. This is already the case within the nation-state. Unsurprisingly, Article 72 of the Constitution was amended and watered down in Germany following unification. The new version no longer refers to 'uniformity', but only to 'equivalent' living conditions.[4] Apart from the obvious semantic difficulties – when are social and economic conditions 'equivalent'? – enormous problems arise in applying even such a compromise formula on a European scale.

Inequality thus constitutes a *three-dimensional field of tension* in Europe in which individual, social and geographical differences collide. The first, immediate consequence of this new constellation is a pluralization of forms of inequality. Individual, social and territorial disparities can be combined, refracted and played out against one another in many different ways. Inequality in Europe resembles a large hall of mirrors in which proportions and perspectives are constantly shifting. Moreover, they must be redefined politically; Europeanization entails a *politicization* of inequality. A meta-power game over inequality has begun in which differences are legitimized and delegitimized, equalities constructed and deconstructed. Everything seems to be up for grabs in this power game and a whole series of fundamental questions are thrown up. Is it possible to define a poverty line for the whole of Europe? Or must there be a plurality of poverty lines for different national and regional contexts? Who decides based on what authority and with what arguments for or against which of these alternatives? And if poverty is relative, what are the units of reference for relative poverty in Europe? And here, too, the same question arises: Who decides, how, and on the basis of what evidence and authority, which units of reference are relevant and which irrelevant for determining poverty in Europe?[5]

At this point, it is possible to develop further some of the central assumptions of the theory of reflexive modernization, grouping them together into three theses:

- First, with Europeanization, the importance of social strata and classes is further relativized. For example, the life chances of a factory-worker in Munich may be far better than those of a factory-owner in southern Spain or eastern Poland.
- Second, Europeanization relativizes and reactivates individual inequalities. Social inequalities that have been levelled out over a country by welfare-state policies may acquire renewed importance through comparison with other countries.
- Third, geographically defined forms of inequality (regions) acquire importance through Europeanization, also as targets of government policy. Regional policy becomes European social policy. In this way, the European institutions stoke up regionally oriented distributional contests, which 'fragment', relativize and gloss over the national lines of conflict and internal differentiations.

The following supportive argument draws attention to how close the connection is between politics and inequality also in the European conflict scenarios. For all of these questions can ultimately be resolved only through political decisions. Hitherto, European regional and structural policy has had a marked national bias: on the one side, the 'poor' member states upheld the claim of the nation-state to uniformity also at the European level, i.e., they Europeanized the national perspective. By contrast, the 'wealthy' member states were extremely wary of European redistribution programmes out of (considerations of) 'national interest'. As a result, European regional and structural policy was transformed into a huge bazaar in which there is constant haggling over budgets and development zones – with frequently absurd results (see chapter 5).

The important point is that this is not simply further evidence of the ineptitude of European bureaucracy or of the irreconcilability of the conflicts of interest between the member states. In fact, this enables us to analyse some of the central contradictions which are disrupting the familiar patterns of social inequality in the process of Europeanization in magnified form. These contradictions will become considerably more acute as a result of the eastern enlargement of the EU. For if the existing criteria of the European regional and structural policy were to be applied to the enlarged EU, it would entail a far-reaching redefinition of social and economic conditions. The 'poor' Spanish farmer would suddenly be relatively 'rich', though nothing in his conditions of life would have changed, simply because he is no longer being compared only with a German farmer but now also with a new fellow EU citizen in the Baltic states, Poland or Slovakia. But this poses another problem: How can such political decisions on the dynamics of inequality and conflict within the EU be legitimized?

4   Mobile 'We' and mobile 'Others'?

We saw how the denationalization and transnationalization of conflicts over social inequality and conflicts over recognition of differences give rise to the pan-European conflict dynamic. The questions this throws up concern, first, the relationship between recognition conflicts and inequality conflicts and, second, the differences which emerge in the dynamic of recognition and inequality conflicts when they are viewed through the European lens instead of the national lens, through which they have hitherto been debated and investigated almost exclusively in the social sciences.

Recognition conflicts and inequality conflicts involve two interlinked but nevertheless analytically distinct ways of understanding *injustice*. In the one case, it is conceived as *socio-economic* injustice grounded in a society's politico-economic structure. The other understanding of injustice relates to *the social treatment of otherness*. In this case, injustice is rooted in the devaluation and exclusion of minorities, of different national, ethnic and religious traditions and identities, as a result of the 'sectional universalism' of the dominant group.

The solution to material inequality and justice problems resides in redistribution policy. The resolution of issues relating to the social recognition of difference, by contrast, generally involves profound social transformations and reforms in participation, representation and self-interpretation in history, politics and religion, which ultimately alter the self-understanding of each individual.

Here the realization that the relationship between issues of inequality or redistribution and issues of recognition at the national and the European levels appears entirely different is of central importance. In the methodological nationalism of the sociology of inequality and research on the welfare state, redistribution means *national* redistribution and therefore presupposes recognition of equality – more precisely, of national equality. Inequality conflicts and redistribution issues are raised and investigated, both socially and sociologically, exclusively within national frontiers, on the model of inequality or redistribution among nationally equal classes, between nationally equal men and women or nationally equal minorities and majorities. Inequality and distributional conflicts, to the extent that they are conducted and investigated within the boundaries of the nation-state, have an *ethnic* background component that is both hidden and constitutive. It is not the recognition of difference but the converse principle – namely, recognition of the (national) equality of the equal – that is the *sine qua non* which produces the qualitative difference between the really existing inequalities and politically relevant inequalities. Even where redistribution and not recognition is at stake, recognition and redistribution are in a certain sense fused. The national framework, the national outlook, is what makes redistribution at once possible and limits it. The methodological nationalism of sociology sets the seal on the suppression, forgetting and the contrived naturalness of 'national recognition' as a precondition for inequality and distributional conflicts.

This fusion of recognition and inequality conflicts within the nation-state is precisely what disintegrates at European level. Accordingly, the pan-European conflict dynamic can be developed and investigated theoretically and empirically as a conflict-ridden decoupling of

- postnational and transnational struggles for recognition;
- postnational and transnational inequality and redistribution conflicts; and
- the intersections of recognition and inequality conflicts with the dilemmas resulting from them.

The conflict dynamic of cosmopolitan Europe – this is the argument which we will develop in what follows – results from the fact that the social dynamic of recognition conflicts is gaining a new explosiveness in relation to redistribution conflicts. Yet, this is not all bad news. In a Europe capable of conflict, a cosmopolitan sensitivity to recognition of difference might well contribute to tempering the intensifying redistribution conflicts in Europe and, moreover, to enabling Europe to become more European.

Europe's ethno-cultural self-conception exhibits *perverse* traits when measured by the criteria set by political Europe for itself. The more the frontiers inside the 'We-Europe' are dismantled, the more persistently they are invoked and strengthened in relation to Europe's others. EU citizens enjoy internal freedom of domicile and, thanks to the Schengen Agreement, there are no longer any identity checks at most internal frontiers. In anticipation of this freedom of domicile, the fortification of the external border, checks on illegal migration, as well as the expulsion of persons belonging to third-party states, are being vigorously pursued.

This might be called the *paradox of 'frontier-mobile' Europe*. While the frontiers between 'Europe' and 'non-Europe' are becoming mobile as nowhere else in the world, social integration is simultaneously being re-ontologized into an exclusion mode, so to speak, so as to render the borders secure. Is the European Union to remain a Christian club? Will it determine its territorial boundaries to the outside by renewing what Europe wants and is supposed to overcome, namely, the 'transcendental community of common descent'? The latter is now being extolled by national politicians and historians to repudiate Turkish membership or the even more remote prospect of Russian membership. Are the boundaries between 'Europeans' and 'non-Europeans', in particular, to be determined by religion and ethnicity? Are we thereby in danger of repeating at the European level the mistake which has just been overcome at nation-state level and which is so profoundly contrary to the cosmopolitan founding principle?

In this way, displacements in power are in a sense being undertaken preventively in the enlarged EU by being transferred onto the discourse over a shared European descent. Turkey's accession to the European Union would entail a substantial shift in power within the European Union due to its demographic development. As an EU member, Turkey would soon 'disempower' the currently most densely populated country in the EU, Germany. It would also mean the end of the dominance of the Christian religion in Europe. Thus, the concern over human rights and democracy in Turkey masks a considerable amount of hypocrisy.

There is no denying that major differences exist between Turkish society and most European countries. However, those who stress these differences and adduce them in opposition to Turkey's accession to the EU misconstrue European reality. The number of Muslims in Europe is now approaching the population of some European countries. A total of 15 million Muslims live in Western Europe, more than 5 million in France alone and more than 3 million in Germany. Thus, on the one hand, the issue is not recognition of difference at all, but recognition of reality. To be consistent, those who would keep Turkey out of the European Union would have to do away with the Turkey which already exists within the European Union.

On the other hand, the criterion of cultural difference is an inappropriate yardstick for drawing the boundary between 'Us' and the 'Others' in Europe. After all, the differences that also exist between the member states are precisely what make Europe attractive. Let us assume that Canada or the USA were toying with the idea of joining the EU. One would be ill-advised to stress the 'cultural difference' between these countries and Europe in making a case for rejection. An application for membership from the US would probably be a chess move by which the European Union could be checkmated through 'over-enlargement' – so, at least, many Europeans would think and react. At the same time, however, the differences between Amsterdam and Philadelphia, Frankfurt and New York or Paris and Montreal are slighter than those between many parts of the EU. What, then, does recognition of Others' otherness mean in the relation between 'Europeans' and 'non-Europeans' – given that this frontier structure is conceived in principle as variable and is politically determined?

Cosmopolitan Europe must guard against two temptations. The first is the notion that ethnic identity is an *essence*, something which is predetermined, specific and objective. The contrary temptation is to assume that ethnic difference is nothing more than a *pure illusion*, which will become transparent as such and dissolve with advancing modernization – Europeanization.

To pose the question of Europe's ethnic identity, some distinctions are necessary – in the first place, that between 'multinational', 'polyethnic' and 'multination-state'. A country that is home to more than one nation is in this sense not a nation-state, but a multination-state, and smaller cultures are designated 'national minorities' and are integrated with varying degrees of conflict. The incorporation of different nations in a state can be *coerced*, for example, when a nation is conquered or colonized. Many Western democracies are multinational in this sense (e.g., there is a whole series of national minorities in the USA, the American Indians, for example, or certain Mexican groups who were living in the southwest when the United States annexed Texas, New Mexico and California after the Mexican war).

A second source of cultural diversity is *immigration*. The more immigrants of different cultural and religious provenances who pour into a country, the greater the country's cultural and religious diversity becomes (as again exemplified by the USA).

A third reason, however – and this reason represents the EU's internal plurality – lies not in the conquest or colonization of other nations, or even in mass immigration, but in the fact that ever more countries and states are joining a community of states. In this process, the people remain where they are, but the collective entities – countries, states – 'immigrate'.

The American experiment is: How can immigrants, i.e., deterritorialized groups, be reterritorialized, rooted nationally in a 'new country', and be fused together into one nation? The European experiment is: How can historically deeply rooted, territorial ethnicities, nationalities and regional and religious identities, whose differences are deeply etched in memory in the bloody language of power, be made receptive to and interwoven with one another so that a cosmopolitan empire or cosmopolitan state cooperative results? In the American case, people are mobile, whereas in the European case, states are mobile and people remain rooted in their own territorial allegiance.

Although the EU is permanently wrestling with immigration and emigration policy, unlike the United States it did not come into being as a country of immigration, but rather as an immobile community of 'immigration *states*'. In this sense, the EU is anything but a large multinational nation-state – not a 'melting pot' but rather a mosaic of states and societies resulting from a radical contradiction between mobility and immobility. These states and countries are completely immobile but they are at the same time also completely mobile (often without really being aware of it). The political innovation – the political 'invention' – of Europe lies in making this permanent contradiction liveable, indeed grasping it as a solution. The European miracle is *the reconciliation of traditional enemies!* This kind of 'enemy integration' into a cooperative network of states, into a 'consensual empire', is utterly different from a multinational, multicultural, polyethnic form of state, as exemplified, for example, by the United States, Canada or Switzerland.

At the same time, however, the EU's self-understanding is paradoxically 'racist'. This statement may be surprising and strike many as exaggerated. But we are dealing here with the (Eurocentric) racism of a white-skinned global minority still unruffled by doubt, in which dominance, invisibility and ignorance are mingled. The struggle for recognition in Europe is directed against the (concealed) racism of Eurocentrism, the authoritative construction of norms that conform to the 'whiteness' of Western Europeans and accord it privileged status. The other side of this coin is the completely unreflected exclusion and devaluation of people and projects regarded as 'black', 'brown' and 'yellow', hence of all 'non-whites', as 'non-European' or 'un-European'. The notion of black Europeans, Turkish Europeans, Muslim Europeans, etc., is perceived in this white racism as an 'absurdity', as a 'contradiction', and thus dismissed and devalued.

Two strategies for acknowledging and responding to this European racism can be distinguished. First, there is the position of *colour-blind universalism.* In this it is assumed that race or ethnicity is not a morally admissible reason for treating one person differently from another. One may register ethnic differences (just as difference of sex, etc.), yet these must not entail differences in treatment and action. The basic principle is: *Our actions must be colour-blind.* This position becomes entangled in the contradictions of universalism. On the one hand, the other's difference is overcome by viewing and treating him or her as an equal. On the other hand, however, the reality of otherness is at the same time denied. Those who are not willing to abandon the position of otherness are excluded. People defend the ideal of others' equality, while simultaneously spreading the cloak of secrecy over the fact that blacks, people of colour, Muslims, etc., are excluded from Europe's participation opportunities precisely by its social structure. The ideal of universal humanity without social distinction enables the dominant groups to ignore their own particularity. Blindness to difference perpetuates cultural domination.

The second position could be called '*self-critical racism*'. This recognizes that ethnic and religious differences play a central part both in Europeans' conduct and in European institutions. It criticizes the grave differences both within European institutions which themselves discriminate (unintentionally and imperceptibly) according to ethnic attributes, and within the institutions that seek to minimize or overcome such forms of ethnic discrimination. Self-critical racism focuses on the fact that European civil society also has a fundamental ethnic conflict dimension – in the interactive relationship between social players, as well as in the conduct of the European public authorities and their representatives. It acknowledges that European decisions and actions in the past and present have treated people very differently depending on their ethnicity and that, consequently, the European authorities cannot simply shirk their responsibility in this matter. Europe cannot suddenly declare itself 'colour-blind' – without actually prolonging the cultural imperialism which has hitherto been sustained by appeals to 'colour-blindness'.

In this sense, key Europe-wide conflicts will turn on the questions: 'What is your attitude to difference?' and 'How can and should the borders between "Europeans" and "non-Europeans" be drawn and legitimized without the political Europe of human rights openly contradicting itself?'

5   The recognition–inequality dilemma: on the intersection of conflicts
    over inequality and conflicts over the recognition of difference

Methodological nationalism construes the conflict dynamics of modern national societies in terms of the dynamic of the *inequality of equals*, both in practice and in scientific theory. This means that the national sociology of inequality and welfare-state research always deal exclusively with inequalities between fellow citizens and the recognition of difference among fellow citizens. The national *a priori* dominates even in relation to territorial and geographical inequalities. Territorial inequalities are thematized only within national frontiers and as a subsidiary differentiation of national differentiations of class, social stratum and social and economic situation. The line of argument sketched above, by contrast, states that what sets the pan-European conflict dynamic apart is that what appeared to be fused once and for all in the national *a priori* is becoming uncoupled. The results of this process can be grouped under three headings.

First, the struggle for recognition cannot be brought to an end either by 'national assimilation' or by 'European descent'. It erupts transnationally in European space and in the European sense, that is, beyond the distinction between the national and the international. A dialectic of cosmopolitanism and anti-cosmopolitanism is in this way set going (see Beck 2006, chapter 5). The careers and failures of Jean-Marie Le Pen and Jörg Haider, for example, demonstrate both how spectacular and how flawed are the actions of the anti-cosmopolitanism movement. In many countries, responses to the cultural, linguistic and religious differences ranging from defensive to hostile, and an almost fascist enthusiasm for 'cultural purity', are closely allied in patriotic rhetoric and appeals to national equality. These are reactions to the imminent future and not, as often assumed, about reviving the past. But the demands for the new 'purity of the European' by which Europe's others are constructed and excluded is encouraged not least by official European policy, which is constructing a 'Fortress Europe'. This means that a perverse coalition is forming *between the official multiculturalism of the European fortress builders and the anti-cosmopolitanism of the European neonationals*. Both groups complement each other in their indifference and intolerance towards the presence of refugees, asylum seekers or other 'immigrants', many of whom, viewed more closely, are not immigrants at all, but recognized/non-recognized 'resident citizens' whose living and employment conditions have long been bound up with the history and culture of their inhospitable host country, Europe.

The absurdity of the 'Fortress Europe' project is apparent not least from the fact that Europe's former and new 'barbarians' have long since been living inside its gates. Samuel Huntington's 'clash of civilizations' prognosis is mistaken not least because it ignores the fact that it has long since ceased to be possible to make the frontiers of cultural differences congruent with the borders of the nation-state. In the European capitals – London and Paris, Berlin and Madrid, Athens and Warsaw – (ex-)colonizers mingle with the (ex-)colonized, European 'applicant' nationalities with 'not-yet' and 'never' member ethnicities and nationalities. The cosmopolitan flux of these cities is a product of the legitimate yet illegal variation of cultural hybridity – mixtures and movements – generated precisely by coexistence and the growing indistinguishability from Europe's so-called others. Here it becomes apparent that otherness is not only marketable, that it not only produces an economic added value, but that it also generates a cultural and political added value. These are, after all, liberal-minded places where the important future experiment is being conducted into how human rights and citizens' rights can be linked in new ways in the public arena across the boundaries between nations, ethnic groups and religions.

Second, to the extent to which Europe becomes a social reality, the exclusion associated with national zones of inequality is eroding. An environment in which hitherto nationally incomparable inequalities can be compared is taking shape with immense explosive political potential. Not least, a *Europe-wide* sociology of inequality and conflict might also play a major part in

this, not just by waking sleeping dogs, so to speak, but by drafting method-
ologically a neither/nor and a both/and point of view. It should not simply
adopt either the categories of nation-state politics or those of European
politics, but would have to incorporate both the European and the nation-
state perspective into its own autonomous conception of Europe-wide conflicts, develop them conceptually and examine them empirically from that
vantage point.

Third, beyond the nation-state *a priori*, not only do the European recognition conflict and the transnational inequality dynamic take on a life of their
own but a new *territorial-geographic* conflict pattern is also developing. This
pattern – contingent on European policy – intensifies, disrupts or tempers the
recognition and inequality conflicts. This raises the urgent question of how
these different conflict dynamics relate to each other.

There are good reasons for studying such intersection effects. Conflicts that
have flared up over the recognition of difference aim to underscore the distinctiveness and high cultural value of a group and its traditions. Recognition
presupposes (the construction of) boundaries between groups. On the other
hand, those who focus on inequalities appeal to the recognition of equality;
for only on this condition do inequalities become a political problem, a political question of the redistribution of resources and rights, and hence politiciz-
able. In other words, the politicizability of recognition conflicts presupposes
the (construction of) *diversity*, whereas the politicization of social inequality
implies the (construction of) *equality*. Recognition politics and redistribution politics – it becomes apparent here – pursue conflicting aims. Nancy
Fraser speaks accordingly of a 'redistribution–recognition dilemma': 'People
who are subject to both cultural injustice and economic injustice need both
recognition and redistribution. They need both to claim and to deny their
specificity. How, if at all, is this possible?' (Fraser 1995: 74).

There are two possible strategies for dealing with this dilemma. One could
be called *strategic essentialism* or *multiculturalism*. Here the difference is
'essentialized' in order to establish a basis for its recognition.

A second strategy turns against such an affirmative recognition of existing
group boundaries and group distinctiveness. This *transformative* strategy
of recognizing difference aims at destabilizing the existing differences and
directing attention to the actually existing instances of interpenetration and
mixture (see Fraser 1995). The affirmative strategies are traditionally associated with the national welfare state. The transformative strategies, by contrast, can be linked to cosmopolitan realism. After all, they aim, first, to raise
awareness of actually existing cosmopolitanisms in Europe and, second, to
transform the self-conception of *all* of the groups involved in the spirit of a
cosmopolitan 'common sense'.

These transformative strategies represent a twofold opportunity for a
European perspective and policy: on the one hand, they are not tied to the

welfare state, which has developed in only a rudimentary form in the EU; on the other, a Europe-wide conflict conducted both within Europe and in the public arenas of the nation-states in which the struggles for recognition of difference might bring about a 'fragmentation' of nation-state integration which would help a European social awareness of the recognition of difference to make a breakthrough.

Even if this assessment of such a Europe-wide conflict scenario is over-optimistic, however, the intersection of recognition, inequality and redistribution conflicts nevertheless creates room for a *cosmopolitan option* that is clearly different from the neoliberal and neonational options. This cosmopolitan option rests on three principles.

- First: redistribution conflicts endanger, whereas recognition conflicts may hone, European identity; politically they have the highest priority ahead of inequality and redistribution conflicts. A politics of recognition may invigorate political Europe.
- Second: detaching recognition conflicts at least partially from conflicts over material inequality and redistribution opens up new opportunities for action *beyond* welfare-state responsibilities and resources for European politics. The latter reside especially in the extension of European civil society, which is perfectly feasible through a fragmentation of the national societies.
- Third: this cosmopolitan Europe is characterized not by what it wants, but by what it does *not* want, namely, no universalist enforced conformity; no essentializing of difference; no violation of human rights and human dignity either inside or outside Europe; but no violation of human dignity through 'absolute' poverty either. A welfare-state minimum is integral to the European understanding of political freedom and democracy.

The idea of absolute poverty as a negative consensus of a European cosmopolitanism may be surprising. 'Absolute' as used here denotes a standard that counters the pluralism and relativism of the 'relative' poverty lines in Europe with a clear-cut conventional stipulation that holds for all Europeans: *no political freedom without basic subsistence.*

The universal content of cosmopolitanism thus proves itself in the negative, in what must on no account be allowed to come about. *Only* (but this 'only' comprehends an enormous political programme) by stipulating a universalist minimum do recognition, inequality and redistribution issues intermesh in Europe.

The strategy of uncoupling and of selective coupling of these different dimensions of Europe-wide conflicts could lead to a situation where conflict-shy Europe discovers and develops the politically productive potential of conflicts. To what extent this is 'realistic' and how great are its prospects of success, however, are matters that can only be resolved *politically*.

6   To what extent can and should a cosmopolitan Europe
promote solidarity?

The extent to which Europe can and should show solidarity is one of the
key questions in the European project (Leibfried and Pierson 1998; Streeck
1995; Offe 2000). It is striking that this question is discussed principally by
Eurosceptics concerned about the national welfare state. In the prevailing
neoliberal discussion, by contrast, this question is not posed at all. The result
is that not even the rudiments of a positive vision of a *social* Europe in which
the *European* dimension is taken seriously are as yet discernible!

Yet, such a vision is indispensable. The claim to social solidarity – to 'fraternity' – is part of the stock of indispensable European values, on a par with
the ideas of liberty and equality. A European civil society and a cosmopolitan Europe are conceivable only as solidary associations. But, first, we must
clarify what 'solidarity' and 'fraternity' mean. How can and must national
and cosmopolitan conceptions of solidarity be distinguished? Only then can
we address the question 'To what extent can and should a cosmopolitan
Europe show solidarity?'

The question of a cosmopolitan understanding of solidarity can be formulated more precisely by contrast with the approach of Claus Offe (2000).
Europe, Offe argues, is not a historically evolved community of common
destiny. It follows that solidarity between its citizens is only weakly developed and that redistributive welfare policies, as we know them from the
national welfare states, are not feasible at the European level. He concludes
that Europe can foster solidarity only to a very limited extent and for the
foreseeable future this cannot be changed because a greater European nation
is unrealistic. A second conclusion is that, because Europe cannot ultimately be solidary, it should not be weighed down with excessive political
expectations.

Here we are dealing with a theoretically ambitious concept of national
solidarity, which is, however, entirely under the sway of methodological
nationalism. Non-solidarity and anti-solidarity towards those who are culturally different, which is linked to it both inwardly and outwardly, are
tacitly overlooked. Refusing to show solidarity towards people born outside
of one's own officially defined regional boundaries is part of the integral
conception of 'national solidarity'. This solidarity of *equality* must be distinguished from the solidarity of *diversity* associated with a conception of
'cosmopolitan solidarity'.

The notion of national solidarity is simplistic, because it takes for granted
what the concept of cosmopolitan solidarity distinguishes.

- First, the national concept does not allow a differentiation between solidarity among equals and solidarity with others, such as is made by the
  cosmopolitan perspective. For the former there is either solidarity or

no solidarity; this solidarity monopoly of the national already excludes analytically the question: How much solidarity do you show towards cultural others? Thus, the understanding of solidarity is *expanded* on the cosmopolitan outlook. In addition to the question of solidarity with equals, the following questions arise: What consequences does this solidarity with equals have for those who are culturally demarcated and excluded as a result? To what extent can and must solidarity with those who are culturally different be made into an integral part of solidarity with equals?

• Second, national solidarity with equals, precisely because in it the ethnic constitutive element is implicitly given, concentrates primarily or exclusively on the dimension of *material* justice. In the cosmopolitan view, by contrast, the questions of cultural recognition of difference stand out, sometimes intertwined with this dimension and sometimes independently. For one thing, the concept of national solidarity is thus blind to the ethnic recognition issues which it itself presupposes; for another, the complexity and dilemmas arising from the intersection of material and cultural justice issues are left aside or played down. The question 'How do national redistribution campaigns relate to the struggles for recognition of cultural distinctiveness?' can be treated systematically only within a cosmopolitan conception of solidarity.

• Third, national and cosmopolitan solidarity also rest on contrasting valuations of sameness and diversity. In the cosmopolitan view, neither sameness nor unity is the supreme value (as the concept of national solidarity assumes), but multiplicity. The aim is not to suppress or gloss over the differences (e.g., within the EU) in order to maximize the differences between an 'essential' national community and its others. Cosmopolitan solidarity is directed against over-integration into a nation and is sensitive not only to one's own particularity, but also to the particularity of all Europeans! It is a community of particularity, a solidarity of particularity, that expressly does not believe in the equality of the equal as the paramount aim and supreme value. Rather, it accords high value to equality within diversity and the equality of difference and sees in it a source of satisfaction and cultural productivity.

• Fourth, whereas national solidarity is essentially concerned with issues of material justice and for the most part disregards questions of cultural justice, cosmopolitan solidarity strives for a new kind of historical compromise between material and cultural justice. To measure these by the criteria of national solidarity and to reject them (as Claus Offe does) betokens a fundamental misapprehension of European reality. Here, surely, only the concept and criteria of cosmopolitan solidarity are capable of depicting appropriately the more complex relations between transnational inequality conflicts, redistribution conflicts and recognition conflicts.

Two steps must be taken if we are to arrive at a vision of a solidary Europe. First, the conception of national solidarity must be stripped of its monopoly position and its inadequacy for explaining European conditions must be demonstrated. Second, there is the problem of how resilient a cosmopolitan, European solidarity actually is in view of the tensions, dilemmas and contradictions inherent in it.[6] How much solidarity can we expect from the citizens in a cosmopolitan Europe in the two dimensions – the love of recognition of difference, on the one hand, and the willingness to accept redistribution to achieve a *social* Europe, on the other?

7

On the Dialectic of Globalization and Europeanization: External Contradictions of Cosmopolitan Europe

In chapter 6, we inquired into the *internal* contradictions of cosmopolitan Europe; here we will examine its *external* contradictions. Why Europe at all? Why not 'the West'? Why not the 'Atlantic community'? Why not the world? Isn't it anachronistic to accord global interdependence central importance, on the one hand, while seeking to replace the nation-state unit by the 'European unit', on the other? Doesn't such an attempt repeat all the errors which have been criticized so extensively in this book, only at another level, namely, the European level? Doesn't the talk of *European* globality become trapped in a contradiction, namely, that of starting from Europe as an illimitable, yet limited, global regional unit?

The formula 'European cosmopolitanism' exhibits a structural ambiguity. It can be oriented inwards or outwards. Whereas in the foregoing chapters we explored the issue of a *European* cosmopolitanism, here we will inquire into a European *cosmopolitanism*. We will proceed in four steps.

First, we want to criticize Europe's cosmopolitan deformations, the fact that the European gaze is introverted, that European cosmopolitan thought and action are oriented inwards – at best – rather than outwards.

Second, we want to inquire to what extent the dynamics of world risk society contribute to the cosmopolitanization of Europe. To what extent does coping with 'risks without passports' create lineaments of a global public in Europe? To what extent do the uncertainties produced by civilization force the European empire of consensus to adopt the cosmopolitan external perspective?

Third, what is the relation between European cosmopolitanism and American hegemony? To what extent are American unilateralism and the notion of a 'European counterforce' tenable in view of the globalization of risks and the challenges of world risk society?

Finally, fourth, what contribution does European cosmopolitanism make to global cosmopolitanism?

1   The cosmopolitan deficit: critique of the Eurocentric outlook
in the debate on Europe

The European Union is a hybrid of the market and bureaucracy but not a cosmopolitan actor with visionary force, regarding neither the shape of the European world of states nor Europe's position relative to other global regions. Do Europeans want to participate in the key historical experiment in Islamic democracy through the accession of Turkey or do they want to shut themselves off from it? Do Europeans want to incorporate Russia or to turn it into a kind of Latin America? How does Europe deal with its colonial or quasi-colonial tradition in its relations with Africa and the Arab world? What is Europe's effective, not merely rhetorical, contribution to defusing the local–global Israeli–Palestinian powder keg? How will Europe respond to the self-confident versions of modernity of other cultures, especially those in the Asian world? Will it throw off the nostalgia of its long since fictional universalistic claim to a monopoly on modernity and open itself up to the controversies and challenges of multiple modernities, especially in the sense of a resolute self-criticism of European modernity whose side effects represent a danger to all parts of the world? What is Europe's contribution to the global debate over the redefinition of modernity in light of struggles for recognition and justice, of growing poverty and unrestricted terrorism?

Hence, is 'Europe' more than a cartographic concept with indistinct borders, more than an introverted, petty-minded spirit preoccupied only with the smooth functioning of the engine of economic growth? What perspective does Europe offer to the masses of the global poor who are doubly disadvantaged in the global power game by their powerlessness and their lack of a public voice?

There is currently much talk of an 'American Empire' whose unilateralism and arrogance are criticized and denounced. However, this overlooks the fact that the end of the Cold War created a power vacuum. Who is supposed to fill it? The United Nations? If it is to perform the function of a quasi-world power, it is not just the UN that is in need of reform but also the nations that support and authorize it. The European Union? The Europeans are preoccupied with themselves. They are neither able nor willing to play a responsible role in global politics alongside their economic role – not up to now, at any rate. Is the power vacuum supposed to be filled by Russia or China?

A 'cosmopolitan' Europe strictly speaking does not exist. But even though it does not yet exist, its absence is at least painfully felt. This nostalgic awareness of the non-existence of Europe seems to emerge especially in situations of danger. The era of global dangers is plunging Europe into an existential crisis. Either the politically inconsequential caterpillar Europe will finally mutate into a cosmopolitan butterfly with a global political voice and vision, or the European experiment will founder on its own petty-mindedness and Europe will fall back into paltry national rivalries. The latter's shifting coalitions and self-righteous double standards have as little to offer the extra-European world as they do the hyper-power America.

Characteristic of the debate on Europe until now has been that these questions were either ignored or given extremely unsatisfactory answers. If Europe has a pet topic, then it is Europe itself. The discussion concerning Europe until now – as well as large areas of Europe research – have been literally introverted, *Eurocentric*, and in Western Europe have even been conducted in an EU-centric fashion. Its gaze was almost exclusively oriented inwards. Interest was focused on domestic conditions within the EU, its institutions and institutional reforms, the internal distribution of tasks, the admission of new members, and so on. The notion that domestic European conditions could also, even especially, be influenced by externally oriented activities, by global political participation – that European foreign policy, for example, could not and should not be produced primarily by creating a new post of the European foreign minister but through European initiatives for democratizing Iraq – has completely escaped this European autism. The refashioning of internal–external relations necessitated by Europeanization, the role of the EU in the creation of a new world order – all of this was thematized at best at the margins. Europe succumbed to the illusion that it could concentrate on building a 'home of its own' and in the process leave fundamental questions of foreign and security policy, not just to its own member states, but also to the much-criticized 'hegemon USA'.

This has a long tradition. During the Cold War, Western Europe, notwithstanding the threat, found itself in quite a comfortable situation. Under the protective umbrella of the United States, it 'only' had to solve its own problems, such as creating the welfare state and upholding democracy. However, from the Eastern European standpoint of Imre Kertész, the deceptive security of Western Europe, however productive it may have been, rested

on an amoral foundation, if by amorality we understand disrespecting one's own, self-imposed moral norms. For, viewed from our eastern side of the Wall or the Iron Curtain, the lack of solidarity with which the small states on our side were unconditionally delivered over to the great buccaneer from the East, the Stalinist Soviet Union, and the smugly conformist way in which this act was then declared to be an unshakeable foundation of global stability and world peace, seemed immoral. To tend one's garden in the shadow of a despicable (though admittedly, perhaps unavoidable) pact may well be a pleasant activity, even a useful one; but there can be no doubt that the idea of Europe could not flourish in such a garden. (Kertész 2003: 169)

Although in this way Europe developed its economic prosperity and strength, it neglected to translate this into global political responsibility and power. It cultivated its moral rigorism but lost its sense of the reality that, when the chips are down, others do the military dirty work, namely, the Americans, who were simultaneously accused of political naïvety, militarism and arrogance of power. Conversely, the Americans reproached the Europeans with hypocrisy, weakness and appeasing dictators. It is hardly surprising, therefore, that Europe is treated in 'realist' analyses of the great power politics of the twenty-first century as a *quantité négligeable* (Mearsheimer 2001). The EU currently possesses neither the will nor the competences and means to pose as the adversary of the sole remaining superpower. Here power, there weakness – the division of roles between the United States and Europe seems clear (see Kagan 2003).

News broadcasts provide almost daily evidence that we have entered a new era of precarious disorder – 'world risk society' – be it North Korea's withdrawal from the Nuclear Non-Proliferation Treaty, Palestinian suicide bombings in Israel, or the al-Qaeda attacks first on the perimeter of Europe in Istanbul, then at its centre in Madrid – and where next? – or be it instability in Afghanistan and guerrilla war in Iraq.

And what is Europe's global political response? Self-pity, declarations of helplessness and criticism of others. We complain that the United States does not consult us, or not sufficiently. The United States doesn't accept our offers of cooperation. Washington would pursue its own national course anyway, if necessary unilaterally. At times Europe sulks in the corner, at times it shuns global politics. But nowhere does it make its presence felt as an ordering influence in global politics, neither in restricting weapons of mass destruction, nor in the conflict with Iraq, in the war on terror or in overcoming the conflicts in the Middle East. (Weidenfeld 2003: 3f.)

Europeans assume that it is right to leave the world as it is, that any change is harmful, largely because they have achieved an unparalleled level of prosperity over the last fifty years, and hence also enjoy an extraordinarily high level of social security and peace. In fact, this is a very European perspective. It combines introvertedness with 'peace politics', understood as status quo politics. In this idyllic projection of internal conditions onto the world, the United States becomes the global troublemaker against which the Muslim counterforce defends itself with a certain amount of justification, as long as it doesn't resort to the instruments of apocalyptic terror – just like the European counterforce, in fact! The rejection of global political perspectives and the resulting paradoxical global political defence of the status quo in the major lines of conflict of the present and future have deep roots. But how can Europe help to prevent large parts of the world from disappearing into black holes because they are being cut off from investment?

In essence, Europe not only lacks a centre of operations for global political initiatives but above all it lacks strategic thinking. The major European powers have all forfeited their global political components – Great Britain, France and Spain with the loss of their empires and colonies, Germany with its fits of belligerent madness that led to a taboo on thinking in terms of categories of global political interests. None of these states has developed sufficient leadership to counterbalance the loss of their national global political horizons by creating European ones. Thus, the dearth of strategic thinking proves to be Europe's real Achilles heel. Europe has no agenda by which it can orient itself in times of crisis and conflict. This holds for transatlantic conflicts as well as for the Middle East, for the ethnic explosions in the Caucasus and in South-East Asia, for the Kashmir conflict and for state failure in Africa. Only when Europe succeeds in developing a culture of global political thinking will it acquire a pronounced constructive relevance. (Weidenfeld 2003: 14f.)

The enlargement of the EU and the resulting distribution conflicts are also likely to foster an inward-looking view of the future. Europe is the living embodiment of the contradiction of a self-obsessed empire, where the contradiction lies not least in the fact that the variability of borders, and the resulting pressure to think beyond borders to bring zones of insecurity under control, makes an external orientation indispensable (more on this later). EU domestic policy is almost always simultaneously EU foreign policy because the EU is a flexible geographical construct. Thus the European Union is filling the vacuum left by the collapse of Soviet power in the western region of the former USSR; this also renders a geopolitical commitment indispensable, for example in conflicts over corresponding regions in the south, such as in the issue of linking Central Asia to the West. And how does the EU deal with 'states at risk', that is, the possible power implosion in North Africa? At the same time, it is true that the new EU states are defending their sovereignty. The necessary renunciation of sovereignty in the legal and economic domains could be counterbalanced by an insistence on sovereignty in foreign policy that runs counter to a cosmopolitan definition of Europe's role in world politics.

Europe's introverted relation to itself has not even paid off in the core domain of the economy. The EU was built in part on an illusion, namely that with 'Europe' a domain of political action is being created that will enable the European states to meet the inordinate demands of economic globalization effectively. The EU is supposed to accomplish what the nation-states can no longer achieve, thus coming to the rescue of the nation-state (Milward 1994). But this is a mistake. A larger, integrated internal market, a strong single currency, common and exacting production standards – to mention just a couple of examples – do in fact produce competitive advantages for European companies that improve their chances of survival on globalizing markets; but this does not bring about the greater national, European 'economic community' dreamt of by many.

European industrial and technology policy during the 1990s clearly showed that economic globalization obeys its own logic and can no longer be contained within a single continent. The notion that European companies would cooperate in order to be better able to compete with American and Japanese firms, which still dominated thinking in the European Commission in the 1980s, was quickly refuted by the global architectures of transnational company networks. In an era of economic globalization, there can no more be

'European' corporations than there can be national – 'American', 'German' or 'French' – corporations.

This is by no means an isolated example. European cosmopolitanism in general must be protected from the illusion that it could help to build Europe into an 'Isle of the Blessed' that offers effective protection against the multiple dangers of world risk society. However, it is also a mistake to assume that, because civilizational dangers have become boundless, the always-limited European experiment has become a fiction. Paradoxically, both the risks and the opportunities of world risk society can open Europeanization up to the outside and force Europeans to make use of their cosmopolitan outlook.

2   World risk society: outline of a theory

The dominant attitude among intellectuals in general, but also among social scientists, involves a kind of reflex flight from a world situation that is so fundamentally flawed that all familiar theoretical instruments, all traditional expectations concerning the future, and especially all classical political means are powerless to deal with it. The theory of a 'second modernity' is our attempt to respond to the problem. This requires not only new concepts but also a different social and political grammar in order to understand and explain the fluid and explosive dynamics of a reality that no longer corresponds to the image of self-reproducing structures. In this context, we place particular emphasis on the theoretical construct of world risk society derived from the theory of reflexive modernization (see chapter 2). Our aim is to clarify the question of what it means to conceive of European society as 'regional world risk society'. To what extent can the conflict dynamics of world risk society force Europeans to make use of their cosmopolitan outlook? We will proceed in five steps. Following (1) a general outline of the theory of world risk society, we will examine, in turn, (2) to what extent the contradictory perceptions of risk in the United States and Europe are responsible for their drifting apart and (3) the distinct logics of environmental, economic and terrorist risks. Then we will ask (4) to what extent world risk society contributes to producing a European global public arena; and (5) to what extent security interests are compelling the European Empire to view itself from an external perspective. We will then attempt to draw some conclusions for a 'cosmopolitan realism' (see chapter 7, sections 3 and 4).[1]

2.1   General theorems

To begin with, we will examine through a set of twelve theorems what distinguishes new risks from old risks and dangers, and why the conflict dynamics within world risk society should be understood in terms of a second, reflexive phase of radicalized modernization (Beck 2007).

Global risks as a social construction

New risks are perceived as transnational or global risks. This means that, even though disasters always strike a particular place and produce a horrifically large, but ultimately limited toll of dead and wounded, the risk is nevertheless perceived as unlimited; ultimately, anyone could be affected. In this sense global risks must be distinguished from 'problems that know no frontiers' (such as illiteracy, poverty, etc.), because they universalize the probabilities of destruction.

We must distinguish clearly between the (physical) event of a disaster (or an ongoing process of destruction) and the global risk as the *unlimited expectation* of such disasters. Whether a possible destructive event counts as a global risk not only depends on the number of dead and wounded or the scale of the devastation of nature, but is also an expression of how the event comes to be recognized by society. Environmental issues, for example, were long thought of as a German fad, but that is no longer the case since the 1992 conference in Rio de Janeiro. Now those who deny the reality and urgency of environmental issues in principle, rather than those who defend it, have to justify themselves. Such processes of social recognition may be quite protracted, but they can also be sudden and dramatic. The terror risk, for example, achieved global recognition in one fell swoop, under the impact of the terrifying television images of 11 September 2001 (though its urgency and position in the hierarchy of global problems are as hotly debated as the responses to it).

Global risk as reflexive globality

Global risks are an expression of global interdependence and heighten it.[2] Unlike global food or production chains, which may remain latent, global risks overcome this latency by virtue of their physically and politically unlimited explosiveness. One of their peculiarities lies in their combination of global interdependence with an awareness of global interdependence, that is, their reflexive globality. By this we mean that global risks potentially create a public domain (at least under certain conditions). They attract the attention of the mass media because they threaten everyone, converting the whole world into prisoners and voyeurs of disasters, and also – not least – because they boost newspaper sales and television audiences.

War without wars

Global risks possess a destructive potential equal to, or perhaps even greater than, that of wars (as the scenarios of the impacts of creeping climate change demonstrate). We are dealing here in a sense with wars without war, which, first, stem from the side effects of *peace* (from the *success* of modernization) and, second, should be attributed not to the state but rather to non-state actors.

The paradigmatic threat to security has not become obsolete since the end of the Cold War; there are still states that compete for territory and resources and threaten each other militarily. But the dangers which are more clearly perceived since the end of the East–West conflict are of quite a different order. They often lack a clearly identifiable agent, a hostile intent or a military potential. The danger is not direct, intentional and definite, but indirect, unintentional or indefinite. In short, it is a question not of threats but of risks. . . . What distinguishes security risks from security threats is, on this account, the certainty of expectations which is lost when at least one quantity in the classical security calculation – actor, intent or potential – becomes an unknown. As a result, the security triangle gives way to a multiplicity of risk factors and the number of potential dangers increases. (Daase 2002: 15f.)

Manufactured uncertainty

A crucial difference between the international system of the first modernity and the international system of the second modernity resides in the fact that the former was in principle predictable because states held one another in check, whereas the latter is *in principle unpredictable*. For not only do we not know if and when a suicide bomber will blow himself up in Hamburg-Altona train station or fly an aircraft into a nuclear reactor and trigger a full-scale disaster, or if and when climate change will produce floods in one place and desertification in another, and so forth; we cannot know these things because probability calculations no longer function. They are 'unknown unknowns' (Beck 1999; Wehling 2002). In this sense, the international system of the second modernity is beset by transnational dangers 'which undermine the evolved stability of the international system. International politics is no longer marked primarily by threats – by the intention and capacity of actors to inflict significant damage on each other – but to an increasing extent by risks' (Daase, Feske and Peters 2002: 267). However, this uncertainty fabricated by civilization by no means relieves, but actually increases, the pressure to make decisions: 'Overcoming boundaries compels decision' (Beck, Bonss and Lau 2001).

Uncertainty authorizes perception

The more apparent it becomes that global risks strip scientific methods of their predictive power, the greater becomes the influence of perceptions of risk. The distinction between actual risks and perceptions of risk is becoming blurred (Douglas and Wildavsky 1983; Hajer and Wagenaar 2003). As a result, the reasons why certain groups of people believe in a risk become more important than the probability scenarios thought up by experts. In other words, research on cultural perceptions of risk in the social sciences is acquiring central importance.

Blurred lines of conflict

Global risks open up a meta-power game involving the deconstruction and reconstruction of boundaries, rules, responsibilities, Us-and-Them identities, domains of action and practical priorities. The paradox is that the prevailing uncertainty and the indeterminable risk shake old certainties but create new ones in their place, namely, the clear conscience that one is apprised of the real global risk, whereas the risk awareness of others is evidently paranoid, irrational and highly dubious and obfuscates their true interests. Different cultural perceptions generate secular-religious risk *certainties*, according to which my risk is urgent and good and overshadows all others, whereas your risk reflects a *betrayal* of the ethos of Western rationality. Reality changes with one's individual 'risk religion'. Are you a climate disaster realist or a terrorism realist? We should not fool ourselves: choosing between risks is not only a choice between different risks but also one between two worldviews. At stake is who is to blame and who is innocent, who is in the ascendant and who is in decline: the military or human rights, the logic of war or the logic of treaties. A perverse kind of apocalyptic 'beauty contest' takes place over the most terrible or senseless threat to civilization. Does the prize go to climate change or to al-Qaeda? Or is the most genuine and most beautiful risk of human decline still lurking undetected in human genetics and nanotechnology?

The politics of empowerment

Recognized civilizational risks represent an extraordinary, extra-democratic source of legitimacy. Countervailing measures across sovereign frontiers, even when they infringe the norms of international law and democracy, can always invoke the need to ward off physical or moral dangers to humanity. This politics of empowerment can be observed, in quite different forms, among both super-powerful and powerless actors, among states and social movements. However, this policy of (self-)enablement is so fragile and risky, so controversial, and yet of such global existential significance, that public examination and constant re-examination of its justification is imperative.

The failure of national and international regulatory systems

The dynamic of world risk society is thus a perfect example of reflexive modernization: the national basis for the calculation and prevention of manufactured uncertainty has been dissolved. The term world risk 'society' should therefore be understood in a 'postnational' sense, since neither national nor international politics and society contains rules governing how to deal with the new risks, what level of urgency should be attributed to each of them, and what political or military strategies should be adopted in response to them. In this way, concrete risk conflict becomes the locus of a meta-power game over future rules for coping with such indeterminate and uncontrollable risks.

The new politics of uncertainty

Global risks are inherently ambivalent. They are uncontrollable, second-order risks (because of institutional failure) but at the same time (by virtue of their political perception) they are in principle controllable. They necessitate a new politics of uncertainty. They call for a distinction between *inherent uncontrollability* and *actual lack of control*. They are emphatically *not* dangers in the premodern or postmodern sense because they rest upon *decisions* and therefore raise issues of attributability, responsibility and conflicts over the distribution of guilt, costs and justice. At any rate, they always necessitate political decisions and responses. No uncontrollable destiny frees national and international politics (and under certain circumstances transnational corporations) from any necessity to act; rather, the cosmopolitan public discourse of risk puts them under intense pressure to justify themselves and to take appropriate action. They are, so to speak, condemned to respond. This expectation of practical responses means that a counterfactual belief that the risks are controllable persists even if all of the available kinds of responses fail. To do nothing in the face of acknowledged risks is *politically* out of the question, regardless of whether the actions undertaken reduce or increase the risks or are completely ineffectual. The anonymity of uncontrollable risks must be broken, global risks must be given a recognizable face. Bin Laden's face is the face of the terrorist risk. The uncertainty of recognized global risks – *fortuna* in classical political theory – which is not susceptible to political control, is here translated into *virtù*, for which political instruments and institutions must be invented and implemented. This generates at the same time a hierarchy of modes of political action, in which greater value attaches to proactive than to reactive policy.

The politics of risk construction and risk minimization

In this context, we must distinguish between two forms of 'risk politics': (a) a politics of risk *construction* (social construction of risks) and (b) a politics of risk *minimization* (precaution, prevention, minimization and corresponding interventions across borders). The latter presupposes the former: (a) contributes to defining the scope for action of (b). Both forms involve a definition of reality, a cognitive one in the case of (a), in terms of political action in the case of (b); (a) is characteristic of sociological constructivism, (b) is more characteristic of realism in political science.

Side effects of side effects: risk paradoxes

The logic of the side-effects argument leads to the question of which side effects are or can be produced by the political construction of risks or by various strategies of risk minimization. Here different risk paradoxes can be distinguished.

(a)   Side effects of side effects produce a public sphere. Regardless of what goes wrong, the more extreme and disastrous the consequences, the more likely it is that they will become objects of public reports and discussion, with varying degrees of distortion.

(b)   Political action and decision aimed at reducing or avoiding risks may, in accordance with the law of side effects, actually exacerbate the dangers that it is supposed to minimize. Thus the 'war on terror' in Iraq, for example, has transformed Iraq into a happy hunting ground for transnational terror networks.

Implications for the social sciences

World risk society poses new kinds of challenges not only for politics and everyday life but also for the social sciences. On the one hand, they have to recognize that social interactions are no longer as clearly defined in space and time as the nation-state paradigm assumed. On the other hand, world risk society points to a model of global socialization that, contrary to the usual image of positive integration based on shared values and norms, rests specifically on conflict over *negative* values (risks, crises, dangers of destruction). It is not a matter of multiplying the uncontrollable risks of interdependence but of removing the limits on them. This is true in three senses: spatial, temporal and social.

Spatially, we are confronted with risks that pay no heed to national or other frontiers: climate change, atmospheric pollution and the hole in the ozone layer concern us all (though not all to the same degree). Something similar holds for the removal of *temporal* limits. The long latency period of global problems such as the disposal of nuclear waste or the repercussions of genetically modified foodstuffs makes them immune to the usual routines for coping with industrial dangers. Finally, *socially*, the attribution of risk potentials, and hence the question of liability, becomes problematic. It is difficult to determine who in a legally relevant sense actually 'causes' environmental pollution or a financial crisis, when these arise only through the interaction of large numbers of individuals. Civilizational dangers, therefore, prove to be for the most part deterritorialized, and hence are difficult to attribute to specific agents and escape the control of the nation-state. As it happens, the utility of Europeanization in this way also shows itself to be limited. This also contains the formula of 'European cosmopolitanism'. It points beyond the European project and uncovers its external contradictions and its inadequacies – yet always underlines its necessity.

Both the unrestricted character and the incalculability of the new risks have been the object of numerous controversies. The 'residual risk' culture is locked in a perpetual public dispute with a 'culture of uncertainty'. The sociologically significant aspect, however, is that the latter seems to be gaining the upper hand. As previously in the Chernobyl disaster or the BSE crisis, the terrorist attacks of 11 September 2001 in New York and 11 March 2004 in Madrid show that the real issue is ultimately not to calculate risks to the third decimal place. The decisive issue is how the *global public perception and construction* of new threats develops. What held until recently, especially within the US cultural horizon, namely, that the consequences were defused by a kind of 'preventive thoughtlessness', no longer holds. But now, for the consciousness of the present shaken by catastrophes, a proactive alarm seems to race ahead of the risks and to lend them a universal significance and political urgency relatively distinct from a specific attack or the events.

The reason for this lies in a twofold failure: the failure of our concepts and theories vis-à-vis the civilizational effects, dangers and attacks; and the failure of national and international institutions that claim (and ostensibly take action) to protect citizens from these dangers. This was the novel aspect that recently dawned on people following the terrorist attacks. We face a 'different kind' of risk, whose full implications cannot be grasped by contemporaries. World political reactions were correspondingly hieratic and confused, and the pronouncements of intellectuals were correspondingly bewildered. The terrorist attacks not only cost thousands of people their lives and highlighted the vulnerability of the invulnerable American nation; they also made apparent our death of concepts and disorientation. The idea of deterrence on which the military security system was built is no longer applicable. Nevertheless – or for that very reason – some action, or pretence of action, must be taken. At every level of world risk society, therefore, in national and international politics, in law, science and economics and in everyday life, the problem is to tame the contradictory compulsion to control the uncontrollable.

2.2   The reality and unreality of global risks as a product of cultural perceptions

The broad lines of conflict during the Cold War were politically open and owed their explosive potential to questions of national and international security. The geopolitical lines of conflict in world risk society run between different risk perception cultures. We are experiencing an invasion of politics by culture. The clearer it becomes that expert knowledge is inadequate to define the indefinable, or fails completely in the face of 'unknown unknowns', the greater becomes the role that cultural perceptions play in deciding which enormous civilizational risks count as real and which as unreal, which priorities should accordingly be set and which political strategies should be pursued.

Denis Tänzler (2002) asks what role cultural perceptions play in the fact that negotiations over international responses to climate risk have thus far failed. As is well known, the United States and the EU propose different policy instruments for tackling the challenges of climate change. But, according to Tänzler's study, this can no more be the decisive factor than the reference to different interests, since the conflict between the USA and the EU is a rare clear case of 'different positions coupled with congruent interests':

Scientific findings concerning the regional effects in North America and Europe indicate that these regions will have to face considerable changes, even if they are less in danger than small island states, for example. Their economic activity and energy-intensive lifestyle mean that both bear a considerable degree of responsibility for the fact that the international community has to confront this risk at all. Moreover, measures to protect the climate could enable both regions to reduce their dependence on fuel imports and to play a leading role in environmental technology markets, since both have a high potential for innovation in this area. Crucial to the policy divergences between the United States and the EU during international climate negotiations is rather how the risks of global climate change are perceived. (Tänzler 2002: 89)

As a consequence, although it is true that so-called hard factors (such as economic-industrial utility, strategic power calculations, oil, etc.) play a role, social and cultural factors are decisive in determining the different perceptions of risk of different societies, cultures and states (Daase, Feske and Peters 2002: 269).[3]

Thus risk perception also draws new boundaries. Those groups, countries, cultures and states which share the same definition of a threat may be said to 'belong'; they form the 'inside' of a 'transnational risk community' that acquires its profile and institutional structure (national and international actors and institutions) in an ultimately preventive defence against the sources of danger. Those who, for whatever reasons, do *not* share this definition of a threat constitute the 'outside' of the risk community and, even if they want to remain 'neutral', can easily become part of the threat to be combated. In this way, geopolitical lines of conflict crystallize under the aegis of risk perception between regions that enter the terrain of world risk society with very different histories, experiences and expectations.

An outstanding example of this is the conflicting urgency, indeed reality, which Europe and the United States attribute to the dangers of climate change and to transnational terrorism. We should not overlook the possibility of a sudden *change* in perception, however, i.e., the so-called *conversion effect*. Before 11 September 2001, conflicting perceptions and evaluations of the climate risk, but *not* of the terrorist risk, prevailed on the two sides of the Atlantic. Only as a result of September 11 did North America (if one can speak in such blanket terms) abandon its general agnosticism towards the 'collapse of civilization' scenarios mostly emanating from Europe and transform itself, in the specific domain of transnational terrorism, from an exporter of optimism into an exporter of pessimism. Thus the asymmetry in perceptions of risk, which has played an important role in tensions and splits between the United States and Europe, first crystallized as a result of the radical change in perception that the United States, though not Europe, underwent in response to the attacks in New York and Washington.

However, the conversion-like change of perception in the United States, and its rejection in Europe, must be seen in the context of the institutional structure specific to each region (or, to put it in sociological terms, a social-constructivist approach must be combined with a neo-institutionalist approach.) As Christopher Daase (2002) has shown in a study, the conversion phenomenon in the United States was based not only on an overnight transformation of risk sceptics into risk believers, but also on the fact that it could break through a 'reform logjam of the 1990s' in US foreign and defence policy:

What appears to outsiders as a rapid and dramatic shift in American foreign policy is the result of an impeded adaptation to a changed security situation. The decisive factor is that, for all the reform proposals and strategic recommendations, the 'national security architecture . . . remained fundamentally a product of the Cold War' and remained fixated on a reactive strategy. September 11 overcame the bureaucratic and institutional hurdles and made it possible to implement a proactive strategy, thereby smoothing the way for a comprehensive risk policy. (Daase 2002: 115)

In Europe, by contrast, the experience of shock did not open the often invoked 'window of opportunity' for military reform plans lying around waiting to be implemented (Kingdon 1995). On the contrary, acknowledging the international terrorist risk profoundly contradicts Europe's institutionalized peace mission both internally and externally, whereas the prioritization of climate change is fully in line with it. Therefore, the missionary zeal with which the Bush administration embraced a strategy of military prevention, and hence of foreign intervention, inevitably appeared as an attack on the premises of Europe's risk certainty, which is committed to peaceful change through global climate change reforms.

The terrorist attack has restored to US military and foreign policy the long sought-for enemy image that enables it to give the mobilization of consent and support at home and abroad a clear focus, across the boundaries and camps of political parties and states. With the construction of militarily oriented 'global risk communities', 'anti-terror coalitions' take shape by forcing all states and countries to decide whether they are for or against them. In the process, the geopolitical landscape is ploughed up. Traditional opponents, such as Russia or China, can be bound into an 'alliance against terrorism', whereas traditional allies such as France or Germany mobilize international resistance to the Iraq War and, in the eyes of Americans fighting for their existence, exclude themselves from the alliance – and are duly excluded.

Not only are European and American cultural perceptions and definitions of risk and threat drifting far apart; Europeans and Americans are living in different worlds *because* their perceptions and definitions of risk are drifting far apart. For Europeans, issues such as climate change, maybe even the dangers posed by global financial flows for certain countries, play a much greater role than the threat of terrorism in their perception of risks. In American eyes, Europe seems to suffer from environmental hysteria, whereas many Europeans see Americans as afflicted with terrorism hysteria. Their respective definitions of danger generate different images of the actors 'behind' and 'responsible' for them, different strategies for action and, not least, different 'antagonisms'. Thus the drifting apart of risk cultures on the two sides of the Atlantic threatens to lead to a cultural break between America and Europe. Hence, the global character of world risk society finds expression in a contradictory dynamic: unity and disintegration are experienced at one and the same time. The 'civilizational shared fate', a politically important idea if ever there was one, is fracturing over the question of who shares which definitions of risk and of how the threats should be overcome. The critical issue here is less how many terrorist attacks result in how many deaths or how dramatic the climatic, and hence the social and political, catastrophes which are creeping or galloping towards us are, or will become. Crucial is rather the extent to which the terrorist risk comes to shape perceptions of international politics, and whether it fosters a preventive military or a preventive political view of the world. A primarily military change in perception would force Europe into the role of an outsider preoccupied with luxury problems. Thus, new lines of conflict and new alternatives are taking shape which ultimately track the fault lines between different constructions, dimensions and potential sources of global risks.

2.3   *Divergent logics of global risks: on the distinction between economic, environmental and terrorist risks*

In this context, at least three axes of conflict must be distinguished in world risk society: first, *environmental risk conflicts* that trigger a global dynamic; second, *global financial risks*, which are initially conceived in individual and national terms; and, third, the *threat from state-supported terrorist networks*.

To begin with environmental risks that represent a physical threat, there is, on the one side, *wealth-related* environmental destruction such as the hole in the ozone layer or the greenhouse effect, which may be laid at the door of the Western industrial world, though its impact is of course global. From this we must distinguish *poverty-related* environmental destruction such as the clearing of the rainforest, which is limited to specific regions but is of such import that it is no less alarming.

Then there are the global *economic* risks, the imponderabilities of currency and finance markets that in recent years have commanded increasing public attention in world risk society. They also conform to the model of the new uncontrollable risks that shape world risk society. They exhibit the stark contradictions between the distributional logics of 'goods' (property, income) and 'bads' (probabilities of illnesses and catastrophes) of risky decisions. They highlight the limits of a quantitative calculation of risks; they can hardly be contained spatially or institutionally and hence explode the boundaries of private insurance options. Thus, they are largely deterritorialized, at least as regards their costs; it is difficult to locate blame for them and they resist the control of nation-states.

Granted, economic crises are as old as the markets themselves. And, since the global economic crisis of 1929 at the latest, it has been clear to everyone that financial crashes can have catastrophic effects – especially for politics. The Bretton Woods institutions established following World War II were conceived in this sense as global political answers to global economic problems, and the fact that they functioned was an important key to the development of the welfare state in Europe. Since the 1970s, however, those institutions have been in large part dismantled and replaced by a succession of ad hoc solutions. As a result, we currently face the paradoxical situation that, whereas markets are more liberal and more global than ever, the global institutions that monitor their effects have experienced drastic curtailments of their powers. Against this background, the possibility of a worldwide financial disaster on the scale of 1929 cannot be ruled out.

In contrast to environmental and technological risks, whose physical effects first acquire social relevance 'from outside', financial risks also affect a directly social structure, namely, the economy or, more precisely, the guarantee of solvency which is indispensable to its normal functioning. This means, first, that the impact of financial risks is also much more strongly mediated by other social structures than the impact of global environmental risks. Hence, it is easier to 'individualize' and 'nationalize' it and it generates larger differences in the respective perceptions of risk. Finally, global financial risks – not least in their worldwide (statistical) perception – are also attributed, as *national* risks, to particular countries or regions (e.g., South Asian countries, Russia or, to cite the most recent example, Argentina). Of course, this does not at all imply that risks of economic interdependence are any less risky. Since all of the subsystems of modern society must rely on the proper functioning of other subsystems, a failure of the financial system would be catastrophic. No other functional system plays such a prominent role in the modern world as the economy. Thus, the world economy is without doubt a key dimension of world risk society.

We must distinguish, in addition, between environmental and financial dangers, on the one hand, and the threat from global terrorist networks, on the other. Environmental and economic conflicts can be conceived on the model of the *side effects* of radical modernization. Both result from the accumulation and distribution of 'bads' that goes along with the production of 'goods'. Terrorist activities, by contrast, must be understood in terms of *intentional* catastrophes. Here the effects, which are triggered unintentionally as side effects on the model of environmental and economic risks, become *deliberately planned acts*. Hence, the principle of deliberately exploiting the obvious vulnerability of modern civil society replaces the principle of chance and accident. Terrorists only have to target so-called residual risks and the civic consciousness of a highly complex and interdependent world to produce a general awareness of danger that paralyses modern society and literally causes it to freeze with panic.

The connection between trust and risk must also be rethought accordingly. As a general rule, the less trust, the greater the perception of risk. But the terrorist threat must be understood as an inflationary destruction of trust. If it is treated as a matter of life and death, the terrorist threat replaces active trust with active mistrust. It places in question trust in neighbours and fellow citizens, foreigners and governments. Since the dissolution of trust magnifies (the perception of) risks, the terrorist threat multiplies risks by triggering every conceivable (and inconceivable) risk fantasy.

Terrorist networks are, as it were, 'violence NGOs'. Whereas military attention used to be directed to military organizations in other countries and to ways of averting their attacks, now the whole world of states is challenged by transnational threats from substate actors and networks. As previously in the cultural realm, we are now experiencing the 'death of distance' in the military realm, indeed the end of the state monopoly on the means of coercion in a highly civilized world where almost anything can become a lethal weapon in the hands of ruthless fanatics. The peaceful symbols of civil societies can become diabolical weapons. In principle, this is nothing new, but it is now an omnipresent experience.[4] The terrorist attacks of recent years have heightened general awareness of the vulnerability of advanced civilization. More precisely, whereas we are insured in varying degrees against accidents of various kinds, we are completely defenceless against the planned catastrophes of anonymous transnational terrorist networks that intentionally exploit the susceptibility of advanced civilizations to chance and accident in order to plunge them into a self-crippling culture of fear. A world in which preventive fantasies of danger are disconnected from chance and accident and focused on the deliberate triggering of catastrophes threatens to undermine the very foundations of freedom and democracy.

For all their differences, environmental, economic and terrorist interdependence risks have two key features in common. First, they all promote or compel a *politics of proactive counteraction*, which annuls the basis of the existing forms and alliances of international politics, compels redefinitions and reforms and inspires new political philosophies. This means that the premises of what counts as 'national' and 'international', of how these dimensions should be related to and demarcated from each other, are disintegrating and must now be renegotiated within the framework of risk prevention in the meta-power game of global and national security policies. Here we must ask, among other things: Does a Europe enamoured of its pacifist worldview (of environmental risks) recognize that Islamic terrorists are not anti-America (as many Europeans believe) but anti-Western, anti-Europe and anti-cosmopolitan? Will a clandestine coalition develop between Islamic-terrorist anti-Americanism and European anti-Americanism based on the maxim 'the enemy of my enemy is my friend'? Or will Europe side with America because it recognizes that Islamic terrorist fundamentalism hates and wants to destroy everything that Europe stands for, namely, non-religious liberal-mindedness, loss of binding traditions, an agnostic ethos of respect among those who recognize uncertainty as part of the human condition?

Second, it is equally true of environmental, economic and terrorist risks that they cannot be foisted onto the environment as *external* threats; they must be understood, rather, as consequences, actions and uncertainties produced by civilization. Accordingly, the risks of civilization can potentially sharpen a global normative awareness, creating a public sphere, and perhaps even a cosmopolitan outlook. In world risk society, one might argue, a new European transnational public space is emerging in the controversy over the causes and agents of global dangers. In other words, disputes over definitions and responsibilities can promote internationalized cosmopolitanism.

2.4   The European public sphere and civil society can be understood and developed as a response to world risk society

The theory of world risk society questions and replaces one of the premises of political theory. For public attention is aroused less by decisions than by perceptions of their consequences as problematic and dangerous. Decisions as such remain a source of indifference. Only perceptions of, and communication concerning, problematic effects make people anxious and get them worked up, shake them out of their apathy and egoism and create the communal and social dimensions of a transnational, postnational public space of action (see Dewey 1991; Beck 2005). In other words, dangers are not merely dangers, and they differ from one another not only in their social and political 'logics' depending on whether conflicts are constructed as economic, environmental or terrorist. Indeed, constructions of danger have their own side effects: *they create a public sphere*. And this public awareness reaches as far as the awareness of dangers staged by the media. This is true in both space and time, in both a positive and a negative sense: the more the threat becomes omnipresent in the mass media, the greater becomes the political power of the risk perception to explode boundaries; but the 'reality' of the threat disappears almost immediately once the media change the subject.

This makes clear that the theory of world risk society can throw an important light on the emergence of transnational public spaces in Europe. Global risks set free a moment of reflection and communication. Organizations and individuals must identify the consequences of other people's actions which affect them, ascribe responsibility for them to the correct source, and thus seek agreement concerning the nature of the problem and what can be done to address it. This also contains a political element. For, in order to act politically, and hence to minimize the risks that threaten everyone, those affected have to organize politically across borders in one way or another, or urge the established political institutions and players to take corresponding measures. It makes no difference whether this promises to be successful or not. It does not give rise to a great new non-ontological 'We', but it does have a *transnational resonance* in which external perspectives become internal and the excluded are included. Global interdependence risks transform uninvited and absent others into fellow inhabitants, neighbours, troublemakers, in a world that has become a trap. Acknowledged risks force people to construct communication bridges where none, or almost none, existed before, between self-enclosed arenas and sectoral subpublics, across systemic and linguistic boundaries and conflicts of opinion, interest, class, nation and denomination.

The forced, involuntary character of this 'side-effects public' can mitigate or overcome the classical problems of deliberately created publics, i.e., the lack of target groups, problems in mobilizing participation and lack of willingness to cooperate. Global risk is infectious; it seeks out potential targets, opens up publics and compels attention and (at least symbolic) cooperation. It short-circuits isolated, policy-specific communications networks and publics.

Here we are dealing with the mobilization of affected groups neither from above nor from below but through the power of unintended side effects, and thus, in a sense, with an *involuntary* public that invalidates the axioms of compartmentalized responsibilities, criteria of relevance and channels of communication. Risk publics disaggregate and re-aggregate democracy. They disprove the postulate of the nation-state that democracy is possible only within the national social container. They create a public space and frame of reference in which the issues affecting people can be defined across frontiers, so that pressure for action can be brought to bear in appropriate ways.

It follows that the political locus of world risk society is not the street but *television* (television becomes the street). Its political subjects are the transnational advocacy movements which, in view of current and impending horror scenarios, are able to stage the cultural symbols that raise the latent threat to consciousness in the media. This is true of *European* risk awareness, but less so of its counterpart in America, which reflects the staging of the terrorist risk in the mass media by the state.

In neither Europe nor America is it the case that global dangers aggravate a general sense of emptiness or meaninglessness in the modern world. Rather, they create a horizon of meaning dominated by avoidance, resistance and assistance, a moral climate that intensifies with the scale of the perceived danger, but which can also become so overheated that it can trigger pogroms. In this hothouse of fear, the classical roles of hero and troublemaker acquire a new political meaning, so that xenophobic, anti-Semitic stereotypes and movements may experience a fatal revival. Perception of the world within the coordinates of a self-endangering civilization combine morality, religion, fundamentalism, hopelessness, tragedy and tragicomedy – always connected with their opposites: salvation, help and liberation – into a universal drama. The established players – states and the economy – are free to assume the role of villain and poisoner in these global tragicomedies, but also to slip into the role of hero or friend in need. This provides the precise background against which advocacy movements can profile themselves through the cunning of weakness. These advocacy movements of global civil society practise a kind of *judo politics* whose goal is to turn the superior strength of environmental miscreants or human rights violators against themselves.

Advocacy movements are, as it were, 'multinational media professionals' who know how to set the traps of self-contradiction between proclamation and violation of human rights and of security and surveillance norms, so that the powers that be (corporations, governments) stumble blindly into them and thrash around telegenically for the entertainment of the global public. Henry David Thoreau and Mahatma Gandhi would have been delighted to see the advocacy movements infiltrating the mass media and established parties and using the instruments of the media age to stage worldwide mass civil disobedience. Greenpeace, for example, is a veritable forge of political symbols in which cultural transgressions and symbols of transgression are artfully produced using the media of black-and-white conflicts, which are capable of concentrating protests and making them into lightning rods for a collective humanitarian or environmental bad conscience. However, this global power game conducted through the mass media can also be played under the opposite sign. As the approach to the terrorist danger demonstrates, powerful states can develop a kind of 'functional equivalent' to these advocacy movements by themselves stirring the global conscience through graphic depictions of danger, and in this way tapping into the source of legitimacy for global action by claiming to 'save the world from self-destruction'.

Through the awareness of dangers, world risk society becomes self-critical in a certain sense. Its foundations, coordinates and ready-made coalitions become fluid. Politics assumes new, unfamiliar forms and directions at odds with the established institutions, alliances and political groupings within and across national borders.

In this context, the EU, as an alliance of civil society and state actors, can gain a new foundation and a sharper political profile. Europe can become the advocate of a global public renaissance of modernity through the latter's self-criticism. Civilizational dangers are a manifestation of alienated, bundled subjectivity and history. They are a kind of collective compulsory reminder of the fact that our own decisions and mistakes underlie the problems we face. Global threats are the avatars of the mistakes of a whole era of the first modernity. They are a kind of collective return of the repressed. In the process of raising them to consciousness, which also propels reflexive risk modernity, resides the opportunity to dispel the curse of fatalism produced by globalization. World risk society contradicts the territorial conception of Europe and makes possible a transnational, cosmopolitan Europe that thematizes the global impacts of European modernity self-critically before a global public.

2.5   World risk society, the European Empire and the contradictions of a proactive security policy

Whereas during the Cold War the European Community found itself threatened by a Warsaw Pact armed to the teeth with nuclear and conventional weapons, the threat today comes not from strong states but from *weak* states. The security of the European empire is currently threatened by the breakdown of states, by state *failure*. The EU no longer faces a rival military power with corresponding hostile intentions, institutions and persons whose identities are known, who wear uniforms, hold verifiable positions and can therefore be systematically spied upon through a network of secret services and counter-espionage services. Instead, it is confronted with 'risk states', whose hazardousness derives from the fact that their structures are dysfunctional or are falling apart. Such states are becoming a source of concern for a European Empire geared to controlling uncertainty.

The risk of state collapse is no longer confined to sub-Saharan Africa and other distant regions – Somalia, Sierra Leone, Liberia, Cambodia and Haiti being well-known examples of complete collapse. It has come to affect virtually the whole of the European periphery. Thus, it no longer merely represents a challenge to Europe's humanitarian ideals; it has become a tangible security problem for Europe itself. The EU fears deleterious effects on security from the failure and collapse of states on its southern and south-eastern periphery. In a 1993 document commissioned by the European Council on a new policy for the Middle East, the European Commission expressed its concern over an already developing trend towards internal political crises: 'Political, economic and social conditions in many of these countries [i.e., the southern and eastern rim of the Mediterranean plus the Middle East] currently endanger stability and are leading to mass emigration, fundamentalist extremism, terrorism, drug addiction and organized crime. This harms both the region itself and the Union.' Chris Patten, the EU Commissioner for External Relations, considers the present and future of the EU to be 'inseparably bound up' with those of the southern Mediterranean countries. In his view, peace, stability and welfare have 'the highest priority of all'. In virtually all documents on the Mediterranean, the EU underlines its urgent interest in stability and in this way makes it plain that it regards the region as unstable. (Wolf 2002: 243)

Characteristically, the risk perception of the member states differs sharply from that of the European Empire. States tend to localize risks and view global risks through the lens of the welfare state; their gaze is inward-looking. Here the primary question (in view of the eastern enlargement, for example) is: What changes are to be expected in terms of the heterogeneity of the population, relations between domestic majorities and minorities and the resulting distributional problems, as well as for the problems posed by sealing the country off from the outside and patrolling its borders? Risk policy is conceived and practiced as welfare state administrative policy.

The outlook of empire, by contrast, is 'categorially' geared to the variability of relations between the inside and the outside. Indeed, the policy of variable geometry must be understood as proactive security policy. It serves to bring zones of insecurity under control and thus faces a twofold dilemma: on the one hand, it runs the risk that cross-border policies designed to minimize risk can produce precisely the opposite of what they aim at by contributing to maximizing insecurity; on the other hand, the policy of integration through expansion risks internalizing global social conflicts through its very *success*. Either way, this justifies the need to break with an abridged form of domestic cosmopolitanism and to develop an external perspective and orientation.

When asked why German soldiers are on active duty in Afghanistan, the German defence minister has consistently responded that it is because Germany's security must be defended on the Hindu Kush. This is clearly false as far as Germany is concerned, but it makes sense when viewed from the cosmopolitan perspective of the European Empire. Then the question really does arise concerning Europe's possible role in controlling zones of insecurity in world risk society that crucially affect its own security interests. As was the case in the past, if such risk policy strategies are to be successful, it is imperative that the EU and Washington agree in their perceptions of zones of insecurity. After initially deep differences over Bosnia in the early 1990s, the United States and Europe ultimately agreed on a common definition of risk to stem the bloody conflicts in the Balkans in 1995 and again in 1999. Under US leadership, NATO expanded to include the countries of Central Europe, with the goal of establishing peace and security in the zones of insecurity created by the end of the Cold War. Although Russia has not become a formal member as a result, it has nevertheless been 'externally integrated' into the new NATO in a partnership that resembles membership. Thus, after the collapse of the bipolar Cold War order, Europe has been made more democratic, peaceful and secure (especially with regard to its internal–external borders) than ever before in history. For the first time since World War II – indeed, since the beginning of the twentieth century – neither Europeans nor Americans need fear an outbreak of military conflict in Central

Europe. This is due not least to the success of transatlantic risk policy since the end of the Cold War.

In 1995, the EU established the Euro-Mediterranean Partnership (EMP) with an eye to the twelve countries on the southern and eastern rim of the Mediterranean.[5] The European imperial strategy to bring zones of insecurity in North Africa (Morocco, Algeria, Tunisia and Egypt) under control includes economic and political liberalization, the gradual creation of a free trade zone by the year 2010, a further liberalization of markets and extensive subventions for private enterprises. All this is supposed to improve conditions in these countries, not only economically but also in terms of civil society and human rights. Thus, economic aid is tied to progress on human rights and democratization and to the development of civil society structures. This is meant as a proactive response to the risks for Europe of the failure and collapse of states, in cooperation with NATO, the CSCE and other organizations. Material economic interests are not at the forefront here, since the region in question is hardly important for Europe's external trade.[6]

Given all of this, European policy can easily become entangled in what one might call the *globalization circle*. Good intentions – economic liberalization and the underpinning of democracy in civil society – have the paradoxical effect of combining to accelerate the breakdown of unstable nation-states and redoubling the security risks for Europe they were supposed to check. This may lead to serious human tragedies and wars, such as those of the 1990s in Somalia, West Africa, Yugoslavia, Albania and parts of the former Soviet Union. Even if liberalization measures and support for civil society activities are not the triggering causes because internal developments and complications play a central role, they can nevertheless produce a hidden vacuum of state power and legitimacy that can suddenly break out into the open. Thus, national compromises among ethnic groups can lose their binding force and latent conflicts can in the end explode into civil wars. In the circle of globalization, therefore, 'exigencies' of economic liberalization and the 'good intentions' of global civil society combine with a chain of 'unintended consequences' which, in this case, produce the very opposite of what they were supposed to achieve. Zones of insecurity grow larger and thus the obligation of 'humanitarian intervention' to bring the insecurity under control, if need be with a UN mandate and with the use of NATO military power. Correspondingly, the security policy of the strategic European Empire can easily mutate into a negative risk paradox, like trying to extinguish the smouldering embers of political conflagrations with petrol.

3   The Iraq War and its lessons for cosmopolitan realism

Europe's self-indulgent disregard for the external cosmopolitan perspective has another problematic consequence. It obscured the fact that from the outset the process of European integration was contingent on a particular constellation in foreign and security policy, namely, the external threat from the Soviet Union and its allies, coupled with the military protection afforded by the United States. Together they forced the Western European countries to band together. The American military shield created the space in which Europe's soul, wounded by two world wars, could convalesce. In building a community, Europe was able to concentrate on economic harmonization, reconciliation and democracy, while allowing itself a position of military weakness. The end of the Cold War meant the dissolution of these historical coordinates of European integration, although Europeans have not yet taken cognisance of this. The collapse of the Soviet Union and the threat of wars on all sides have exposed the contradictions between the United States and Europe, but also those between various member states of the current or potential EU, because their vital security interests and strategies were defined in conflicting ways. It would be both unhistorical and unrealistic simply to project the success story of EU integration policy into the future. The writing on the wall tells a different story. As things stand, there is no single European view on the vital issues of war and peace. If this is the signature of the future, it means that the experiment in European unification could also end in failure. The more the world of civilizational threats develops in a belligerent direction, the greater is the danger that the European consensual empire geared to reconciliation and the rule of law will be destroyed from within. Whereas the old Cold War constellation forced the countries of Western Europe to band together, the new constellation of world politics is threatening to tear the EU apart.

What does 'integration' mean in view of the 'abstract enemy' of the civilizational threats of world risk society? Or, to put it more pointedly, what does 'Europe' mean amid the new risks of the global situation, where the old external stabilizers of integration have fallen away, spatial (and hence also 'substantive', geostrategic) frontiers are expanding, and new kinds of global risk have emerged to which no one has an answer, not to speak of a patent remedy? Europe stands at a crossroads where debate has become essential on basic issues of political order and positions in world risk society far beyond the issues addressed in the Draft European Constitution. What we call 'cosmopolitan realism' (Beck 2005, 2006) can suggest some answers to the question of what will hold Europe together in the future and what strategic contribution it is willing and able to make to solving global problems. These answers are also the key to the future of Europe.

The wars in Afghanistan and Iraq are the first wars against global risk. For Americans a new threat to humanity has altered the security situation fundamentally since September 11, whereas Europeans have long considered this new threat to humanity as a case of American hysteria. In the American view of things, it would have been sufficient in the pre-September 11 world to do what France, Germany, Russia or China demanded, i.e., to disarm

Saddam Hussein step by step; but in the post-September 11 world this is foolish and irresponsible, because even a 1 per cent chance that 'evil' dictators or failed states could supply chemical, biological or nuclear weapons to suicide attackers is so unacceptable that there is no other option but military action. Otherwise, a stateless, socially atomized atomic age could develop in which the very survival of humanity is jeopardized by ruthless terrorists. For Americans, then, it is the horror of terror that stares us in the face, for Europeans, the horror of war. In fact, what has happened in Iraq demonstrates the paradoxical character of a proactive military risk politics.

Not long ago, revolutionary pamphlets were being written about the American military empire and fiery calls were being made for the construction of a counterforce to American power. In terms of descriptive and political content, both models were already obsolete before the printer's ink had even dried on the paper on which they were printed.

Without underestimating America's unparalleled military superiority, we can say that the dream or nightmare that the United States could rule the world through military force has been shown by the Iraq War to be an illusion. The predicted 'eternity' of the new empire has proved to be the shortest in history. The United States has 'designed a military that is better suited to kick down the door, beat up a dictator, and go home than to stay for the harder work of building a democratic polity' (Nye 2003: 72). 'Nation-building' is not working; in fact, the United States has barely managed to pacify central Iraq. The south of the country is being ruled by mullahs, the north by Kurdish warlords. The situation is grimly reminiscent of Afghanistan. Worst of all, the Iraq War is threatening to go down in history as a textbook example of a risk paradox: the 'war against terror' is *creating* breeding grounds of terrorism.

Roughly 80 per cent of Americans believe that war can create justice. However, this conviction has lost some of its purity in light of the experience of the Iraq War. Even Robert Kagan, who a short while ago thought that Europe was living on the planet Venus while the US had to deal with the dirty business of the planet Mars (Kagan 2003), has come around to the view that the vague but important question of legitimacy in world politics is essential both to American power and to overcoming global challenges (Kagan 2004a; see Beck 2005). Kagan has accordingly criticized President Bush's national security adviser, Condoleezza Rice, who on assuming office immediately announced that the Clinton administration had concerned itself too little with 'national interests' and too much with 'humanitarian interests'.

Pursuing the 'national interest' always sounds right. But in fact the idea that the United States can take such a narrow view of its 'national interest' has always been mistaken. For one thing, Americans had 'humanitarian interests' two centuries before that term was invented, as well as moral, political and ideological interests for which Americans have historically been willing to fight. Beyond that, the enunciation of this 'realist' view by the dominant power in a unipolar era is a serious foreign policy error. A nation with global hegemony cannot proclaim to the world that it will be guided only by its own definition of its 'national interest.' That is precisely what even America's closest friends fear: that the United States will wield its vast power only for itself. (Kagan 2004a)

Political *realism* itself compels us to subordinate national interests to the cosmopolitan goal of promoting democracy and freedom. 'It is a common observation . . . that our cause is the cause of all mankind, and that we are fighting for their liberty in defending our own', wrote Benjamin Franklin. This early luminous principle could lend impetus to the realistic cosmopolitanism of the United States at the beginning of the twenty-first century. Power stems not only from military superiority, however overwhelming, but also from the legitimacy that accrues to it from its interplay with the global public and the principles of international law. Only when power is converted into international cooperation can it escape the process of self-endangerment and dissolution triggered by global risks. In the meantime, the policies of the United States (more against its will than voluntarily) have little to do with unilateralism – only yesterday still the battle cry of the Bush administration. Washington is conducting its negotiations on arms control with North Korea in close cooperation with other affected nations, such as Japan, Russia, China and South Korea. In other words, radical unilateralism has given rise to the need for multilateral cooperation.

Another cornerstone of American unilateralism, the power play with the distinction between 'old' and 'new' Europe, has also begun to totter. There is an increasingly strong view that, in the elections following the terrorist attack in Madrid in March 2004, the Spanish government was punished for its alliance with US President Bush in the so-called coalition of the willing. According to this logic, the other governments which signed up to the 'coalition' – Blair in Britain and Berlusconi in Italy – had good reason to be nervous. First, their re-election was in jeopardy and, second, attacks in the run-up to elections were a distinct possibility. Of course, it remains possible that the US administration will continue to employ classical 'divide and rule' tactics to rein in the EU, and hence that the former integrative power, the United States, will fan the flames of national rivalries and continue to juggle with shifting coalitions. However, as American unilateralism in Iraq demonstrates, such a course will destroy the basis of its own power and legitimacy.

However, on this side of the Atlantic, this invalidates the preconditions under which the EU is supposed to serve as a counterforce to the United States. This idea rests on four premises.

1 It is not global risks but the unbridled lust for power of the US government which represents the real threat facing the world.

218 The Dialectic of Globalization and Europeanization

2 After the end of the Cold War, the military threats to Europe dissolved; therefore, Europe no longer needs American military protection or agreement with the United States; it is largely autonomous in its defence policy.
3 The sense of a European 'We' can be honed and secured especially by demarcating itself from the United States.
4 To make this counterforce to the United States effective, the integrationist vanguard must take the initiative, which means retreating into the shell of the founding members of the European community. Only then can Europe regain its capacity for action at home and abroad.[7]

These fantasies of a counterforce are unreal, both because they ignore the dominance of global risks (including the potential of invisible transnational terrorism to inflict violence and social change) and because they fail to recognize that such risks can be transformed into a source of cooperation for a legitimate global political order. In addition, the politics that conceives of Europe as a counterforce commits the same error for which it rebukes the US administration, namely unilateralism. In this way, it cuts itself off from cosmopolitan sources of cooperation and legitimacy of global power.

Furthermore, any attempt to build the expanded EU on an anti-American basis threatens to split Europe. The counterforce model entails a strategic split with the United States. But Europe would increase the danger to itself through an internal split or an external break with the Atlantic alliance.

A final point that is overlooked is that American power need not be the cause of the world's problems, but can be, or be turned into, the indispensable means for overcoming those problems. The mega-power need not be resisted but can be channelled by setting common strategic objectives. No US president, from whichever party, will accept that the formation of a counterforce to the United States can be the basis for cooperation with the United States.

However, it also holds from the US perspective that any power that combats the global terrorist risk in the name of *national* security *endangers* the legitimacy and effectiveness of its action, even if it has all the military means to impose its national defence policy. The United States can legitimize, and thereby expand, its power in the cooperation with the EU and the UN. To tackle the global threats facing the world, the Americans need the legitimacy which Europe may be able to provide. Conversely, only if the EU – and the UN – cooperate with the United States will they – and the whole world – have a chance of finding an answer to the global risks. However, if Europe makes reining in the superpower its priority, it will lose sight of the growing risks that face the world. 'Right now, many Europeans are betting that the risks posed by the "axis of evil", from terrorism to tyrants, will never be as great as the risk posed by the American Leviathan unbound' (Kagan 2004b).

4   What European cosmopolitanism can contribute to global cosmopolitanism

Over the past sixty years, a special case of cosmopolitan realism – 'the West' – has taken shape in the transatlantic relationship under US leadership (though, to be sure, under the pressure of the communist threat). This broke with the exclusive logic of realism or neorealism. All participating nations and governments could experience for themselves that cooperation among states has the additional political benefit of making a mutual increase in sovereignty possible, also for settling national conflicts. Here the combination of renunciation of autonomy with acquisition of sovereignty only appears paradoxical. This cosmopolitan realism rests on the fact that the asymmetry of power and the egoisms of sovereignty can balance each other out or be held in check through a kind of transnational social contract from which everyone involved stands to gain. This establishes a twofold self-restriction, which conforms – this is the point of cosmopolitan realism – not to a fanciful idealism but to the maxim of maximizing national interests.

The hegemonic power – i.e., the United States – must forego applying its hegemonic power because this is what its own national interests (properly understood) require. At the height of its power following World War II, the 'Great Generation' of the United States owed its fame not least to the fact that it produced cosmopolitan entrepreneurs on a historically unprecedented scale. American internationalism helped European cosmopolitanism onto its feet, based on a system of transnational alliances, organizations and legislation represented by a multitude of abbreviations: UNO, IMF, GATT, OECD, NATO, World Bank, WTO, as well as sub-alliances such as ANZUS, SEATO and CENTO. The United States is strong *because* it drew its power from cosmopolitan realism. It enhanced its power by binding itself to coalitions and it promoted international regulations that legally civilized and legally legitimized the asymmetry of power through a procedural consensus. The self-restraining ('liberal') hegemon respected, indeed served, the national interests of its alliance partners, offered them military protection, cultivated the art of diplomacy and strengthened the international organizations that provided a legal framework to ensure fairness and equality. In return, the allies pledged their loyalty and reliable diplomatic and logistic support. The result was a pre-established harmony of security, prosperity and democracy unprecedented in world history. In his essay 'Dead Souls: The Denationalization of the American Elite', Samuel Huntington laments the fact that, in spite of the Iraq War of 2003, nothing essential has changed in this respect. On the contrary: 'The central distinction between the [American] public and [American] elites is not isolationism versus internationalism, but nationalism versus cosmopolitanism' (Huntington 2004: 5). According to Huntington, the cosmopolitanism of the American elites decries patriotism and nationalism as 'evil forces' and attaches greater moral value to international law and international regimes and norms than to the sovereignty of individual nations.

That the power asymmetry was not overcome but only 'restricted' is apparent from the exit option. This is available *only* to the sole world power, the United States, since the associated costs virtually rule it out for the other members of the alliance. Herein lies a crucial difference between the transatlantic community and the EU. If the criterion for hegemonic power is the exit option, there is no 'real' hegemon in the EU. For the exit option represents a threat to the survival of *all* of the member states and governments alike. America's hegemony, by contrast, finds expression, indeed an outlet, in the fact that it always has the option of breaking loose and ignoring international treaties and institutions, and that it can even celebrate this as a 'liberation', as the Bush administration demonstrates.

Thus, cosmopolitan realism means that national interests are not annulled at all, much less extinguished, but are bound in and are at once tamed, transformed *and* more powerful through the Atlantic community or Europeanization. Cosmopolitan realism refutes both empirically and theoretically what the national perspective assumes, i.e., the zero-sum game, in which European politics wins what its member states lose (and vice versa). It becomes apparent that a positive-sum game expands the power of *all* within national and European space.

During the Cold War, it was not climate disaster or the terrorist threat to global civil society but the 'nuclear stalemate', humanity's possible *atomic suicide*, which provided the pioneers of *Ostpolitik*, Willy Brandt and Egon Bahr, and later the reformer Gorbachev, with the context and 'means' to transcend frontiers and create new commonalities. As the transnational peace movements alerted and honed people's perception of the nuclear threat to humanity as a whole, they undermined the dominance of the past and relativized national and ideological walls and replaced them with an orientation to the future in which the primacy of risk prevention was in each country's national interest. In this way, the interests of humanity as a whole could be fused with national, European and ideological interests.

This historical experience teaches us that it is not the asymmetry of power itself that is unbearable but that the absence of a common strategic goal makes it unbearable. At one time common strategic goals enabled the creation of organizations and procedures that made it possible not only to compensate for the asymmetry in power but also to transform it into a clear benefit for all. This is precisely where the Bush administration has failed. It has ultimately ridiculed the idea on which the Atlantic alliance is founded, namely, that the United States makes a legitimate use of its power only when it employs it in the name of someone else or for other objectives. 'To be sure', writes Condoleezza Rice, 'there is nothing wrong with doing something that benefits all humanity, but that is, in a sense, a second-order effect' (Rice 2000: 46). This 'second-order effect' cost the Bush administration its legitimacy and effectiveness and fed the aspiration for a 'European counterforce'.

Nevertheless, the environmental, economic and terrorist dangers of world risk society can give rise to new strategic commonalities. In the world post-September 11, 2001, and post-March 11, 2004, the old name for the Middle East in political geography, the *Near* East, has taken on a new and dangerous relevance. For, whereas during the twentieth century Europe was the region from which the gravest dangers to international security emanated, this title must now be accorded to the Middle East. Regardless of what standards we use, the countries of this region are threatened with collapse, tyranny, fundamentalism and terrorism, and hence represent an acute problem for Europe's *internal* security.

To meet this challenge, however, the West needs more than a military campaign plan. It needs an approach that addresses the root causes of these problems by changing the dynamics that produced such monstrous regimes and groups in the first place. Otherwise, the names of the terrorist groups and rogue states might change, but the long-term threat will not. Thus, the West must move beyond a strategy of simply trying to manage a crumbling status quo. Instead, it must actively try to help the region transform itself into a set of societies that can live in peace with one another and that no longer produce ideologies and terrorists who desire to kill in large numbers and who increasingly have access to the technology needed to do so. (Asmus 2003: 25)

The distinction between *political* and *military* risk policy is central to the construction of such a common strategic goal. As we have seen, *both* strategies are threatened by the risk paradox. This applies not only to military strategy, for the Iraq War has shown that combating the terrorist risk with military means can lead to a multiplication of the heads of the fire-breathing terrorist dragon. It can also apply to the strategy of political prevention, because the danger of countermeasures increases with the depth of the intended intervention and the complexity and contradictoriness of the social and political conditions. The distinction between genuine and non-genuine cosmopolitanism acquires key importance for such a strategy. In other words, what matters is 'taking Arab public opinion seriously' (Lynch 2003: 82). This includes a serious systematic, and not merely a rhetorical, attempt to defuse, and as far as possible to pacify, the barbaric conflict between the Israelis and the Palestinians. The use of military means may be necessary to achieve this strategic goal; but if the point is to help countries to help themselves, then political and economic means are crucial. Besides, the 'West' has no shortage of military means (given that the United States spends more on its military budget than the rest of the world put together). On the contrary, the Achilles heel of the West is its political paralysis and the lack of concepts and visions for containing global risks and, as regards the Arab world, promoting an alternative model of society that is at once Muslim and democratic. However, here the contribution of a cosmopolitan Europe acquires central importance, for instance in the issue of Turkish membership of the EU. This no longer appears as a question of identity, as in the national outlook on Europe, but as a necessary contribution to Germany's and Europe's internal security.

The political goal of building bridges in the Middle East and helping the Islamic world to modernize itself represents a European supplement, an alternative and a necessary corrective to America's policy of changing the world by military means. In its own interests, the US hegemonic power could no longer withhold recognition and material and political support from such an outwardly oriented European cosmopolitanism. For this expansion of the EU would be part of an expansion of their common power for defusing global risks, in a different yet comparable form to that which the founding generation used to create the Western alliance.

Against this background, cosmopolitan realism in international politics may be summed up in the following five points.

1 World risk society exhibits the new historical reality that no nation can master its problems alone. This is no longer an idealist principle of utopian internationalism or ivory tower social theory but a concrete political insight. It is the fundamental law of cosmopolitan realism, which contradicts the unilateralism of the US administration as much as the counterforce fantasies of Europeans.

2 Global problems create transnational commonalities. Anyone who plays the national card will lose. Only those who understand and conduct national politics in a cosmopolitan manner will survive. National states, whether weak or strong, are no longer the primary units for solving national problems. Interdependence is not a scourge of humanity but the precondition for its survival. Cooperation is no longer a means but the end. Individual states act for the most part both unilaterally and multilaterally, according to the issue they address and the domain in which they operate. The more globality is consciously recognized, and the more cultures, countries, governments, regions and religions are as a consequence affected by it, the more ineffective and unrealistic it becomes to act unilaterally. For the likelihood of failure is greater because both effectiveness and legitimacy are the result of cooperation among states.

3 International organizations are not just the continuation of national politics with different means. They bundle and transform national interests. They give rise to a positive-sum game among the states concerned that can supersede the negative-sum game of national autonomy. National (neo)realism maintains that international organizations serve primarily national, not international interests. Cosmopolitan realism asserts that international organizations serve neither national (in the old sense) nor primarily international interests, but *change*, *maximize* and *extend* national into transnational interests and open up new transnational spaces of power and action for diverse global political players, including individual states. Who or what will sustain this cosmopolitan integration among states? It will certainly be

maintained by 'national' calculation on the part of states and governments concerned (as realism in political science asserts), though one changed to its core by a *cosmopolitan supplement*. This is ultimately to everyone's benefit, because only thus can global problems, which are also national problems, be, if not solved, then at least reined in within expanded national political spaces. The creation of international organizations presupposes that the United States will automatically limit its power as a strategy for the legitimation and cooperative expansion of power. Something new and different comes into being when states that stand in asymmetrical power relations cooperate to confront global threats within the rule of law and with respect for democratic values.

4 This is the reason why two institutions that have an affinity with each other – the EU and the UN – are so important for the effectiveness and legitimacy of global risk politics. The refusal of certain European countries and the UN Security Council to act as rubber stamps for US military unilateralism has not led to a loss of power of the EU and the UN, as some commentators suspected. On the contrary, both have gained in global credibility. The legitimacy of global risk politics rests essentially on a global division of powers between the ability to deploy military force and the procedural power of global public consensus. The autonomy of the EU and UN from unipolar US military power can equip the latter with the requisite legitimacy. The apparently necessary direct link between national power and national legitimacy in the national sovereignty paradigm is counterproductive at the global level. If the United States seeks agreement with the EU, it will maximize its chances of gaining UN support and as a result the political premium generated by the unanimity of the US, the UN and the EU.

5 Unilateralism is uneconomic. Cosmopolitan realism, by contrast, is also *economic* realism. It reduces and redistributes costs, not only because military expenditures are many times higher than the costs of a strategy of political prevention, but also because costs rise exponentially with a loss of legitimacy. Conversely, shared responsibility and shared sovereignty also mean shared costs. For example, it might be possible to fund the same US experts from the UN budget and to deploy them with the seal of international law. Such options of transnational politics are ruled out by national unilateralism. In other words, cooperation among states – an important component of cosmopolitan realism – is also good business.

8

Cosmopolitan Visions for Europe

The cosmopolitan vision teaches us that the microcosm and the macrocosm can no longer be separated. Simple questions, such as: 'What is a couple?', 'What is a family?' or 'What is a society?' no longer admit of clear answers because the social units in terms of which we used to think, and which continue to underlie our actions and our institutions, are becoming blurred and indistinct. The most local and the most global politics are alike confronted with an era of disorder, crises and ambivalence. Indeed, we do not even know whether the concepts 'disorder' and 'crisis' are the correct ones, because they hold out the false prospect of a return to normality that is precisely becoming uncertain. All of this now also applies to 'Europe' – that is the message of this book. However, the question which reality still poses even though nobody wants to ask it, much less to answer it, is not: 'What "is" Europe?' but rather: 'In which Europe do we want to live?' In fact, the European question, in all immodesty, is: 'In which world do we want to live and what contribution can Europe make to it?'

We have answered this question with the aid of the concept of cosmopolitanism and have reconstructed and criticized the process of Europeanization to date from this perspective. We have seen that three features are constitutive if a self-critical European cosmopolitanism is to serve as a model.

First, the European dream, the European miracle, is that enemies can become neighbours. The implicit lesson here is that the path leading to a cosmopolitan network of cooperating states presupposes not only political freedom, democratic institutions and a market economy, but also a new understanding of history. Democracy can only take root if we succeed in breaking open the national 'container' conception of history and replacing it with institutionalized forms of transnational memory in which the roles of victims and perpetrators are redefined through a systematic change in perspective. In a world in which ethnic conflagrations are everywhere erupting, or threatening to erupt, into war, we must pay heed to the maxim of cosmopolitan Europe that neither democracy nor peace nor security is possible in the long run without a concerted policy of reconciliation. This maxim essentially determines the security policy of a European Empire with variable internal and external borders.

Second, the level of civilizational self-endangerment reached, and the degree to which this has permeated global public consciousness and people's everyday practices, makes two positions (until now the dominant ones) seem absurd, even dangerous: on the one hand, the *postmodern reaction* which dissociates itself from modernity's claim to rationality and control; and, on the other, the *posture of the first, straightforward modernity* that the civilizational self-endangerments can be mastered by the very methods of the first modernity (more technology, more market, more national controls, etc.) that gave rise to them. In this spirit, the 'European way' can be developed as a path of *reflexive modernization* that acknowledges *alternative modernities* against the background of different historical approaches to, and ways of dealing with, specific principles of modernity. This would represent an alternative to the 'American way', which globalizes the first modernity and categorically refuses to recognize other modernities.

Third, the dangers produced by civilization are two-faced. They give rise to transnational and even global publics and risk communities, in which contestation over solutions is possible because they defuse the claims to control of the national first modernity. A cosmopolitan Europe in this sense can use the legitimation potential of civilizational dangers before a global public to construct or strengthen the coalition of European and global civil society and cosmopolitan cooperating states. It is the *opportunities* of the global risk society which can found the synthesis of civil society movements and the European Empire of consensus.

In this chapter, we now want to apply the reflections developed above to the most important current problems of 'European integration'. The question is what 'Europe' can and will mean, what it could and should mean, and what it could achieve in an ambivalent world that has lost its coordinates. We will address these issues in a number of steps.

Three scenarios concerning the further development of Europe provide a starting point. Then we will address in detail the question of how a cosmopolitan Europe could be realized. To this end, we will depict four building blocks of a European cosmopolitanism – namely, civil society, democracy, differentiated integration and the renewal of a transatlantic security community – in greater detail. Redefining and reformulating national interests in a European cosmopolitan spirit is, as we have seen, a precondition for constructing a cosmopolitan Europe. This requires that we pose and answer the question of who defines Europe's cosmopolitan interests and cosmopolitan responsibility and what they entail. Finally, we must warn against a common overestimation of Europe. Even the cosmopolitan European Empire is not a machine for producing global happiness but is marked by contradictions, ambivalences and paradoxes. In the concluding section, we will at least address some of the resulting dilemmas, though we cannot resolve them.

1   Three scenarios of the future Europe

How should the European project proceed from here? How will it cope with its internal tensions and conflicts? Will it succeed in integrating the twelve new member states politically and economically? Will the new constitution, should it materialize, improve the scope for action of the institutions; and could the EU survive if the constitution actually fails? What role will Europe play in a new global order? And, not least, how should Europe respond to the environmental, economic and terrorist perils of the global risk society? We want to make an initial approach to these questions with the aid of three scenarios through which the possibilities for the further development of Europe can be staked out. These scenarios, although fundamentally different from one another, rest on two assumptions justified in detail in the previous chapters. They assume, first, that Europe can no longer proceed on the basis of business as usual. Europe is changing – indeed, Europe must change! The direction of this change and its goal – this is the second assumption – remain open. Europe's future is not pre-programmed. The internal and external dynamics of Europeanization cannot be brought to a standstill.

The decay scenario

The decay scenario assumes that the EU is collapsing under its internal and external contradictions. On this scenario, the EU would not succeed in integrating the new Eastern European member countries economically, in advancing the 'positive', market-correcting integration of the Community and in reforming and democratizing the European institutions. The result would be that the neoliberal market logic would hollow out the national welfare states and that the political forces which advocate a renationalization of politics would gain new adherents in both the 'old' and the 'new' member states.

European politics would become trapped in a *nationalistic vicious circle*. Strong nationalistic parties and movements would paralyse the European institutions and block supranational decisions. Moreover, this would be taken at the national level as an excuse to restore more powers to the member states. The irony is that this process of decay would probably be accelerated by a failure of the Constitutional Treaty rather than being stayed, as suggested by its critics in France and the Netherlands.

This process of internal disintegration would be favoured and reinforced by the fact that the EU member states are deeply divided over the goals and strategies of their foreign policy. There are three opposed camps: a 'continental European camp' led by France and Germany that wants to build the EU into a unified and independent power centre in global politics to compete with the United States and China; a 'transatlantic camp' led by Great Britain that conceives of the EU primarily as part of the 'Western community of values' under the leadership of the United States, and whose aim is to create a political counterweight to the supremacy of France and Germany within the Union; and a 'neutrality camp' consisting of a number of the smaller countries, such as Finland, Austria and Sweden, that defends the independence of the EU in foreign policy, though it also wants to deny it any independent role in global politics so as to prevent the large member states from dominating foreign policy as well, rather than just economic policy. As a result of these internal conflicts, the EU would ultimately fragment into a larger number of strategic state alliances and regional regimes with at best modest supranational powers.

The stagnation scenario

The stagnation scenario assumes that the EU will succeed in integrating the Eastern European countries into the Community economically and in maintaining a (more or less) functioning internal market. However, the greater heterogeneity in the ranks of the member states will make it impossible to agree on market-correcting policies at the European level. Any further deepening of integration, as well as any extension of the competences of the Community in the area of foreign and security policy, would be blocked by the member states on account of their divergent interests. The Constitutional Treaty, once enacted in a watered-down version, would not enable the national resistances to further integration to be overcome. The EU would be frozen in the condition of a neoliberal free trade zone lacking any fartherreaching political claims and with dubious democratic legitimacy. However, a father-reaching disintegration would be prevented not only by the economic advantages of a single market but also by the support in foreign policy offered by the United States, for whom the weakness of the EU in foreign and security policy provides the assurance that no competing hegemonic power can develop in Europe.

The cosmopolitanization scenario

Finally, the cosmopolitanization scenario is based on the assumption that Europe has arrived at a turning point at which conflicts over fundamental questions are becoming imperative. What holds a postnational Europe together and what contribution is it able and willing to make to the process of creating a new global system? One concern of cosmopolitan Europe will be to integrate the EU economically in the wake of the eastern enlargement and to liberate it from the fetters of the neoliberal internal market project. A further concern will be to lend it a distinctive profile and to strengthen it in the domain of foreign and security policy and transform it into a second global centre of power that succeeds in committing its ally, the United States, to a cosmopolitan global order, that is, one based on the recognition of otherness. Such a cosmopolitan Europe will not be free from contradictions, but it will find ways and means of dealing with these tensions and of preventing the Community from being fragmented and politically stymied by the unavoidable ambivalences of the second European modernity. However, this scenario presupposes that Europeans reinvent and reconstitute Europe at the beginning of the twenty-first century. The renewal of Europe is based on four pillars:

- first, strengthening a *European civil society* based on universally shared constitutional norms;
- second, the transition to a new *postnational model of democracy* that, instead of incapacitating the European citizens, accords them an active role in the European decision-making process;
- third, introducing a new *cosmopolitan approach to integration* that is no longer geared to 'harmonizing' rules and overcoming (national) differences but to acknowledging them;
- fourth, establishing Europe as the driving force of a global cosmopolitanism and as a member of a new transatlantic security community.

2   Reflexive constitutionalism: constitution and civil society in Europe

Cosmopolitan Europe needs a constitution! To preclude misunderstandings, it does not need a constitution because the European integration process would create a state – or, as some fear, even a 'superstate' – that would thereby acquire an independent source of legitimacy; nor does it need a constitution to finalize the integration process. Neither goal is compatible with the vision of a cosmopolitan Europe. Cosmopolitan Europe does not supersede the nation-states but recognizes and integrates them; and cosmopolitan Europe remains an open, variable and flexible entity that resists clear and final determination. From the perspective of a cosmopolitan Europe, therefore, two of the most important arguments that have been advanced in support of a European constitution completely miss the target.[1]

But why then does Europe need a constitution? From the perspective of a European cosmopolitanism, primarily for two reasons: first, to lay the normative foundation for *the constitution of a European civil society*; and, second, to *institutionalize the cosmopolitan regime* in European politics. What does this mean in more concrete terms?

As we have already explained, cosmopolitanism is based on two principles, namely, on the principle of the recognition of difference and on a minimum store of shared substantive and procedural norms. This store of shared norms directs the search for solutions to the two fundamental problems of cosmopolitanism, namely, the maintenance of social integration, on the one hand, and the effective protection of difference, on the other. Shared norms are supposed to prevent the recognition of difference from becoming a purely arbitrary matter and a source of disintegration; at the same time, they are supposed to protect those who are socially and culturally different from suffering unjust forms of homogenization and assimilation.

We do not need to spell out in detail here what this minimum store of norms should look like. The important point for the present is that this normative foundation *cannot* be traced back to a 'common origin' or to a shared 'Western culture'. These values must be derived instead from the conscious break with the national 'container' conception of history and from the self-critical commemoration of the Holocaust, on the one hand, and of Europe's colonial history, on the other. The experience of absolute negativity ('crimes against humanity') alone can establish substantive norms (human rights, conditional sovereignty).

The validity of the normative foundation of cosmopolitan Europe is at the same time tied to two general conditions: first, there must be mutual recognition (on the part of the states involved as well as their citizens) and, second, this recognition must be the product of a discursive process. The crucial point is that the process of founding a constitution then fulfils a dual function. It not only lays down shared norms for organizing a political community; through this discursive process, civil society at the same time constitutes itself as a political subject. The second aspect is of particular importance for our argument, and the procedure of formulating and agreeing upon a European constitution can also be critically elucidated in this context.

Although the Constitutional Convention represented a considerable improvement on the previous procedure of treaty revisions, the deficiencies of the latter could not be completely overcome. Despite attempts to open its deliberation to social groupings of various kinds, the Convention remained in its decisive stages essentially an exclusive club of dignitaries who exercised their functions almost completely unnoticed by the citizens of Europe. The findings of an opinion poll covering more than 16,000 citizens conducted by the European Commission in March and April 2003 – hence shortly before the conclusion of the deliberations of the Convention – tell a clear story. The result of the survey was that more than half (57 per cent) of the citizens questioned were *completely unaware* that the Convention was working on a draft constitution for Europe at all (see *Frankfurter Allgemeine Zeitung*, 18 June 2003: 2)!

Whatever one may think about the detailed shape of the European constitution, one thing is already clear: Europe has thus far recklessly squandered the opportunity to link the process of drafting a constitution with the activation and mobilization of a European civil society. The Convention could not prevent the strategies and power tactics which distorted the European project in the past from dominating the process of constitution founding as well. The whole procedure was thoroughly symptomatic of the European malaise. The participants did not conduct debates over political visions but engaged in the most petty quarrels over the weighting of votes, decision-making procedures and the division of powers; and in the end the whole array of techniques of power – threats, vetoes, extortions, etc. – were employed to break down remaining resistance. This spectacle had no need of the European citizens, even as spectators.

However, the national referendums on the Constitutional Treaty in France and the Netherlands clearly demonstrated that citizens do care about Europe, its policies, how it is organized and its future development. It would be a fatal mistake to place the blame for the failure of these referendums solely on national political rivalries or on citizens' ignorance concerning Europe. Rather, the French and the Dutch 'No' revealed a 'birth defect' of the European Constitution, namely its lack of public deliberation and citizens' participation. This birth defect can only be rectified, if at all, by the active involvement of European citizens in a European decision-making process, i.e., by a *pan-European* referendum in which the citizens of Europe would have to give *their* assent to *their* Constitution. In this way, the European Constitution could at least be freed from the blemish of being primarily the product of pre-democratic arcane diplomacy, rather than an expression of the democratic will of the European citizenry. Regardless of the prospects and the outcomes of such an enterprise, the strengthening of European civil society and the establishment of a European public sphere must be accorded a prominent place on the agenda of cosmopolitan Europe.

3 Cosmopolitan democracy: possibilities for legitimating the European Empire

From the outset, the process of European community-building suffered from a serious design flaw. The transfer of sovereign rights to the supranational level deprived democratically elected national parliaments of some of their control and decision-making powers, without ensuring in turn that the supranational institutions acquired adequate democratic legitimacy. There have been constant complaints about this 'European democratic deficit' in the past; however, it remains to be rectified. The powers of the European Parliament are still insufficient, although they have been extended several times, whereas the European Commission completely lacks democratic legitimacy and even the European Council enjoys only indirect democratic legitimacy.

The democratic deficit of the European policy process was always problematic; but it was accepted as long as the tasks of the EC remained narrowly circumscribed and all essential political decisions were taken at the national level. However, this situation became untenable with the transfer of additional powers through the Single European Act and the Maastricht Treaty. Moreover, the increasingly vehement public criticism in recent years clearly shows that further steps in the integration process can no longer be implemented without a concurrent democratization of the EU. Otherwise, the European project would be seriously impaired. This had already become apparent in the early 1990s. Towards the end of his second period in office, the former president of the Commission, Jacques Delors, remarked that the phase of 'benign despotism' in Europe was definitively over. It is no accident that the preamble to the Maastricht Treaty expresses not only faith in the fundamental principles of democracy but also the desire 'to enhance further the democratic and efficient functioning of the institutions'. However, this has remained an empty wish. The democratic deficit remains the Achilles heel of the European project.

Why is the democratization of Europe such a fraught endeavour? After all, the member states of the EU are all democracies, and the protection of human rights and the democratic organization of government are among the most important criteria for accepting a country into the EU. Under these circumstances, shouldn't democracy at the European level be a straightforward matter? Shouldn't the member states have a 'natural disposition' to democratize the EU? Clearly not, and there are at least two reasons for this. First, there is political opposition. The form of Europeanization pursued to date not only weakened the parliaments but also simultaneously strengthened the executives, both at the national and at the European level. The executives are the major beneficiaries of the transfer of power within Europe, and they occupy the control centre for institutional reforms. Hence, a democratization of the EU along the established path of treaty revision would presuppose something highly improbable, namely, the voluntary self-disempowerment of the various executives. Nevertheless, there is an additional, even more fundamental, reason for the difficulties facing a democratization of the EU: the need to rethink democracy in Europe from the ground up.

The fundamental problem of democracy in the EU resides in a twofold lack of conceptual clarity. First, it is unclear what kind of political authority actually exists in the EU, and hence *what* needs to be democratized; and, second, it also remains unclear which of the numerous models of democracy known to us best fits Europe, assuming that any of them fits, and hence *how* Europe should be democratized. We have already removed the first of these sources of unclarity with the aid of the concept of empire. Our thesis is that Europe is not, and it is not set to develop into, a state but a (cosmopolitan) empire and that this imperial tendency will become more, rather than less, pronounced in the future. Consequently, all reflections on the democratization of the EU must take this as their starting point. They must ask how the European Empire can be democratized.

To be more precise, they must ask whether the European Empire can be democratized at all. As is well known, empires are regarded as unsuitable for *any* form of democracy not only because of their high degree of concentration of power but also because of their specific organization of power. The principal evidence for this is the Roman Empire, which changed from a republic into a monarchy with the consolidation of imperial power. And it is no accident that the following questions have been asked with regard to American global domination: 'Can America remain a republic and a democracy if it becomes an empire? Or does the one preclude the other?' (Bender 2003: 251). These questions could be posed with even greater justification regarding Europe. Have the European states renounced democracy – unintentionally and irredeemably – in the process of constructing an empire? Did the political endeavours to rescue democracy in Europe from totalitarian and nationalistic excesses by using supranational institutions to tame politics lead to precisely the opposite result, namely, the weakening of democracy? These queries are clearly well founded. The problem of the democratic organization of the European Empire, however, does not result from the magnitude of its sovereign territory or the high level of concentration of ruling power, but from the peculiar way in which its sovereign territory is organized, on the one hand, and its specific power structure, on the other.

Fundamental to the problem of democracy in the European Empire is, first, the *asymmetry* of its constituent units. Europe, as we have seen, is not congruent with the EU; and, even within the Union, a variable geometry of memberships has evolved. The inevitable result is an asymmetry of rights and forms of participation among states. Not all the states, their governments and citizens integrated into this empire have equal rights; rather, rights and entitlements exhibit a whole variety of gradations. To put it bluntly, the European Empire is based on difference, it must be founded on difference and it must constantly produce and reproduce this difference. Democracy, by contrast, is based on equality; democratic participation can be realized only among equals, and the primary goal of democratic politics must, as a consequence, be constantly to produce and to guarantee equality.[2]

However, democracy in the European Empire still confronts a second structural problem, one which results from the peculiar way in which power is organized. Political power in the EU is not concentrated and centralized, as is assumed by the Hobbesian concept of absolute sovereignty, but is fragmented in various ways and distributed among numerous institutions and several levels of political decision-making. In most areas, political decisions involve a number of ministries in the member states, the Council of Ministers responsible for specific policy areas, the European Commission together with various cabinets and directorates general, the national parliaments and the European Parliament, not to mention numerous committees, subcommittees, working groups and task forces. Under these institutional conditions, it would be presumptuous to expect that the democratic sovereign, the electorate, should even be able to identify the responsible political actors and agencies, let alone exercise effective control over them. Even under the most favourable conditions, the European political process exhibits a structural gap in responsibilities that makes an effective exercise of control over political decision-makers by the citizens an unreasonable, indeed an impossible, expectation.

How is democracy possible under such conditions? How can appropriate avenues for political participation be established in these circumstances? And how can political authority be effectively controlled? The answer to these questions depends crucially on what normative standards one adopts. The history of political authority has generated an abundance of models of democracy that place a whole range of different requirements on the scope of political participation and control. The 'procedural minimal definition' of democracy (Collier and Levitsky 1997), which is frequently employed in research on democratic transitions, focuses primarily on free and fair elections under conditions of universal suffrage in combination with guarantees of civil liberties (i.e., freedom of speech, assembly and association). As the 2004 elections to the European Parliament have shown, on such an understanding of democracy the EU would undoubtedly already be a fully developed democracy, one which might even have to be rated as superior in this respect to some of the new member states and accession candidates. The picture already changes considerably when the threshold is raised further and an 'extended procedural minimal definition' of democracy is adopted which demands, in addition, that governments elected in this way must also possess effective governing power. In the EU, governmental functions are not only highly fragmented and dispersed among numerous institutions; the member states also place various restrictions on them and, finally, the members of these institutions are not elected by the European Parliament. The democratic character of the EU would be extremely doubtful judged by this criterion. If we set the threshold even higher and adopt the usual demand on parliamentary democracy – namely, that elected governments should be entirely responsible to parliament – then the EU clearly fails to measure up to the standards of a modern democracy. Moreover, neither the EU nor its member states satisfy more demanding models of participatory democracy.

There is broad agreement in research on Europe that the quality of democracy within the EU should be measured by the elevated standard attained by the member states before the eastern enlargement; and there is equally broad agreement that the EU does not satisfy these requirements.[3] Fundamental disagreement breaks out, however, once the question is posed as to how the democratic character of the EU can be enhanced. Two main *democratization strategies* can be identified:

- the first strategy, that of parliamentarization, seeks to democratize the EU primarily by extending the rights of the European Parliament. It is based on the model of parliamentary democracy and wants to apply this as far as possible to Europe. Its ultimate goal is to establish a bicameral parliamentary system of the kind familiar from federal states (see Maurer 2002; Rittberger 2005);

- the second strategy attempts to close the democratic deficit with the help of new models of 'postnational' or 'post-parliamentary' democracy. It takes its orientation from a variety of different concepts, such as 'associative democracy', 'deliberative democracy', 'participatory democracy' and 'consociational democracy', which it combines into various new models of 'cosmopolitan democracy' (see Greven and Pauly 2000).

Here we want to defend the claim that not only the EU but also the European Empire can indeed be organized in a democratic way, but that the Westminster model of parliamentary-majoritarian democracy is inadequate in this regard. The models of 'postnational' or 'post-parliamentary' democracy which have been proposed thus far are also insufficiently attuned to the peculiar features of the European Empire. They either focus too much on the global 'cosmopolis' and take insufficient account of the peculiar circumstances of Europe, like the concept of cosmopolitan democracy developed most notably by Daniele Archibugi and David Held (see Archibugi and Held 1995; Held 1995, 2004; Archibugi 2003a), or they are too fixated on the EU, and hence take insufficient account of Europe's imperial character (e.g., Abromeit 1998; Schmitter 2000).[4] However, in what follows we will take these concepts as a point of departure and argue that the democratization of Europe must pursue four main strategies: (1) *intervention* strategies; (2) *inclusion* strategies; (3) strategies of *recognition of otherness*; and (4) *control* strategies. In short, the democratization of Europe must combine elements of democratic cosmopolitanism with the special requirements for controlling imperial power in Europe.

Intervention strategies

The key to the democratization of Europe resides in reconfiguring political participation from the principle of representation to a new principle of participation, i.e., the *principle of intervention*. This takes account of the fact that the preconditions for applying the principle of representation in the European Empire cannot be realized sufficiently. Previous attempts to democratize the EU have demonstrated this clearly. They essentially pursued a dual strategy designed to strengthen the principle of representation. On the one hand, the principle of political representation was reinforced by direct elections to the European Parliament and the extension of its legal powers; on the other hand, it was complemented by additional forms of representation, namely, functional representation in the Economic and Social Committee and numerous consultative bodies and territorial representation in the Council of Ministers and the Committee of the Regions. However, this dual strategy has not achieved its goal. With the exception of the Council of Ministers, functional and territorial forms of representation have remained largely irrelevant in the EU. And although the power of the European Parliament has increased, its democratic legitimacy has not. As the participation in European elections has made clear, the European Parliament still lacks the recognition of the citizens as a site of legitimate representation of *their* political goals and interests. It is seen as part of the Brussels power apparatus and not as an effective instrument of citizen control. And this perception is completely correct. Who even knew the name of their European representative before the last European electoral campaign? Who felt adequately informed concerning their activities? Granted, these are chronic problems of all parliamentary democracies. Nevertheless, they acquire additional weight at the European level because the distances from the citizens are especially large. Moreover, the intermediaries which are supposed to bridge these distances in national parliamentarism (inadequate though they be) – namely, the political parties and the political public sphere – are especially weak at this level. This leads to the schizophrenic situation that European elections remain dominated by national political forces and tend to be misused as 'second-order national elections' (see van der Eijk and Franklin 1996), while the members of the European Parliament nevertheless continue to work primarily at the European level – at a great distance from their voters, the national parties and the national parliaments.

But aren't these transitional problems? Isn't the low turnout in European elections simply an expression of the weakness of the powers of the Parliament? Why should the European citizens vote for a parliament that cannot even elect a government? And won't the legitimacy of the European Parliament necessarily increase in tandem with its powers? Those who argue in this way overlook the institutional peculiarities of network power in the European Empire. Due to the distribution of power among several independent levels of decision-making, the European Parliament could control at most only part of the whole decision-making process. As a consequence, the democratic control of European politics by a European Parliament is subject to structural limits that are to a large extent independent of its range of powers. More than that, even a European Parliament equipped with the maximum possible powers would be made responsible for political decisions that it can control only to a limited extent.

In these circumstances, the parliamentarization strategy necessarily leads to a dead end. The European democratic deficit can be eliminated only if the citizens are granted the possibility of intervening directly in the European political process. The introduction of direct forms of political participation is the key to the democratization of the EU (see Grande 1996, 2000b; Zürn 1996; Abromeit 1998; Hug 2002). This does not mean the total replacement of an indirect, representative democracy by a Rousseauean form of direct democracy. Rather, it is a matter of creating independent possibilities of articulation and intervention for the citizens that complement existing institutions of parliamentary democracy. The most important means to this end are *Europe-wide* referendums. If we really want to democratize Europe, there is no way around their introduction. In this way, not only can the distance between the European institutions and the European citizens be bridged and control over European politics improved; it is also likely that the deliberative processes set free by such referendums will enhance the political integration of Europe 'from below'. Properly designed, referendums could develop a considerable 'community-creating potential' (Zürn 1996: 49), and contribute to the strengthening of Europe 'from below'.

However, not all referendums are alike (Butler and Ranney 1994; Gallagher and Uleri 1996). If Europe is to be strengthened rather than weakened by referendums, they will have to satisfy at least five conditions.

1   They must be genuinely *European* referendums and not a series of unco-ordinated national referendums, as in the case of the ratification of the Maastricht Treaty, the eastern enlargement or the Constitutional Treaty. In this way, the danger that referendums will be misused for national purposes, or even for renationalizing politics, can be minimized.

2   The issues to be decided upon in European referendums should not be restricted. It should be possible to hold them on *any issue* proposed by a qualified number of European citizens. In order to ensure that initiating a referendum already becomes a process of transnational deliberation, however, a referendum initiative should have the support not only of a minimum number of citizens but also of citizens from a sufficient number of states.

3   European referendums should be initiated by the citizens as a general rule, not by supranational institutions, such as the European Commission, or by national governments, in order to minimize the danger of their being instrumentalized for European power games.

4   The results of European referendums should be *binding* for the suprana-tional institutions. They should confer effective decision-making power on the European citizenry; citizens should not appear as mere petitioners, as envisaged by the Constitutional Treaty.

5   The supranational institutions should retain the *possibility of reacting* to the results of a referendum and integrating them into their own proposals. Thus referendums should not merely be blocking mechanisms but also have the potential to initiate political learning processes.

European referendums, conceived in this way, could serve as effective instruments for transforming the European citizens from passive objects into the active subjects of European politics. The provisions of the treaty estab-lishing a Constitution for Europe concerning the introduction of European referenda by no means satisfy these requirements. Article 47, in which the EU commits itself to the principle of 'participatory democracy', envisages only an extremely vague and non-binding right of the European citizens to take initiatives. It states: 'Not less than one million citizens who are nationals of a significant number of Member States may take the initiative of inviting the Commission, within the framework of its powers, to submit any appropriate proposal on matters where citizens consider that a legal act of the Union is required for the purpose of implementing the Constitution' (Art. I-47, 4). Regardless of how these provisions are concretized, they will not confer effective decision-making power on the citizens of Europe.

Given all of this, one should not forget, of course, that any such activation of the citizenry can be a double-edged sword. As the record of national referendums demonstrates, a referendum can function both as a source of political innovation and as a conservative, conserving element. Their concrete use would determine which direction the further development of the European Empire would take and whether European cosmopolitanism assumes repressive or emancipatory features.

Inclusion strategies

However, European referendums as the central element of a strategy of 'subpolitical' intervention have a defect that they share with the elections to the European Parliament, namely, that participation is restricted to EU citizens. Hence, they cannot overcome the asymmetry of rights and opportunities to participate within the European Empire; on the contrary, they threaten to exacerbate it further. For now, it is no longer merely a question of abstract rights but of concrete opportunities to participate that are granted to some but denied to others. This problem cannot be solved within the logic of political authority of the European Empire; but this does not mean that existing inequalities must simply be accepted as a matter of fate.

If the European Empire is to be reconciled with the postulates of cosmopolitan democracy, then intervention strategies must be supplemented by inclusion strategies. In short, we must find ways of including those who are at present excluded and of counterbalancing unequal participation opportunities. Such inclusion strategies could start within the EU and its institutions as well as outside them. In the former case, the idea would be to create participation and involvement opportunities for the citizens, civic associations, parties and governments of countries located in the empire's external power zone. The European Convention on a constitution could serve as a model here, for it expressly included representatives of the accession countries. Another institutional platform could be the Council of Europe with its forty-six member states. What is to prevent its institutions and procedures from being extended so that it can function as an effective link between the EU and its external power zones? A further possibility, at times already realized, would be to include civil society groups from non-member states in the deliberations and hearings of the EU institutions.

However, inclusion strategies need not be based solely on the receptivity of the EU institutions to the aspirations of external actors to participate. They can also gain a foothold within the countries of the external power zone themselves. Through strategies of deliberate self-inclusion, the citizens of the non-member countries and their governments can define themselves into European politics, as it were – they can contribute to constructing Europe by bringing their vision of Europe into the construction process. Here, too, there are numerous possibilities, ranging from public debate and mobilization to diplomatic intervention. The decisive issue in all of them is to counteract the exclusive 'either/or' logic of EU membership. One does not become a member of Europe, of the European Empire, only through formal membership in the EU, but also by actively defining oneself into Europe.

Strategies of recognition of otherness

Cosmopolitan democracy is faced with yet another problem, however. In contrast to liberal models of democracy, it cannot rest content with according equal participation rights. The latter cannot be fully realized within the asymmetrical power structure of the European Empire in any case. A Europe of difference must, in addition, give effect to the recognition of otherness through democratic procedures. Granting equal rights of participation is undoubtedly important in this regard but it is not sufficient. Cosmopolitan democracy must at the same time ensure that this formal equality is not used to eliminate substantial differences – i.e., to destroy differences that ought to be preserved.

Here, the most serious danger is posed by a procedure that is regarded as being fundamental to democracy, namely, majoritarianism. As is well known, the strength of the majoritarian principle resides in the fact that it can be applied in a whole variety of ways and is extremely undemanding from a procedural point of view. It requires in the first instance nothing more than mutual acceptance of a couple of universal political norms designed to ensure that all participants abide by the (commonly agreed-upon) rules of the game governing the acquisition and exercise of political power. The obvious drawback of the majoritarian principle for our purposes is that it is insensitive to difference: a majority is a majority! However, the majoritarian principle can serve as a source of legitimacy only if majorities can change and majority decisions can be reversed. Where this is not the case, where structural majorities develop or irreversible effects are generated, the majoritarian principle exacerbates political conflicts instead of founding legitimacy. A cosmopolitan Europe is vulnerable to just this danger.

Consequently, cosmopolitan democracy in Europe needs strategies for recognizing otherness that restrict the use of majority votes as a decision-making procedure. The most promising alternative is to replace majority voting in all important political issues by a different decision rule, namely, the principle of consensus. This is the strategy employed by most socioculturally heterogeneous states in an attempt to guarantee the political recognition of difference – i.e., of minority positions – in political decision-making. Comparative research on democracy has shown that an overwhelming number of modern democracies have in the meantime supplemented, or even replaced, majority voting by a wide variety of consensual conflict-resolution procedures. As a consequence, they have mutated into forms of 'consensus' or 'negotiation democracy' rather than majoritarian democracy (see Lijphart 1984, 1999; Lehmbruch 2003).

This is of even greater importance for a cosmopolitan Europe founded on the recognition and preservation of difference than for any national democracy. In major political controversies, cosmopolitan democracy cannot operate on the majoritarian principle but must seek consensus. This implies that the constant extension of majoritarian decision-making within the EU creates problems. Although it enhances the room for manoeuvre and decision-making capacity of the European institutions, this is increasingly achieved at the expense of the democratic legitimacy of decisions. Obviously, the EU is trapped in an effectiveness–legitimacy dilemma from which there is no easy escape. However, it is at least possible to mitigate this dilemma, and two such possibilities are especially compatible with the basic principles of cosmopolitan democracy.

- First, the introduction of a *'qualified right of veto'*, as proposed by Renaud Dehousse (1995: 133). On this proposal, veto rights would not be accorded to individual member states, as has been the case to date, but to a (small) group of (for example, three) states. This would have several advantages. First, it would prevent individual member states from blocking decisions and blackmailing other member states; but it would also enhance the deliberative moment in the decision-making process. Any side that wanted to make use of its right of veto, therefore, would have to convince at least some of the other states of the legitimacy of its cause.[5]
- Second, the introduction of a *'reflexive loop'* into the decision-making process, as suggested by Claus Offe (1982: 332). This means that the rule for arriving at a decision in a particular area would not be laid down in advance but would be deliberately left open. Those involved in the decision-making process could then decide on a case by case basis on how to arrive at the decision; and that means, importantly, whether to accord priority to the greater effectiveness of a decision-making process or to its legitimacy. In this way, at least the either/or dead end – either majority decisions or unanimity – in which the debates over reform of the EU constantly end up, could be avoided.

Control strategies

At least some of the problems of democracy within the European Empire – in particular, those of participation and integration – could be solved by enhancing citizens' opportunities for political participation, the inclusion of non-members and the recognition of difference in decision-making procedures. This is not enough, however. It would be presumptuous to assume that adequate control over the political power which is constituted and organized within the European Empire can be secured in this way. Neither the European Parliament nor the national parliaments – not to speak of the citizens – are in a position to do this on account of the multi-level structure of the European Empire. How, then, can political authority within the European Empire be controlled? How can we prevent an anonymous, impenetrable and uncontrollable power complex from emerging within Europe? The answer is through new strategies of control, more specifically, by reconfiguring the control principle from individual to *institutional* control and by expanding and optimizing institutional controls within the EU political system. The logic of this principle of control was trenchantly formulated as early as 6 February 1788 by James Madison, in the 51st Federalist Paper. There, Madison outlines the basic features of a system of overlapping powers whose goal is the reciprocal institutional control of power. The problem of the misuse of governmental power should be solved by 'so contriving the inner structure of the government as that its several constituent parts may, by their mutual relations, be the means of keeping each other in their proper places' (Madison 1941: 336). Madison summed up the principle underlying his reflections in the pithy formula: 'Ambition must be made to counteract ambition' (ibid.: 337).

Our argument is that this basic principle not only must be made a central pillar of a European model of democracy, but at the same must time serve as one of the guiding principles for institutional reforms. For this purpose, it can be expressed more concretely as at least two principles:

- first, the principle of equality of institutional power, which states that the most important institutions of the EU system of governance should possess at least approximately equal ranges of powers in order to facilitate effective mutual control;
- second, the principle of institutional interdependence, which states that no relevant institution should be located outside of the system of mutual institutional control of power.

In this context, the proposal to extend the powers of the European Parliament and to expand the existing system of institutions into a bicameral system – as proposed, among others, by Joschka Fischer in his Humboldt University speech (see Fischer 2000) – makes a lot of sense. For, as is well known, a bicameral system is an effective option for counterbalancing and holding in check the interests of different political units, especially in federal systems. This is not to suggest that the establishment of a bicameral system alone would represent an optimal solution to the problem of the division and control of powers within the European political process. The system of European institutions as a whole must be examined with a view not only to improving the effectiveness of decisions, as was the case in the recent constitutional deliberations, but also to optimizing institutional controls within the European multi-level system.

The foregoing reflections suggest that the democratization of the European Empire is no easy task. Yet, it is neither impossible nor utopian. In principle, the European Empire is entirely compatible with the requirements of modern democracies; however, none of the proposals for solving the European democratic deficit which have dominated the political reform debate to date goes far enough. A 'full parliamentarization' of the EU, the extension of majority decisions and greater transparency of decision-making procedures alone are insufficient. On the contrary, in this way the existing problems would merely be displaced or even exacerbated. The transition to cosmopolitan democracy in Europe cannot be achieved by pursuing the well-trodden paths of business-as-usual democratization or simply by sticking with the established, conventional national models of democracy. It calls for radical institutional and procedural innovations – Europe cannot be reinvented without the reinvention of democracy in Europe.

4 The principle of the cosmopolitan integration of Europe

Reinforcing democracy in Europe does not go far enough. Cosmopolitan Europe has a chance only if the EU, which forms the institutional core of the European Empire, is made receptive to a new philosophy of integration that accords with the idea of *cosmopolitan integration*, both internally and externally. The principle of cosmopolitan integration modifies and reinterprets the highly creative, persistent tension between unity and diversity, which runs through European history (Le Goff 2003: 168; Reinhard 2002: 613ff.), for the challenges of the interdependent world. Within the European Empire, cosmopolitan integration, as differentiated integration, serves as the counter-principle to the dominant principle of European integration, the so-called Community Method (dimension of internal integration). Towards the outside, it regulates the expansion of the European Empire and its integration into the political problem-solving contexts of world risk society (dimension of external integration). Thus, the processes of internal and external integration are fused in the principle of cosmopolitan integration, in which the ambivalence of European cosmopolitanism becomes particularly apparent.

Internally, differentiated integration overcomes the fatal alternative between European and national integration. *Unity* is no longer confused with *uniformity*; precisely the converse holds, namely, Europe's strength is seen to reside in the fact that it acknowledges its own differences. This poses the question: Doesn't embracing a confusing multiplicity of speeds and special alliances with shifting compositions lead of necessity to the self-obstruction of Europe, or even to its disintegration? Our answer to this problem is 'external integration'. This conceives of the expansion of the EU as a part of the expansion of the shared power to cope with global risks, where the point is that external integration both enables and limits differentiated integration. In what follows, we will outline these two sides of the argument (and the tension between them).

4.1　Internal integration: the principle of differentiated integration

A brief examination of the history of the process of European integration shows what is meant by – or, better, what cannot be meant by – differentiated integration. For many years, the latter primarily took the form of the *abolition of difference*. The model of European community-building was – and remains – 'uniform integration': national regulations are 'harmonized' by being replaced by uniform European regulations. In its pure form, uniform integration means that: 'A community regulation is applied by *all* member states *at the same time* and with *the same technical content*' (Scharrer 1984: 12). The 'everybody or nobody' principle holds: 'Either all member states march together and in step along the path towards integration or they abandon a Community regulation altogether.' To put it bluntly, this means: 'Better a bad regulation for all member states than a better one for just some' (ibid.: 5, 12). Clearly, this observance follows the logic of exclusive disjunction: *either* a single European regulation *or* different national regulations.

This 'harmonization policy' confuses unity with uniformity or assumes that uniformity is a necessary precondition for achieving unity. Unity in this sense became the highest regulative principle of modern Europe. The principles of classical constitutional law were simply applied to the European institutions. The institutional reality of the new Europe which resulted was measured by the extent to which this uniformity through harmonization was successfully achieved in all policy domains, the Common Agricultural Policy, market regulation, competition policy, environmental policy, research policy and many others. The more successfully EU policy operated under this primacy of uniformity, the greater the resistances it inspired and the more apparent its counterproductive effects became.

Cosmopolitan integration, by contrast, is based on a paradigm shift resting on the principle that *diversity is not the problem but the solution*. Affirming cultural distinctiveness rescues Europeanization from the stigma that the individual countries and regional identities must commit 'cultural suicide', as it were, if they are not to count as troublemakers within the EU. This fear of being condemned to self-destruction provoked by the Europe of harmonization is overcome and is replaced by the promise of finding one's own difference affirmed in the difference of others. Cosmopolitan integration means that you do not have to betray yourself in order to become a European; rather, you are a European because you acknowledge the profusion of multiple identities even in your own social environment!

Associated with this is a series of 'liberations'. In particular, the EU itself is liberated from the drudgery of founding unity. The confusion between unity and uniformity contributed essentially to the legendary caricature of Europe according to which, for example, the mania for regulation emanating from Brussels meddled with the resin content of the Greek wine retsina until it became flat, dull, 'uniform' and ultimately tasted of nothing at all. More precisely, the compulsion to uniformity has bequeathed three problems to the European integration process:

- first, the *problem of over-integration*: due to the compulsion to integrate that is built into the Community Method, areas are brought under the control of the Community and rules are standardized in which harmonization and European cooperation is not appropriate in all member states;
- second, the problem of deformed integration: because of the compulsion to achieve consensus inherent in the Community procedures, agreements often represent the lowest common denominator among participants and the results are more often than not 'suboptimal policies' (see Scharpf 1988);
- third, the problem of under-integration: in areas in which individual member countries are either unwilling or unable to accept Community policies based on the principle of uniformity, there is the danger that the potential for cooperation between the European states is not completely exploited.

Briefly, Europe suffers from the fact that there is at once too little and too much European policy and too much of it is bad. And although it may sound paradoxical, with progressive deepening and enlargement, the EU with its rigid model of integration is in danger of becoming a *brake* on further integration and cooperation in Europe. Europe is obstructing Europe!

The EC/EU has hitherto had two main 'safety valves' in dealing with the problems generated by the Community Method in ways favourable to integration and cooperation: internal differentiation and externalization. However, the first avoidance strategy, namely, internal differentiation, initially featured only in the form of innumerable exceptional permissions, saving clauses, interim regulations and postponements for individual member states. These deviations from the rule enable the claim to uniform regulation to be upheld in principle, although it was actually implemented only at a low level (see Grabitz and Iliopoulos 1984). The other avoidance strategy is externalization, in other words, cooperation outside the Community framework. The EU member states employed this in numerous forms from the outset to evade the pressures towards integration and consensus within the European Community.[6] In this way, an institutionally and geographically highly differentiated network of cooperation between states was erected around the European Community. It differed from community-building in two principal respects: first, it respected the sovereignty of the European nation-states, for these forms of intergovernmental cooperation did not require a transfer of powers to supranational institutions; and, second, it was highly flexible in its geographical scope and took into account the marked variations in the willingness and ability of the European states to cooperate across policy areas.

Thus, Europeanization was shaped from the outset by a *tension between integration and expansion*, and hence always (and not beginning with its various enlargements) had an imperial tendency, even though this was certainly not intended by the protagonists of European integration. What is more, the European Empire is in a sense the unintended product of a process of European state-building that was flawed in its conception and was condemned to failure. If we want to understand the history of European integration, we need to grasp the following paradox: the founding fathers of the European Communities (Monnet, Hallstein) wanted a European (federal) state and created – as a side effect of their policy – an empire.

But wasn't this imperial tendency reversed with the expansion of the powers of the EU and with its various stages of enlargement? Isn't the EU absorbing the competences of its member states, as well as the intergovernmental alliances and unaligned states that have emerged beside it and along its borders? Isn't the end state of Europeanization, therefore, a European federal state, whereas the imperial phase represents just a brief interlude?

Those who argue in this way overlook two things. First, they ignore the fact that even the new Europe, with its twenty-seven member states, is not in a position to solve the problems of world risk society unilaterally and to exert complete control over the zones of insecurity along its borders. The pressure towards imperial expansion, towards *external imperialization*, may have weakened with the eastern enlargement, but it has not disappeared. But those who argue in this way also overlook something else. Now that the others who were previously excluded have been included, the 'either/or' approach to integration in the EU has finally run up against its limits. The tension between integration and expansion has not been overcome but rather has been internalized, and a process has been instituted that could be called *internal imperialization*. There are two reasons for this internal imperialization of the EU. On the one hand, with the progressive deepening of the integration process, the hitherto established approach of 'uniform integration' is overtaxing the *will* of the member states for standardization, which means nothing other than the renunciation of national particularities, identities and traditions. On the other hand, this approach tends to overstrain the *ability* of the individual member states to participate in uniform European policies and to apply uniform European rules.

As we have seen, there is nothing new in the practice of differentiated integration in Europe; rather, it has shaped Europeanization from the outset. As a political concept, by contrast, differentiated integration was only worked out in the latter half of the 1970s in an attempt to overcome the stagnation of the integration process.[7] It was rediscovered – hesitantly, because tainted with the stigma of being a highly problematic second-best solution – in the mid-1990s, when the Community undertook to bring its institutions, policies and procedures into compliance with the economic and monetary union agreed upon in the Maastricht Treaty and to prepare them for the imminent eastern expansion. In this context, the principle of differentiated integration was assigned the role of 'last resort' (Art. 43, 1); it was supposed to function as a 'rescue concept' (Janning 1998: 209), as the 'dynamic preliminary and intermediate stage towards complete integration' (Weinstock 1984: 352).[8] In a similar spirit, the concept of 'enhanced cooperation' was included in the Constitutional Treaty (Art. I-44). It is still viewed as a 'last resort' (Art. I-44, 2) which should only be used if other forms of cooperation cannot be realized within a reasonable period of time. However, the requirements and procedures for its utilization are now less demanding.

This is still insufficient. Our argument is that the principle of differentiated integration must be radicalized and extended in a cosmopolitan Europe. In developing and applying it, we should not take the traditional notions of uniformity within a European 'federal state' as our frame of reference; instead, we should take the irreducible diversity of the European Empire as our point of departure. We should regard difference not as a problem, as a disruptive factor to be minimized, but as a potential to be preserved and exploited. Moreover, we must overcome the 'EU-fixation' and 'EU-blindness' of European policy and conceive Europe within the context of the global risk society.

Therefore, the principle of differentiated integration must be developed in both directions. It must be conceived towards the outside as a strategy for enhancing the integration of Europe into new forms of transnational politics. Internally, the principle of differentiated integration is an indispensable precondition for realizing the recognition of otherness in a cosmopolitan Europe. Only in this way can two at first sight mutually exclusive demands be reconciled, namely, the recognition of *difference*, on the one hand, and the *integration* of the different, on the other.

How, then, can the claim to uniformity – in particular, to legal uniformity – which is constitutive for modern states, be secured in an integrated Europe without impairing the autonomy of its constitutive elements? Numerous answers of the most diverse kinds have been proposed to this question. The crucial point is that the potential of the concept of differentiated integration can be fully exploited only if it is spelled out completely in both of its dimensions, namely, differentiation *and* integration. Thus, we can distinguish two principal varieties of differentiated integration.

- First, forms of *difference-friendly integration* (for example, the principle of mutual recognition, procedural integration). Here the claim to complete integration is upheld but is put into effect in ways sensitive to difference; thus, it is more tolerant towards national, regional and local peculiarities than the usual harmonization approach.
- Second, forms of *integration-friendly differentiation* (e.g., functional differentiation, geographical differentiation). Here the claim that all member states must accomplish everything simultaneously is abandoned. Integration is restricted accordingly and the claim to complete integration is subjected to spatial, temporal and material restrictions.

We would like to illustrate this with three examples: (1) the principle of mutual recognition; (2) the method of open coordination; and (3) the concept of variable geometry.

1 The *principle of mutual recognition*, which has hitherto been applied primarily in regulatory policy, is based on the principle of the *qualified* recognition of difference (see Scharpf 2003: 242ff.). In this case, the EU renounces the aspiration to harmonize national regulations completely at the European level and allows national regulations to be maintained on the condition that they satisfy specific requirements stipulated at the European level. Among the latter is the requirement that they be compatible with each other and satisfy the functional demands of European regulation. In this case, the member states commit themselves to recognizing their respective national regulations and thus to Europeanizing them. In this way, it becomes possible in the area of regulative policy to arrive at cosmopolitan, i.e., *inclusive*, solutions, hence at regulations that satisfy both the requirement of *European* regulation and the desire to preserve *national* difference.[9]

2 The *method of open coordination* points in the same direction. It was agreed upon by the heads of state and government of the EU member states in March 2000 at their summit in Lisbon, initially for the area of employment and social policy, but in the meantime in an ever increasing number of policy areas (among others, education, health care, nursing and pensions).[10] The essence of this method consists in the fact that, although the formal competences for the individual policy areas remain the preserve of the member states, common guidelines are formulated at the European level which are supposed to be realized through 'soft', i.e., non-legal, steering mechanisms ('benchmarking', 'monitoring' and 'evaluation'). This takes place primarily outside of the formal Community framework. The aim is to make possible common European policies even where a further transfer of legal authority to the EU is unwelcome or unrealistic. The method of open coordination announces a new form of internal imperialization of the EU. Europeanization no longer occurs primarily by means of law and its goal is

no longer 'legal uniformity'; instead it occurs through informal pressures, self-accommodation and learning, and its goal is a politically 'effective unit'. From the perspective of European cosmopolitanism, such an approach to integration has obvious advantages. This method is extremely sensitive to national, regional and local differences because it places them under the protection of the sovereignty of the member states.

3 *Geographical differentiation* is at once the most important and the most controversial possible form of differentiation. Geographical differentiation is geared to the varying territorial scope of rules and policies. By contrast with the 'Community Method', rules and policies in this case do not hold for all, but only for states that expressly agree to them. This enhanced cooperation can take different forms, though the process of Europeanization has shown that the boundaries between them are fluid. Geographical differentiations can (a) occur in different power zones of the Empire (i.e., inside or outside the Community framework), (b) embrace a varying circle of members and (c) exhibit a variable time horizon (temporary or permanent). Using these differentiations, various models of 'tiered' or 'differentiated' integration can be constructed, among others the model of 'different speeds' (Tindemanns), the concept of an 'à-la-carte' Europe (Dahrendorf), that of 'variable geometry' (Delors) or the idea of a 'core Europe' (Lamers and Stoiber; Derrida and Habermas) (for early concepts of differentiated integration, see the survey in Scharrer 1984).

The best-known example of a variable geometry of European integration is the economic and monetary union, a form of differentiated integration within the Community framework, but involving just twelve (of the at the time fifteen) EU members. Participation is not completely open but is tied to commonly agreed-upon conditions (the stability criteria). The non-participation of Denmark, Great Britain and Sweden is formally only temporary but has no fixed time limit; these countries – as well as the new member states – can opt to join the economic and monetary union at any time as long as they have fulfilled the stability criteria. A second variant is the European agency for research coordination, EUREKA, which was established in the 1980s outside of the Community framework and at first competed with the research programmes of the EU. EUREKA's circle of participants extended from the outset beyond the EU and currently embraces not only all members of the EU but also countries such as Switzerland, Norway, Russia and Turkey. Finally, a third variant is the Schengen Agreement, which was initially negotiated outside of the European treaty complex by a handful of EU member states (Belgium, Germany, France, Luxembourg and the Netherlands). The Agreement has in the meantime been signed by twenty-eight states and implemented by fifteen, including, with Norway, Iceland and Switzerland, three non-members of the EU, whereas two EU member states, Great Britain and Ireland, have not signed the Agreement.

These examples show that the European Empire already exhibits a highly 'variable geometry'. The vision of a uniform Europe has long since been overtaken by reality, and from the perspective of European cosmopolitanism there are good reasons for thinking that this principle of integration will exert even more pronounced effects in the future. For what speaks against taking more account of the different geographical, cultural, historical and climatic conditions in an enlarged Europe by creating different zones of cooperation in areas such as agricultural, transportation and environmental policy (e.g., Western Europe, the Southern European Mediterranean countries, the Eastern European countries, the Northern European countries)? And couldn't European social policy become more responsive to the different 'welfare state models' in the Community and correspondingly become more differentiated?

In principle, there exist a multiplicity of possibilities for creating new, functionally and regionally based zones of cooperation between the EU and its member states – and beyond – as a way out of the dead end of the 'Community Method'. In this way – and only in this way – could the European Empire develop into a 'new large European stability zone' (Weidenfeld 2000: 6), assimilate its greater internal diversity and heterogeneity, and promote peace outside its borders.

If, during the 1950s, the existence of the United Nations and of the North Atlantic Alliance did not prevent the states involved from founding the EEC, the ECSC and Euratom, then likewise the existence of the EU should not prevent the states from creating regional subcommunities in the future. Efficient partial groupings will emerge within the large stability framework; they are already foreseeable through participation in the economic and monetary union or, in the future, in the defence union. In the final analysis, these subcommunities would represent a gain in capacity for efficient action that can no longer be achieved in an EU of the 28. (Weidenfeld 2000: 8)

En route towards this goal, however, we will have to clear away one thing above all, the 'notion of a federal Europe with state-like characteristics' (Weidenfeld 2000: 6).

However, differentiated integration has two sides that at first sight seem to conflict with each other. On the one hand, this principle holds cosmopolitan Europe together through the commitment to difference and constitutional tolerance; on the other hand, it splits Europe apart and could ultimately promote a movement of political movements which can agree on nothing, or it could be used as an excuse for reviving the old national power game within Europe, i.e., precisely what the philosophy of integration wanted to overcome. Without a doubt, the principle of differentiated integration, taken to an extreme, can end in disintegration. Hence, it must be restricted – but how? This is the question to which we will now turn.

4.2 *External integration: on the dialectic of differentiation and expansion*

Cosmopolitan integration, as we have seen, combines internal, differentiated integration with external integration. Our argument is that external integration unites, facilitates and limits differentiated integration. This holds in the twofold sense of cultural and strategic policy (on this, see also chapter 4, section 3.2).

Cosmopolitan integration, understood as external integration, means that the European outlook must be directed not only inwards but also outwards, because the external problems have long since also become internal European problems. The assumption that integration is only possible through demarcation has been shown to be questionable. Conversely, it becomes necessary to break with the primacy of domestic policy, to open up the national-historical self-understanding to the outside and to become practised in cultural and cognitive border-crossing. Processes of assimilation and translation between societies, ethnicities and religions must become an everyday affair, especially when it comes to guaranteeing the 'internal security' of both Europe and its member states. The more heterogeneous societies become, the more explosive living together becomes and the more important become such capacities for intercultural interaction. European integration oriented to uniformity and based on the false model of nation-like integration has hitherto failed to take this important but thorny question seriously.

In addition, there is the danger that the European vision will bring about a renaissance of the demarcation and exclusion of others by appeal to civilization. Seen through the conceptual lenses of civilization, others would be perceived from the outset as *collectively different* insofar as they enter the visual field only as part – and as prisoners – of the construct 'civilization' rather than as responsible agents acting on complex motives and interests who bother about the boundaries between civilizations, however they are defined, only to a limited extent. 'The step to the essentialization and ontologization of difference is then but a short one. In conflicts with people from different cultures and with their history, we would again find ourselves where we were during the period of colonialism and imperialism' (Wirz 2001: 491). Thus, the pressure to engage in intercultural interaction can lead to the very opposite – namely, anti-cosmopolitan eruptions – owing to the ubiquity of cultural and religious differences.

Thus, here, too, the question arises of what makes (internal and external) cosmopolitan integration *realistic*. All we can do at this point is to reiterate our answer – namely, the absence of satisfactory alternatives. There is simply no apparently provincial German solution to apparently provincial German problems any longer. Indeed, there is no provincial European solution to provincial European problems any more either, at least not if we take the challenges of world risk society seriously. Faced with the threat of terrorist attacks throughout Europe, even the earth-shattering disputes over milk quotas and the weighting of votes in the EU lose much of their relevance. At the same time – and this is the decisive point – it becomes apparent that unity can and must be achieved through the recognition of others rather than through uniformity.

A good illustration of this is the dispute over Turkey's prospective membership of the EU. Global, anonymously operating terrorist networks have made the latter necessary for domestic security in Germany (as in other member states of the EU) and Europe. Those who advocate purely 'domestic' responses to global terrorism, such as more restrictive immigration laws, reinforcing border controls or making national records and police files available for European exchange, are like those whose response to violence raging on the streets is to shut their blinds. To repeat, no provincial German or provincial European solution is possible if terrorists are determined to kill regardless of time or place. The only answer is to internalize the 'outside'. In the case of Islamic terrorism, this means that domestic security in Europe must be recovered through the experiment of a European-Muslim democracy in Turkey. A European continent that defined itself in anti-Turkish terms would become a hazard to itself.

But does Turkey have to become a member of the EU to achieve this? Hasn't it long since become part of the European Empire, if only of its external power zone, through its membership in NATO? And isn't Turkey's NATO membership founded primarily on the geopolitical security interests of the 'West' in any case? This is all true, but it fails to recognize the novelty of the new threats. The terrorist risks of world risk society can no longer be countered with military means and the old military alliances of the Cold War era. They call for a broader understanding of security – or, to be more precise, of insecurity. The question of the EU membership of Turkey must be answered in the context of the European Empire's extended security needs.

It is the internal operation of external pressure that fosters cooperation between the states, buttresses the Brussels institutions and imposes simplified decision-making procedures. The affirmation of the European Turkey, the affirmation of diversity, therefore, makes possible the differentiated integration of the EU through *external* integration.

Where do the integrating forces of external integration come from? There can be no doubt that the common strategic goals of a proactive world risk politics create the benefit of the transatlantic political alliance through which the national anxieties (and resistances) produced by the European experiment of a European-Muslim Turkey can be overcome. A Europe that openly embraces cosmopolitanism in this way could be sure of external integration, i.e., of the extension of its power through the United States (more on this later).

However, the courage needed to integrate Turkey into the EU in the face of fierce opposition in several member states makes clear that external integration depends in turn on pioneering strategies, and hence on forms of differentiated integration. If we uphold the rule that everyone must wait until all are ready to move, this will only maximize veto power and increase the likelihood that decisions will be postponed or blocked. Thus, the *logic of political mobilization* holds especially for a *political* Europe that has to prevail over blocking coalitions. A few states must take the initiative in order to drag along those who have their foot on the brake. This is exactly what Jacques Derrida and Jürgen Habermas (2003) had in mind with their plea for a 'core Europe'. What was problematic about their proposal was not the idea of a small group of states that are highly motivated to cooperate in pushing ahead with the European project; the main problem was the intention to position Europe as a counter-power to the United States instead of conceiving it as a transatlantic cooperating power. It remains true, however, that only an avant-garde committed to integration can break down Europe's national self-misunderstanding and open up a common transnational European space of action for all. 'There is no other way: two, three or four, even five or six governments must simply start with a policy designed to reflect the specifically "European"' (Hofmann 2004: 3; on this, see also chapter 5, section 5 above).

 5   Power and weakness in world risk society – Europe's cosmopolitan realism in a new world order

The reader may well wonder whether our arguments for a cosmopolitan Europe are nothing more than pious wishes in a world in which neither international norms, nor transnational cooperation, but military power seems to be the key factor and in which nation-states and their military capabilities are ultimately decisive. Doesn't the key to realizing a cosmopolitan Europe reside in constructing and extending its own military capacities, however paradoxical this may seem? Won't Europe have to become a military power if its civil power is to have worldwide impact? For neorealist political thinkers such as Robert Kagan (2002, 2003), the answer to these questions is obvious: the relation between America and Europe is marked by fundamental oppositions: 'The United States and Europe are fundamentally different today', he writes. He identifies two mutually reinforcing sources of these differences. The first is the growing power differential between Europe and the United States. They see the world from different perspectives, the United States from a position of strength, Europe from a position of weakness. Second, this power differential has opened up an 'ideological gap' between the United States and Europe: 'American military strength has produced a propensity to use that strength. Europe's military weakness has produced a perfectly understandable aversion to the exercise of military power' (Kagan 2002: 9). In Kagan's view, the problem is not a matter of temporary differences of opinion or the usual intergovernmental conflicts:

the problem is not Bush or any American president. It is systematic. And it is incurable. Given that the United States is unlikely to reduce its power and that Europe is unlikely to increase more than marginally its own power or the will to use what power it has, the future seems certain to be one of increased transatlantic tension. The danger – if it is a danger – is that the United States and Europe may become positively estranged. (Kagan 2002: 17)

From a 'realistic' perspective, there is only one solution to this problem, namely that Europe must enhance its military power. Such a strategy has hitherto failed not only because of the Europeans' lack of willingness fully to integrate their defence policies. In view of the restricted financial room for manoeuvre of the European states and the almost complete absence of supranational authorities empowered to make decisions in foreign and security policy, it is especially 'unrealistic'. However, the alternative solutions to this problem proposed by liberal and constructivist approaches remain extremely vague and anodyne (see Mayer, Rittberger and Zelli 2003).

If we want to solve this problem, we must first expose and criticize the *antiquated concept of power* on which realist thinking is based. Within this perspective, power is exclusively military power. Quite apart from whether such an understanding of power was ever adequate, it is certainly hopelessly obsolete in the era of world risk society with its global threats and interdependencies.

In the first place, 11 September 2001 is the Chernobyl of the military conception of power. The Cold War equation 'military build-up = security' no longer holds. Granted, dangers and insecurities are not a distinguishing characteristic of the second modernity. Human beings and cultures have been confronted by them throughout history. What is specifically new, what has first arisen with the terrorist dimension of world risk society, is that even the most powerful states are almost defenceless when faced with the attacks of unknown, anonymous, unpredictable and uncontrollable aggressors – in spite of their absolute military superiority. This undermines the neorealist premise: the strongest is no longer immune from attacks by the weakest.[11] Rather, the opposite holds: the weakest is strong enough to threaten the most powerful, richest, most secure – indeed, the only – world power. Even the most highly armed, most perfect military power in world history is helpless in the face of terrorist attacks for which the principle holds neither of deterrence nor that the enemy strikes from outside one's own territory (instead of operating simultaneously inside and outside of the society under attack). A world power could not increase its security even by conquering the most distant corner of the globe by military means; on the contrary, it would increase its vulnerability. This is already evident in the case of the 'defeated' Iraq. The institutionalized and perfected instruments of military power of the most highly armed state *fail* in the face of the terrorist threat. The global dangers of world risk society are destroying nothing less than the promise of security provided by military power on which the modern state was founded – namely, the greater its military power, the more powerful and invulnerable the state. Human beings and cultures have always been prey to paranoid fears; the historical novelty in the context of the dangers of world risk society is that this now also holds for state (mega-)power and for governments convinced of their own power.

2 Second, neorealism and its military autism of power are afflicted with a further birth defect. It assumes that law and legitimacy are founded on violence and consequently fails to recognize that, in world risk society, the sources of legality and legitimacy of power have been displaced from the national to the global level. This transformation must be understood as a paradigm shift from the first to the second modernity. On the one hand, the struggle against civilizational dangers becomes a basis of *legitimate* global power. In other words, in addition to the sources of legitimacy of authority identified by Max Weber which are all located in the context of the nation-state, in the era of global dangers the proxy struggle against the latter becomes a source of legitimacy of the transnational – no longer merely national – exercise of power and political authority. The beneficiaries are transnational advocacy movements, but also, for example, corporations that effectively criticize child labour and transnationalize labour rights, not to mention states committed to implementing global environmental norms, combating terrorist networks and opposing violations of human rights and genocides. On the other hand, the 'rule of law' in international relations acquires a novel, global effectiveness. This can be shown by the example of the human rights regime.

Over the past decades, the rhetoric and legitimacy-founding power of humanitarian law have grown exponentially. This can be seen from its spatial and temporal extension, from changes in the understanding of individual liberties and from new forms of institution-building. The human rights regime escapes the older territorial logic of nation-state law. In contrast to traditional humanitarian law, it no longer holds exclusively in times of war. On the contrary, it is now applied quite generally, in peacetime and across national borders, to internal conflicts within sovereign states. All of this finds expression in the new treaties, institutions, controls and tribunals, including the International Criminal Court. Consequently, the legitimacy of the exercise of transnational military power does not follow automatically from military strength. Indeed, just the opposite holds. It depends on compliance with the emerging global principles of law, consensus and consultation and on the associated procedures. Hence, global political power in world risk society does not derive from military strength, on the equation: the greater a country's military superiority, the greater its political power. Rather, only the ability to deploy means of military force coupled with the rule of law in the global arena generates political power.[12]

3 Third, those who try to follow the example of the United States and apply the national perspective to global problems (terrorism, disarmament,

climate change, etc.) become entangled in global interdependencies. National approaches for combating transnational terrorism – closing borders, patrolling harbours, increasing airline security, introducing new forms of 'homeland security' – literally do not go far enough. They represent the 'phantom reactions' of the national in an era in which the causes of the problems no longer conform to the national schema. If, in addition, the causes of terrorism, which are located outside of the national territory, are likewise combated with a national, i.e., a military strategy, and hence the world of states is deprived of cosmopolitan cooperative answers, then this is not a strategy of strength, but one of weakness. In other words, in world risk society military strength easily mutates into weakness because, instead of solving problems, it contributes to producing and exacerbating them.

Fourth, neorealism fails to recognize new power opportunities that result *not* from military strength but from the art of cooperation and the concerted exploitation of the new, non-military sources of legitimacy of global power. The dangers threatening states are in principle two-faced: they annul the boundaries between the national and the international, but at the same time also relativize the power asymmetry among states.[13] Even the most powerful nation in the world is powerless against this threat. Unilateral actions are ineffective or counterproductive. If states want to preserve and enhance their power, they must (a) cooperate, (b) negotiate international rules and (c) establish corresponding international institutions. In other words, because they want to survive, states must cooperate. However, permanent cooperation transforms the self-definition of states from the ground up. Their egoism to survive and to extend their power compels them to unite and transform themselves. National interests are maximized not through rivalry but through cooperation. Thus, there is a self-destructive way of pursuing national interests (national autism) and one which maximizes them (cosmopolitanism).

Fifth, world risk society demands a more complex understanding of state power in which the military components are no longer decisive although they continue to play an important role. It is also insufficient simply to distinguish between different dimensions of power (military power, economic power, cultural power), 'hard power' and 'soft power', as Joseph S. Nye (2002) proposes, and then to use these forms of power strategically to promote one's national interests, properly understood. Although these differentiations are important, this approach does not throw sufficient light on the interdependencies, the reciprocal limitations and the contradictions between these different forms of power. The key question is not even posed, namely, what are the sources of legitimacy, and hence the stabilizing factors, of global power? To what extent do the globalized rule of law, the publicly perceived civilizational dangers, their causes and originators, contribute essentially to the exercise of military power?

Sixth, Kagan's formula 'power and weakness' must therefore be applied differently if we are to understand the actual power relations between the

United States and Europe in world risk society. The world is not ordered in such a way that power and weakness can be ascribed consistently to one side or the other, power to the United States, weakness to the Europeans. On closer inspection, both sides are both strong and weak at the same time. Although the United States possesses the military capabilities, it lacks moral and legitimating power; the Europeans are militarily weak, but they possess the legitimating power of morality and law. This strangely complementary constellation of power *and* weakness on either side of the Atlantic cannot be changed so easily. Although it is unlikely that Europe will catch up with the United States in military terms in the foreseeable future, it is equally improbable – especially in light of the political fallout from the Iraq War – that the United States will be able to overcome its worldwide deficiency of legitimate authority.

The point is that this could provide the basis for a new 'transatlantic division of labour' (Maull 2003), a 'new transatlantic project' (Asmus and Pollack 2002): 'America urgently needs allies who can help to establish a workable international order. Conversely, for the foreseeable future America represents Europe's only realistic chance for a world order worthy of the name' (Maull 2003: 1476).

6   In the European interest: Europe's cosmopolitan interest and cosmopolitan responsibility

A new transatlantic division of labour also presupposes an answer to the question: What is the European interest? What is meant exactly when the old formula of 'European interests', which cannot be equated with the sum of the 'national interests' of the member countries and member governments, is again dug out? The question acquires urgency when, on the one hand, armed conflicts are escalating throughout the world and, on the other, European soldiers are being sent into action, whether under the aegis of NATO or, more recently, as part of a European operation in zones of conflict in Africa. Almost 9,000 German soldiers, for example, are currently deployed on a wide variety of missions in Bosnia, in Kosovo and Macedonia, in Afghanistan, in Uzbekistan and Georgia, in the Horn of Africa and in Kuwait, and now also in the Congo and Uganda. Thus Europe's national armies, including the Bundeswehr, are undergoing a latent, as it were, *internal* cosmopolitanization – 'latent' because the goals and interests underlying these military operations remain indeterminate or undetermined. Even the simple question 'What are German soldiers dying for in Afghanistan?' can no longer be answered in the customary categories of national patriotism. The fall-back formula that 'German security interests' are being defended in the Hindu Kush or in the Horn of Africa points not only to the constitutionally prescribed formula of 'national security interests' but also to the fact that, in the age of world risk society, even 'German security' issues have spread across borders, and hence are no longer territorially and nationally determined (neither at home nor abroad). Moreover, the decision concerning the deployment of troops is taken against the background of a peculiar vagueness and unacknowledged non-sovereignty. As the debate over the German government's refusal to participate in the Iraq War in the global public arena shows, 'unavoidable' pressures are developing. Refusal of a military engagement, by contrast, requires explicit legitimation, whereas there is at the same time a general expectation that a rejection is ultimately motivated not by legitimate but by egoistic national reasons.

Precisely insofar as a cosmopolitan Europe becomes a reality, we urgently require convincing answers to the questions: When does a cosmopolitan Europe want to undertake an intervention and when not? With what means, under what conditions – and under what conditions on no account? With which allies and for what goals? In which regions? To achieve what ends (for itself and for others)? And who is to decide how such an intervention should be undertaken? It will no longer be possible to postpone answers to these questions once the so-called European rapid strike force is ready for deployment. For then 60,000 troops will be available, a considerable force whose operational range is ultimately global in scope and which requires that the political goals and conditions under which it would be deployed be clearly defined. Europeans must take a clear cosmopolitan stand not only in foreign and security policy but also in global politics! Since the relation between the available capacities and possible occasions for deployment is, realistically speaking, approximately that of a drop to the proverbial bucket of water, we need a new European-cosmopolitan Magna Carta if we are to be able to justify positive or negative answers and the conditions underlying them. This is precisely what is lacking:

Europe's real Achilles heel is its deficiency of strategic thinking. There is no agenda to provide Europe with orientation in times of crisis and conflict. This holds as much for transatlantic conflicts as for the Middle East, for ethnic expulsions in the Caucasus and in Southeast Asia, for the Kashmir conflict and for state failure in Africa. Only when Europe succeeds in developing a culture of reflection on world politics will it acquire a distinctive profile and relevance. Europe needs a rational calculation of its global political interests. (Weidenfeld 2003: 21)[14]

The principles of European cosmopolitanism developed in this book provide five (provisional) standards:

1   European cosmopolitanism can no longer take its orientation from the principle of national self-determination and of 'nation-building' (which entails a multiplication of ethnic conflicts and national pseudo-sovereignties) but rather from the *principle of regional cosmopolitanization*

inspired by the model of cosmopolitan Europe itself. Cosmopolitanization cannot be pursued as an isolated strategy of individual states, however; it presupposes, rather, that various states and 'quasi-states' come to see themselves as collective cosmopolitan actors in light of their respective historical backgrounds and of shared conceptions of world risk society in the great meta-power game of world politics. Such new forms of collective actors beyond the state and civil society arise out of regional state alliances – 'networked state cooperatives' encompassing non-state global actors such as NGOs, international organizations, etc. Only in such transnational, but at the same time regionally circumscribed, state networks can the traumas of war and ethnic violence be overcome in the long run, thus providing the soil in which the principles of democracy can take root. Applied to the explosive Arab–Israeli conflict – as well as to Afghanistan, Iraq, Iran, etc. – this implies that European cosmopolitanism must seek a non-national, transnational conception that encompasses the whole region and orients its policy both independently and consensually.

2   Cosmopolitan Europe can bring its historical experience of how enemies can become neighbours to bear in the contest of voices. In other words, it can lend its voice to the priority of a *political*, as opposed to a primarily military, world risk politics and practise the politics and art of translation. Europe's cosmopolitan interest is also a limited self-interest to the extent that the resources of peacemaking and peacekeeping must be deployed with special concern for Europe's changing neighbouring states, that is, its actual and potential neighbours. There is, after all, a *principle of proximity*: the European Empire must be especially concerned with the successor states of the Soviet Union, the dual membership of Turkey, as well as with the eastern and southern Mediterranean countries, because its own security and the costs of waves of refugees, criminality, etc., are in play. 'Cosmopolitan responsibility' in this sense means that the European Empire of consensus unfolds its binding force through overlapping multiple memberships.

3   Cosmopolitan Europe strives for the recognition of global problems, especially in the dimensions of environmental, economic and terrorist threats. In so doing, it also acts completely 'egoistically' in the sense that, in this way, it opens up new global markets, sources of legitimacy and interdependencies. Threats are perceived not only as threats but also as sources and instruments for creating the legitimacies and institutions of a cosmopolitan order.

4   Cosmopolitan Europe negates the notions of a one-best-way modernity and of an American-way modernity and advocates the existence, recognition and fostering of *alternative* paths of modernity that remain interwoven with each other while respecting different historical backgrounds and situations. Closely bound up with this is the idea of a cosmopolitan democracy, that is, of a democracy that is valid not only for domestic

affairs of states but also for relations between states. Hence, there must be alternatives and oppositions on a global scale if the paradox of a democratic dictatorship in world society is to be avoided.

5   A Europe that wants to live up to its cosmopolitan responsibility will no longer block the recognition of others through a development policy of mere charity but will open itself up, and in particular its markets, to the products and initiatives of others. Therefore, Europe's contribution to a more just, and hence a cosmopolitan, new world order begins within Europe itself. It is a matter of overcoming economic and political – and narcissistic – protectionism. In Europe, being white means the privilege of not noticing that one is white. Colour-coded colour-blindness is the order of the day. Europe's at once white and colour-blind universalism exerts pressure on its ethnic and religious minorities to abandon the position of difference: the genuinely black European is the non-black; the genuinely Jewish European is the non-Jew; the genuinely Muslim European is the non-Muslim European. The good and true white European sees the other, the alien, as the universalized self – *that* is the essence of the closure to the world from which Europe must liberate itself if it is to become cosmopolitan.

7   Dilemmas of cosmopolitan Europe

In conclusion, we would like to raise the question concerning the *dilemmas* of cosmopolitan Europe which had been rumbling just below the surface throughout this book. This reflects an attempt to apply cosmopolitan realism to itself: the second modernity does not solve the problems created by the first modernity but it uncovers the resulting contradictions, ambivalences and paradoxes and it reveals new perspectives as well as their inbuilt dilemmas. This conforms to our understanding and practice of critical theory as self-critical theory. In this spirit, we want, if not to investigate, then to illustrate by way of example five closely interconnected dilemmas of cosmopolitan Europe: (1) the universalistic dilemma; (2) the integration dilemma; (3) the insecurity dilemma; (4) the boundary dilemma; and (5) the peace dilemma.

The universalistic dilemma

A question running through our whole argument is: How much universalism, and how much *critique* of European universalism, is required to make cosmopolitan Europe possible and to reinforce it? As we have repeatedly argued, universalistic basic norms, a universalistic minimum, is indispensable. However, this immediately throws up four extremely tricky questions.

1   How many such basic norms does cosmopolitanism require? How 'thick' and how strong must be the unifying bond of cosmopolitan norms? Do

they include substantial norms or are a couple of procedural principles sufficient?[15]

2   Which norms should be counted among the core basic norms of cosmopolitan Europe? Is the whole catalogue of basic values listed in the 'Charter of Basic Rights of the European Union' really necessary? Or mustn't these cosmopolitan norms be reformulated in any case in light of future enlargements of the EU?

3   Who decides on these norms? A convention, parliaments, the citizens? And how should they decide? Can these norms be adopted by decision at all or don't they have to prove themselves through their acceptance in daily practice?

4   How does European cosmopolitanism cope with those who reject and fight against it?

The initial reaction to the racist argument that those who are different are inferior, and hence cannot be members of the national community, is not that we should respect difference; the answer is rather a universalistic one, namely, that all human beings are equal and as such should enjoy equal rights. For example, Carl Popper in his book *The Open Society and its Enemies* (1945) updated Immanuel Kant's cosmopolitanism in this sense within the framework of political liberalism and, as a consequence, took on board the problem of Kantian universalism. Followed through to their logical conclusion, Kant's and Popper's universalism suppress diversity. In constructing a federation of republics, Kant reinforced uniformity and excluded states and individuals that did not conform to the template of the rational (world) citizen. In Kant's vision, there can be only *one* cosmopolitanism, because there is only one global community of human beings.

This raises the question: How many cosmopolitanisms are there? How cosmopolitan are the various world religions in theory and in practice? Moreover, we must ask: Is Kant's postulate that there can only be one cosmopolitanism still true today with respect to human rights? Is it possible to proclaim *human* rights, that is, rights for everybody, on the one hand, while accepting a Muslim, African, Jewish, Christian or Asian charter of human rights, on the other? Acknowledging the difference of others and respecting their history demands that we view them as members of one and the same humanity and not of another, second-class humanity.[16]

But isn't it also true that those who support the universal validity of human rights open up new horizons for state power in space and time? Existing frontiers between nations are undermined, states and NGOs who make themselves advocates of human rights meddle in what were previously 'internal affairs' of states, contest their claim to do what they like within their own territory, and hence interfere in the core domains of what used to be called 'sovereignty'. The human rights regime and empire-building complement each other so well that it would not be an exaggeration to speak of the emergence of a 'human rights empire'. The very moral superiority of the discourse on human rights can reinvigorate both a strategic-geopolitical and a moral imperialism.

The integration dilemma

In cosmopolitan Europe, the fundamental tension running through European history, which could only be repeatedly pacified through compromises specific to particular eras but never be really overcome, is breaking out in the new form. This tension is expressed in the question: How can we renegotiate and reconnect the polarity between unity and diversity in the cosmopolitan constellation? In this question there lurks an *imperial* dilemma of the post-hegemonic empire: Where are the limits of the controlled self-integration of states, regions, ethnicities and nations in the EU? What are the boundaries of differentiated integration, in particular if we consider that the perception and relevance of European inequalities might be aggravated by the collapse of borders? And how will the losers in the process of Europeanization be integrated?

Looking outwards: How could the United States be persuaded to engage in a new transatlantic give and take? Doesn't this presuppose that the United States would grant the Europeans a certain amount of influence over how American power is exercised? And mustn't the Europeans in return use this influence wisely by not playing the counter-power card and using their influence to support the legitimacy of a global pre-emptive risk politics? For example, could a transformed NATO again serve as such an external integrating link in the future? What role could a reformed UN and the relations between the UN and the EU play in this context?

The insecurity dilemma

World risk society confronts *all* social and political actors at *all* levels with a new kind of insecurity and uncontrollability. At stake are, on one hand, *manufactured* uncertainties – that is, uncertainties are not held in check, but rather aggravated, by the available institutional answers; on the other hand, in international politics there are as yet no rules for dealing with these new threats. Both of these things may also have been true in the past. However, their novel historical character results in large part from the fact that the quality of the insecurity, which questions the basic foundations of the modern understanding of state and society, is now a matter of open discussion and controversy for a global public.

This can be seen from the attempts to cope with terrorism, the 'elusive' transnationally operating 'enemy'. The utter contingency with which the victims are indiscriminately targeted throughout the world conveys the message that anyone can become a target at any time, and this leads to a globalization of the *awareness* of uncertainty. The eeriness of the terrorist threat consists in the very fact that this constitutive vagueness, and the resulting uncontrollability, are intentional.

Generalizing our argument, on the one hand, global risks elude the institutionalized, national controlling mechanisms of the first modernity *in principle*; on the other hand, this shattering of the basic confidence in political and social institutions calls for the very opposite of these mechanisms, namely, the permanent renewal of the state's political claim to control. As a consequence, the 'security policy' designed to thwart this deep insecurity can no longer rely on the traditional institutions but must employ ad hoc, experimental means to promote new forms of cooperation gradually.

To the extent that the terrorist threat is taken seriously within states, it leads to a *security-democracy dilemma* within states. The greater the threat posed by the immediate enemy appears to be, the more strident become the calls for security at any price, even in mature democracies, and the greater the readiness to restrict, or even sacrifice, basic rights.

The immediate implication of this problem for external relations is a classic imperial dilemma. On the one hand, the empire must extend its sphere of influence in order to bring the emerging zones of insecurity under control; on the other hand, in so doing it internalizes the very global social conflicts that it is trying to tame and stem. This entails at the same time a highly modern intervention dilemma. European cosmopolitanism involves two opposing impulses – to intervene and not to intervene – *both* of which are open to criticism in the global public arena. Failure to intervene in Rwanda inspires just as much moral criticism as the attempt to hold off an ethnic genocide in the collapsing Yugoslavia by military means.

The boundary dilemma

Our argument could easily succumb to a postmodern misinterpretation of European cosmopolitanism that affirms the difficulty, or even impossibility, of preserving or reconstructing borders (in the old sense) because of the logic of interdependence and globality. But this is not our position! Interpreted in terms of second modernity, cosmopolitanism underscores the resulting conclusion and countermovement: *opening borders necessitates closing borders.* This dialectic of opening and closing borders gives rise to the boundary dilemma of cosmopolitan Europe according to which the national must be both overcome *and* preserved. How is this possible? Or: Where does cosmopolitan Europe end? When Moscow nominates an EU Commissioner? How is it possible both to include and exclude Russia? Can we conceive of an association between the European Union and a state that is bigger than itself, such as Russia? What reasons speak for or against this?

If the interconnection between inside and outside becomes the norm, how can cosmopolitan Europe be determined? In contrast with whom or what can it define its identity? Or is this question outdated because the concept and question of identity continually lead us into the trap of thinking in terms of exclusive disjunctions, and thus fail to do justice to the reality of the inclusive Europe?

The peace dilemma

Has the peace mission of cosmopolitan Europe been exhausted by its own successes? Hasn't the peace, which has become a matter of course over half a century, become a comfortable reality to which Europe has become accustomed, which it does not want to relinquish, and which condemns it to inactivity and passivity when the values for which it stands actually call for active engagement? Wasn't the peace mission the driving force behind the birth of the new Europe, whereas today it has turned into its opposite, namely, the defence of the status quo which justifies European self-indulgence while horror is festering at its boundaries and in other parts of the world?

Doesn't the history of the Holocaust, in particular, teach us that the illusion involved in defining oneself as a member of a cosmopolitan community can be shattered by violent ethnic or racist definitions of self or others that force one to be a Jew? What, then, if an elusive enemy declares war on cosmopolitan Europe? Not war in the old sense but an ubiquitous, systematic terrorist threat that annuls the difference between war and peace? Is it then enough to maintain peace within Europe and for the rest to erect electronic guard fences? Or mustn't the EU distance itself from its policy of inertia and of defending every national front garden?

What exactly is Europe's peace mission in view of the new world war of terror? Is the interpretation that it is the president of the United States who has declared war on terror and, hence, that the terrorist attacks are essentially anti-American, but not anti-Western, anti-European or anti-cosmopolitan, really tenable? Or is there after all such a thing as a cosmopolitan Europe and its *enemies*?

If this avalanche of question marks gives the impression that the authors of the present book do not have answers to these questions, then that is correct. The theory of the second modernity is not a theory of simple solutions or theoretical relief. Its intention is rather to formulate a conceptual and empirical framework for making sense of the realities of the second modernity and its dilemmas. Of course, the most important question then is: How do the various social actors – organizations, political parties, governments, world religions, global economic players, trade unions, national legal and educational systems, the various national and international winners and losers, social movements, the social sciences and, last but not least, all of us! – deal with these dilemmas, paradoxes and contradictions? Do they provide reasons for retreating into the shell of the national outlook (or methodological nationalism), and hence for reinvoking the evaporating certainties of the straightforward first modernity through a politics of nostalgia? Or do they provide the starting points and impulses for a culture of *shared uncertainties* and *shared dilemmas*? And, in view of this uncertainty concerning uncertainty, mustn't we act *as if* the latter were at least possible?

Beyond arrogance and self-betrayal: culture of shared ambivalence

That shared dilemmas need not represent a hindrance to action, that they can, on the contrary, establish bonds and justify action, is nothing new. Rather it is the clear message conveyed by Europe's myth of origins, Europe's anti-original, anti-essentialistic and, in the true sense, cosmopolitan origin. 'Europa', recounts Homer, was the daughter of Phoenix, the king of Phoenicia, a country in the Middle East. The god of the Greeks, Zeus, was so enamoured of her beauty that he approached her in the shape of a white bull and abducted her to Crete, where she became the mother of King Minos. Here we encounter all the ingredients of a transgressive myth. Boundaries between the divine, the human and the animal, as well as those between spheres of power, are disrespected; there is talk of metamorphosis, enchantment, conquest and abduction; the charming Europa is robbed of her autonomy and violated; she must live 'between cultures', hence is 'uprooted' and 'alienated'; but these 'dilemmas', this *difference as existence* or *existence as difference*, are not presented as a history of loss, as weakness or a hindrance to action, but instead establish Europe's strength and power to act: Europa, whose beauty compels even the god Zeus to humble himself by adopting a half-human, half-animal form, becomes the queen. Her children and grandchildren establish a political realm in which inside and outside, familiarity and strangeness, intermingle.

The cosmopolitan Europe, which is aware of its dilemmas and paradoxes, can avoid or overcome *both* the combination of arrogance and ignorance towards cultural others *and* the counter-romanticism that consists in idealizing the alien and in demonizing itself. Jacques Derrida must have had this in mind when he wrote in *The Other Heading*:

it is necessary to make ourselves the guardians of an idea of Europe, of a difference of Europe, *but* of a Europe that consists precisely in not closing itself off in its own identity and in advancing itself in an exemplary way toward what it is not, toward the other heading or the heading of the other, indeed – and this is perhaps something else altogether – toward the other *of* the heading, which would be the beyond of this modern tradition, another border structure, another shore. (Derrida 1992: 29)

The capacity to act and the global influence exerted by the cosmopolitan Europe, therefore, are founded on the responsibility of shared dilemmas.

On the one hand, Europe must avoid falling into the traps of arrogance *and* of self-betrayal while, on the other, deriving its pride and self-consciousness from the same source – as well as from the unique historical lesson which it teaches the world, namely, how enemies can become neighbours. Then there exists a global alternative to the *American way*, namely, a *European way* that accords priority to the rule of law, political equality, social justice, cosmopolitan integration and solidarity.

Notes

Chapter 1   Introduction

1   All quotations are from the essay by Winfried Schulze (2004).
2   The cardinal error of 'constructivism' in research on Europe lies in the fact that it understands the 'construction of Europe' primarily as an intentional, rational process, and thereby overlooks the importance of unintended processes and the power of side effects.
3   To anticipate misunderstandings, it should be emphasized that this does not imply that we construe Europe as a pan-nationalist project. We are exclusively interested in conceptual affinities between research on nationalism, on the one hand, and research on Europe in the social sciences, on the other.
4   Joerges (2003: 191–2) points out that, in making their decisions, the actors concerned were guided not only by the 'internal logic' of law, but also by an extra-legal ('ordo-liberal') 'vision' of Europe.
5   This concept of 'Europeanization' goes far beyond the concept of Europeanization in recent research on Europe, which is focused primarily on the internal side of the process of European integration, whether at the European level or within the member states (for a summary, see Eising 2003).
6   On the critique of multiculturalism, see Beck (2006: 66f.).
7   Needless to say, here the devil is in the details. Who lays down the procedures in accordance with which these minima are determined? Who imposes them in the face of opposition? How are conflicts resolved in which one or both sides are not ready to renounce the use of organized violence which violates the minimal norms of civilization? These questions already make clear that cosmopolitanism does not provide any magic formulas but is replete with dilemmas.
8   For this reason, orthodox Marxist philosophy does not regard cosmopolitanism as opposed to, but instead as the 'reverse side' of 'bourgeois nationalism and chauvinism'. According to the dominant Marxist doctrine, it is 'the reactionary response to socialist internationalism' (Klaus and Buhr 1975: 667).
9   The distinction between the premodern period and modernity is intended here only in a heuristic sense and in full awareness that it is encumbered by an extremely problematic distinction between tradition and modernity. It is also true that the hierarchy of difference in the guise of colonialism was the *integral* of the process of European nation-state formation in the eighteenth and nineteenth centuries. The terrorist attacks of 11 September 2001, are also being used to replace the lost 'communist enemy' with an 'Islamic enemy'.

10   This involves a strange irony. Postmodernity, which was developed to unmask and overcome essentialism, in fact revives it in the guise of a postmodern quasi-essentialism of the incomparability of others. This shares with the premodern, 'natural' essentialism of difference the notion that one must accept things as they are.

11   Exemplary for the former approach is the pan-European movement of Count Richard N. Coudenhofe-Kalergi (Coudenhofe-Kalergi 1953), for the latter, the functionalism of David Mitrany (Mitrany 1966).

12   We will discuss this question in detail in chapter 8, section 3. On the EU's problems concerning democracy and possible ways of resolving them, see, especially, Abromeit (1998), Chryssochoou (1998), Greven and Pauly (2000), Kohler-Koch (1998), Schmitter (2000) and Zürn (1996).

Chapter 2   The Reflexive Modernization of Europe

1   For an overview of the theory of reflexive modernization and its possible applications, see, in particular, Beck, Giddens and Lash (1994), Beck and Bonss (2001), and Beck and Lau (2004, 2005); for discussions, see among others Latour (2003), Lash (2003), Adam (2003), Urry (2003), Poferl and Sznaider (2004), Soziale Welt (2005) and Böschen, Kratzer and May (2006).

2   The role of the ECJ in the European process of integration reveals especially clearly the weaknesses of a purely intergovernmental theory of integration. Its attempts to trace the adjudication of the ECJ back to the preferences of the 'largest' member states (specifically Garrett 1992, 1995; Garrett, Keleman and Schulz 1998) must be regarded as complete empirical failures (see, in particular, Stone Sweet and Brunel 1998; Stone Sweet and Caporaso 1998; Alter 2001).

3   These key decisions form the main focus of research of the (liberal) intergovernmentalists; Moravcsik (1998) is exemplary in this regard.

4   Useful overviews of the development and the current state of integration theory are to be found in Caporaso and Keeler (1995), Rosamond (2000) and Loth and Wessels (2001), in several contributions in Schieder and Spindler (2003) and in Wiener and Diez (2004). The studies of Giering (1997) and D. Wolf (1999), among others, are prime examples of explicit attempts to fuse neofunctionalist and intergovernmentalist integration theories.

Chapter 3   Cosmopolitan Empire

1   Most recently, Siedentop (2001); for a critical view, see previously Lübbe (1994).

2   Of course, there have been repeated attempts to analyse the EU using these categories, for example, as a 'distinctive kind of international regime' (Lepsius 1992: 189) or as a 'complex international organization' (Gehring 2002). However, it has proved impossible to grasp the peculiarities of the EU adequately in this way.

3   In this context, the neofunctionalist analyses of the EEC provided by US authors during the 1960s were especially innovative. They benefited from the fact that the functionalist theory of political systems, on which their analyses were based, had already abandoned the concept of the state during the 1950s and replaced it with the general concept of the 'political system' (see Haas 1958, 1964; Lindberg 1963; Lindberg and Scheingold 1970). Such a concept not only offered better

opportunities for comparing different national political system but also opened up new perspectives for research on Europe.

4 Note, however, that this is a description of the current power structure of the EU, hence of deformed cosmopolitanism, and not of the cosmopolitan Europe which we will outline in what follows.

5 For an excellent overview of the more recent discussion concerning the *American Empire*, especially in North America, see Speck and Sznaider (2003); for a critical assessment of attempts to equate contemporary US politics with historical forms of imperial power, see Calhoun, Cooper and Moore (2006).

6 Doyle defines empire as a 'system of interaction between two political entities, one of which, the dominant metropole, exercises political control over the internal and external policy – the effective sovereignty – of the other, the subordinate periphery' (Doyle 1986: 12). By contrast, hegemonic powers control only the external actions of states, while leaving their internal activities unaffected.

7 One of the limitations of the current discussion of the imperial character of the United States after 11 September 2001, is that it reduces the function of empires to the aspect of security. Conversely, the left-wing critique of nineteenth-century imperialism primarily emphasizes the economic function of empires. Historical comparison shows that empires for the most part performed both functions simultaneously and that their development was shaped by how and with what specific emphases they exercised these functions (see Doyle 1986: 19).

8 Herfried Münkler even argues that 'imperial orders . . . possess a capacity for problem-solving far greater than that of states. Empires are subject to different expectations: they have to solve problems on which states inevitably founder on account of their greater internal obligations' (Münkler 2003: 113).

9 This feature of empires was emphasized by Karl Ferdinand Werner, in particular: 'A kingdom is a country, perhaps a large and powerful country. At any rate, it ideally tends towards unity and hence could prepare the way for the unity of the nation, especially in France. An empire, in its intention, is never a single country but a world, and indeed it has always been paired in the West with the term *orbis*' (Werner 1980: 190f.).

10 However, this does not mean that they can also be easily surmounted from outside. On the contrary, the idea of universal power in an open space is quite compatible with the attempt to close oneself off permanently from the outside, from 'chaos' and 'barbarism', by means of walls and other kinds of fortifications (see Duverger 1980b: 17).

11 The importance of centre–periphery relations for the internal organization of empires was emphasized in particular by Eisenstadt (1963) in his seminal book on the political systems of empires.

12 The asymmetry in the internal relations of power and authority is also an essential characteristic of empires for Doyle: '[Unlike] both federations and confederations, the imperial state is not organized on the basis of political equality among societies or individuals. The domain of empire is a people subject to *unequal rule*' (Doyle 1986: 36; our emphasis). The Roman Empire, for example, was divided into three zones of influence in its first phase: a 'zone of direct control' with Rome as centre, an 'inner zone of diplomatic control' through which the subject states were integrated into the empire, and an 'outer zone of influence' which was composed of dependent tribes (see Mann 1986: 275).

13   Duverger points out: 'Empires of their nature are multinational. They unite several ethnicities, several communities, several cultures, that were previously separated and remain distinct' (Duverger 1980b: 10).

14   The concept of hegemony features in quite different variants in the literature. In distinguishing between empire and hegemony, Doyle focuses primarily on the different range of control: 'Control of both foreign and domestic policy characterizes empire; control of only foreign policy, hegemony' (Doyle 1986: 40). Czempiel, by contrast, tries to distinguish the two models of order in terms of the instruments of the exercise of power, namely, force and voluntarism: 'Imperialism prevails where obedience is demanded and forced. Characteristic of hegemony are the offers of co-operation and the consensus produced through power' (Czempiel 2003: 1004). On our understanding, empire combines both, and consequently differs from both.

15   Niall Ferguson (2003) has recently demonstrated this very impressively with reference to the British Empire.

16   This is by no means only a theoretical possibility. Given the rapid disintegration of the postcolonial states in Africa, it is quite conceivable that their political authority will have to be organized differently – that is to say, in a postmodern way – if it is not to regress to a condition of premodern tribal rule.

17   It is those who try to answer this question in historical terms, that is, with reference to the Christian culture and tradition of the West, who think in decidedly unhistorical terms. For 'we can only speak of "Europe" when the states that comprise this continent no longer regard themselves exclusively as the heirs of the Roman Empire or as a religious community with a global mission, when the Christian component of European reality has been so far banished from the secular domain that, although it remains a supporting foundation, it no longer constitutes its sole authoritative substance – in short, once the state has liberated itself from ecclesiastical supremacy' (Foerster 1963: 11).

18   An exception to this is the European Court of Justice, whose decisions are binding on member states in a hierarchical manner (Stone Sweet 2000), as well as certain competition policy powers of the Commission, which the latter can exercise without the formal involvement of the member states (see Schmidt 1998).

19   Hardt and Negri illustrate the repressive character of cosmopolitanism with the example of the early twentieth-century New England factories and the Appalachian coal mines: 'The factories and mines were dependent on the labor of recent immigrants from various European countries, many of whom carried with them traditions of intense worker militancy. Bosses, however, did not shy away from bringing together this potentially explosive mixture of workers. They found, in fact, that carefully managed proportions of workers from different national backgrounds in each workshop and each mine proved to be a powerful formula of command. The linguistic, cultural, and ethnic differences within each work force were stabilizing because they could be used as a weapon to combat worker organization. It was in the bosses' interest that the melting pot not dissolve identities and that each ethnic group continue to live in a separate community maintaining its differences' (Hardt and Negri 2000: 200).

20   In order to avoid misunderstandings, we should emphasize that we use the concept of the 'cosmopolitan state' with reference to the transformed

nation-states and to signify a quite specific form of 'transnational state', whereas the concept of the (cosmopolitan) empire refers to the transnational political system into which these states are integrated.

21 The Roman Empire after its foundation was exemplary in this regard: 'the Roman people, the sovereign of so many nations, was for ever delivered from the weight of taxes. The increasing revenue of the provinces was found sufficient to defray the ordinary establishment of war and government, and the superfluous mass of gold and silver was deposited in the temple of Saturn, and reserved for any unforeseen emergency of the state' (Gibbon 1896: 158). It was only under Augustus that taxes were reintroduced for Roman citizens; under Caracalla the increasing financial needs of the Roman ruler led to the extension of the right to Roman citizenship as a means of broadening the tax base.

22 This is not to imply that in premodern empires and modern colonial systems no resources flowed back from the centre to the periphery. It is a well-known fact that in the British Empire the export of capital from the centre was an important aspect of the imperial economy from the middle of the nineteenth century onwards, though it nevertheless remained subordinate to the needs of the centre (see Hobsbawm 1968: 121f.). In the case of the Roman Empire, Gibbon reports gifts and payments of tribute to the 'allies': 'After the wealth of nations had centred in Rome, the emperors displayed their greatness, and even their policy, by the regular exercise of a steady and moderate liberality towards the allies of the state. They relieved the poverty of the barbarians, honoured their merit, and recompensed their fidelity. These voluntary marks of bounty were understood to flow, not from the fears, but merely from the generosity or the gratitude of the Romans; and whilst presents and subsidies were liberally distributed among friends and suppliants, they were sternly refused to such as claimed them as a debt' (Gibbon 1896: 250–1).

23 Exceptions to this are, specifically, agricultural, trade and, most recently, monetary policy. These policy areas belong to the zone of complete integration of the European Empire.

24 Tax policy is among the policy areas which have proved to be especially resistant to Europeanization (see Genschel 2002). Here the role of the EU is restricted to the more or less successful harmonization of national taxes and tax regimes. The EU was denied independent tax revenue, even though the Commission has made repeated attempts to create an EU tax.

25 It is easy to recognize that such a delegation of governance functions is risky. It always involves the danger of being misused by individual member states to repatriate tasks back from the EU.

26 The self-taming of the military by the military, as secured in an exemplary way through the overlapping of memberships between the EU and NATO, however, has only qualified success and that primarily internally, as the 'war against terrorism' and the Iraq War have most recently demonstrated. Once the either/or order of the Cold War dissolved and the enemy images became more flexible, a dynamic of internal tensions and splits could take hold.

27 The distinction between 'legal' and 'material' sovereignty plays an important role in fostering a more differentiated understanding of the effects of globalization on the room for manoeuvre of nation-states in the recent literature on globalization in particular (see Reinecke 1998; Krasner 1999; Grande and Risse 2000).

28   The Eastern European states also suffered this fate after the collapse of the Soviet Empire. Their newly won independence, important though it is, is far from sufficient to guarantee the security and welfare of their citizens under the conditions of globalization. Hence it is no surprise that these states immediately used their independence to apply for admission into another, more peaceful and prosperous imperium.

29   This also holds for older concepts in the field of international political economy, for which economic interdependence did not entail pressure to cooperate with other states. They focused primarily on strategies for an improved domestic adaptation to international economic imperatives and on non-cooperative strategies towards the outside (see, in particular, Cooper 1968). In the 1980s, research in this field emphasized cooperative strategies; however, it focused primarily on cooperation within the state (especially between governments, trade unions and employer associations) (see Katzenstein 1984, 1985; Gourevitch 1986).

30   In the second half of the 1980s, the Cecchini Report represented at least an attempt to calculate the costs of 'non-Europe', i.e., of the non-completion of the internal market, in order to provide arguments in support of the project of a single internal market (see Cecchini 1988).

31   This does not preclude the possibility that there could be secessionist movements in certain countries in the future, though these would have a high price, as is shown by the Canadian province of Quebec.

32   To date, Greenland represents the only instance of a secession from the EC/EU. Since 1953, it has been an equally entitled part of Denmark, and joined the EC – against the will of the majority of the population of Greenland – with Denmark's accession to the EC in 1973. In 1982, the Greenlanders voted in a referendum by a slender majority to secede from the EC, which duly occurred in 1985.

33   On the concept of the transnational state, see Beck 2005: 262–3.

34   Or, as in the Swiss and Norwegian cases, voluntary renunciation of these gains.

35   Hence, changes in the German Basic Law, for example, necessitated by European integration relate primarily to procedural aspects of the participation of the Federation [*Bund*] and States [*Länder*] in the European decision-making processes (in particular, the new formulation of Art. 23 of the Basic Law). Until now, this has not affected the organization of parliament, government and administration and citizens' scope for political participation.

Chapter 4   European Social Space

1   '27 + 1' refers to the current number of member states; to be more precise we should speak of the 'x + 1' logic, since only then is the variability of borders thematized.

2   A good example of this is the special issue of the *Kölner Zeitschrift für Soziologie und Sozialpsychologie* which, although it bears the title 'Europeanization of National Societies', deals with this topic mainly in just three areas, namely, citizenship, the political public sphere and migration (see Bach 2001).

3   Two characteristics in terms of which Benedict Anderson (1991) defines national identity.

4   This number is an estimate of the German Federal Office of Statistics (*Statistisches Bundesamt*).

5   Excluding Luxembourg and Greece.

6   In EU countries (excluding Luxembourg and Greece) and Hungary, Norway, Switzerland, the Vatican, Romania and Poland.

7   From the numbers presented, one can form a comprehensive picture of horizontal Europeanization via the *professional* mobility – for example, immigration into Germany or emigration from Germany to other countries – of individuals with higher-level qualifications. However, important clues are provided by employment statistics in Germany (Federal Office for Employment) and the European Union (Eurostat), as well as by a careful analysis of the investigation of European university graduates (Teichler 2002). This study presents the educational and employment biographies of individuals who completed their studies in 1995, for example, during the first four years following graduation. The central focus of the analysis is the international mobility of European university graduates before their studies, during their studies and in working life. This survey largely confirms the picture already presented by educational mobility.

8   Niklas Luhmann already distanced himself from the territorially and nationally determined concept of society in sociology at the beginning of the 1970s. For Luhmann, modern society exists only in the singular, as world society. He contrasts this with the 'old European' concept of society of the nation-states. He even indirectly anticipates the critique of the 'zombie categories'. 'It may be that we fail to perceive the newly emerged world society because we anticipated it under the wrong categories, for example under the idea of the global empire' (Luhmann 1975: 53). 'But world society is, evolutionarily speaking, a completely new phenomenon. It is not possible to assess the chances of success of such a system with the available conceptual tools, since they are presumably beyond the latter's field of vision' (ibid.: 57). Nevertheless, the concept of world society, both in its orientation and in its exposition, is a purely theoretical implication, an artificial product of the conceptual elaboration of Hegelianism into a systems theory, founded on the certainty of the idea of functional differentiation as a global or universal ordering idea. This apodicticity and self-sufficiency of the theory, its prior conceptual orientation to a world society in the singular, can easily lapse into blindness concerning the new empirical reality of globally and locally mixed relations and dynamics.

9   Here we draw on arguments and motifs from Geyer and Bright (1995).

10 Here European 'society' must always be thought of in scare quotes.

11 On this, see the discussion of 'globality' in Robertson (1992, 1995) and Albrow (1996) in which a close interconnection between global interdependence and global awareness of interdependence is highlighted. The concept of global interdependence (originally developed in opposition to realism) also belongs to the canon of the theory of international relations, although it was for many years geared to economic interdependences in a one-sided way (see Cooper 1968; Keohane and Nye 1972, 1977; Nye 2003; Spindler 2003 provides an overview; on the empirical analysis of global interdependences, see above all Held et al. 1999).

12 We owe the argument concerning 'integration through expansion' to Georg Vobruba (2003).

Chapter 5   Strategies of European Cosmopolitanization

1   The questions posed in this paragraph represent, respectively, numbers 2, 7, 8, 25, 42 and 44 of the catalogue of questions presented to the Convention by the European Council of Laeken.

2   To what extent these different 'varieties of capitalism' still exist, or whether they are being eroded by Europeanization and the globalization of the economy, has been an object of lively scholarly debate for a number of years (see, among others, Crouch and Streeck 1997; Hall and Soskice 2001). Uncontroversial is the fact that French 'statism' has undergone considerable modifications since the 1980s and the role of the state in France has diminished considerably (see Schmitt 1996); German corporatism, too, seems to be on the wane, as the failure of the '*Bündnis für Arbeit*' [Alliance for Work] recently indicated. As a consequence, normative political conflicts within the EU have lost some of their edge, but they have not disappeared entirely.

3   On this, see also Offe (2001); on the interconnection between social cleavages and process of state-building in Europe in general, see Lipset and Rokkan (1967).

4   This constellation corresponds to three key variables in research on Europe in political science: 'state preferences and strategies', 'domestic actors and structures' and '(supranational) institutions'. The different approaches either focus on one of these key variables or combine them in different ways. These approaches do not take into account the influence of norms and ideas, which are central to constructivist approaches.

5   On the conceptualization of the supranational institutions as 'corporate actors', see Schneider and Werle (1988); on liberal intergovernmentalism in general, see Moravcsik (1993, 1998).

6   It is worth noting as an aside that the justification of the French veto offered by de Gaulle bears an amazing resemblance to the arguments currently being brought against the EU accession of Turkey: 'The Treaty of Rome', wrote de Gaulle, 'was concluded between six continental States – States which are, economically speaking, one may say, of the same nature . . . England. . . . is an insular, maritime country. . . . England's nature, England's structure, England's very situation differs profoundly from those of the Continental countries' (de Gaulle 1970–71: 107).

7   Margaret Thatcher formulated this intergovernmentalist logic in similar terms in her famous Bruges speech: 'Willing and active co-operation between independent sovereign states is the best way to build a successful European Community' (Thatcher 1993: 745).

8   To prevent misunderstandings, we should emphasize that we do not understand capital strategies in an actor-specific sense; they can be pursued either by economic actors or by states, political parties, etc.

9   In his analysis of the administration of justice of the ECJ, Joerges concludes: 'The ECJ has based all of its assertions concerning the quality and contents of Community law on "strictly legal" operations. Explications of methodological premises or theoretical reflections on the preconditions of validity of the European "constitutional charter" are nowhere to be found' (Joerges 2003: 190).

10   On the distinction between input and output legitimacy, see especially Scharpf (1999).

11 This by no means contradicts the observation that economic globalization not only destroys diversity but at the same time creates it. What is questionable, however, is whether this artificial 'cultural mélange' can also function as a motor for cosmopolitanization in a similar way to historical identities.

Chapter 6   Inequality and Recognition

1 This does not mean, of course, that the member states are not interested in getting back as large a share as possible from the EU budget. The British prime minister Margaret Thatcher's demand 'I want my money back' is still legendary. A crucial determining factor in the nature and intensity of distributional conflicts within the EU, however, is the fact that *there is no contractual entitlement* to a 'just' return of funds. At least in principle, funds are allocated in accordance with other criteria, for example, according to the principle of excellence in the case of European research and technology policy.

2 Little would be altered in this finding even if one were to construe the European Agricultural Policy as disguised social policy (see Rieger 1998), since in comparison with other social security systems the latter is strictly limited to a particular sector and is quantitatively not of major consequence.

3 The controversy surrounding the EU 'Posted Workers Directive' demonstrated that under the conditions of a unitary internal market this could only be achieved at a high political cost (see Eichhorst 1998).

4 The English translation of the German Basic Law issued by the Federal Ministry of the Interior glosses over the authors' point by speaking of 'equal living conditions' (*Trans.*).

5 From the scholarly literature addressing these questions, the following studies can be highlighted by way of example: Rainwater (1992) poses important questions concerning transnational inequality research (though without really answering them); Rothenbacher (1994) gives an overview of various statistics in Europe; Ebbinghaus (1998) offers some reflections on how Europeanization should be analysed theoretically and argues for the inclusion of comparative research and international relations; Layte, Whelan and Nolan (2001), but primarily Vogel (1999), Capucha, Bernardo and Castro (2001) and Whelan et al. (2001), have presented initial empirical studies.

6 Thus Robin Blackburn (2004: 8) proposes establishing a European basic insurance scheme modelled on the American social security card. Furthermore, he advocates (together with the European Trade Union Confederation) a European social fund, 'with resources to invest to generate productive employment and underwrite future welfare expenditure . . . Such funds could help to protect productive enterprises from financial exploitation, to promote socially responsible business objectives and assert some popular control over wealth accumulation.' It would be funded by an EU-wide levy of 10 per cent on company profits.

Chapter 7   On the Dialectic of Globalization and Europeanization

1 On the theory of world risk society, see Beck 1992, 1997, 1999, 2002, 2006: chs 1 and 4; Giddens (1994); Münch (1996); Adam, Beck and van Loon (2000); Franklin (1998); Baker (2003); Bougen (2003); Ericson and Doyle (2003); and, on their

implications for international politics, Zürn (1998) and Daase, Feske and Peters (2002).

2   See the discussion of 'globality' in Robertson (1992, 1995) and Albrow (1996), where a close link is made between global interdependence and global awareness of interdependence. In international relations theory, too, the concept of global interdependence (originally developed in opposition to realism) is part of the theoretical canon, although for a long time it was one-sidedly geared to economic interdependence. (See Cooper 1968; Keohane and Nye 2003; the overview in Spindler 2003; and, for empirical analysis of global interdependence, especially Held et al. 1999.)

3   Grace Skogstad (2005) reaches a similar conclusion in her study of the European–American trade dispute over the EU ban on imports of genetically modified foodstuffs. Different regulatory approaches and philosophies also played a role, of course, but the crucial factor was different perceptions of risk in the United States and in Europe. The expanded possibilities of democratic participation in the EU have further exacerbated the conflict, since it has increased the likelihood of the views of European citizens finding institutional expression and implementation.

4   In future, risk analysis will also have to address the malicious triggering of disasters – a 'logic' which instrumentalizes the hitherto ignored 'residual risk' of disaster in order to maximize its impact. This poses the dilemma for risk analysis that, whereas it must anticipate events and think the unthinkable, this good intention to enlighten may actually open Pandora's box by suggesting to terrorists possible new forms of attack. In this way, analysis of residual risk itself becomes risky because thinking of hitherto unthinkable dangers can unintentionally produce these very dangers.

5   On the following, see especially Wolf (2002).

6   With the 'wider Europe' strategy, this policy has in the meantime acquired a conceptual framework and has been extended to the Eastern European countries for which accession to the EU is not (currently) envisaged (see European Commission 2003a).

7   See the debate over the concept of a 'core Europe' launched by Jacques Derrida and Jürgen Habermas in Summer 2003 (Derrida and Habermas [2003] 2006), as well as the earlier special issue of the journal *Merkur* entitled 'Europa oder Amerika? Zur Zukunft des Westens' (Bohrer and Scheel 2001).

Chapter 8   Cosmopolitan Visions for Europe

1   Here we do not offer a detailed account of the debate over a constitution for the European Union. The basic positions were already staked out in the mid-1990s in the controversy between Dieter Grimm (1995) and Jürgen Habermas ([1995] 1998b). On the more recent discussion, see also Fossum (2000), Habermas (2006), Weiler (1999), Scharpf (2002) and Asbach (2002), as well as the contributions in Joerges, Mény and Weiler (2000) which take critical aim at the Humboldt University speech of the former German foreign minister Joschka Fischer (Fischer 2000).

2   It is highly controversial in modern democratic theory whether this postulate of equality relates only to the formal equality of rights of participation or whether it also extends to the material equality of opportunities for participation.

3 Of course, there have been repeated attempts to play down or even completely deny the problem of democracy in the EU (see most recently, Crombez 2003, Moravcsik 2003, among others). Two main lines of argumentation are pursued in this context. One claims that, because of its more limited competences and tasks, the EU is also less in need of democratic legitimation than the member states, so that the legitimation produced by the European Parliament is entirely adequate; the other argues that the legitimation of European policy continues to be generated primarily by the national parliaments. The latter line of argument is exemplified by the German Constitutional Court, which took the following position in its Maastricht judgement: 'If an association of democratic states performs sovereign tasks and thereby exercises sovereign authority, the latter must be democratically legitimized in the first instance by the peoples of the member states through their national parliaments' (Bundesverfassungsgericht 1993: 155).

4 Here we do not need to deal further with the argument that the EU cannot be completely democratized because it lacks the decisive presupposition for any democracy, namely, a 'demos'. This argument has already been convincingly refuted in recent years (see, in particular, Habermas 1998a, 2006; Weiler 1995; and Weiler, Haltern and Mayer 1995).

5 Expressed in the language of negotiation theory, the actors would not be able to get by without at least a minimum of 'arguing'; hence, the chances of success of a negotiation strategy based solely on 'bargaining' would be minimized.

6 Of course, we should not forget possibilities for circumventing the pressures to uniformity exercised by the Community Method and their consequences that do *not* promote integration and cooperation, such as intentional violations of treaties or national unilateralism. These, too, were, and still are, frequently employed by the member states.

7 On the history of the concept of differentiated integration and its variants, see, in particular, Scharrer (1984). In Germany, the concept of differentiated integration has in recent years been promoted and further developed primarily by Werner Weidenfeld and his collaborators (see, especially, Bertelsmann Stiftung 1997; Weidenfeld and Janning 1997; Weidenfeld 2000).

8 The introduction of options for flexible integration was supposed to overturn neither the existing store of Community rules, the *acquis communautaire*, nor the guiding model of 'complete integration'. As a result, the concept of differentiated integration has remained trapped in the old exclusive dichotomies and in the old categories of unified statehood. Particularly symptomatic of this outdated mindset is the Amsterdam Treaty, for, although it introduced the principle of 'enhanced cooperation' (to give it its official title) into the European treaty complex, it restricted this principle so radically that it has yet to be applied on a single occasion even five years after the treaty was signed (Deubner 2003: 29; on the criticism of the Amsterdam Treaty, see also Janning 1998; Wessels 1998).

9 Here the difference between second modernity and postmodernity, i.e., between cosmopolitan and postmodern solutions to this problem, becomes apparent. In contrast to postmodern approaches, the principle of differentiated integration does not relinquish the claim to common norms completely but attempts to satisfy the claim of modern statehood to internal uniformity in a new, differentiated manner.

10   In recent years, the 'method of open coordination' has been one of the pet projects of Europe research (see, among others, Hodson and Maher 2001; Bauer and Knöll 2003; Héritier 2003; Behning 2004; Eberlein and Kerwer 2004).

11   Of course, realists do not assume that states can achieve absolute security through military means. This is unattainable in principle in an 'anarchic' Hobbesian world of states. Moreover, they realized early on that this structural insecurity of the world of states is under certain circumstances even magnified by military armament because this spurs other states to enhance their military capabilities as well. Nevertheless, it remains true that in a 'realist' world risks are calculable and can be held in check by military means. However, neither is possible any longer given the terrorist risks of world risk society (see Daase 2002).

12   It speaks for Robert Kagan's realism that, in light of the American pyrrhic victory in Iraq, he in the meantime at least acknowledges the importance of the legitimacy of state action in international politics (cf. Kagan 2004b).

13   More precisely, they introduce a new type of asymmetry into global conflicts, one which privileges the weak contenders against great military powers. This is one of the main characteristics of the 'new wars' in world risk society (see Münkler 2005).

14   The strategy paper 'A Secure Europe in a Better World' of the High Representative for the Common Foreign and Security Policy of the EU, Javier Solana, from 2003, represents a first attempt to address this deficit (see Solana 2003).

15   Rainer Forst, for example, has formulated a 'reflexively and morally' grounded theory of tolerance 'in which no other values are made the foundation of tolerance than the superordinate principle of justification itself' (Forst 2003: 20).

16   On the distinction between universalism and cosmopolitanism, see Beck 2006, ch. 2.

References and Bibliography

Abromeit, Heidrun (1998) *Democracy in Europe: Legitimizing Politics in a Non-State Polity*. Oxford: Berghahn Books.

Abromeit, Heidrun (2000) Kompatibilität und Akzeptanz: Anforderungen an eine 'integrierte Politie'. In Edgar Grande and Markus Jachtenfuchs (eds), *Wie problemlosungsfähig ist die EU?* Baden-Baden: Nomos, pp. 59–75.

Adam, Barbara (2003) Reflexive modernization temporalized. *Theory, Culture and Society* 20/2: 59–78.

Adam, Barbara, Beck, Ulrich, and van Loon, Joost (eds) (2000) *The Risk Society and Beyond*. London: Sage.

Albrow, Martin (1996) *The Global Age*. Cambridge: Polity.

Alter, Karen (2001) *Establishing the Supremacy of European Law*. Oxford: Oxford University Press.

Anderson, Benedict (1991) *Imagined Communities*. London: Verso.

Andretta, Massimiliano, DellaPorta, Donatella, Mosca, Lorenzo, and Reiter, Herbert (2003) *No Global – New Global: Identität und Strategien der Antiglobalisierungsbewegung*. Frankfurt am Main: Campus.

Ansell, Chris (2000) The networked polity: regional development in Western Europe. *Governance* 13: 303–33.

Appadurai, Arjun (1991) Global ethnoscapes: notes and queries for a transnational anthropology. In R. G. Fox (ed.), *Recapturing Anthropology*. Santa Fe: School of American Research Press, pp. 191–200.

Archibugi, Daniele (2003a) Cosmopolitical democracy. In Archibugi (ed.), *Debating Cosmopolitics*. London: Verso, pp. 1–15.

Archibugi, Daniele (ed.) (2003b) *Debating Cosmopolitics*. London: Verso.

Archibugi, Daniele, and Held, David (eds) (1995) *Cosmopolitan Democracy: An Agenda for a New World Order*. Cambridge: Polity.

Archibugi, Daniele, Held, David, and Köhler, Martin (eds) (1998) *Re-imagining Political Community: Studies in Cosmopolitan Democracy*. Cambridge: Polity.

Arendt, Hannah, and Jaspers, Karl (1985) *Briefwechsel*. Munich: Piper.

Asbach, Olaf (2002) Verfassung und Demokratie in der Europäischen Union: Zur Kritik der Debatte um eine Konstitutionalisierung Europas. *Leviathan* 30/2: 267–97.

Ash, Timothy G. (1993) *In Europe's Name: Germany and the Divided Continent*. New York: Random House.

Asmus, Ronald D. (2003) Rebuilding the Atlantic alliance. *Foreign Affairs* (Sept/Oct): 20–31.

Asmus, Ronald D., and Pollack, Kenneth M. (2002) The new transatlantic project. *Policy Review* 115 (Oct/Nov): 3–18.

Axelrod, Robert (1984) *The Evolution of Cooperation*. New York: Basic Books.

Axtmann, Roland (2003) State formation and supranationalism in Europe: the case of the Holy Roman Empire of the German nation. In Mabel Berezin and Martin Schain (eds), *Europe without Borders: Remapping Territory, Citizenship, and Identity in a Transnational Age*. Baltimore: Johns Hopkins University Press, pp. 118–39.

Bacevich, Andrew J. (2002) *American Empire: The Realities and Consequences of U.S. Diplomacy*. Cambridge, MA: Harvard University Press.

Bach, Maurizio (1992) Eine leise Revolution durch Verwaltungsverfahren: Bürokratische Integrationsprozesse in der Europäischen Gemeinschaft. *Zeitschrift für Soziologie* 21: 16–30.

Bach, Maurizio (1995) Ist die Europäische Einigung irreversibel? Integrationspolitik als Institutionalisierung in der Europäischen Union. In Birgitta Nedelmann (ed.), *Politische Institutionen im Wandel*. Opladen: Westdeutscher Verlag, pp. 368–91.

Bach, Maurizio (2000) *Die Bürokratisierung Europas: Verwaltungseliten, Experten und politische Legitimation in Europa*. Frankfurt am Main: Campus.

Bach, Maurizio (ed.) (2001) Die Europäisierung nationaler Gesellschaften. *Kölner Zeitschrift für Soziologie und Sozialpsychologie, Sonderheft 40*. Opladen: Westdeutscher Verlag.

Baker, Tom (2003) *Insurance, Law and Policy: Cases, Materials, and Problems*. New York: Aspen.

Bauer, Michael W., and Knoll, Ralf (2003) Die Methode der offenen Koordinierung: Zukunft Europäischer Politikgestaltung oder schleichende Zentralisierung? *Aus Politik und Zeitgeschichte* 12: 33–8.

Beck, Ulrich (1992) *Risk Society: Towards a New Modernity*. London: Sage.

Beck, Ulrich (1996) Wissen oder Nicht-Wissen? Zwei Perspektiven 'reflexiver Modernisierung'. In Ulrich Beck, Anthony Giddens and Scott Lash (1996) *Reflexive Modernisierung: Eine Kontroverse*. Frankfurt am Main: Suhrkamp, pp. 289–315.

Beck, Ulrich (1997) *The Reinvention of Politics: Rethinking Modernity in the Global Order*. Cambridge: Polity.

Beck, Ulrich (1999) *World Risk Society*. Cambridge: Polity.

Beck, Ulrich (2002) *Ecological Politics in an Age of Risk*. Cambridge: Polity.

Beck, Ulrich (2005) *Power in the Global Age*. Cambridge: Polity.

Beck, Ulrich (2006) *The Cosmopolitan Vision*. Cambridge: Polity.

Beck, Ulrich (2007) *Weltrisikogesellschaft*. Frankfurt am Main: Suhrkamp.

Beck, Ulrich, and Bonss, Wolfgang (eds) (2001) *Die Modernisierung der Moderne*. Frankfurt am Main: Suhrkamp.

Beck, Ulrich, and Lau, Christoph (eds) (2004) *Entgrenzung und Entscheidung: Was ist neu an der Theorie reflexiver Modernisierung?* Frankfurt am Main: Suhrkamp.

Beck, Ulrich, and Lau, Christoph (2005) Second modernity as a research agenda. *British Journal of Sociology* 56/4: 525–58.

Beck, Ulrich, Bonss, Wolfgang, and Lau, Christoph (2001) Theorie reflexiver Modernisierung – Fragestellungen, Hypothesen, Forschungsprogramme. In Ulrich Beck and Wolfgang Bonss (eds), *Die Modernisierung der Moderne*. Frankfurt am Main: Suhrkamp, pp. 11–59.

Beck, Ulrich, Giddens, Anthony, and Lash, Scott (1994) *Reflexive Modernisation: Politics, Tradition and Aesthetics in the Modern Social Order*, Cambridge: Polity.

Beck, Ulrich, Holzer, Boris, and Kieserling, Andre (2001) Nebenfolgen als Problemsoziologischer Theoriebildung. In Ulrich Beck and Wolfgang Bonss (eds), *Die Modernisierung der Moderne*. Frankfurt am Main: Suhrkamp, pp. 63–81.

Beck, Ulrich, Levy, Daniel, and Sznaider, Natan (2004) Erinnerung und Vergebung in der Zweiten Moderne. In Ulrich Beck and Christoph Lau (eds), *Entgrenzung und Entscheidung: Was ist neu an der Theorie reflexiver Modernisierung?* Frankfurt am Main: Suhrkamp.

Beck-Gernsheim, Elisabeth (1999) *Juden, Deutsche und andere Erinnerungslandschaften: Im Dschungel der ethnischen Kategorien*. Frankfurt am Main: Suhrkamp.

Beck-Gernsheim, Elisabeth (2004) *Wir und die Anderen*. Frankfurt am Main: Suhrkamp.

Behning, Ute (2004) Die 'neue Methode der offenen Koordination': Versuche der integrationstheoretischen Klassifizierung einer neuen Form des sozialpolitischen Regierens in der Europäischen Union. *Österreichische Zeitschrift für Politikwissenschaft* 2: 127–36.

Bender, Peter (2003) *Weltmacht Amerika: Das Neue Rom*. Stuttgart: Klett-Cotta.

Benz, Arthur (1984) Zur Dynamik der föderativen Staatsorganisation. *Politische Vierteljahresschrift* 25: 53–73.

Benz, Arthur (1985) *Föderalismus als dynamisches System: Zentralisierung und Dezentralisierung im föderativen System*. Opladen: Westdeutscher Verlag.

Benz, Arthur (1998) Politikverflechtung ohne Politikverflechtungsfälle – Koordination und Strukturdynamik im Europäischen Mehrebenensystem. *Politische Vierteljahresschrift* 39: 558–89.

Benz, Arthur (2000) Entflechtung als Folge von Verflechtung: Theoretische Überlegungen zur Entwicklung des Europäischen Mehrebenensystems. In Edgar Grande and Markus Jachtenfuchs (eds), *Wie problemlosungsfähig ist die EU? Regieren im Europäischen Mehrebenensystem*. Baden-Baden: Nomos, pp. 141–63.

Benz, Arthur (2001) *Der moderne Staat: Grundlagen der politischen Analyse*. Munich: Oldenbourg.

Benz, Arthur (2003) Mehrebenenverflechtung in der Europäischen Union. In Markus Jachtenfuchs and Beate Kohler-Koch (eds), *Europäische Integration*. 2nd edn, Opladen: Leske & Budrich, pp. 317–51.

Bertelsmann Stiftung (ed.) (1997) *Das neue Europa – Strategien differenzierter Integration*. Gütersloh: Verlag Bertelsmann Stiftung.

Bittner, Jan (2002) Finanzmärkte: Von der vorsorgenden zur vorbeugenden Risikopolitik der G7. In Christopher Daase, Susanne Feske and Ingo Peters (eds), *Internationale Risikopolitik*. Baden-Baden: Nomos, pp. 191–213.

Blackburn, Robin (2004) Un espoir persistant mais déçu. (This is not the Europe that the World Needs.) *Le Monde diplomatique* (Jan): 8.

BMBF, Bundesministerium für Bildung und Forschung (2002) *Deutsche Studierende im Ausland: Statistischer Überblick 1991–2000*. Bonn: Bundesministerium für Bildung und Forschung, Referat für Öffentlichkeitsarbeit.

Bohrer, Karl-Heinz (2000) *Die Europäische Differenz*. Merkur, Special Edition 9/10: 991–1003.

Bohrer, Karl-Heinz, and Scheel, Kurz (eds) (2001) *Europa oder Amerika? Zur Zukunft des Westens*. Merkur, Special Edition 617/618.

Boje, Thomas P., van Steenbergen, Bart, and Walby, Sylvia (eds) (1999) *European Societies: Fusion or Fission?* London and New York: Routledge.

Bonss, Wolfgang, and Kesselring, Sven (2004) Mobility and the cosmopolitan perspective. Discussion paper, Munich.

Bornschier, Volker (1994) The rise of the European Community: grasping toward hegemony? Or therapy against national decline? *International Journal of Sociology* 24: 62–96.

Böschen, Stefan, Kratzer, Nick, and May, Stefan (2006) *Nebenfolgen: Analysen zur Konstruktion und Transformation moderner Gesellschaften*. Weilerswist: Verbrück.

Bougen, Philip D. (2003) Catastrophe risk. *Economy and Society* 31: 253–74.

Brennan, Timothy (1997) *At Home in the World: Cosmopolitanism Now*. Cambridge, MA: Harvard University Press.

Brenner, Neil (1999) Beyond statecentrism? Space, territoriality, and geographical scale in globalization studies. *Theory and Society* 28: 39–78.

Brubaker, Rogers W. (1992) *Citizenship and Nationhood in France and Germany*. Cambridge, MA: Harvard University Press.

Brunn, Wolfgang (2002) *Die Europäische Einigung von 1945 bis heute*. Stuttgart: Reclam.

Bundesverfassungsgericht (1993) *Entscheidungen des Bundesverfassungsgerichts* 89; www.bverfg.de/.

Burckhardt, Jacob (1957) *Historische Fragmente*. Stuttgart: Koehler.

Burley, Anne-Marie, and Mattli, Walter (1993) Europe before the court: a political theory of legal integration. *International Organization* 47: 41–76.

Butler, David, and Ranney, Austin (eds) (1994) *Referendums around the World: The Growing Use of Direct Democracy*. Basingstoke: Macmillan.

Buzan, Barry, and Waever, Ole K. (2003) *Regions and Powers: The Structure of International Security*. Cambridge: Cambridge University Press.

Calhoun, Craig, Cooper, Frederick, and Moore, Kevin W. (eds) (2006) *Lessons of Empire: Imperial Histories and American Power*. New York: New Press.

Caporaso, James A., and Keeler, John T. S. (1995) The European Union and regional integration theory. In Carolyn Rhodes and Sonia Mazey (eds), *The State of the European Union*, Vol. 3: *Building a European Polity?* Boulder, CO: Lynne Rienner, pp. 29–62.

Cappelletti, Mauro, Seccombe, Monica, and Weiler, Joseph H. H. (1986) *Integration through Law: Europe and the American Federal Experience*, Vol. 1, Bk 2. Berlin: De Gruyter.

Capucha, L., Bernardo, J., and Castro, J. (2001) Social exclusion and poverty in Europe: new social problems and new priorities for social research. In Max Haller (ed.), *The Making of the European Union: Contributions of the Social Sciences*. Berlin and New York: Springer.

Castells, Manuel (1998) *End of the Millennium*. Oxford and Malden, MA: Blackwell.

Cecchini, Paolo (1988) *1992: The European Challenge: The Benefits of a Single Market*. Aldershot: Gower.

Cheah, Pheng, and Robbins, Bruce (eds) (1998) *Cosmopolitics: Thinking and Feeling Beyond the Nation*. Minneapolis: University of Minnesota Press.

Chryssochoou, Dimitris N. (1998) *Democracy in the European Union*. London: Tauris.

Churchill, Winston S. (1948) *The Sinews of Peace: Post-War Speeches*. London: Cassell.

Coakley, John (ed.) (1992) *The Social Origins of Nationalist Movements. The Contemporary West European Experience*. London: Sage.

Cohen, Jean L. (1999) Changing paradigms of citizenship and the exclusiveness of the demos. *International Sociology* 14/3: 245–68.

Cohen, Michael, March, James, and Olsen, Johan (1972) A garbage can model of organizational choice. *Administrative Science Quarterly* 17: 1–25.

Collier, Paul, and Levitsky, Steven (1997) Democracy with adjectives: conceptual innovation in comparative research. *World Politics* 49/3: 430–51.

Commission of the European Communities (1998) First European community framework programme in support of culture 2000–2004, COM 266 final.

Commission of the European Communities (2000) Enhancing democracy in the European Union, SEC 1547/7 final, http://europa.eu.int/comm/governance/work/en.pdf [3 May 2001].

Commission of the European Communities (2001) European governance, COM 428 final, http://europa.eu.int/comm/governance/whitepaper/index_en.htm [25 Sept 2001].

Cooper, Richard N. (1968) *Economic Policy in an Interdependent World: Essays in World Economics*. Cambridge, MA: MIT Press.

Cooper, Robert (2003) *The Breaking of Nations: Order and Chaos in the Twenty-First Century*. London: Atlantic Books.

Coudenhofe-Kalergi, Richard N. (1953) *Die Europäische Nation*. Stuttgart: DVA.

Council of Europe (1997) *In from the Margins: A Contribution to the Debate on Culture and Development in Europe*. Strasbourg: Council of Europe.

Crombez, Christophe (2003) The democratic deficit in the European Union. *European Union Politics* 4/1: 101–20.

Crouch, Colin (1999) *Social Change in Western Europe*. Oxford and New York: Oxford University Press.

Crouch, Colin, and Streeck, Wolfgang (eds) (1997) *Political Economy of Modern Capitalism*. London: Sage.

Crozier, Michel, and Friedberg, Erhard (1979) *Macht und Organisation: Die Zwänge kollektiven Handelns*. Königstein im Taunus: Athenäum.

Cutler, A. Claire, Haufler, Virginia, and Porter, Tony (1999) *Private Authority in International Affairs*. New York: State University of New York Press.

Czempiel, Ernst-Otto (2003) Pax Americana oder Imperium Americanum. *Merkur* 57: 1003–14.

Daase, Christopher (2002) Internationale Risikopolitik – ein Forschungsprogramm für den sicherheitspolitischen Paradigmenwechsel. In Christopher Daase, Susanne Feske and Ingo Peters (eds), *Internationale Risikopolitik*. Baden-Baden: Nomos.

Daase, Christopher, Feske, Susanne and Peters, Ingo (eds) (2002) *Internationale Risikopolitik*. Baden-Baden: Nomos.

Dann, Otto (1993) *Nation und Nationalismus in Deutschland, 1770–1990*. Munich: Beck.

De Gaulle, Charles (1970–71) *Discours et messages*. Paris: Plon.

Dehousse, Renaud (1995) Constitutional reform in the European Community: are there alternatives to the majority avenue? *West European Politics* 18/3: 118–36.

Delanty, Gerard (1995) *Inventing Europe: Idea, Identity, Reality*. Basingstoke: Macmillan.

Delanty, Gerard (2003) The making of a post-Western Europe: a civilisational analysis. *Thesis Eleven* 72: 8–25.

Delgado-Moreira, José M. (2000) Cohesion and citizenship in EU cultural policy. *Journal of Common Market Studies* 38/3: 449–70.

Deubner, Christian (2003) Differenzierte Integration: Übergangserscheinung oder Strukturmerkmal der künftigen Europäischen Union. *Aus Politik und Zeitgeschichte* 1–2: 24–32.

Derrida, Jacques (1992) *The Other Heading: Reflections on Today's Europe*. Bloomington: Indiana University Press.

Derrida, Jacques, and Habermas, Jürgen ([2003] 2006) February 15, or: What binds Europeans. In Habermas, *The Divided West*. Cambridge: Polity, pp. 39–48.

Dewey, John (1991) *The Public and its Problems*. Athens, GA: Swallow Press.

Diner, Dan (2003) *Gedächtnis-Zeiten: Über jüdische und andere Geschichten*. Munich: Beck.

Douglas, M., and Wildavsky, A. (1983) *Risk and Culture*. Berkeley: University of California Press.

Doyle, Michael W. (1986) *Empires*. Ithaca, NY: Cornell University Press.

Duverger, Maurice (ed.) (1980a) *Le Concept d'empire*. Paris: Presses Universitaires de France.

Duverger, Maurice (1980b) Le Concept d'empire. In Duverger (ed.), *Le Concept d'empire*. Paris: Presses Universitaires de France, pp. 5–23.

Ebbinghaus, Bernhard (1998) Europe through the looking-glass: comparative and multi-level perspectives. *Acta Sociologica* 41/4: 301–14.

Eberlein, Burkard, and Kerwer, Dieter (2004) New governance in the European Union: a theoretical perspective. *Journal of Common Market Studies* 42: 121–42.

EG-Kommission (1970) Die Industriepolitik der Gemeinschaft (Memorandum der Kommission an den Rat). Brussels: Kommission der EG.

EG-Kommission (1979) Die Europäische Gesellschaft und die neuen Informationstechnologien: Eine Antwort der Gemeinschaft, Brussels: KOM(79) 650 endg. Brussels: Kommission der EG.

Eichhorst, Weiner (1998) Europäische Sozialpolitik zwischen supranationaler und nationaler Regulierung: Die Entsendung von Arbeitnehmern im Rahmen der Dienstleistungsfreiheit innerhalb der Europäischen Union. Diss., Universität Konstanz.

Eisenstadt, S. N. (1963) *The Political Systems of Empires*. New York: Free Press.

Eising, Rainer (2001) Policy learning in embedded negotiations: explaining EU electricity liberalization. *International Organization* 56/1: 85–120.

Eising, Rainer (2003) Europäisierung und Integration: Konzepte in der EU Forschung. In Markus Jachtenfuchs and Beate Kohler-Koch (eds), *Europäische Integration*. 2nd edn, Opladen: Leske & Budrich, pp. 387–416.

Elster, Jon (1983) *Sour Grapes: Studies in the Subversion of Rationality*. Cambridge: Cambridge University Press.

Ericson, Richard V., and Doyle, Aaron (2003) *Risk and Morality*. Toronto and London: University of Toronto Press.

Eriksen, Erik Oddvar, and Fossum, John Erik (1999) The European Union and postnational integration. ARENA Working Papers. Research Council of Norway.

Esping-Andersen, Gøsta (1990) *The Three Worlds of Welfare Capitalism.* Cambridge: Polity.

European Commission (2001) European governance: a White Paper. COM(2001) 428 final. Brussels: European Commission.

European Commission (2003a) Wider Europe-neighbourhood: a new framework for our eastern and southern neighbours. COM(2003). Brussels European Commission.

European Commission (2003b) Third European report on science & technology indicators 2003. Towards a knowledge-based economy. Luxembourg: Office for Official Publications of the European Communities.

European Council (2000) Charter of Fundamental Rights of the European Union. *Official Journal of the European Communities* 364 (2000/C): 1–22.

European Union (2000) Economic and monetary affairs: transition to the third stage and introduction of the euro. http://europa.eu.int/scadplus/leg/en/s01020.htm.

Eurostat (2003) *Science and Technology in Europe: Statistical Pocketbook: Data 1991–2001.* Luxembourg: Office for Official Publications of the European Communities.

Faist, Thomas (2000) *The Volume and Dynamics of International Migration and Transnational Social Space.* Oxford: Oxford University Press.

Falkner, Gerda (1998) *EU Social Policy in the 1990s: Towards a Corporatist Policy Community.* London: Routledge.

Favell, Adrian (1998a) A politics that is shared, bounded, and rooted? Rediscovering civil political culture in Western Europe. *Theory and Society* 27: 209–36.

Favell, Adrian (1998b) The Europeanisation of immigration politics. European integration online papers 2, http//eiop.or.at/eiop/texte/1998-101.htm.

Featherstone, Kevin (1994) Jean Monnet and the 'democratic deficit' in the European Union. *Journal of Common Market Studies* 32: 149–70.

Ferguson, Niall (2003). *Empire: How Britain Made the Modern World.* London and New York: Alan Lane.

Fischer, Joschka (2000) Vom Staatenverbund zur Föderation – Gedanken über dir Finalität der europäischen Integration. Speech by Joschka Fischer at Humboldt University in Berlin, 12 May 2000, http://www.auswaertigesamt.de/diplo/de/Infoservice/Presse/Reden/Archiv/2000/000512-EuropaeischeIntegrationPDF.pdf.

Foerster, Rolf Hellmut (ed.) (1963) *Die Idee Europa 1300–1946: Quellen zur Geschichte der politischen Einigung.* Munich: dtv.

Fontaine, Pascal (2000) *A New Idea for Europe: The Schuman Declaration, 1950–2000.* Luxembourg: Office for Official Publications of the European Communities.

Footitt, Hilary (2002) *Women, Europe and the New Language of Politics.* London and New York: Continuum.

Forst, Rainer (2003) *Toleranz im Konflikt: Geschichte, Gehalt und Gegenwart eines umstrittenen Begriffs.* Frankfurt am Main: Suhrkamp.

Forsthoff, Ernst (1971) *Der Staat der Industriegesellschaft: Dargestellt am Beispiel der Bundesrepublik Deutschland.* Munich: Beck.

Fossum, John (2000) Constitution-making in the European Union. In Erik Eriksen and John Fossum (eds), *Democracy in the European Union – Integration through Deliberation?* London: Routledge, pp. 111–63.

Franklin, Jane (ed.) (1998) *Politics of Risk Society.* Cambridge: Polity.

Fraser, Nancy (1995) From redistribution to recognition? Dilemmas of justice in a 'postsocialist' age. *New Left Review* 212 (July/Aug): 68–93.

Friedrich, Carl J. (1964) Nationaler und internationaler Föderalismus in Theorie und Praxis. *Politische Vierteljahresschrift* 5: 154–87.

Gallagher, Michael, and Uleri, Pier Vincenzo (eds) (1996) *The Referendum Experience in Europe*. Basingstoke: Macmillan.

Garrett, Geoffrey (1992) International cooperation and institutional choice: the European Community's internal market. *International Organization* 46/2: 533–60.

Garrett, Geoffrey (1995) The politics of legal integration in the European Union. *International Organization* 49/1: 171–81.

Garrett, Geoffrey, Keleman, R. Daniel, and Schulz, Heiner (1998) The European Court of Justice, national governments, and legal integration in the European Union. *International Organization* 52/1: 149–76.

Gehring, Thomas (2002) *Die Europäische Union als komplexe internationale Organisation: Wie durch Kommunikation und Entscheidung soziale Ordnung entsteht*. Baden-Baden: Nomos.

Gellner, Ernest (1983) *Nations and Nationalism*. Oxford and Malden, MA: Blackwell.

Genschel, Philipp (2002) *Steuerwettbewerb und Steuerharmonisierung in der Europäischen Union*. Frankfurt am Main: Campus.

Genschel, Philipp and Plümper, Thomas (1997) Regulatory competition and international co-operation. *Journal of European Public Policy* 4/4: 626–42.

Gerhard, Victoria, Llobera, Joseph R., and Shore, Chris (eds) (1994) *The Anthropology of Europe: Identity and Boundaries in Conflict*. Oxford: Berg.

Geyer, Michael, and Bright, Charles (1995) World history in a global age. *American Historical Review* (Oct).

Gibbon, Edward (1896) *The History of the Decline and Fall of the Roman Empire*. London: Methuen.

Giddens, Anthony (1994) *Beyond Left and Right: The Future of Radical Politics*. Cambridge: Polity.

Giering, Claus (1997) *Zwischen Zweckverband und Superstaat: Die Entwicklung der politikwissenschaftlichen Integrationstheorie im Prozess der europäischen Integration*. Bonn: Europa Union/VVA.

Gill, Stephen (1998) European governance and new constitutionalism: EMU and alternatives to disciplinary neo-liberalism in Europe. *New Political Economy*.

Goncalves, Veiga, and Rosa Fonseca, Linda (1998) A touchstone of dissent: Euroscepticism in contemporary Western European party system. *European Journal of Political Research* 33: 363–88.

Gottdiener, Mark (2001) *Life in the Air: Surviving the New Culture of Travel*. Lanham, MD: Rowman & Littlefield.

Gourevitch, Peter (1986) *Politics in Hard Times: Comparative Responses to International Economic Crises*. Ithaca, NY: Cornell University Press.

Grabitz, Eberhardt, and Iliopoulos, Constantin (1984) Typologie der Differenzierungen und Ausnahmen im Gemeinschaftsrecht. In Eberhardt Grabitz (ed.), *Abgestufte Integration*. Kehl am Rhein and Strasbourg: Engel, pp. 31–46.

Grande, Edgar (1995) Forschungspolitik in der Politikverflechtungs-Falle? Institutionelle Strukturen, Konfliktdimensionen und Verhandlungslogiken Europäischer Forschungs- und Technologiepolitik. *Politische Vierteljahresschrift* 36: 460–83.

Grande, Edgar (1996) Das Paradox der Schwäche: Forschungspolitik und die Einfluss-slogik europäischer Politikverflechtung. In Markus Jachtenfuchs and Beate Kohier-Koch (eds), *Europäische Integration*. Opladen: Leske & Budrich, pp. 3–39.

Grande, Edgar (2000a) Multi-level governance: Institutionelle Besonderheiten und Funktionsbedingungen des europäischen Mehrebenensystems. In Edgar Grande and Markus Jachtenfuchs (eds), *Wie problemlosungsfähig ist die EU? Regieren im europäischen Mehrebenensystem*. Baden-Baden: Nomos, pp. 11–30.

Grande, Edgar (2000b) Post-national democracy in Europe. In Michael T. Greven and Louis W. Pauly (eds), *Democracy Beyond the State? The European Dilemma and the Emerging Global Order*. Lanham, MD: Rowman & Littlefield, pp. 115–38.

Grande, Edgar (2003) How the architecture of the European Union political system influences European Union business associations. In Justin Greenwood (ed.), *The Challenge of Change in EU Business Associations*. Basingstoke: Palgrave Macmillan, pp. 45–59.

Grande, Edgar, and Jachtenfuchs, Markus (eds) (2000) *Wie problemlosungsfähig ist die EU? Regieren im europäischen Mehrebenensystem*. Baden-Baden: Nomos.

Grande, Edgar, and Pauly, Louis W. (eds) (2005) *Complex Sovereignty: Reconstituting Political Authority in the Twenty-First Century*. Toronto: University of Toronto Press.

Grande, Edgar, and Risse, Thomas (2000) Bridging the gap: Konzeptionelle Anforderungen an die politikwissenschaftliche Analyse von Globalisierungsprozessen. *Zeitschrift für Internationale Beziehungen* 7: 235–66.

Grande, Edgar, Prange, Heiko, and Wolf, Dieter (2004) Die Wahl der Qual? Staatliche Handlungsmöglichkeiten im Zeitalter der Globalisierung. MS, Munich, Berlin and Bremen.

Greenwood, Justin (1997) *Representing Interests in the European Union*. New York: St Martin's Press.

Greenwood, Justin (ed.) (2002) *Inside the EU Business Associations*. Basingstoke: Palgrave Macmillan.

Greenwood, Justin (ed.) (2003) *The Challenge of Change in EU Business Associations*. Basingstoke: Palgrave Macmillan.

Greven, Michael T., and Pauly, Louis (eds) (2000) *Democracy Beyond the State? The European Dilemma and the Emerging Modern Order*. Lanham, MD: Rowman & Littlefield.

Grewlich, Klaus W. (1992) *Europa im globalen Technologiewettlauf: Der Weltmarkt wird zum Binnenmarkt*. Gütersloh: Bertelsmann Stiftung.

Grimm, Dieter (1987) *Recht und Staat in der bürgerlichen Gesellschaft*. Frankfurt am Main: Suhrkamp.

Grimm, Dieter (1993) Mit der Aufwertung des Europaparlaments ist es nicht getan: Das Demokratiedefizit der EG hat strukturelle Ursachen. In Thomas Ellwein, Dieter Grimm, Joachim Jens Hess and Gunnar Folke Schuppert (eds), *Jahrbuch zur Staats- und Verwaltungswissenschaft*, Vol. 4. Baden-Baden: Nomos, pp. 11–18.

Grimm, Dieter (1995) Does Europe need a constitution? *European Law Journal* 1/3: 282–302.

Gurr, Ted Robert (1993) *Minorities at Risk. A Global View of Ethnopolitical Conflicts*. Washington, DC: United States Institute of Peace Press.

Haas, Ernst B. (1958) *The Uniting of Europe: Political, Social, and Economic Forces, 1950–1957*. Stanford, CA: Stanford University Press.

Haas, Ernst B. (1964) *Beyond the Nation-State: Functionalism and International Organization*. Stanford, CA: Stanford University Press.

Haas, Peter M. (1992) Introduction: epistemic communities and international policy coordination. *International Organization* 46/1: 1–36.

Habermas, Jürgen (1998a) *The Inclusion of the Other*. Cambridge: Polity.

Habermas, Jürgen ([1995] 1998b) Does Europe need a constitution? Response to Dieter Grimm. In Habermas, *The Inclusion of the Other*. Cambridge: Polity, pp. 155–61.

Habermas, Jürgen (1998c) The European nation-state: on the past and future of sovereignty and citizenship. In Habermas, *The Inclusion of the Other*. Cambridge: Polity, pp. 105–28.

Habermas, Jürgen (2001) *The Postnational Constellation: Political Essays*. Cambridge: Polity.

Habermas, Jürgen (2006) Does Europe need a constitution? In Habermas, *Time of Transitions*. Cambridge: Polity, pp. 89–109.

Hajer, Maarten A., and Wagenaar, Hendrik (eds) (2003) *Deliberative Policy Analysis: Understanding Governance in the Network Society*. Cambridge: Cambridge University Press.

Hale, John (1993) The renaissance idea of Europe. In Garcia Soledad (ed.), *European Identity and the Search for Legitimacy*. London: Pinter, pp. 46–63.

Hall, Peter A., and Soskice, David (2001) *Varieties of Capitalism: The Institutional Foundation of Comparative Advantage*. Oxford: Oxford University Press.

Hammar, Tomas (1990) *Democracy and the Nation-State: Aliens, Denizens and Citizens in a World of International Migration*. Aldershot: Avebury.

Hansen, Peo (2000) European citizenship, or Where neoliberalism meets ethnoculturalism; analysing the European Union's citizenship discourse. *European Societies* 2: 139–65.

Hardt, Michael, and Negri, Antonio (2000) *Empire*. Cambridge, MA: Harvard University Press.

Harrison, Jackie, and Woods, Lorna (2000) European citizenship: can European audio-visual policy make a difference? *Journal of Common Market Studies* 38: 471–96.

Hartenberger, Ute (2001) *Europäischer Sozialer Dialog nach Maastricht: EU-Sozialpartnerverhandlungen auf dem Prüfstand*. Baden-Baden: Nomos.

Hedetoft, Ulf (1994) National identities and European integration 'from below': bringing people back. *Revue d'integration européenne* 18: 1–28.

Heine, Heinrich (1985) *Romantic School and Other Essays*. New York: Continuum.

Held, David (1995) *Democracy and the Global Order: From the Modern State to Cosmopolitan Governance*. Cambridge: Polity.

Held, David (2004) *Global Covenant*. Cambridge: Polity.

Held, David, McGrew, Anthony G., Goldblatt, David, and Perraton, Jonathan (1999) *Global Transformations: Politics, Economics and Culture*. Cambridge: Polity.

Heller, Agnes (2004) European master-narrative about freedom. Discussion paper for the conference 'Beyond East and West': Europe in a Changing World. Elmau, Germany.

Héritier, Adrienne (2003) New modes of governance in Europe: increasing political efficiency and policy effectiveness? In Tanja Börzel and Rachel Cichowsky (eds), *The State of the European Union*, Vol. VI. Oxford: Oxford University Press.

Hobsbawm, Eric J. (1968) *Industry and Empire: An Economic History of Britain since 1750*. London: Weidenfeld & Nicolson.

Hobsbawm, Eric J. (1987) *The Age of Empire 1875–1914*. London: Weidenfeld & Nicolson.

Hobsbawm, Eric J. (1990) *Nations and Nationalism since 1780: Programme, Myth, Reality.* Cambridge: Cambridge University Press.

Hobsbawm, Eric J. (1992) Ethnicity and nationalism in Europe today. *Anthropology Today,* 8/1: 3–8.

Hodson, Dermot, and Maher, Imelda (2001) The open method as a new mode of governance: the case of soft economic policy co-ordination. *Journal of Common Market Studies* 39/4: 719–46.

Höffe, Ottfried (1999) *Demokratie im globalen Zeitalter.* Munich: Beck.

Hofmann, Gunther (2004) Des Rudels Kern. *Die Zeit* 14 (25 March): 3.

Honneth, Axel (1995) *The Struggle for Recognition: The Moral Grammar of Social Conflicts.* Cambridge: Polity.

Hooghe, Lisbeth, and Marks, Gary (2001) *Multi-Level Governance and European Integration.* Lanham, MD: Rowman & Littlefield.

Hooghe, Lisbeth, and Marks, Gary (2003) Unravelling the central state, but how? Types of multi-level governance. *American Political Science Review* 97: 233–43.

Hug, Simon (2002) *Voices of Europe: Citizens, Referendums, and European Integration.* Lanham, MD: Rowman & Littlefield.

Huntington, Samuel (1993) The clash of civilizations? *Foreign Affairs* 72/3: 22–49.

Huntington, Samuel (1996) *The Clash of Civilizations and the Remaking of World Order.* New York: Simon & Schuster.

Huntington, Samuel (2004) Dead souls: the denationalization of the American elite. *National Interest* 75 (spring): 5–18.

Huntington, Samuel P. (2005) *Who Are We? America's Great Debate.* New York: Free Press.

Immerfall, Stefan (ed.) (1999) *Territoriality in the Globalizing Society: One Place or None?* Heidelberg: Springer.

Ipsen, Hans Peter (1972) *Europäisches Gemeinschaftsrecht.* Tübingen: Mohr.

Ipsen, Hans Peter (1987) Europäische Verfassung – Nationale Verfassung. *Europarecht* 22: 195–213.

Jachtenfuchs, Markus (1997) Democracy and governance in the European Union. European integration online papers 1(2), http://eiop.or.at/eiop/texte/1997-002a.htm [May 2001].

Jachtenfuchs, Markus and Kohler-Koch, Beate (eds) (2003) *Europäische Integration.* 2nd edn, Opladen: Leske & Budrich.

Jänicke, Martin (eds) (1973) *Politische Systemkrisen.* Cologne: Kiepenheuer & Witsch.

Janning, Josef (1998) Differenzierung als Integrationsprinzip: Die Flexibilität im neuen EU-Vertrag. In Werner Weidenfeld (ed.), *Amsterdam in der Analyse.* Gütersloh: Verlag Bertelsmann Stiftung, pp. 203–17.

Jellinek, Georg (1960) *Allgemeine Staatslehre.* 3rd edn, Darmstadt: Wissenschaftliche Buchgesellschaft.

Jensen, Ole, and Richardson, Tim (2004) *Making European Space: Mobility, Power and Territorial Identity.* London: Routledge.

Joerges, Christian (2003) Recht, Wirtschaft und Politik im Prozess der Konstitutionalisierung Europas. In Markus Jachtenfuchs and Beate Kohler-Koch (eds), *Europäische Integration,* 2nd edn, Opladen: Leske & Budrich, pp. 183–218.

Joerges, Christian, Mény, Yves, and Weiler, Joseph H. H. (eds) (2000) *What Kind of Constitution for What Kind of Polity? Responses to Joschka Fischer.* Florence:

Robert Schuman Center for Advanced Studies at the European University Institute; Cambridge, MA: Harvard Law School.

Joppke, Christian (ed.) (1998) *Challenge to the Nation-State: Immigration in Western Europe and the United States*. Oxford and New York: Oxford University Press.

Judt, Tony (2002) Its own worst enemy. *New York Review of Books* 49/13 (15 Aug).

Kagan, Robert (2002) Power and weakness: why the United States and Europe see the world differently. *Policy Review* 113 (June–July): 3–28.

Kagan, Robert (2003) *Of Paradise and Power: America and Europe in the New World Order*. New York: Alfred A. Knopf.

Kagan, Robert (2004a) A decent regard. *Washington Post* (2 March): A21.

Kagan, Robert (2004b) America's crisis of legitimacy. *Foreign Affairs* 83/2 (March–April): 65–87.

Kaldor, Mary (1999) *New and Old Wars: Organized Violence in a Global Era*. Cambridge: Polity.

Kaldor, Mary, Anheier, Helmut, and Glasius, Marlies (2003) *Global Civil Society. Yearbook 2003*. Oxford: Oxford University Press.

Katzenstein, Peter J. (1984) *Corporatism and Change: Austria, Switzerland and the Politics of Industry*. Ithaca, NY: Cornell University Press.

Katzenstein, Peter J. (1985) *Small States in World Markets: Industrial Policy in Europe*. Ithaca, NY: Cornell University Press.

Katzenstein, Peter J. (2005) *A World of Regions: Asia and Europe in the American Imperium*. Ithaca, NY: Cornell University Press.

Keohane, Robert O., and Hoffmann, Stanley (1990) Conclusions: community politics and institutional change. In William Wallace (ed.), *The Dynamics of European Integration*. London: Pinter, pp. 276–300.

Keohane, Robert O., and Nye, Joseph S. (eds) (1972) *Transnational Relations and World Politics*. Cambridge, MA: Harvard University Press.

Keohane, Robert O., and Nye, Joseph S. (1977) *Power and Interdependence: World Politics in Transition*. Boston: Little, Brown.

Keohane, Robert O., and Nye, Joseph S. (2003) Redefining accountability for global governance. In Miles Kahler and David Lake (eds), *Governance in a Global Economy: Political Authority in Transition*. Princeton, NJ: Princeton University Press.

Kertész, Imre (2003) *Die exilierte Sprache*. Frankfurt am Main: Suhrkamp.

Kesselring, Sven, and Vogl, Gerlinde (2004) Mobility pioneers: networks, scapes and flows between first and second modernity. Discussion paper: Munich.

Kingdon, John W. (1995) *Agendas, Alternatives and Public Policies*. 2nd edn, New York: HarperCollins.

Kitschelt, Herbert, and McGann, Anthony J. (1995) *The Radical Right in Western Europe*. Ann Arbor: University of Michigan Press.

Klaus, Georg, and Buhr, Manfred (eds) (1975) *Philosophisches Wörterbuch*. 2nd edn, Leipzig: VEB Bibliographisches Institut.

Kleingeld, Pauline (1999) Six varieties of cosmopolitanism in late eighteenth-century Germany. *Journal of the History of Ideas* 60: 505–24.

Knill, Christoph (2001) *The Europeanisation of National Administrations: Patterns of Institutional Change and Persistence*. Cambridge: Cambridge University Press.

Koebner, Richard (1961) *Empire*. Cambridge: Cambridge University Press.

Kohler-Koch, Beate (ed.) (1998) Regieren in entgrenzten Räumen. *PVS-Sonderheft* 29. Opladen: Westdeutscher Verlag.

Kohler-Koch, Beate, and Eising, Rainer (eds) (1999) *The Transformation of Governance in the European Union.* London: Routledge.

Koser, Khalid, and Lutz, Helma (eds) (1998) *The New Migration in Europe: Social Constructions and Social Realities.* London: Macmillan Press.

Krasner, Stephen D. (1999) *Sovereignty: Organized Hypocrisy.* Princeton, NJ: Princeton University Press.

Kriesi, Hanspeter (2001) Nationaler politischer Wandel in einer sich denationalisierenden Welt. *Blätter für deutsche und internationale Politik* 2: 206–13.

Kriesi, Hanspeter, and Grande, Edgar (2004) Nationaler politischer Wandel in Entgrenzten Räumen. In Ulrich Beck and Christoph Lau (eds), *Entgrenzung und Entscheidung: Was ist neu an der Theorie Reflexiver Modernisierung?* Frankfurt am Main: Suhrkamp.

Krüger, Herbert (1966) *Allgemeine Staatslehre.* 2nd edn, Stuttgart: Kohlhammer.

Laffan, Brigid (1998) The European Union: a distinctive model of internationalisation. *Journal of European Public Policy* 5: 235–53.

Landfried, Christine (2002) *Das politische Europa: Differenz als Potenzial der Europäischen Union.* Baden-Baden: Nomos.

Lash, Scott (2003) Reflexivity as non-linearity. *Theory, Culture and Society* 20/2: 49–58.

Latour, Bruno (2003) Is remodernization occurring? And if so, how to prove it? A commentary on Ulrich Beck. *Theory, Culture and Society* 20/2: 35–48.

Latour, Bruno (2004) Whose cosmos, which cosmopolitics: two comments on the peace terms of Ulrich Beck. *Common Knowledge* 10/3: 456–62.

Layte, Richard, Whelan, Christopher T., and Nolan, Brian (2001) Explaining levels of deprivation in the European Union. *Acta Sociologica* 44/2: 105–21.

Le Goff, Jacques (2003) The roots of European identity. In Susan Stern and Elizabeth Seligmann (eds), *Desperately Seeking Europe.* London: Archetype Publications, pp. 159–68.

Lehmbruch, Gerhard (2003) *Verhandlungsdemokratie: Beiträge zur vergleichenden Regierungslehre.* Wiesbaden: Westdeutscher Verlag.

Leibfried, Stephan, and Pierson, Paul (eds) (1998) *Standort Europa: Sozialpolitik zwischen Nationalstaat und Europäischer Integration.* Frankfurt am Main: Suhrkamp.

Lepsius, M. Rainer (1992) Zwischen Nationalstaatlichkeit und westeuropäischer Integration. In Beate Kohler-Koch (ed.), *Staat und Demokratie in Europa.* Opladen: Leske & Budrich, pp. 180–92.

Lepsius, M. Rainer (1997) Bildet sich eine kulturelle Identität in der Europäischen Union? *Blätter für deutsche und internationale Politik* 8: 948–55.

Lepsius, M. Rainer (2000) Die Europäische Union als Herrschaftsverband eigener Prägung. In Christian Joerges, Yves Mény and Joseph H. H. Weiler (eds), *What Kind of Constitution for What Kind of Policy? Responses to Joschka Fischer.* Florence: Robert Schuman Center for Advanced Studies at the European University Institute; Cambridge MA: Harvard Law School, pp. 203–12.

Levy, Daniel, and Sznaider, Natan (2001) *Erinnerung im globalen Zeitalter: Der Holocaust.* Frankfurt am Main: Suhrkamp.

Lieven, Dominic (2002) *Empire: The Russian Empire and its Rivals.* New Haven, CT: Yale University Press.

Lijphart, Arend (1984) *Democracies: Patterns of Majoritarian and Consensus Government in Twenty-One Countries*. New Haven, CT: Yale University Press.

Lijphart, Arend (1999) *Patterns of Democracy: Government Forms and Performance in Thirty-Six Countries*. New Haven, CT: Yale University Press.

Lindahl, Hans (2000) European integration: popular sovereignty and a politics of boundaries. *European Law Journal* 6/3: 239–56.

Lindberg, Leon N. (1963) *The Political Dynamics of European Economic Integration*. Stanford, CA: Stanford University Press.

Lindberg, Leon N., and Scheingold, Stuart A. (eds) (1970) *Europe's Would-Be Polity: Patterns of Change in the European Community*. Englewood Cliffs, NJ: Prentice-Hall.

Linklater, Andrew (1998) *The Transformation of Political Community: Ethical Foundations of the Post-Westphalian Era*. Columbia: University of South Carolina Press.

Lipgens, Walter (ed.) (1985) *Documents on the History of European Integration*, Vol. 1: *Continental Plans for European Union 1939–1945*; Vol. 2: *Plans for European Union in Great Britain and in Exile 1939–1945*; Vol. 3: *The Struggle for European Union by Political Parties and Pressure Groups in Western European Countries 1945–1950*; Vol. 4: *Transnational Organizations of Political Parties and Pressure Groups in the Struggle for European Union 1945–1959*. Berlin: Walter de Gruyter.

Lippolis, Vincenzo (1998) European citizenship: what it is and what it could be. In Massimo La Torré (ed.), *European Citizenship: An Institutional Challenge* (European Forum 3). The Hague: Kluwer Law International.

Lipset, Seymour M., and Rokkan, Stein (1967) Cleavage structures, party systems, and voter alignments: an introduction. In Seymour M. Lipset and Stein Rokkan (eds), *Party Systems and Voter Alignments: Cross-National Perspectives*. New York: Free Press, pp. 1–64.

Longford, Graham (2002) Net gain: e-government in Canada, the US and the UK: dilemmas of public service, citizenship and democracy in the digital age. Conference paper, International Studies Association, New Orleans.

Loth, Werner, and Wessels, Wolfgang (eds) (2001) *Theorien der europäischen Integration*. Opladen: Leske & Budrich.

Lübbe, Hermann (1994) *Abschied vom Superstaat: Vereinigte Staaten von Europa wird es nicht geben*. Berlin: Siedler.

Luhmann, Niklas (1975) *Soziologische Aufklärung*. Opladen: Westdeutscher Verlag.

Lynch, Marc (2003) Taking Arabs seriously. *Foreign Affairs* (Sept/Oct): 81–94.

Maalouf, Amin (2000) *In the Name of Identity*. Harmondsworth: Penguin.

McNeill, Daniel, and Freiberger, Paul (1993) *Fuzzy Logic*. New York: Simon & Schuster.

Madison, James (1941) Federalist no. 51, February 8, 1788. In Alexander Hamilton, John Jay and James Madison, *The Federalist*. New York: Modern Library, pp. 335–41.

Maier, Hans (1995) *Eine Kultur oder viele? Politische Essays*. Stuttgart: de Gruyter.

Majone, Giandomenico (1996) *Regulating Europe*. London: Routledge.

Malcolm, Noel (1995) The case against 'Europe'. *Foreign Affairs* 74/2 (March/April): 52–68.

Mann, Michael (1986) *The Sources of Social Power*, Vol. 1: *A History of Power from the Beginning to AD 1760*. Cambridge: Cambridge University Press.

Marks, Gary (1997) A third lens: comparing European integration and state building. In Jytte Klausen and Louise Tilly (eds), *European Integration in Social and Historical Perspective: From 1850 to the Present* (Lanham, MD: Rowman & Littlefield), pp. 23–44.

Marks, Gary, Scharpf, Fritz W., Schmitter, Philippe C., and Streeck, Wolfgang (1996) *Governance in the European Union*. London: Sage.

Mattli, Walter (1995) *The Logic of Regional Integration: Europe and Beyond*. Cambridge: Cambridge University Press.

Maull, Hanns W. (2003) Die 'Zivilmacht Europa' bleibt Projekt: Zur Debatte um Kagan, Asmus/Pollack und das Strategiedokument NSS 2002. *Blätter für deutsche und internationale Politik* 12: 1467–78.

Maurer, Andreas (2002) *Parlamentarische Demokratie in der Europäischen Union: Der Beitrag des Europäischen Parlaments und der nationalen Parlamente*. Baden-Baden: Nomos.

Mayer, Peter, Rittberger, Volker, and Zelli, Fariborz (2003) Risse im Westen? Betrachtungen zum transatlantischen Verhältnis heute. *Leviathan* 31/1: 32–52.

Mearsheimer, John J. (2001) *The Tragedy of Great Power Politics*. New York: Norton.

Meinecke, Friedrich (1907) *Weltbürgertum und Nationalstaat: Studien zur Genesis des deutschen Nationalstaats*. Munich: Oldenbourg.

Milward, Alan S. (1994) *The European Rescue of the Nation-State*. London: Routledge.

Minc, Alain (1994) *Das neue Mittelalter*. Hamburg: Hoffmann & Campe.

Mitrany, David (1966) *A Working Peace System*. Chicago: Quadrangle Books.

Mokre, Monika (ed.) (2003) *Europas Identitäten: Mythen, Konflikte, Konstruktionen*. Frankfurt am Main: Campus.

Moravcsik, Andrew (1993) Preferences and power in the European Community: a liberal intergovernmentalist approach. *Journal of Common Market Studies* 31/4: 473–524.

Moravcsik, Andrew (1994) Why the European Union strengthens the state. Center for European Studies working paper 52. Cambridge, MA: Harvard University.

Moravcsik, Andrew (1998) *The Choice for Europe: Social Purpose and State Power from Messina to Maastricht*. Ithaca, NY: Cornell University Press.

Moravcsik, Andrew (2003) The EU ain't broke. *Prospect* (March): 38–45.

Münch, Richard (1998) *Globale Dynamik, lokale Lebenswelten: Der schwierige Weg in die Weltgesellschaft*. Frankfurt am Main: Suhrkamp.

Münkler, Herfried (2003) Das Prinzip Empire. In Ulrich Speck and Natan Sznaider (eds), *Empire Amerika: Perspektiven einer neuen Weltordnung*. Munich: DVA, pp. 104–25.

Münkler, Herfried (2005) *The New Wars*. Cambridge: Polity.

Münkler, Herfried (2007) *Empires: The Logic of World Domination from Ancient Rome to the United States*. Cambridge: Polity.

Murphy, Craig N. (1994) *International Organizations in Industrial Change: Global Governance since 1850*. New York: Oxford University Press.

Nassehi, Armin (2003) Identität als europäisches Konzept. MS, Munich.

Neumann, Iver B. (1998) European identity, EU expansion, and the integration/exclusion nexus. *Alternatives* 23: 397–416.

Neuss, Beate (2000) *Geburtshelfer Europas? Die Rolle der Vereinigten Staaten im europäischen Integrationsprozess 1945–1958*. Baden-Baden: Nomos.

Niblett, Robin (1997) The European disunion: competing visions of integration. *Washington Quarterly* 20: 91–109.

Nicolaïdis, Kalypso, and Howse, Robert (eds) (2001) *The Federal Vision: Legitimacy and Levels of Governance in the United States and the European Union*. Oxford: Oxford University Press.

Niess, Frank (2001) *Die Europäische Idee – aus dem Geist des Widerstands*. Frankfurt am Main: Suhrkamp.

Novalis (Baron Friedrich Leopold von Hardenberg) (1844) *Christianity in Europe*. The Catholic Series.

Nugent, Neill (2001) *The European Commission*. Basingstoke: Palgrave.

Nye, Joseph S. (2002) *The Paradox of American Power – Why the World's Only Superpower Can't Go it Alone*. New York: Oxford University Press.

Nye, Joseph S. (2003) U.S. power and strategy after Iraq. *Foreign Affairs* 82/4: 60–73.

O'Brien, Robert, Goetz, Anne Marie, Scholte, Jan Aart, and Williams, Marc (2000) *Contesting Global Governance: Multilateral Economic Institutions and Global Social Movements*. Cambridge and New York: Cambridge University Press.

Offe, Claus (1982) Politische Legitimation durch Mehrheitsentscheidung? *Journal für Sozialforschung* 22/3: 311–36.

Offe, Claus (2000) The democratic welfare state in an integrating Europe. In Michael T. Greven and Louis Pauly (eds), *Democracy Beyond the State? The European Dilemma and the Emerging Modern Order*. Lanham, MD: Rowman & Littlefield, pp. 63–89.

Offe, Claus (2001) Is there, or can there be, a 'European Society'? In Aleksander Koj and Piotr Sztompka (eds), *Images of the World: Science, Humanities, Art*. Kraków: Jagellonian University, pp. 143–159.

Ohmae, Kenichi (1990) *The Borderless World: Power and Strategy in the Interlinked Economy*. New York: Harper Business.

Ohmae, Kenichi (1995) *The End of the Nation-State: The Rise of the Regional Economies*. New York: Free Press.

Oppermann, Thomas (1977) Die Europäische Gemeinschaft als parastaatliche Superstruktur. In Rolf Ströter and Werner Thieme (eds), *Hamburg, Deutschland, Europa: Festschrift für Hans Peter Ipsen zum 70. Geburtstag*. Tübingen: Mohr, pp. 685–99.

Osterhammel, Jürgen (2001) Transnationale Gesellschaftsgeschichte: Erweiterung oder Alternative? *Geschichte und Gesellschaft* 27: 464–79.

Painter, Joe (2001) Multi-level citizenship, identity and regions in contemporary Europe. In James Anderson (ed.), *Transnational Democracy*. London: Routledge.

Parker, Ken W. (2002) Making connections: travel, technology and global air travel networks. MS, Queensland University.

Peters, B. Guy (1992) Bureaucratic politics and the institutions of the European Community. In Alberta M. Sbragia (ed.), *Euro-Politics: Institutions and Policymaking in the 'New' European Community*. Washington, DC: Brookings Institution, pp. 75–122.

Peterson, John, and Bomberg, Elizabeth (1999) *Decision-Making in the European Union*. Basingstoke: Macmillan.

Poferl, Angelika, and Sznaider, Nathan (eds) (2004) *Ulrich Becks kosmopolitisches Projekt: Auf dem Weg in eine andere Soziologie*. Baden-Baden: Nomos.

Pogge, Thomas W. (1992) Cosmopolitanism and sovereignty. *Ethics* 103: 48–75.

Popp, Susanne (2004) Auf dem Weg zu einem europäischen 'Geschichtsbild': Anmerkungen zur Entstehung eines gesamteuropäischen Bilderkanons. *Aus Politik und Zeitgeschichte* 7–8: 23–31.

Popper, Karl R. (1945) *The Open Society and its Enemies*. London: Routledge.

Preuß, Ulrich K., and Requejo, Farran (1998) *European Citizenship: Multiculturalism, and the State*. Baden-Baden: Nomos.

Puchala, Donald J. (1971) Of blind men, elephants and international integration. *Journal of Common Market Studies* 10: 267–84.

Quaritsch, Helmut (1970) *Staat und Souveränität*, Vol. 1. Frankfurt am Main: Athenäum.

Rabinow, Paul (1989) *French Modern: Norms and Forms of the Social Environment*. Cambridge, MA: MIT Press.

Racké, Cornelia (2004) The historical roots of the Bologna process. MS, University of Maastricht.

Rainwater, Lee (1992) Changing inequality structure in Europe: the challenge to social science. In Meinolf Dierkes and Bernd Bievert (eds), *European Social Science in Transition: Assessment and Outlook*. Frankfurt am Main: Campus.

Raphael, Lutz (1999) Nationalzentrierte Sozialgeschichte in programmatischer Absicht. *Geschichte und Gesellschaft* 27: 489–98.

Reinecke, Wolfgang H. (1998) *Global Public Policy: Governing without Government*. Washington, DC: Brookings Institution.

Reinhard, Wolfgang (2002) *Geschichte der Staatsgewalt: Eine vergleichende Verfassungsgeschichte Europas von den Anfängen bis zur Gegenwart*. Munich: Beck.

Rice, Condoleezza (2000) Campaign 2000: promoting the national interest. *Foreign Affairs* 79/1: 45–62.

Rieger, Elmar (1998) Schutzschild oder Zwangsjacke: Zur institutionellen Struktur der Gemeinsamen Agrarpolitik. In Stephan Leibfried and Paul Pierson (eds), *Standort Europa: Sozialstaat zwischen Sozialpolitik und Europäischer Integration*. Frankfurt am Main: Suhrkamp, pp. 240–80.

Risse-Kappen, Thomas (ed.) (1995) *Bringing Transnational Relations Back In: Non-State Actors, Domestic Structures and International Institutions*. Cambridge: Cambridge University Press.

Rittberger, Berthold (2005) *Building Europe's Parliament: Democratic Representation beyond the Nation State*. Oxford: Oxford University Press.

Robbins, Kevin, and Aksoy, Asu (2001) From spaces of identity to mental spaces: lessons from Turkish-Cypriot cultural experience in Britain. *Journal of Ethnic and Migration Studies* 27/4: 685–711.

Robertson, Roland (1992) *Globalization, Social Theory and Global Culture*. London: Sage.

Robertson, Roland (1995) Glocalization: time-space and homogeneity and heterogeneity. In Mike Featherstone, Scott Lash and Roland Robertson (eds), *Global Modernities*. London: Sage, pp. 25–44.

Rodriguez-Pose, André (2002) *The European Union: Economy, Society and Polity*. Oxford: Oxford University Press.

Rokkan, Stein (1999) *State Formation, Nation-Building, and Mass Politics in Europe: The Theory of Stein Rokkan*. Oxford: Oxford University Press.

Rosamond, Ben (2000) *Theories of European Integration*. Basingstoke: Macmillan; New York: St Martin's Press.

Rosen, Stephen Peter (2003) Ein Empire auf Probe. In Ulrich Speck and Natan Sznaider (eds), *Empire Amerika: Perspektiven einer neuen Weltordnung*. Munich: DVA, pp. 83–103.

Rothenbacher, Franz (1994) Social reporting in Europe. In Peter Flora, Franz Kraus, Heinz-Herbert Noll and Franz Rothenbacher (eds), *Social Statistics and Social Reporting in and for Europe*. Mannheim: Mannheimer Zentrum für Europäische Sozialforschung, pp. 9–98.

Rumford, Chris (2003) European society or transnational social space? *European Journal of Social Theory* 6/1: 25–43.

Sandholz, Wayne, and Stone Sweet, Alec (eds) (1998) *European Integration and Supranational Governance*. Oxford: Oxford University Press.

Sasse, Christoph, Poullet, Edouard, Coombes, David and Deprez, Gerard (1977) *Decision Making in the European Community*. New York: Praeger.

Sassen, Saskia (2003) Globalization or denationalization. *Review of International Political Economy* 10/1: 1–22.

Scharpf, Fritz W. (1988) The joint decision trap: lessons from German federalism and European integration. *Public Administration* 66: 239–78.

Scharpf, Fritz W. (1992) Europäisches Demokratiedefizit und deutscher Föderalismus. *Staatswissenschaften und Staatspraxis* 3: 293–306.

Scharpf, Fritz W. (1993) Autonomieschonend und gemeinschaftsverträglich: Zur Logik der europäischen Mehrebenenpolitik. MPIfG discussion paper 93/9. Cologne: Max-Planck-Institut für Gesellschaftsforschung.

Scharpf, Fritz W. (1994) Community and autonomy: multi-level policy-making in the European Union. *Journal of European Public Policy* 1: 219–42.

Scharpf, Fritz W. (1999) *Governing in Europe: Effective and Democratic?* Oxford: Oxford University Press.

Scharpf, Fritz W. (2000) *Interaktionsformen: Akteurzentrierter Institutionalismus in der Politikforschung*. Opladen: Leske & Budrich.

Scharpf, Fritz W. (2002) Regieren im europäischen Mehrebenensystem – Ansätze zu einer Theorie. *Leviathan* 30/1: 65–92.

Scharpf, Fritz W. (2003) Politische Optionen im vollendeten Binnenmarkt. In Markus Jachtenfuchs and Beate Kohier-Koch (eds), *Europäische Integration*. Opladen: Leske & Budrich, pp. 219–54.

Scharrer, Hans-Eckart (1984) Abgestufte Integration – eine Einführung. In Eberhard Grabitz (ed.), *Abgestufte Integration*. Kehl am Rhein and Strasbourg: Engel, pp. 1–30.

Schieder, Siegfried, and Spindler, Manuela (eds) (2003) *Theorien der Internationalen Beziehungen*. Opladen: Leske & Budrich.

Schimmelfennig, Frank (2003) Osterweiterung: Strategisches Handeln und kollektive Ideen. In Markus Jachtenfuchs and Beate Kohler-Koch (eds), *Europäische Integration*, 2nd edn, Opladen: Leske & Budrich, pp. 541–68.

Schlereth, Thomas (1977) *The Cosmopolitan Ideal in Enlightenment Thought*. Notre Dame, IN: University of Notre Dame Press.

Schlögel, Karl (2003) Tragödie der Vertreibungen: Über das Erfordernis ein europäisches Ereignis neu zu erzählen. *Lettre* 60: 78–83.

Schmidt, Manfred G. (2000) Der konsoziative Staat: Hypothesen zur politischen Struktur und zum politischen Leistungsprofil der EU. In Edgar Grande and Markus Jachtenfuchs (eds), *Wie problemlösungsfähig ist die EU?* Baden-Baden: Nomos, pp. 33–58.

Schmidt, Susanne K. (1998) *Liberalisierung in Europa: Die Rolle der Europäischen Kommission.* Frankfurt am Main: Campus.

Schmidt, Vivien A. (1996) *From State to Market? The Transformation of French Business and Government.* Cambridge: Cambridge University Press.

Schmidt, Vivien A. (2002) *The Futures of European Capitalism.* Oxford: Oxford University Press.

Schmitter, Philippe C. (1996) Imagining the future of the Euro-polity with the help of new concepts. In Gary Marks, Fritz W. Scharpf, Philippe C. Schmitter and Wolfgang Streeck (eds), *Governance in the European Union.* London: Sage, pp. 121–50.

Schmitter, Philippe C. (2000) *How to Democratize the European Union – and Why Bother?* Lanham, MD: Rowman & Littlefield.

Schneider, Volker, and Werle, Raymund (1988) Regime oder korporativer Akteur? Die EG in der Telekommunikationspolitik. MPIfG discussion paper 88/4. Cologne: Max-Planck-Institut für Gesellschaftsforschung.

Schulze, Winfried (2004) Mutatio-Innovatio – Zugänge zur Wahrnehmung von Veränderung in der Frühen Neuzeit. MS, Munich.

Schwarz, Hans-Peter (1994) *Adenauer: Der Aufstieg, 1876–1952,* Vol. 1. Munich: dtv.

Seitz, Konrad (1990) *Die japanisch-amerikanische Herausforderung: Deutschlands Hochtechnologie-Industrien kämpfen ums Überleben.* Stuttgart: Bonn Aktuell.

Servan-Schreiber, Jean-Jacques (1968) *Die amerikanische Herausforderung.* Munich: Hoffmann & Campe.

Shaw, Josephine (1997) The many pasts and futures of citizenship in the European Union. *European Law Review* 22: 554–72.

Shaw, Martin (2002) Post-imperial and quasi-imperial: state and empire in the global era. *Millennium* 31/2.

Sheller, Mimi, and Urry, John (2006) The new mobilities paradigm. *Environment and Planning A* 38/2: 207–26.

Shepsle, Kenneth (1979) Institutional arrangement and equilibrium in multidimensional voting models. *American Journal of Political Science* 23: 27–60.

Shore, Cris (1997) Governing Europe: European Union audio-visual policy and the politics of identity. In Cris Shore and Susan Wright (eds), *Anthropology of Policy: Critical Perspectives on Governance and Power.* London: Routledge.

Shore, Cris (2000) *Building Europe: The Cultural Politics of European Integration.* London: Routledge.

Siedentop, Larry (2001) *Democracy in Europe.* New York: Columbia University Press.

Sinn, Gerlinde, and Sinn, Hans-Werner (1991) *Kaltstart: Volkswirtschaftliche Aspekte der deutschen Vereinigung.* Tübingen: Mohr.

Skogstad, Grace (2005) Contested political authority, risk society, and the transatlantic divide in genetic engineering regulation. In Edgar Grande and Louis W. Pauly (eds), *Complex Sovereignty: Reconstituting Political Authority in the Twenty-First Century.* Toronto: University of Toronto Press.

Slaughter, Anne-Marie (2004) *A New World Order*. Princeton, NJ: Princeton University Press.

Smith, Anthony D. (1995) *Nations and Nationalism in a Global Era*. Cambridge: Polity.

Smith, Jackie, Chatfield, Charles, and Pagnucco, Ron (eds) (1997) *Transnational Social Movements and Global Politics: Solidarity beyond the State*. Syracuse, NY: Syracuse University Press.

Solana, Javier (2003) A secure Europe in a better world. European Council, Thessaloniki, 20 June.

Soysal, Yasemin N. (1994) *Limits of Citizenship: Migrant and Postnational Membership in Europe*. Chicago: University of Chicago Press.

Soysal, Yasemin N. (2001) Changing citizenship in Europe: remarks on postnational membership and the nation-state. In Janet Fink, Gail Lewis and John Clarke (eds), *Rethinking European Welfare*. London: Sage, pp. 65–75.

Soysal, Yasemin N. (2002) Locating Europe. *European Societies* 4/3: 265–84.

Soziale Welt (2005) *Theorie und Empirie reflexiver Modernisierung* [special issue] 56/2–3.

Speck, Ulrich, and Sznaider, Natan (eds) (2003) *Empire Amerika: Perspektiven einer neuen Weltordnung*. Munich: DVA.

Spindler, Manuela (2003) Interdependenz. In Siegfried Schieder and Manuela Spindler (eds), *Theorien der Internationalen Beziehungen*. Opladen: Leske & Budrich, pp. 89–116.

Spinelli, Altiero (1986) *Altiero Spinelli: Speeches in European Parliament 1976–1985*, ed. Pier Virgilio Dastoli. Rome: D.C.F.

Spruyt, Hendrik (1994) *The Sovereign State and its Competitors: The Analysis of Systems Change*. Princeton, NJ: Princeton University Press.

Starbatty, Joachim, and Vetterlein, Uwe (1990) *Die Technologiepolitik der Europäischen Gemeinschaft: Entstehung, Praxis und ordnungspolitische Konformität*. Baden-Baden: Nomos.

Statistisches Bundesamt (2002) *Datenreport 2002: Zahlen und Fakten über die Bundesrepublik Deutschland*. Bonn: Bundeszentrale für politische Bildung.

Stoiber, Edmund (2002) Draußen vor der Tür: Der Türkei-Beitritt würde die EU verändern. *Süddeutsche Zeitung* (11 Dec): 15.

Stone Sweet, Alec (2000) *Governing with Judges: Constitutional Politics in Europe*. Oxford: Oxford University Press.

Stone Sweet, Alec, and Brunell, Thomas L. (1998) Constructing a supranational constitution: dispute resolution and governance in the European Community. *American Political Science Review* 92: 63–81.

Stone Sweet, Alec, and Caporaso, James A. (1998) From free trade to supranational polity: the European Court and integration. In Wayne Sandholtz and Alec Stone Sweet (eds), *European Integration and Supranational Governance*. Oxford: Oxford University Press, pp. 92–133.

Streeck, Wolfgang (1995) From market making to state building? In Stephan Leibfried and Paul Pierson (eds), *European Social Policy: Between Fragmentation and Integration*. Washington, DC: Brookings Institution, pp. 389–431.

Tänzler, Denis (2002) Klimawandel: Divergierende Perzeptionsbedingungen als Ursache gescheiterter Klimaverhandlungen. In Christopher Daase, Susanne Feske and Ingo Peters (eds), *Internationale Risikopolitik*. Baden-Baden: Nomos, pp. 87–112.

Taylor, Charles (1992) The politics of recognition. In Amy Gutmann (ed.), *Multi-culturalism and the Politics of Recognition*. Princeton, NJ: Princeton University Press, pp. 25–73.

Teichler, Ulrich (ed.) (2002) *Erasmus in the Socrates Programme: Findings of an Evaluation Study*. Bonn: Lemmens.

Thatcher, Margaret (1993) *The Downing Street Years*. New York: HarperCollins.

Thielking, Sigrid (2000) *Weltbürgertum: Kosmopolitische Ideen in Literatur und politischer Publizistik seit dem achtzehnten Jahrhundert*. Munich: Fink.

Tindemans, Leo (1977) European Union. In A. H. Robertson (ed.), *European Yearbook 23*. The Hague: Martinus Nijhoff, pp. 1–93.

Todd, Emmanuel (2003) *After the Empire: The Breakdown of the American Empire*. New York: Columbia University Press.

Töller, Annette Elisabeth (2002) *Komitologie: Praktische Bedeutung und Arbeitsweise von Durchführungsausschüssen in der Europäischen Union am Beispiel der Umweltpolitik*. Opladen: Leske & Budrich.

Tömmel, Ingeborg (2003) *Das politische System der EU*. Munich: Oldenbourg.

Toulmin, Stephen (1990) *Cosmopolis: The Hidden Agenda of Modernity*. New York: Free Press.

Tsoukalis, Loukas (1997) *The New European Economy Revisited*. Oxford: Oxford University Press.

Urry, John (2003) Introduction: thinking society anew. In Ulrich Beck and Johannes Willms, *Conversations with Ulrich Beck*. Cambridge: Polity.

Van der Eijk, Cees, and Franklin, Mark (eds) (1996) *Choosing Europe? The European Electorate and National Politics in the Face of Union*. Ann Arbor: University of Michigan Press.

Venables, Tony (2000) The time has come to turn the rhetoric on 'European citizenship' into a reality. *European Voice* 6/1.

Vertovec, Steven, and Cohen, Robin (2002) *Conceiving Cosmopolitanism: Theory, Context, and Practice*. New York: Oxford University Press.

Vobruba, Georg (2003) The enlargement crisis of the European Union. *Journal of European Social Policy* 13/1: 35–62.

Vogel, Joachim (1999) The European 'welfare mix': institutional configuration and distributive outcome in Sweden and the European Union: a longitudinal and comparative perspective. *Social Indicators Research* 58/3: 245–97.

Walzer, Michael (2000) *Just and Unjust Wars: A Moral Argument with Historical Illustrations*. New York: Basic Books.

Weber, Max (1978) *Economy and Society*, 2 vols. Berkeley: University of California Press.

Weber, Max (1992) *The Protestant Ethic and the Spirit of Capitalism*. London and New York: Routledge.

Wehling, Peter (2002) Was kann die Soziologie über Nichtwissen wissen? Antwort auf Klaus Japp. *Zeitschrift für Soziologie* 31: 440–44.

Weidenfeld, Werner (1996) *Kulturbruch mit Amerika? Das Ende transatlantischer Selbstverständlichkeit*. Gütersloh: Verlag Bertelsmann Stiftung.

Weidenfeld, Werner (2000) Erweiterung ohne Ende? Europa als Stabilitätsraum strukturieren. *Internationale Politik* 55/8: 1–10.

Weidenfeld, Werner (2003) Das strategische Defizit – die Achillesferse Europas. MS, Munich.

Weidenfeld, Werner, and Janning, Josef (1997) Strategiepapier für das Internationale Bertelsmann Forum. In Bertelsmann Stiftung (eds), *Das neue Europa – Strategien differenzierter Integration*. Gütersloh: Verlag Bertelsmann Stiftung, pp. 139–68.

Weiler, Joseph H. H. (1991) The transformation of Europe. *Yale Law Journal* 100: 2403–83.

Weiler, Joseph H. H. (1995) Does Europe need a constitution? Reflections on demos, telos, and the German Maastricht decision. *European Law Journal* 1/3: 219–58.

Weiler, Joseph H. H. (1999) *The constitution of Europe: 'Do the new clothes have an emperor?' and other essays on European integration*. Cambridge: Cambridge University Press.

Weiler, Joseph H. H., Haltern, Ulrich R., and Mayer, Franz C. (1995) European democracy and its critics. *West European Politics* 18/3: 4–39.

Weinstock, Ulrich (1984) Abstufung als Realität und Chance. In Eberhard Grabitz (ed.), *Abgestufte Integration: Eine Alternative zum herkömmlichen Integrationskonzept?*. Hamburg: Schriftenreihe Europaforschung, pp. 345–85.

Werner, Karl Ferdinand (1980) L'Empire carolingien et le Saint Empire. In Maurice Duverger (ed.), *Le Concept d'empire*. Paris: Presses Universitaires de France, pp. 151–202.

Wessels, Wolfgang (1996) Verwaltung im EG-Mehrebenensystem. In Markus Jachtenfuchs and Beate Kohler-Koch (eds), *Europäische Integration*. Opladen: Leske & Budrich, pp. 165–92.

Wessels, Wolfgang (1998) Verstärkte Zusammenarbeit: Eine neue Variante flexibler Integration. In Mathias Jopp, Andreas Maurer and Otto Schmuck (eds), *Die Europäische Union nach Amsterdam*. Bonn: Europa Union Verlag, pp. 187–218.

Wessels, Wolfgang, and Dietrichs, Udo (1997) A new kind of legitimacy for a new kind of parliament – the evolution of the European Parliament. In European integration online papers 1/6, http://eiop.or.at/eiop/texte/1997-006a.htm [10 May 2001].

Wessels, Wolfgang, Maurer, Andreas, and Mittag, Jürgen (eds) (2000) *Fifteen into One? The European Union and Member States*. Manchester: Manchester University Press.

Whelan, Christopher T., Layte, Richard, Maître, Bertrand, and Nolan, Brian (2001) Income, deprivation, and economic strain: an analysis of the European Community household panel. *European Sociological Review* 17/4: 357–72.

Wiener, Antje (1998) *'European' Citizenship Practice: Building Institutions of a Non-State*. Oxford: Westview Press.

Wiener, Antje, and Diez, Thomas (eds) (2004) *European Integration Theory*. Oxford: Oxford University Press.

Winkler, Heinrich August (2002) Ehehindernisse: Gegen einen EU-Beitritt der Türkei. *Süddeutsche Zeitung* (23–4 Nov): 13.

Wirz, Albert (2001) Für eine transnationale Gesellschaftsgeschichte. *Geschichte und Gesellschaft* 27/3: 489–98.

Wittel, Andreas (2001) Towards a network sociality. *Theory, Culture and Society* 18: 51–76.

Wolf, Dieter (1999) *Integrationstheorien im Vergleich: Funktionalistische und intergouvernementalistische Erklärung für die Europäische Wirtschafts- und Währungsunion im Vertrag von Maastricht*. Baden-Baden: Nomos.

Wolf, Eric R. (1999) *Envisioning Power: Ideologies of Dominance and Crisis*. Berkeley: University of California Press.

Wolf, Jörg (2002) Staatszerfall: Die riskante Stabilisierungsstrategie der Europäischen Union für den südlichen Mittelmeerraum. In Christopher Daase, Susanne Feske and Ingo Peters (eds), *Internationale Risikopolitik*. Baden-Baden: Nomos.

Wolf, Klaus Dieter (2000) *Die Neue Staatsraison – Zwischenstaatliche Kooperation als Demokratieproblem in der Weltgesellschaft*. Baden-Baden: Nomos.

Yataganas, Xénophon A. (2001) The Treaty of Nice: the sharing of power and the institutional balance in the European Union: a continental perspective. Jean Monnet working paper, http://www.jeanmonnetprogram.org/papers/01/010101.html [17 May 2001].

Zolo, Danilo (1997) *Cosmopolis: Prospects for World Government*. Cambridge: Polity.

Zuleeg, Manfred (1984) Die Europäische Gemeinschaft als Integrationsverband. In Bodo Börner, Hermann Jahrreiß and Klaus Stern (eds), *Einigkeit und Recht und Freiheit: Festschrift für Carl Carstens zum 70. Geburtstag*, Vol. 1. Cologne: Carl Heymanns Verlag, pp. 289–303.

Zürn, Michael (1996) Über Staat und Demokratie im europäischen Mehrebenensystem. *Politische Vierteljahresschrift* 37: 27–55.

Zürn, Michael (1998) *Regieren jenseits des Nationalstaats: Globalisierung und Denationalisierung als Chance*. Frankfurt am Main: Suhrkamp.

Index